REDEEMED BY BEAUTY

The Life of Brother Andrew
Co-founder with Mother Teresa
of the Missionaries of Charity Brothers

Make the time

En Route Books and Media, LLC
5705 Rhodes Avenue
St. Louis, MO 63109

ISBN: 979-8-88870-038-9
Library of Congress Control Number: 2023933621

This book has been reprinted by En Route Books and Media, LLC, with permission of ST PAULS. All rights reserved. No part of this booklet may be reproduced, stored in a retrieval system, or transmitted in any form, or by any means, electronic, mechanical, photocopying, or otherwise, without the prior written permission of Better Yourself Books & Media Private Limited.

REDEEMED BY BEAUTY

The Life of Brother Andrew
Co-founder with Mother Teresa
of the Missionaries of Charity Brothers

Carmel Duca, MC.

Republished with permission by

En Route Books and Media, LLC

St. Louis, MO

Copyright © 2022 Better Yourself Books & Media Private Limited

ST PAULS ISBN 978-93-92340-06-2

Cover: Pishon Fernandez

The writings of Brother Andrew MC © by the Missionaries of Charity Brothers. Used with permission.

The Writings of Mother Teresa of Calcutta © by the Mother Teresa Center, exclusive licensee throughout the world of the Missionaries of Charity for the works of Mother Teresa. Used with permission.

Bible quotations are taken from The Jerusalem Bible, Reader's Edition, Doubleday & Company, Inc. Garden City, New York, 1968.

ST PAULS is an activity of the members of the Society of St Paul, who proclaim the Gospel through the media of Social Communication.

The books published reflect the views of their authors, and do not necessarily reflect the official position of the Society of St Paul, as we are open to publishing also works that enlighten the mind, nourish the spirit, challenge the conscience and invite discussion, debate and dialogue.

Contact:

Editorial	:	editor@stpauls.in
Sales	:	sales@stpaulsbyb.com
		sales@betteryourselfbooks.com
Marketing	:	marketing@stpauls.in
Website	:	www.stpaulsbyb.com

Printed at St Paul Press Training School, Bandra,
and published by ST PAULS,
58/23rd Road, TPS III, Bandra, Mumbai – 400 050
2022

*The only story worth
telling is that of
the beauty and the suffering.*

– BROTHER ANDREW

Dedicated to the

*humiliated, hard-pressed,
embarrassing people,
struggling with a disgrace,
a failure, a fall
in their own lives or in their dear ones —
a painful break-up of a relationship,
abandonment, a lonely pregnancy,
a police case, being written off.*

– BROTHER ANDREW

TABLE OF CONTENTS

ACKNOWLEDGEMENTS 11
FOREWORD 13
PREFACE 15
INTRODUCTION 17

PART – I

IAN – EARLY LIFE AND VOCATION TO THE JESUITS (1928 – 1954)

Childhood and School Years 35
Vocation to the Jesuits 42

PART – II

TRAVERS – AS A JESUIT IN INDIA (1954 – 1966)

The Australian Jesuits In India 65
Ranchi — Studying Hindi 66
Poona—Philosophy Studies 69
The Niyogi Report 73
Sitagarha — Teachers' Training Institute 75
Poona — Theology Studies 80
Vocation Promoter 81
The Writer 83
Priesthood 85
B.A. Santamaria and Social Issues 95
31 July 1964 98
Tertianship—From Sitagarha to Calcutta 100

PART – III

BROTHER ANDREW MC – CALCUTTA
(1966-1972)

Calcutta, 1966 121
Mansatala Row.. 131
Something Beautiful for God, 1969 143
The Bangladesh War.. 146
Inculturation and Indianisation 148
In Australia... 150

INTERLUDE – I

THE VIETNAM – CAMBODIA PERIOD
(1973-1975)

The War in Vietnam 171
Australia and Vietnam Relations..................................... 172
The Interlude Begins 175
30 April 1975 – Fall of Saigon and Aftermath 216
Last Night in Saigon... 230

PART – IV

FROM GENERAL to TROUBADOUR
(1976 – 1986)

Leaving Vietnam.. 247
Opening of Houses.. 249
Andrew and the MC Brothers' Identity............................ 275
Mother Teresa, Brother Andrew and
   Other Male Branches... 280
Australianness... 292
Visits to Australia 298
What I Met along the Way 301
Spirituality of Brother Andrew (1976 – 1987)................. 306

Third General Chapter – 1986 323
After the General Chapter 329

INTERLUDE – II

THE MEETING AND SEPARATION
(1987 – 1988)

The Meeting 357
Separation and Dispensation from Vows 373

PART – V

BROTHER ANDREW – SANNYASI
(1988 – 2000)

The Church in Australia and the "Underground People".... 390
Retreats and Missions in Australia 394
Graziers in Delegate 404
Home for Broken Priests 408
Pilgrims of Mary 414
Retreats outside Australia 417
The Spiritual Journey Continues 431
Friends 439
Beatification of Mother Teresa 443

PART – VI

THE JOURNEY COMES TO AN END

The Last Days 466
Death and Funeral 475
Tributes 479
Posthumous Writings and Possessions 483

PART – VII
THE FIORETTI AND EPILOGUE

The Fioretti of Brother Andrew 493
Epilogue 509

APPENDIX:

    I – MILLER AND TRAVERS-BALL FAMILY TREES ... 518

APPENDIX:

    II – INTERVIEW WITH BROTHER ANDREW 519

NAME INDEX 531

ACKNOWLEDGEMENTS

I would like to thank all the people involved in writing this book, who helped me gain insight into the person of Brother Andrew. They are too many to list them all, but a special thanks goes to the Travers-Ball family in Australia.

Three particular people I am indebted to are Elizabeth Hanink in the USA, Kathryn Spink in the UK and Maria Lourdes Bugelli in Malta for their untiring work of editing the manuscript and transcribing the many interviews and talks. In Australia, I thank Val Noone for his historical expertise.

But above all, I am profoundly grateful to the Missionaries of Charity Brothers who entrusted me with this task, especially to Br Marc Daniel Delapeyre, MC, for his constant and valuable advice.

FOREWORD

As a young Brother, right after my First Profession, I was told to study the letters of Brother Andrew, and that was really the first "contact" I had with him. I quickly became aware that I was in the presence of something great, and I fell in love with Brother Andrew's spirituality. Something on a very deep and personal level inside of me connected with him and identified with him, which seems to be the experience of many quoted in this book.

The Missionaries of Charity Brothers have the great privilege of being founded by two very special people. We have the world acclaimed sanctity of Mother Teresa through whom the Holy Spirit revealed a new charism. But we also have our special identity and spirituality given to us by Brother Andrew, whom I also consider a saint, though a hidden one. Mother Teresa's holiness is so high and obvious to everyone. But Brother Andrew's way of holiness is more hidden, but somehow more reachable, more human, and very easy to identify with. He showed us that the miracle of God's love can work through our weakness and brokenness, and that gives us much hope and strength. I pray that all those who read this book will also feel that hope.

I thank Br Carmel Duca for the years he has put into writing this book. He has done a wonderful job. And I hope that this book will make us all come to know Brother Andrew more, and appreciate him. For the Brothers I desire that through this biography they will give him the rightful honour and recognition he deserves in our Congregation as our Co-Founder. For his family members and friends, I augur it will be a joyful remembrance of a very special person. For all those who are struggling, feeling small, fragile or rejected, may it be a message of hope: God is very close to you.

Brother Andrew never wanted any acclaim or special attention either in his life or at his death. Let this biography be a sign of our deep love and appreciation of him: for all he has been and for all he has given to us. Let us pray for Brother Andrew's intercession, that we may have a greater desire to live the poverty, simplicity and love for the poor that he tried to instil in all of us. Thank you.

Br Paul Eaton, MC
General Servant
Missionaries of Charity Brothers
Kolkata
January 2022

PREFACE

Many years ago, Andrew wrote of what he hoped would be made public of his story and what he believed his life would have been, had he not resolved to seek and surrender to the God who was "the All" of his being:

> I'd like to say that you can hit that (compulsions) as hard as you like in my story as it is really part of me. There was a racing committee in Australia who used to joke about broken down old punters wearing a sandshoe on one foot and a galosh on the other. And that surely would have been me.

We cannot know whether that would in fact have been the case. Andrew's life raises many questions, not all of them answerable. But it is not always the provision of answers that is important but rather, in the words of Jean Vanier, another of Andrew's friends, "walking with the right questions". Carmel Duca has spent five years posing the "right questions" and faithfully following Andrew's journey with all its adversity, thrills, surprises, tears and beauty.

The Andrew that I knew was an unfailing and sensitive source of encouragement and counsel of the kind that stems from that place of quiet surrender to a higher wisdom and purpose. Asked once about the nature of his relationship with God, he responded that he was "inclined to a silent sort of prayer". It was not by techniques or knowledge that we are made holy, he claimed, but by God alone:

"So I bring my poor sullied self into His presence to be made holy. I simply sit before Him. And He transforms me into light, beauty, peace, joy and love." It was, I believe, this transformational, redemptive openness to the touch of God that enabled him not to miss the beauty in the ordinary, to perceive in insecurity and uncertainty the freedom of the sparrow, to feel a joyful song welling inside him even when he sensed that the curtain would come down before too long, and to be a light and life-giver to others.

Mother Teresa, who spoke often of the call of each one of us to holiness but far less frequently of holiness as an accomplished state, once remarked of Andrew, "He is very holy." I am profoundly grateful to Carmel for providing so comprehensive an insight into the progress of an extraordinary pilgrim and for the potent reminder that it is through the cracks that the light gets in.

Kathryn Spink
August 2022
Surrey, UK.

INTRODUCTION

Brother Andrew, an "*unfaithful man used by God*", friend of the poor and the wounded, unsung hero of the broken.[1] Born after the First World War and two weeks after the death of an elder sister; baptised Ian Travers-Ball by a Jesuit priest; matriculated from high school at the end of the Second World War; ordained a priest at the onset of the Second Vatican Council; arrived in India a few years after Independence and subsequent Partition; lived through the 1971 Bangladesh War; experienced the ravages and insecurities of Vietnam during the fall of Saigon. Andrew, a man who loved to gamble, was also an instigator of hope in small souls around the world, especially in his native Australia. Together with a great saint, he was co-founder of a Congregation and a misfit in that same Congregation.

An extremely simple, down-to-earth person, he was nonetheless beset with complexities: a writer and a contemplative; a mystic; a troubadour of beauty and suffering; serious and reserved yet fun-loving with a great sense of humour; a man both austere and deeply compassionate. Together with other great spiritual men and women, he can be considered to "embody an abyss and depth of spiritual significance..... To want to limit them to our interpretation ...is like wanting to grasp a handful of air."[2]

I am no journalist and no professional writer, but I was asked by the Missionaries of Charity Brothers to interview people who knew Brother Andrew. I did not make history. I just "interviewed history", as the journalist, Oriana Fallaci would say. I tried to let Andrew speak for himself through the people I met. There are as many Andrews as there were people to tell the story. Who were these people? Among others, there were nephews and nieces (the only ones of his immediate family still alive), fellow Jesuits who lived with him in communities in Australia and India, Missionaries of Charity Brothers and Sisters (including a few who had left the Congregation), Co-Workers in different parts of the world, friends, people who attended his retreats, missions and days of prayer, and people who received his regular newsletters.[3] In fact it was through Eugene Galea (whom I interviewed in 2017) that in 1982 I was introduced to Brother Andrew's newsletters. That was the year I had joined the *Third World Group*. We were over 60 young men and women who met regularly to study, reflect and act on situations of poverty in our native country Malta and around the world. Amongst the activities, we organised silent demonstrations against Apartheid in South Africa, fasted for twelve hours in solidarity with the famine victims of Ethiopia and helped the MCs and other organisations in Italy, Tunisia, Egypt and England. They were small but significant gestures. We were young, romantic and enthusiastic. A few had already joined the Missionaries of Charity. One of these was Eugene. In 1982, he had returned to Malta from Macau where he had been a novice under the guidance of Brother Andrew. We immediately became friends and he shared with me Andrew's newsletters until 1990 when I then joined the Congregation in Paris.

I never met Brother Andrew so I have no claim on him but for a desire to present him as he was: a man on a journey, a soul in progress towards a precise and yet mysterious aim. As a Jesuit he had one direction in life: to seek God in all things through *magis* — striving for excellence — sharing his gifts with others whilst caring for the individual souls, and this *Ad Maiorem Dei Gloriam*, for the greater glory of God. As a Missionaries of Charity Brother, his aim was to see, love, and serve Jesus in the poorest of the poor whilst trying to live as humbly and simply as he could. As a diocesan priest living in Australia (incardinated under the auspices of the

Archbishop of Calcutta), his life's project was to minister to small, underground souls, fellow suffering pilgrims. This book attempts to follow him on this passage.

It is no easy task to portray a man with paradoxes and nuances: firstly because of some of the events in Brother Andrew's life, especially his decision to leave the Congregation he had helped to build; and then because everyone brings his or her own limitations and preferences to the table. I have to admit that I am unclear as to what Andrew meant by "compulsions" and "unfaithfulness" because gambling was always top of the list whenever he mentioned his addictions, but he never admitted to being an alcoholic. However, he did later on in life hint that he was powerless over other addictions which he never named. It is also natural to want to leave out unpleasant details or include only what is traditionally acceptable and in conformity with personal tastes and opinions. A case in point: in a culture like the Asian, where respect for the elders is one of the most prized values, honest answers to questions about whether there were less likeable aspects to Andrew could and would be interpreted as a lack of respect. Only one person shared her disapproval of a photo of Andrew taken in the late 1960s or early1970s, showing him surrounded by a group of children and carrying a young child in his right arm while holding a cigarette in his left hand.[4]

So how to discover the integral Andrew? Nearly all the Missionaries of Charity Brothers I interviewed perceived a common trait. He was a father-figure for them. Gordon Garrick was a volunteer in Calcutta when he first met Brother Andrew in 1976. "[He was] so different from what I'd imagined. I had thought of him as a forceful and dynamic character, instead he was quiet, meek and unassuming."[5] Andrew was "gentle, kind and well-read. He listened carefully to each person who wanted to visit with him, making them feel — as Mother [Teresa] did — that they were the only ones in the room. His spirituality was contagious and motivating."[6] But, whereas Mother Teresa declined to answer questions about her personal life, her family, her likes or dislikes and her feelings, and lived it all in silence, Andrew, without over-stepping boundaries, was more open about himself. When he knew he could be of help by sharing his struggles with others, he did not hesitate to do so. "He came across as so special, eyes full of Christ, compassionate, caring, holy, a beautiful smile radiating joy."[7]

His fellow Jesuit, Fr Hans Hendriks remembered Travers (as the Jesuits call him to this day) as a very perceptive, thoughtful, unpretentious man:

> Less straightforward, and a benign person. He did not like fuss. I used to say Mass with him in Mansatala Row and there was no, "Oh this is lovely, it is so nice to be together." Not him. He hated that. He didn't like gush. And if any other Brother gushed, he would instinctively be uncomfortable. That was a character trait of his. Very ordinary person and wanted to be like that. They all loved him because he was like that. What you see is what you get. There was no image, he did not put up any image. He had a dislike for show, for fuss. He disliked all that.[8]

At the same time he had an aura of authority, as some MC Sisters witnessed in him.

> You felt like a sense of security or belonging, being accepted in his presence no matter who you were. You didn't feel like out of place or "What will he think of me?" No, never felt that with Brother Andrew. You could feel that he had a very big spirituality and very deep convictions. Brother [had a] great simplicity and great insights into life in general and into what was going on around us.... I think he was able to give people hope even if they felt that they were a failure or they couldn't do anything. He knew that everyone has a mission and no matter how much you fail, no matter how many mistakes you make, you are still very special and God has some special mission for you and you can still do something. You are still a beloved of God. He was able to go down to where the people were. He was able to empathize with them where they were in their brokenness. He was not someone telling them from above what they should

be doing or how they should be dealing with it, but he was with them in it... that ability to be able to go down to the level where the people are and to kind of experience the sufferings with them, and then lift them up.[9]

Quite a number of people shared, "Brother Andrew had a good sense of humour. He was good fun really."[10] He was "very grounded and matter of fact about the MC work ...a very wry sense of humour. We often laughed together, and his humour was distinctively Australian. Quietly spoken, but also able to be decisive and directive, interested in theological ideas, supportive of Vatican II reforms, and liturgical experimentation, [but] not so interested in the bigger picture ideas like political ideologies, India's place in the world, American imperialism."[11] It seems that like most of his family, Andrew was stubborn, and at times touchy.[12] "One day during a retreat, John [Barnes] noticed that Brother Andrew was wearing a pair of purple socks. John jokingly asked him whether that was some kind of promotion [to bishopric]. Andrew never wore them again!"[13] "Earthy", was a word he himself used while stressing that he was very human. Br Nicholas Prinster, OCSO, as quoted by Eileen Egan, long-time friend of Mother Teresa and author of *Such a Vision of the Street,* described Andrew as one whose "outstanding trait [was] his fortitude, or what we Americans call 'guts'. He does not seem to be afraid of anything, especially not afraid to fail. Much of this trait is natural to him, but one can see in it, too, the marks of his training as a Jesuit. This fortitude is in every sense a gift of the Spirit and springs from his inner conviction; faith in and love of God."[14]

"He was a very spiritual person, spiritual on one level but eminently practical on another level. I think starting the Missionaries of Charity and getting the whole thing going was the major thing for him, I don't think he felt he made it to be there forever."[15] He was very good at starting things but it was hard for him to maintain them. In an informal chat with a Jesuit in Hazaribagh (a city in the Indian state of Jharkhand) who was recruited by Andrew, Fr Thomas Joseph told me, "Travers moved into and moved on to." There was a pattern to his life: as soon as "he felt hemmed in, he left."[16]

> By nature he was a chap that had interests; he would be totally absorbed in them and then after some time, depending on what the thing was, he would get a little bit fed up. He would lose interest, it was part of his way, part of what he did in the Teachers' Training College, a part of what he did when he left the Brothers. It is the same, a pattern. That was his character. He would get enthused on something, and then the enthusiasm would die down. That's why when he went to Vietnam ...his enthusiasm for India died down, and the enthusiasm for Vietnam [grew].[17]

Hans Hendriks believed that what saved Andrew was the fact that there was a change of regime in Vietnam and was forced out, otherwise his enthusiasm would have also eventually died and the pattern would have repeated itself.

Jim Smith, one of his nephews recalled, "We used to have good discussions. Ian was very gloomy about the temporal world. He could always say something calming to you if you were concerned about anything. He tried to calm things down and put it in perspective. At the Wednesday lunches when Mary and Lucy (Andrew's sisters) would get a bit growling at each other, Ian used to have a nice knack of calming the waters. 'That's enough of that. I'm only here for an hour.'"[18]

In Andrew's presence everybody felt understood. He could explain things, both to people with little schooling and to university students. His grandnieces, Kate and Jane Simons, remembered,

> When we were kids asking him all sorts of silly questions and he didn't laugh, he just said, "Oh," he popped his eyebrows "Oh." Or he'd give a practical example. You know, I used to love his stories. That was the part of the highlight when he used to come back from his travels. I was very little when he was in India but I remember some of the stories. He always managed to find something really beautiful, in

> extraordinarily awful situations. I am very human, and I wouldn't have the patience for it in a million years. But he'd tell these stories and we just wow! Such a bright person. We're very lucky to have been exposed to him. He was a really special person.[19]

Simplicity, freedom and closeness to the poor were his trademarks. A Missionaries of Charity Sister recalled, "I remember one day when he came to Sydney, he handed me a brown paper bag after Mass, and he said, 'I don't need all these donations. I can't use this.' A brown paper bag looked like a sandwich. I took it. It was ten thousand dollars in that bag! It was a lot of money and he just gave it to me, because he tried to live Divine Providence, and he didn't need anything which somebody needed."[20] "In the community of Sam Seong in South Korea, the Brothers eat with the patients, and there he was, Brother Andrew feeding one of the poor men in bed, while he himself was eating. He stood feeding him and himself eating."[21]

Kathryn Spink, co-author of *Spirit of Bethlehem*, wrote to me:

> My first impression was of an exceptionally humble and holy man who was simultaneously very conversant with the ways of the world and very accessible. What I liked about him were the qualities that I picked up at our first meeting, together with his naturalness in relating to me as a woman. Unlike so many committed to celibacy, he was not afraid to have a friendship with a member of the opposite sex. I never found anything to dislike but then of course it was a relationship conducted largely at a distance. Just a word on the alleged alcohol problem here — on the occasions on which he and my husband and I came together socially (e.g., at our house) he had no difficulty in just having a couple of glasses of wine with a meal and then stopping. This, in my experience, is not the mark of an alcoholic.[22]

Brother Ben Harrison, even though he did not live with him for very long stretches of time, remembered Andrew as a person who left,

A very strong positive impression, as somebody who was humble, compassionate, courageous when facing things, new challenges, strong in faith but aware of his own weakness and that of others involved, very sensitive. He was his own person, he lived the spirit I would say, closeness to the poor and that sense of identification or closeness with the poor and broken people, and poor, broken Brothers also. But he was always a bit of a free spirit, "Don't be afraid to demand obedience of the Brothers. It's good for them." So I mean in some areas he could be tough. Sometimes when he came on a visitation it was very tough. I remember once he came on a visitation and shook everything to pieces and we had already planned a community picnic.... It was supposed to be a nice outing for all the Brothers because there were a lot of brothers at that point probably twenty-five or thirty Brothers altogether.... And we went to that outing and there were little pockets of Brothers in shock, in various corners around the place, licking their wounds and trying to recover, and a couple of Brothers in tears at different points during the day, because of his shaking things up. So yes, interesting combination. I guess it's kind of typical in a way of people who demand a lot of freedom for themselves and are a bit autocratic with others. However, I think generally people felt that he was loving, caring, understanding and even when he was tough that it was for the good.[23]

Two of his closest Australian friends: Sr Margaret Ryan, RSM, and Daven Day, SJ, acknowledged respectively, "When I first met him, I was fairly young. I was twenty-eight. There was something about him that I felt that he was a saint. I'm surprised that it took so long to write his story because I know he never pretended he was other than a flawed character but he was a saint, he was absolutely a saint. And I say he was the saint — he was the male saint of the Australian Catholic Church — absolutely."[24] "He gave himself completely to God.... I think it is worth writing a book about this extraordinary person who so loved God, loved

Introduction

people and he was so loved that everybody thought he was their best friend."[25]

How to convey on paper the intensity of the emotional charge of some of the interviews? It is difficult or practically impossible. But two interviews are worth describing. The first was with an Adibasi Brother in India and the other with a grazier in Australia. Adibasis are the tribal people of the northern part of India, once called Chota Nagpur. They are down-to-earth people, practical, with less schooling than the people of the South, and also less inclined to share. Verbalising and systematising their thoughts is not their forte. So when one Brother came to my room to be interviewed, I was already mentally prepared for a yes/no answers. I was taken aback when, before he sat down, he closed the door and made sure that it was properly bolted! What happened next astounded me. As soon as he started reminiscing about Brother Andrew, tears began streaming down his face. That was worth more than a thousand words or hours of a more verbose interview.

The other interview was with Peter Reed, a grazier from a small town in the outback of New South Wales. The official definition of a grazier is one who tends sheep; he is not a farmer. The unofficial one is that of a tough man who shows emotions only to his dog who helps him tend the sheep for days on end. In my opinion, Peter was a typical grazier — seventy years old, red-faced probably from long hours in the sun — sitting erect in the chair with arms crossed over his chest. Peter was one of about seven with whom I chatted about Andrew together as a group. It was fun! Later when I was on my own with Peter, I mentioned that I had never met Andrew and that, although I had only met him [Peter] a few hours previously, I could imagine them chatting amicably over a cup of tea. Peter's eyes gleamed with tears. He could not comment on the observation. There was no need!

I couldn't possibly have completed this work without the generous help of so many people: all Andrew's nephews and nieces;

friends; Co-Workers; people who helped me with transcribing some of the interviews and talks; our Missionaries of Charity communities; those who gave access to the libraries and archives of the Congregation and the Jesuits; people who gave me permissions; materials, photographs, data and information, CDs and DVDs of so many talks given by Brother Andrew during retreats; people who shuttled me from and to airports, train and bus stations; those who took time to answer my emails, letters, phone calls. The list could go on. This book is definitely their work too.

Ian's journey in this study starts with the death of his grandfather. Oddly, Henry Ball died some hundred years before Ian's death on the same street in Melbourne's Fitzroy neighbourhood. Part I of the book deals with Ian's childhood, schooling and vocation to the Society of Jesus. As a young Jesuit, in Part II he embarked on his journey to India where he began his philosophy and theology studies and was ordained a priest in Ranchi. It is there, in India, that he discovered his call to write. His deepest vocation to be a priest amongst the poor became a reality when he met Mother Teresa and she invited him to take charge of the formation and direction of the newly-founded congregation of the Missionaries of Charity Brothers. Thus Part III introduces Brother Andrew at the helm of the MC Brothers: a task which entailed not only his being their general superior but also giving them an identity as male Religious, while at the same time expanding the scope of their work. Eventually he opted to start opening communities in war-torn Vietnam and Cambodia. The book defines this time of Brother Andrew's life as an Interlude — there was a break. People who knew Andrew during this period all agree that there was an Andrew before Vietnam and an Andrew after Vietnam. When in 1975, Saigon fell at the hands of the Viet Cong and he was evacuated, Andrew made his base in Hong Kong, hoping that one day he could go back to these Indo-Chinese countries, but life would never be the same.

Andrew's journey during the decade between 1976 and 1986 is covered in Part IV. The Congregation expanded substantially both in the number of Brothers and in the number of communities.

Introduction

At the same time, in South Korea, he co-founded, the Chain of Charity — a quasi-religious congregation for young women with physical disabilities. In 1986, while the Missionaries of Charity Brothers were preparing for the General Chapter held every six years, Brother Andrew was stuck in Hong Kong without a visa to enter India. His desire was not to be re-elected as General Servant of the Congregation, but to become a "troubadour" travelling "in a smaller boat", giving retreats and spiritual talks to the Brothers. Instead, he was called for an intervention meeting when the Congregation's leaders became aware that his drinking was becoming heavier. This would be the Second Interlude in Andrew's life. An abrupt change took place. He did not accept the offer to go to a rehabilitation centre, opting instead for a dispensation from his vows as a Missionaries of Charity Brother.

The last stage of his life started now. Part V follows Brother Andrew the *sannyasi*, the ascetic with no fixed abode, who went around Australia and other parts of the world giving retreats and talks to the "underground people". Other projects in Andrew's mind — such as the Home for Broken Priests and the Pilgrims of Mary — never actually took root. The journey came to an end when he discovered he had stomach cancer. In Part VI Andrew comes back to the MC Congregation for care. After disposing of his few possessions and having arranged his last practical legal details, he arrived at the Missionaries of Charity Sisters' home in Fitzroy, Melbourne, where he died peacefully on 4 October 2000. The title of Part VII –Fioretti (little flowers) is a term borrowed from the biography of St Francis of Assisi. Even though the fioretti are not the primary source of the biography, they are still interesting anecdotes, stories which can shed light on the personality, character and spirituality of Brother Andrew. The Epilogue then presents the cause for his possible canonisation.

A note on certain place names: even though Bombay was renamed Mumbai as early as 1995, and Calcutta became Kolkata in 2001, for this book the original names (appearing in letters, books, articles, etc.) Calcutta and Bombay have been retained. The same goes for Poona and any other place names which may have changed during the course of the years. The proper transliteration from the Hindi for "Hazaribagh" is actually "Hazaribag", but in all of Andrew's correspondence and articles the former is used. Thus, that form was kept throughout.

All underlined parts and capitalised words and/or phrases in the text — mostly or entirely — in Andrew's letters, were already underlined and/or capitalised in the original letters. The abbreviation MC refers to Missionaries of Charity Brothers unless otherwise clarified to mean Missionaries of Charity Sisters, Fathers or Contemplatives. All other abbreviations which Brother Andrew used in his letters were left in their original form unless doing so would obscure the meaning. Since some quotes were taken directly from oral interviews, some slight editing in punctuation and grammar was done to preserve clarity.

Carmel Duca, MC
Kolkata
June 2022

Introduction

Endnotes codes are as follows:

"I" and "L" stand for "interview" and "letter" respectively. They are then followed by "F," or "B," or "S," or "P," or "J," or "O," or "G," which stand for "Family," "MC Brothers," "MC Sisters," "Public," "Jesuits," "Others," "General to MC Brothers" respectively. They are then followed by the name of a person. In the case of Interview, it denotes the name of the person being interviewed. In the case of a Letter, it denotes the name of the recipient or sender of the letter. All these are preceded by a date: either of the letter written or when the interview was held.

1. To various Brothers and other people Br Andrew would insist that his story was one of an *"unfaithful man used by God"*. He used the same term in his book 'What I Met along the Way', page 152.
2. The Dark Night, Bk.1, Ch.9 as quoted from *San Juan de la Cruz, Obras Completas,* Burgos: Editorial Monte Carmelo, 2010.
3. From the beginning, Mother Teresa attracted people all over the world who wanted to help her in her service to the poorest of the poor. They are referred to as Co-Workers. The International Association of Co-Workers of Mother Teresa was blessed by Pope Paul VI on 19 March 1969.
4. 20180309 IF Shirley Smart.
5. 20210209 Email Gordon Garrick.
6. 20190224 Email Ed and Dorothy Baroch.
7. 20190711 IF Annie Joseph.
8. 20180227 IJ Hans Hendriks, SJ.
9. 20180325 IS Sister Milada, MC, Sister Hannah, MC, Sister Antonella, MC, Sister Radiance Therese, MC.
10. 20180321 IS Sister Eliezer, MC and Sister Hanahri, MC.
11. 20190129 Email Garry McLoughlin.
12. 20180305 IR Anne and Julian Millership, Jim Smith.
13. 20180303 IF Jenny Barnes.
14. Egan, Eileen, *Such a Vision of the Street, Mother Teresa—The Spirit and the Work,* New York, USA: Image Doubleday, 1985. Eileen Egan, (1912-2000). American journalist, Roman Catholic activist and co-founder of the Catholic Peace group, PAX Christi-USA. She marched with Martin Luther King Jr. at Selma.
15. 20180305 IR Anne and Julian Millership, Jim Smith.
16. 20190118 IJ Thomas Joseph, SJ.

17 20180227 IJ Hans Hendriks, SJ.
18 20180403 IR Jim, Gregory and Gabrielle Smith.
19 20180319 IR Leone, Kate and Jane Simons.
20 20180515 IS Sister Joseph Maria, MC.
21 20180321 IS Sister Eliezer, MC, and Sister Hannahri, MC.
22 20181018 IF Kathryn Spink; Kathryn Spink, born in India in 1953, authorized biographer of Mother Teresa of Calcutta and other spiritual leaders, and translator of many books including City of Joy. She is married and lives in Surrey England. She first met Brother Andrew in the summer of 1985 when he gave an address to the Co-Workers of Mother Teresa to which Kathryn was also invited, but had corresponded about possible books some two years prior to that.
23 20170202 IB Ben Harrison, MC.
24 20180308 IF Margaret Ryan, RSM. Sister Margaret had known Andrew since 1972 when he visited Australia for the first time. Through a mutual friend, Fr Patrick O'Sullivan, she met Andrew at the Mercy Hospital in East Melbourne where she was working and living. What struck her most about that twenty- or thirty-minute meeting was that his attention never deflected throughout: "I have never been in the company of someone who listened so well. I just understood all of a sudden what it meant to be present to someone, and then the next time I met him was when he had been in Vietnam. In the first meeting I had already expressed my desire to go and work in India. He wrote to me in Saigon and said, 'Come.' I couldn't, I always felt badly, that I had family responsibilities and I thought, 'Just right now I can't come.'"
25 20180320 IJ Daven Day, SJ.

PART – I

IAN – EARLY LIFE AND VOCATION TO THE JESUITS (1928 – 1954)

*What I received from my parents and my family growing up,
above all, was the presence of God in our home.
We weren't an overly religious family,
We went to Mass every Sunday, and I remember when I was little
we used to say prayers before I went to bed.
Somehow though God was very present in our family.*

– BROTHER ANDREW

CHILDHOOD AND SCHOOL YEARS

Fitzroy — Victoria — 22 August 1903. Henry Ball, occupation gentleman, died aged sixty-six at 334 Gore Street. Henry had arrived in Victoria from his native Cornwall, United Kingdom, in January 1864 on the SS Great Australia. Around the same time, twenty-year-old, Irish-born Rose Anne Travers also arrived in Victoria from Liverpool where her family had lived for several years.[1] Twelve years later, in 1876, Rose Anne and Henry were married at St Patrick's Cathedral in Melbourne. They lived in an attractive residential area called Fitzroy, an area considered suitable for "city gentlemen", bankers and merchants. The second of their three children, Frederick Henry Travers-Ball, was born on 2 July 1879. On 7 February 1911, Frederick Henry married twenty-two-year-old Anne Margaret Cecilia Miller in the same church in which his parents had been married.

Somewhat earlier, on 13 June 1854, James Miller, a thirty-four-year-old Englishman, his first wife and their five children, had arrived in Melbourne on the *SS Admiral Box*. They were both Church of England people from Northampton, Leicestershire, and they landed in Australia as assisted immigrants, having, like the majority of other British citizens at that time, received financial aid — possibly in the form of their boat passage.

Melbourne had been founded on the Yarra River in 1835, on land infamously "purchased" from Aborigines. It was in 1851 that the gold-rush broke out. The streets of Melbourne, once deserted, were now full of workers, mostly miners, from other parts of Australia and from overseas. By 1854 the population had grown from 80,000 to 300,000. This influx reflected the arrival of free immigrants and also changed the nature of the settlement from a convict colony into a more advanced city. "Marvellous Melbourne" flourished with extraordinary development: new buildings, freshly gravelled streets, the State Library, the first Flinders Railway Station, and Melbourne University, to mention but a few. It was in that same year that the first major exhibition was organized, bringing together the best agricultural, industrial and artistic goods to be sent to the 1855 Paris Exposition Universelle. Melbourne was thriving.

On arriving in Australia, James Miller and his sons took up parcels of land on the Noorilim Estate in the Arcadia district on the Goulburn River near Shepparton and eventually became significant landowners. It is James' second marriage to Mary Ann Daly that is of relevance to our story. Little is known of how fifteen-year-old Mary Ann Daly found employment in 1875 as housekeeper for the Miller family in Arcadia and seven years later married the sixty-three-year-old widower. Of Irish descent, she was born in 1860 in Castlemaine, a small town in the goldfield regions of Victoria. On 13 November 1889, when James was seventy, Mary Ann gave birth to their only child, Anne Margaret Cecilia.

When Anne Margaret Cecilia Miller married Frederick Henry Travers-Ball, she was twenty-one and he was ten years her senior. The marriage certificate lists Frederick's profession as accountant. They lived at Shakespeare Grove in Hawthorn. A year later Mary Vincentia was born (1912), followed by five other children: Leo Thomas (1913), Lucy Arcadius (1915), Joan Beatrice (1916), Brendan Marius (1917), and Aimée Antoinette (1919).[2] By that time the family had moved to 18 Kinkora Road in the same city of Hawthorn. A family photo (in a classic sepia-coloured hue) taken at a studio in 1922 shows the six Travers-Ball siblings in ascending order. Nobody would have thought that about six years later, on 27 August 1928, the seventh and last Travers-Ball would appear almost ten years after Aimée.

In *Such a Vision of the Street*, Eileen Egan claims that "by a strange chance or providence" Ian came into the world eighteen years and one day after the birth of Agnes Bojaxhiu in Skopje, and the same year that Agnes — later known as Mother Teresa of Calcutta — left her native country to join the Institute of the Blessed Virgin Mary, also known as the Loreto Nuns.[3] By a stranger chance or providence Ian was born two weeks after the death of his sister, the twelve-year-old Joan Beatrice who suffered from rheumatic fever and whose death had been imminent for some time. Most probably the arrival of the new baby helped Anne cope with her death.

Ian's birth certificate shows that he was born at 25 Linda Crescent, Hawthorn, a few blocks away from the Travers-Ball residence, possibly in a small, private clinic run by Dr Roy Watson (the doctor who signed the birth certificate) and Matron E.M. Watson. The baby was registered in the District of Hawthorn in the State of Victoria on 9 October 1928. Whether or not it is true is hard to determine, but various people (by hearsay) recounted that Dr Watson, on delivering the little Ian, exclaimed, "This boy is destined for great things."[4] Ian was the only Travers-Ball with no second name. Neither his baptismal certificate nor parish records nor his confirmation certificate lists one.[5] His brother Leo and sister Mary served as Ian's godparents when he was baptised on 15 September 1928, in Immaculate Conception Church, in Hawthorn by Thomas J. O'Mara, SJ.

Hawthorn, situated six kilometres away from Melbourne, with the city of Boroondara as its local government area, had also seen a rapid expansion towards the end of the nineteenth century with the erection of grand Victorian houses. In 1869 the Immaculate Conception Church at 345 Burwood Road was completed and in 1884 the adjoining presbytery was built to house a community of

Jesuit priests. A few metres away on the opposite side of the road stood the Town Hall, opened in 1890.

It was close to this area that the Travers-Ball family moved in the early 1930s, to 5 Howard Street in Kew. Like the adjoining suburb of Hawthorn, Kew was and is to this day an old-established suburb. Other significant landmarks in Kew situated within a few kilometres of each other are Raheen, a nineteenth century Italianate mansion built in 1870 on Studley Park Road, and once the residence of former Archbishop of Melbourne, Daniel Mannix; Genezzano FCJ college for girls on Clotham Road, run by the Faithful Companions of Jesus; the Carmelite Monastery on Stevenson Road; and Xavier College and Burke Hall on Barkers Road and Studley Park Road respectively — both run by the Jesuits.[6]

The Travers-Ball family did not stay long on Howard Street. Soon they moved to 14 Miller Grove in Kew and then to 54 Studley Park Road.[7] It was at 14 Findon Crescent that they would eventually settle in 1938. These moves came as no surprise to the family because Frederick's philosophy was not to buy a house until he'd lived in and was happy with it.

When in 1983 the house on Findon Crescent was up for auction by Abercromby & Beatty Pty. Ltd., it was described as "an extremely charming post-Edwardian attic-style residence, situated in a highly desirable and convenient location, providing spacious comfortable family accommodation with a most appealing sunny aspect on generous land approximately 12,000 sq. ft. within close proximity to schools, transport and recreation areas."[8]

The Travers-Balls were a tightly-knit group. Family members loved each other in a really robust and happy way, always laughing and giggling as children (and even as adults!). They loved both their mother and their father. Anne, or "Nana Ball", as her grandchildren (and later even her children) used to call her, had the Travers-Ball charm that Ian inherited. She was elegant and sophisticated with a sweet demeanour, a woman who got on famously with neighbours.[9] We will never know whether, being the Benjamin of the family, Ian

Part: I – Ian: Early Life and Vocation...

was her favourite but he was surely loved by her. Nana Ball was involved in her son's life, helping to organize fund-raising afternoon teas for her son's school as part of her involvement in the Ladies' Committee. As Ian would later say, "my mother was a very, I would say a saint, was a very wonderful woman."[10] No wonder we find Nana Ball desperately trying to get lipstick off the tuxedo Ian was wearing one night, when he told her he was to wear the same tuxedo on the following evening! Such a scene was witnessed by a young Leone. Leone, the only daughter of Ian's eldest brother Leo, was only twelve years younger than her Uncle Ian. As a young girl she lived in Sydney with her parents, but every school holiday, "my parents would put me on a plane, the old propeller Australian National Airlines, and I'd be taken to the airport with my name slapped on, and my grandmother and usually Mary who was the oldest would pick me up at the airport and I would stay down in Melbourne for a while, which was lovely. I got to know my grandparents and it was wonderful."[11]

Frederick was a man of small stature, strict and at times grumpy. Even Ian's school friends were occasionally scared of him. When they saw him on the road, they would remark to each other, "There he goes!" and cross to the other side. He was not a regular churchgoer, even though as a young man he had been an altar boy. Later, he stopped going entirely, in response apparently to being scolded and publicly shamed by the celebrant when he left Mass early. Ian described his father as, "pretty strict, but he was always there, he was a great provider for the family. He worked very hard to provide for us, for our education."[12] The family was middle class, "of comfortable means and quite respectable".[13] The father worked in the insurance business until the Depression, and even then Ian was able to go to the prestigious Jesuit College at Burke Hall in preparation for his secondary years at Xavier College.

Photos of young Ian show him proudly wearing his Xavier's uniform: white shirt, shorts, red and black striped tie, and black blazer and cap, both emblazoned with the distinctive college crest. Ian entered Burke Hall in 1935 at the age of seven. He was a good student but never made Dux of the Class. He did win awards for spelling, English, religious knowledge, geography, elocution, reading and dictation. During his time at Burke Hall, he engaged in various extra-curricular activities such as being a Mass server, official of the Mission Society, a member of the Society of St John Berchman and of the Sodality. Sport in a Jesuit educational centre was part of the formation and Ian played for the Under 13's football team. Unfortunately, there are no records of his taking part in extra-curricular activities later on when he moved to Xavier College. His nephews and nieces believe that he was in the rowing team, either as a coxswain or as a rower. His tall, thin stature meant that he could easily have made a good rower. Hailing from Hawthorn as he did, throughout his life Ian barracked for the Hawthorn Football Club. He also had a great love of district cricket, a love he shared with his father. When once Julian, one of Frederick's grandsons, turned up at Findon Crescent wearing a Collingwood jumper, his grandfather was quick to admonish him, "Never come into my house again wearing that jumper!"[14]

When the Second World War started, both of Ian's brothers Leo and Brendan — to whom he was very close despite the age difference — were old enough either to be conscripted or to volunteer. In fact, Brendan was eventually captured in 1941 in Athens and spent five years as a prisoner of war. Mary was already married, so Ian was left at home with his parents and Lucy and Aimée, the sisters closest to him in age.

There was no television at that time. Life was slower, with little or no money in people's pockets, and no toys, so the only entertainment boys of Ian's age had was throwing stones into the Yarra River on Saturday afternoons. Fr Tom Keogh — now a Jesuit living in Bokaro Steel City in Bihar, India — who was a couple of years younger than Ian, recalled the Saturday when as a kid he first chatted with him. A truck heading to Melbourne went straight over the bridge down into the Yarra below. Everybody heard about it, and in a place and at a time where little happened, this was big news. People rushed down to see the crashed truck.

Part: I – Ian: Early Life and Vocation... 41

Life was very ordinary. Reminiscing about these days in later life, Brother Andrew related: "I had a good education with the Jesuits, for which I've always been grateful... not a very brilliant [student]. Somehow I got through but not very wonderfully. Somebody [Geoffrey Solomon] was writing about me a few years ago and he asked a few questions to an old Jesuit Fr Stevenson who had taught me and just died a few years ago, and this writer, was asking him about me and he said, 'Oh yes, he was a very unexceptional boy.' And he was right."[15]

At the age of fourteen, on 16 August 1942, Ian received the Sacrament of Confirmation through the hands of Daniel P. Mannix, Archbishop of Melbourne in St Joseph's Church in Malvern, Victoria. As early as this, much of Ian's pocket money was spent betting on horses and aiming more at the big metropolitan tracks at Flemington and Caulfield Racecourses.[16] Because of his eagerness to read and listen to the outcomes of one of his bets, he failed the Matriculation Examination French paper.[17]

Since the Travers-Ball residence at 14 Findon Crescent was between Burke Hall and Xavier College, there was no need for Ian to board. Life at Xavier was uneventful. According to Solomon in *Brothers of Mother Teresa*, "Ian enjoyed the life at Burke Hall rather more than that at the senior school. For one who was still disinclined to push himself forward Xavier was more overpowering and less companionable than Burke Hall had been." It seems that at Xavier Ian enjoyed anonymity. The only class photos of him are from the early years at Burke Hall. Out of all the photos of students displayed on the walls of the Xavier College hallways there is not one showing Ian. There is no mention of him on the honours board or in the archives of Xavier College. There is nothing that could give a clue, shed some light or indicate that Ian was there, that Ian walked those hallways as an adolescent. Nothing. Nothing at all.

But, among the photos of all the rectors of the College on one of the walls on the ground floor of the school, is the likeness of James Hawkins, SJ, (1916–2004) the sixteenth head of Xavier College from 1969-1973. His hope as a rector was "that our students will be warm-hearted people, adding love and generosity to society.... I hope our students will be people for others." These words were typical of many Father Hawkins uttered about education and life in general during the time he spent educating and guiding young men. But it is what he said at the award ceremony for Xavier College students in 1971 that is remarkably striking for this study and provides us with an insight. Speaking about the Christian unselfishness some of the boys had exhibited when collecting money for Pakistani refugees, he expressed the hope that their generosity would endure even after they left the College, and added:

> In this context, I would refer to Br Andrew, a former student of the College who was known to us as a boy as Ian Travers-Ball. Many of you will have heard of his working out of his Christian commitment for the help of the dying and starving in Calcutta and more recently of his endeavours for the refugees of the current political crisis in Pakistan. Time does not allow me to give a full picture of what this man is or does, but I will be happy to go on record as saying — even if Xavier had produced no one else in the course of its history — that such Christianity would have made the enterprise worthwhile.[18]

VOCATION TO THE JESUITS

It was in 1945, at the age of seventeen, that Ian matriculated from Xavier College and left school. That same year, the United States ended World War II with the atomic bomb attacks on Nagasaki and Hiroshima, Japan. Communism was starting to gain momentum in the world, especially in Europe. The United States began to help post-war Europe re-establish its agriculture and industry, but this economic growth brought with it a rise in secularism and anticlericalism. Australia, led then by Prime Minister Robert Gordon Menzies, was facing an additional problem, best summarised by the Australian government's slogan "populate or perish." There was a fear — real or imagined — that if Australia didn't increase

Part: I – Ian: Early Life and Vocation... 43

its population by receiving Britons as part of a mass immigration programme, in fewer than twenty-five years the country would be taken over by the "yellow races", and subsequently by Communism.

How did such a world situation affect our young Ian? Primarily in that he had to consider himself lucky to have a job as soon as he left school. He was an office boy with the General Accident and Assurance Corporation, and stamped letters and delivered them, "for the princely sum of one pound ten a week."[19] By late 1947, Ian had moved to a smaller company called Bankers and Traders Insurance Company. By this time he was thinking of a vocation, and had already signed up with the Benedictines in New Norcia and with the Missionaries of the Sacred Heart. Before long, however, he "chickened out." The one who was happiest was his father Frederick who had hoped that his son would follow him into the insurance business.

But, the spark was already there. When Aimée Antoinette dated Keith Millership, she would take her brother Ian with her as a chaperone. Keith would bring his brother Brian. Eventually the two became friends and one day Brian asked Ian, "What are you going to do in life?" to which Ian's response was, "I would like to do something for the poor."[20]

The other factor that may have had a slight influence on Ian was the fear and rejection of Communism creeping into Australia. He joined the Young Liberals just for their social activities, but the fact remains that he did not join any other party.[21] The Liberal Party in Australia is actually the conservative party in political terms.[22] But he knew that politics was not for him. Deep down, there was that nagging voice insistently calling him to the priesthood.

Early in 1951 Ian left the Bankers and Traders Insurance Company and tried unsuccessfully to sell insurance on his own.

> After a few years, I sort of tried a few things to do. I tried to start a little insurance business on my own, and that failed. Then I had a go at something that was, always had been a bit of a weakness with me — and that was the horses. And I did very well for a while, and I thought, 'Oh, this is a great life,

I don't need to work.' And it went on and of course after a couple of months, the day of reckoning came. I didn't have much to lose but, I lost a lot.... And there I was at 22 or 23 years of age, and I had to think. I had to stop and think what I am going to do. And I started to pray a little and started to go for Mass on weekdays.[23]

When, in 1969, Ian (by then Brother Andrew), was being interviewed by Malcolm Muggeridge in Calcutta as part of *Something Beautiful for God* the documentary about Mother Teresa's work and organisation, and the topic of the horse racing came up, Andrew averred that he could still remember the name of the horse on which he lost everything that Saturday, 9 June 1951. Such was the impact the loss had on him! As Muggeridge would write, "If that horse had won, Ian, by his own admission, would have gone on gambling and his vocation, India, Mother Teresa and 'Brother Andrew' might never have emerged as such a tremendous part of his life."[24] Blessed "*Regent King*"![25]

By now, Ian was opening up to what God was asking of him. He was more susceptible and sensitive to the events around him. He was stuck in a rut and dissatisfied with his life in general, frustrated with the enjoyments he was running after and yet couldn't live without. It was painful! And then:

> ... one afternoon on the steps of the General Post Office, in Melbourne, a very ordinary little drama became a turning point in my life. I saw a young woman with three small children, one of them in a push-chair trying to come down the steps. I went up and carried the push-chair down for her, and immediately we went our separate ways. But I walked off a changed man. Something had happened inside me.... This didn't happen all at once, but I moved in a different direction, with a different step from that moment. It was a beautiful experience.[26]

Was it just a "beautiful experience," or was it a "mystical experience"? The great spiritual writer and Cistercian monk, Thomas Merton

Part: I – Ian: Early Life and Vocation...   45

had a similar mystical experience on 18 March 1958, in downtown Louisville, Kentucky.[27] It would change his life and influence countless others. Experiences like these leave such an indelible mark on those concerned that they recall with precision the day, place and circumstances. Thomas Merton recalled the exact spot at the corner of Fourth and Walnut in the centre of the shopping district, when he was "suddenly overwhelmed with the realization that I [he] loved all those people, that they were mine and I theirs, that we could not be alien to one another even though we were total strangers."[28] Merton's experience happened on an ordinary day when he was running errands for the monastery. In the same way, Ian's mystical experience happened in the middle of an ordinary day on the steps of a post office.

July 1951 was to become a major turning point in Ian's life. Fr Harold Lalor, a prominent Jesuit speaker among Catholics in Melbourne, and an influential personality of *The Movement*, spoke in the parish centre in Kew and Ian attended the event.[29] According to Ian, Harold Lalor was a dramatic and in many ways controversial figure, especially when he gave speeches against Communist infiltration of the trade unions in Australia. The meeting was on this topic and was targeted at all the men in the parish.

> On the Saturday there was an invitation that came from my parish to my father.... There was to be a meeting.... A lot of the men in the parish were invited and my father wasn't one who would go to those things and so he tossed it across, and said, 'You can go if you wanted.' And it was Harold Lalor giving a talk on the struggle of *The Movement*... the constant strikes at the coal mines and transport, dock workers. I remember going to work and for three months there were no trains, had to walk to work.... I was drifting at the time. I had given up my job and here I was. The meeting was on a Monday night.
>
> My mother had given me a couple of pounds and I still had a go at the horses on a Saturday, and I won 25 pounds and Harold Lalor gives this talk and I go up to him and I

> gave him all the 25 pounds. I sort of felt moved and I said to him, 'I'd like to talk to you' and he said 'There's no time now. Come and see me during the week.'[30]

After his personal meeting with Father Lalor, it did not take Ian long to decide that his calling was to the Society of Jesus which had already moulded him in the values and attitudes of Ignatius of Loyola for more than ten years. He quickly contacted the Jesuits and asked to be admitted to the novitiate in October of that same year. His "desire [was] to devote my life to the Glory of God and with His Grace, I want to bring souls to his Most Sacred Heart."[31] Asked whether he had any fears that he might not be suitable for religious life, Ian answered, "None that, I pray, cannot be overcome with the Grace of God."[32] As to whether he had spoken to his parents about his wish, Ian stated affirmatively that they had given him their consent and prayers. To the last question in the same questionnaire, about the reason why Ian wished to become a Jesuit, he wrote, "Because the spirit of the Order would help me to imitate Christ and the scope of the Order's work would enable me to serve God in whatever sphere of activity He should desire."[33]

It was Harold Lalor again, who filled in Ian's *Informatio de Candidato Scholastico* on 4 September 1951. In his opinion Ian would make an excellent candidate for the Society but he suggested that the young man's entry be deferred until February 1952.[34] Was Ian upset? We don't know. One thing is sure, namely that Ian trusted him:

> Father Lalor was a very committed man. He had a great faith. He really believed his faith. He had an enthusiasm, and a great power in his approach and he was the one who directed me, other young people, young women into religious orders at that time, and young men into seminaries.[35]

Unlike other congregations, the Jesuits consider entrance day the first day of belonging to the Order, not the day on which vows of poverty, chastity and obedience are made. This is the date that figures on the tombstones of Jesuits together with those of their

Part: I – Ian: Early Life and Vocation...   47

birth and death. Ian entered the Jesuit novitiate in Watsonia in February 1952. Loyola College in Watsonia, on Melbourne's northern outskirts had opened as novitiate, retreat house and seat of philosophy studies for the Society in Australia in 1934, and novices came from all over the country. Among the nineteen candidates who joined the novitiate that year were Daven Day from Perth, John Harte and Des Walker. Together with Ian, the three of them were to build a long-lasting relationship. At eighteen, Daven was the youngest, while John, a brilliant musician, was nineteen and had already finished a university course. Des was twenty-seven years old when he started the novitiate, a veteran of World War II, and nearest in age to Ian. Hence their immediate closeness. But it was Daven who would eventually be accepted "as part of" the Travers-Ball family. Because he was from Perth he had no immediate family in Melbourne. The local novices could go into the garden to see their parents once a month, and occasionally they could take one of the other novices. In Ian's case it was always Daven. Another fellow novice would recall, "We loved Ian a lot because he was a normal person, he had lived a normal life. He wasn't sort of excessively pious as a novice. Well, Australians in general are not very pious (like some Indians or some Europeans). He used to go to the annual colleges rowing boat race carnivals, he used to drink — he was a normal young man. And that's why we liked him. That was all normal for a young person; that was completely normal."[36]

Life in the novitiate was tough. Some of his companions saw Ian's experience as an advantage and looked up to him, but it may in fact have been harder for one who had already "lived in the outside" world longer than the other novices: "So I went to the Jesuits. In those days, formation was pretty disciplined. We didn't have much scope for wandering off the track. And then I found it hard."[37] Fr Edward (Ned) Riordan — an Irish Jesuit — was the novice director at that time. He was strict and tough.

> I certainly appreciated that rather rigorous novitiate, not at that time so much. Later when I went to India, and lived in traditions that were much more demanding, that

preparation, that training that I got in the discipline and asceticism in the novitiate, certainly stood me in good stead in later years.[38]

Absolute silence and Latin! Latin was spoken at all times during the day except for half an hour after lunch and maybe in the last fifteen minutes of the half hour recreation in the evenings. Everything else, including lectures and classes (not to mention liturgy) was in Latin. During this two-year period of novitiate, the *primi* — the first-year novices — made their long thirty-day retreat according to the Spiritual Exercises of St Ignatius of Loyola.[39]

Mr Ian Travers-Ball, SJ, took his first vows of poverty, chastity and obedience on 2 February 1954. (A month before that, Ian made his will.)[40] It was at the same Loyola College in Watsonia that he began the juniorate programme — his first year in Humanities.

Pondering on his life and these early stages as a young Jesuit, Andrew commented:

What I received from the Jesuits … my experience with them as a boy at school and then later when I joined them as a novice and through my years of training, God, Christ was at the centre of everything. St Ignatius called it the society, when he founded 'The Society of Jesus'. And Jesus was truly at the centre of Jesuit life, Jesus was the centre of the spiritual exercises of St Ignatius.[41]

Part: I – Ian: Early Life and Vocation...

1. Travers-Ball residence —14 Findon Crescent.

2. Frederick Henry Travers-Ball — father of Ian.

3. Anne Margaret Cecilia Miller — mother of Ian.

4. Immaculate Conception Church — Hawthorn.

Part: I – Ian: Early Life and Vocation...

5. *Melbourne 1922 – Aimée, Brendan, Joan, Lucy, Leo, Mary.*

6. *Ian and school friend Brian Grutzner — Fitzroy Gardens, 1939.*

7. The Under 13s football team — Ian standing first on the right.

8. Ian with his mother and sisters c. 1941.

Part: I – Ian: Early Life and Vocation...

9. School photo c. 1942.

10. Possibly a school graduation party — Girl unknown c. 1945.

11. Ian (first on left) with old Xavierans c. 1950.

12. As a young Jesuit in Watsonia with his mother c. 1952.

Part: I – Ian: Early Life and Vocation...

13. Ian in the middle with Michael Doyle and John Hurney. Watsonia c. 1952.

14. Receiving the Missionary Cross — 28 November 1954 – with his sisters Aimée and Lucy and brother-in-law Keith.

15. Remembrance Photo of the Fourth Group of Jesuits to sail to India 1 December 1954.

Part: I – Ian: Early Life and Vocation...

Endnotes

[1] In 1990, during a retreat talk given by Brother Andrew at Gracewood – God's Farm, "I think of my own grandmother. She came out to Australia as a young girl of nineteen — alone, on a sailing boat from Liverpool, God knows how long it took to come out to Australia in the 1840s which must have been a pretty rough thing. Met my grandfather who was some sort of a sailor. She was dead before I came on the scene, but the story was pretty hard news. I suppose we've all suffered a bit from that, but there is a woman of her time. What was she doing in Liverpool, alone, a girl of 19, during the potato famine or something or other? And she comes out here to Australia, the white convict settlement."

[2] Mary Vincentia Ennis née Travers-Ball, born 1912 in Armadale, Victoria. She married in 1934, but had no children. She died in 1988 and is buried in the family tomb at Boroondara Cemetery in Kew.
Leo Thomas Travers-Ball, born 1913 in St Kilda, Victoria. He died in 1985, in Hawthorn, Victoria. He married and had a daughter, Leone Simons née Travers-Ball, currently living in Sydney. She has three children: Timothy, Kate and Jane.
Lucy Arcadius Smith née Travers-Ball, born 1915, in Arcadia, Victoria. She died in 2007, and is buried in Boroondara Cemetery in Kew. Lucy married Harry Smith in 1945 and had two sons: James and Gregory. James is married to Gabrielle and has five children: Thomas, Matthew, Kate, Andrew and Edward; Gregory is not married.
Joan Beatrice Travers-Ball, born 1916 in Brighton, Victoria. She died aged 12 on 14 August 1928 and is buried in the family tomb in Boroondara Cemetery in Kew.
Brendan Marius Travers-Ball born 1917, in Brighton, Victoria. He married in 1948 but had no children and died in 1981, in Rosebud.
Aimée Antoinette Millership née Travers-Ball, born 1919, in Brighton, Victoria. She married Keith Millership in 1948, and had three children: David, Julian, and Anne. (None of them have children). Aimée died in 2017.

[3] Egan, Eileen, *Such a Vision of the Street, Mother Teresa — The Spirit and the Work,* New York, USA: Image Doubleday, 1985.

[4] Related by Yesudas Mannooparampil, MC, who said that Andrew's sister Aimée had told him the story of the doctor in an informal chat, and by Betty Peaker at God's Farm in an interview with the author. (20180328 IF Betty Peaker)

[5] On a trophy cup Ian won at school for a sporting event — and conserved by one of his nieces — the letter "A" appears to be engraved after Ian as if it were his second name: prophetically?

[6] Daniel Mannix, (1864 - 1963), Irish-born Roman Catholic prelate and one of Australia's most controversial political figures during the first half of the twentieth century. He became Archbishop of Melbourne in 1917. After World War II Mannix sought to stop Communist infiltration of the Australian trade

unions; backing the largely right-wing Catholic Democratic Labour Party (founded by B. A. Santamaria). Mannix confirmed Andrew who would often go to pray at his tomb in St Patrick's Cathedral, Melbourne. (https://www.britannica.com/biography/Daniel-Mannix Web. 29 July 2020.)

7. Most probably when Frederick and Anne married as they were living in Shakespeare Grove until the early 1920s. For about ten years they lived at 18 Kinkora Road, Hawthorn, moving in the early '30s to 5 Howard Street in neighbouring Kew.

8. Findon Crescent featured: "entertaining rooms such as a commodious entrance hall leading to drawing room with bay windows and open fire, large dining room, study cum family room opening to rear garden with ample room for a pool. Master bedroom with extensive built-in robes, full bathroom, well-fitted kitchen and walk-in pantry and breakfast area, laundry cum utility room. Upstairs there was a second bathroom with separate W.C. and shower, four generous bedrooms, two of which open to sunroom overlooking front garden. Further features include central heating, garage and an abundance of off-street parking and huge storage areas." It was eventually sold in 1988.

9. Among the Travers-Balls' neighbours was the Menzies family. The father, Sir Robert Menzies became Prime Minister of Australia from 1939 to 1941 and from 1949 to 1966.

10. From a talk given by Brother Andrew circa 1994 or 1995 at Gracewood - God's Farm, Australia.

11. 20180319 IR Leone, Kate and Jane Simons. Leone was almost 78 at the time of this interview. She exuded the charm of Nana Ball, elegant in her simplicity. Married to Peter but widowed, she lived in Sydney. They had three children: Kate, Jane and Timothy Paul. She and her Melbourne-cousins believe that Timothy inherited Uncle Ian's personality.

12. From a talk given by Brother Andrew circa 1994 or 1995 at Gracewood - God's Farm, Australia.

13. 19510904 MJ Entrance Application to novitiate. From the Informatio de Candidato Scholastico when Ian requested permission to join the Jesuit Order in 1951.

14. 20180305 IR Anne and Julian Millership, Jim Smith.

15. From a talk given by Brother Andrew circa 1994 or 1995 at Gracewood - God's Farm, Australia.

16. Most probably betting illegally with a Starting Price bookmaker in his locality since the Totalisator Agency Board (TAB) in Victoria began operating in 1961 as a state enterprise.

17. Solomon, Geoffrey D., *Brothers of Mother Teresa,* Homebush NSW: St Paul Publications, 1987.

18. Laurels, Old Xaverians' Association, Melbourne, 30 November 1971.

19. From a talk given by Brother Andrew circa 1994 or 1995 at Gracewood - God's Farm, Australia.

Part: I – Ian: Early Life and Vocation... 59

20 20180305 IR Anne and Julian Millership, Jim Smith.

21 The Young Liberal Movement was formed in Melbourne in 1945 by Sir Robert Menzies. Its manifesto "encourage[s] members to participate not only in political aspects of the Liberal Party, but also in a regular sporting competition, in community service activities and in numerous social events as part of its broad, all-encompassing charter, as defined in our Movement's By-laws."

22 At this time, there were three major political parties in Australia: the right-wing Liberal Party, the left-wing Communist Party and the Labour Party somewhere in between. In 1954 after a split in the Labour Party, the Democratic Labour Party (DLP) was born. The DLP — a staunch anti-Communist party mostly, but not exclusively made up of Catholics of Irish descent — a was backed by influential members of the Roman Catholic Church, including the then Archbishop of Melbourne, Daniel P. Mannix. The intellectual leader of the Victorian Catholic wing of the DLP was Bartholomew A. Santamaria who had been heading together with Harold Lalor, SJ, the Catholic Social Studies Movement (often known as The Movement) modelled on the Catholic Action groups in Europe.

23 From a talk given by Brother Andrew circa 1994 or 1995 at Gracewood - God's Farm, Australia.

24 Brother Andrew, MC, *What I Met Along the Way*, London, UK: Darton, Longman and Todd Ltd., 1987.

25 The name of the horse was divulged by Andrew during his interview on the BBC with Terry Wogan on 29 April 1987. "I can still remember the name of the horse, it was called "Regent King". It was very, very narrowly picked, there was a young rider on the horse, who, if he'd been a bit smarter, he could have possibly won that race."

26 Brother Andrew, MC, *What I Met Along the Way*, London, UK: Darton, Longman and Todd Ltd., 1987.

27 Thomas Merton, (1915 – 1968). Born in France of a New Zealander father and an American mother — both artists. After a rambunctious youth and adolescence, Merton converted to Roman Catholicism and in 1941 joined the Abbey of Gethsemani, a community of monks of the Order of Cistercians of the Strict Observance (Trappists), the most ascetic of Roman Catholic monastic orders. Friends with Daniel Berrigan, Dorothy Day, and other famous members of the 1960s peace movement, he was also interested in Asian religions, particularly Zen Buddhism. It was during a trip to a conference on East-West monastic dialogue that Merton died near Bangkok in tragic circumstances.

28 Merton, Thomas, *Conjectures of a Guilty Bystander*, New York: Image Classic, 1968. (A plaque marks the event in downtown Louisville — the only one in the United States to commemorate a mystical experience.)

29 Harold Lalor, (1911 – 1969). A well-known public figure in Perth in the 1930s. A contemporary of Cardinal Knox of Melbourne during his seminary days, he

was ordained a priest in 1939 for the diocese of Perth, and in 1946 he asked to start novitiate with the Jesuits in Watsonia. A fiery and sensational speaker, he quickly made both friends and enemies — especially when crusading against Communism, first in Sydney and later with Bob Santamaria in Melbourne through The Movement. 1959 – 1968 he worked with various sodalities and established Indianaid for groups of people who founded special projects within the Jesuit mission in India. For this reason he occasionally travelled to Calcutta and also Hazaribagh. He began the Co-Workers of Mother Teresa in Melbourne a few months before he died in 1969.

[30] From a talk given by Brother Andrew in 1991 at Gracewood – God's Farm, Australia.

[31] Quoted from the entrance application to the Jesuit Novitiate as completed by Ian Travers-Ball.

[32] Ibid.

[33] Ibid.

[34] The original document records the date erroneously as February 1951.

[35] From a talk given by Brother Andrew circa 1994 or 1995 at Gracewood - God's Farm, Australia.

[36] 20180227 IJ Hans Hendriks, SJ.

[37] From a talk given by Brother Andrew circa 1994 or 1995 at Gracewood - God's Farm, Australia.

[38] Ibid.

[39] Also called The Exercises, composed 1522-1524 by Ignatius of Loyola, they are divided into four "weeks", the major themes being sin and God's mercy, episodes in the life of Christ, the Passion of Jesus, and the Resurrection of Jesus together with a contemplation of God's love. This last is often seen as the goal of Ignatian spirituality: to find God in all things.

[40] Ian's will reads as follows: "I, Ian Travers-Ball, Jesuit novice of Loyola, Watsonia Victoria, do hereby certify that I have no debts. I have no personal or real estate. Such chattels and personal effects as I own in the novitiate will become the property of the Domus Probationis at Loyola when I take my vows. Should I after my first vows and before my final vows, become the owner of personal or real estate, under the terms of Epit. 479, par. 1, I hereby promise to cede its administration in accordance with Canon 569 par. 2. I hereby appoint as my administrator from this date to the date of my Renunciation, Mr. F.H. Travers-Ball of 14, Findon Crescent, Kew, Victoria. I hereby appoint that all income accruing to me from my real or personal estate from this date to the date of my Renunciation be paid by my administrator to Rev. Austin Kelly of 130, Power Street, Hawthorn, Provincial for the time being of the Province of Australia for my training and support. In accordance with Epit. 481, par. 1, I promise to make my Renunciation at the time fixed by my Provincial and in the manner prescribed n Epit. 481-490 Art. II. Ian Travers-Ball, Loyola Watsonia, 11th January, 1954."

[41] From a talk given by Brother Andrew circa 1994 or 1995 at Gracewood - God's Farm, Australia.

PART – II

TRAVERS – AS A JESUIT IN INDIA (1954 – 1966)

*I personally owe so much to the Jesuits —
a richness that I received.*

– BROTHER ANDREW

An unexpected event took place in July of that same year, 1954: a film about the life and work of the Columban Fathers working in Burma and the Philippines was shown to the young Jesuits. Ian was so taken and moved by it that he decided to ask to go to the newly-established mission in India. The next day he spoke with his former novice master who in turn advised him to write to the provincial of the Society. Austin Kelly, SJ, had been head of the Jesuits in Australia since the erection of the province in 1951. Things proceeded quite quickly and by September Ian had received a positive answer. Enthusiastically he cycled home to break the news to his parents. Unfortunately, Frederick was still somewhat opposed to his son's vocation (despite Ian's statement that he had both parents' blessing in his application to join the Society), and this disapproval was intensified by Ian's wanting to leave Australia for a faraway mission country. Ian's mother was, moreover, very sick. She died on 6 October, less than two months before her son set sail for India.

On Sunday, 28 November 1954, the Ceremony of Presenting the Crosses for the Melbourne area took place at the Church of the Immaculate Conception in Hawthorn. (The same ceremony had been held in St Mary's North Sydney two days previously for those Jesuits living in the Sydney area due to leave for India.) Father Kelly presented the Missionary Cross to five Jesuits — a tradition started by Ignatius of Loyola when St Francis Xavier left on his missionary journey to the Far East. "Go, set the whole world on fire with the love of God," was Ignatius' mandate. The only photo we have of Ian's receipt of the cross shows him standing with Lucy, Keith and Aimée, a clean-shaven young man wearing a white cassock and holding the cross in his hands. We do not know whether his father was present, but it is reasonable to assume that Frederick did not attend the function to mark his son's despatch to India.

On 1 December 1954 Ian, together with Rev. Michael Doyle, Rev. Stephen Daly, Rev. Michael Mulhearn and Mr John Hurney boarded the P&O Liner *Strathaird*.[1] The five young Jesuits were too enthusiastic to realise that they did not have first-class tickets that would entitle them to cabins on the upper decks. Still they managed to enjoy the voyage. Dr Frank Mobbs who was on the same ship recalled: "We met on the P&O ship *Strathaird* in December 1954." Mobbs remembered the whole group of Jesuits going to India, but particularly young Ian, because, "fortunately he teamed with me to win the deck tennis competition. Without him, I faced certain defeat."[2] The journey took sixteen days. On Tuesday 14, the ship arrived in Colombo, Ceylon, (Sri Lanka) and from that port of call, John Hurney wrote:

> The trip so far has been very enjoyable, one of the best holidays I have ever had, although I have always loved the sea. Fathers Mulhearn and Daly are very well and looking in top form. Mr Travers-Ball and Mr Doyle are also in the best of health and all enjoying themselves no end. The only misadventure was signalled by an alarm at midnight, which brought the passengers tumbling on deck, under the impression that the ship was going down. A 'new-chum' cabin boy had fallen into the sea. The captain was shouting to the victim to catch hold of one of the illumined lifebuoys, and not to be afraid since there were no sharks in the area. The lad did as he was told, and was soon rescued with great efficiency.[3]

Fr Kevin Grogan (who had arrived in India in 1951), and Jim Collins, SJ, were in Bombay to meet the young Jesuits when they arrived at about seven in the morning on 17 December 1954. From there, Fathers Mulhearn and Daly, Mr John Hurney and Ian were assigned to Bihar where they were to start the arduous task of learning Hindi.

THE AUSTRALIAN JESUITS IN INDIA

After the Second World War, the Belgian Jesuits' Ranchi Mission was short of manpower. These priests, part of the Calcutta Province, had first come to India in the middle of the nineteenth century and included the famous Fr. Constant Lievens who had arrived in Chota Nagpur in 1885.[4] Expansion around Ranchi followed, as a consequence of which the bishop there, Oscar Sevrin, SJ, appealed to the general superior of the Jesuits, Jean Baptiste Janssens to send English-speaking Jesuits to his province. Father Kelly, then vice-provincial of the Australian Jesuits, agreed, despite criticisms from some of his colleagues who warned that overextension was looming. Kelly, a man of impossibly high standards and autocratic manner, went ahead with his decision.

The first group of six Jesuit priests was sent from the Australian Province in 1951. Their enthusiasm as young scholastics was quickly evident in their innovative spirit. Right from the beginning they immersed themselves in the life of the native tribal people to the extent that Hans Hendriks, studied the traditional Santal "pagan" ritual of sacrifice, and Phil Crotty, organised a tribal dance competition in an era when it was strictly forbidden for Christians to engage in such activities. Later, they would be introduced as part of the opening rite at feasts and occasional Eucharistic celebrations. Peter Doherty went so far as to live among the *Harijans*, the untouchables, and Bill Dwyer became an expert in Hindi.[5]

Three elements comprised the motivating force in the Ranchi Church:
- The preaching of faith and subsequent formation of believing communities,
- Education through schools to eradicate illiteracy,
- Social uplifting of the poor through cooperative credit societies.

In 1953 the four-page bulletin *Hazaribagh*, was first published to distribute information about the young Jesuits in the Hazaribagh and Palamau districts. (It later changed its name to *News from India* and then *Jesuit Mission News*.)

But there still remained a hurdle at the provincial level: how were the Hazaribagh and Palamau districts' missions to be financed? Father Kelly appointed John Hamilton Smith, SJ, as mission director and in May 1952 the first Maytime Fair was organised at Xavier College in Melbourne, followed, in 1953, by the first India Bazaar at St Ignatius' College in Sydney. The Maytime Fair, with its rides, food stalls, homemade and local delicacies, music and various raffles, soon became the main fundraiser in Victoria for the Jesuit Mission in India.

The Travers-Ball family would actively participate in the Maytime Fair, especially once the youngest brother Ian had travelled to India. The fair, together with the Christmas meeting at the Jesuit Provincialate House on Power Street, during which families were able to talk on the telephone with their loved ones in India, became an annual fixture for the Travers-Balls.

RANCHI — Studying Hindi

By the time the young Australian Jesuits reached their first destination, Ranchi, news had arrived that Harold King, SJ, had joined the Mission Office in Melbourne as procurator and assistant director. In fact, it was to Father King that Ian addressed his first letter from Manresa House in Ranchi. In it he wrote "[we] are settled in by now and up to our ears in Hindi."[6] After some further small talk, Ian came to the main concern of his letter. He was worried about his father:

> Well, Father, perhaps the real reason of my writing is to ask a favour of you. Just before I left my mother died and my father, a man of 75, is living on his own. He could live with my sisters, but feels he could not put up with their young families. For many years, he had not been to the Sacraments, but at my mother's death, he confessed & received Communion. However, he cannot make the effort to go to Mass, fasting — or even to Mass and he has a complex about Confessing. He does say his prayers, however, and says several rosaries each

day. I would like to ask, if you could call on him, with a view to confession and perhaps take him Communion. He is not very happy and the Sacraments would help him so much. He is a bit of "a problem child", Father, and I know I am giving you a tall order. I shall pray for your success however. I shall tell him that you will call on him about the Sacraments. The best time to see him is in the morning of any day except Saturday and Sunday.[7]

This was the first but not the last request young Ian made of Father King. On receipt of Ian's letter the priest did in fact contact Frederick Travers-Ball, whereupon Ian worried about the reception Father King might have had from his father!

My sister wrote telling me that you had been on the phone with Dad, and between us we imagined the reception you probably got. I am sorry for this and thank you for your efforts. Poor Dad is not too happy. Please God he will be alright and in due time will set things right.[8]

Frederick was still not happy about his son's joining the Jesuits, let alone his leaving for India, especially after his mother's death. These disappointments, together with his long-lasting resentment against the Church at large, would take some years to heal — but healing did come when the time was right with God.

All in all, Ian was happy in Ranchi. This was the first time he had left his hometown to live in a new country, new surroundings and especially, a new culture. It was exciting. He was captivated:

Easter was a happy time. We attended the ceremonies at the Cathedral and somehow, you can feel the joy & the peace of the people. I had the happy consolation on Good Friday to help with the Veneration of the Cross after the Stations. It was wonderful the way the mothers would manoeuvre the babies' heads to touch the Cross.[9]

Hindi is not an easy language to learn, and young Ian found it hard and tedious. But if he wanted to be efficient and useful to the people he was going to serve as an ordained Jesuit priest, he had to learn the language. His being Australian helped him to find humour in the classes, and in an article he described a typical day for a Jesuit Hindi scholar in Ranchi. The task of teaching Hindi fell to Fr Peter Shanti, a priest with infinite patience. The students, all Jesuits, came from all over the world — New Zealand, Belgium, Australia, Malta, China and even Goa. It felt "like the United Nations, only more united."[10]

On their day off the young seminarians used to go out with a little box of first aid. One day, Ian recounted:

> When I was still a Jesuit ...a poor man gave me an early lesson in that, as young seminarians we used to go out in India, one day a week on our day off, with a little box of medicine, first aid, very simple stuff and we go to a slum and we do little things for the people and we go on a bike and you have your box of medicines. You didn't have any money in those days, there was no pocket money for seminarians; we were finishing the work and tidying up and this poor man started talking to me and he was telling me about his situation. He didn't have a job, and he had a family and children, and they were having tremendous difficulty, and he was telling me this and I was beginning to get a bit nervous and I said to him, "You know I don't have any money, I can't help you. And I really can't do anything." And that poor man looked at me and said, "I know that," he said, "you can just listen to me."
>
> That was a great lesson. He knew I didn't have money, and he wasn't really asking, but here is this man in desperate need who just wanted to talk.
>
> And so the richness of all those poor people, and the beauty, the beautiful characters, there are poor people like rich people, whose circumstances destroy them and damage them. But there are many who are really wonderful human people and definitely I have been greatly enriched by them.[11]

Four months passed and Ian welcomed a well-deserved break from his Hindi classes. Two things were due: the major vacation and departure for Poona to start philosophy studies.

> Before leaving Ranchi, I was able to spend almost the full time of the Major Vacation at Sarwada [54 km from Ranchi] and it was indeed enjoyable. We stayed in the village school. Conditions were such that, apart for the holiday side, the experience should be valuable for the future. In addition, I went on a two-day cycle tour on which I saw five different Fathers' bungalows and schools, which was very interesting.[12]

POONA—Philosophy Studies

By 21 May 1955, Ian was in Poona after a train journey of more than forty hours. Poona in the west-central Maharashtra state of India was and still is the cultural centre of the Maratha people and a major educational and cultural hub, at times referred to as the "Oxford and Cambridge of India." Nowadays it has at least twenty-three major formation houses for both male and female Religious. "Of course, I am very happy to be starting Philosophy, but I was sorry to leave Ranchi, as my stay there had been pleasant and I shall always have good memories of it," Ian wrote to his provincial in Australia.[13] In Poona he began his scholastic period at the Papal Athenaeum, the history of which goes back to 1893 when Pope Leo XIII founded the Papal Seminary in Kandy, Sri Lanka, and entrusted its direction and administration to the Society of Jesus.[14] While studying at the Papal Athenaeum, Ian lived at the Jesuit Residence, De Nobili College, or as folk around used to call it "Nobility College!"[15]

When Ian arrived in 1955, De Nobili College was still in its beginnings, having been transferred from Sri Lanka. William (Bill) Dwyer, SJ, in an article for *Hazaribagh* No. 26, January-February, 1955, related how while the seminary, a "massive blue-stone building," was already erected, it was still not unusual to see a small army of seminarians planting and caring for trees in the semi-desertic land.

Philosophy classes that year started on 13 June, but before that the scholastics had their annual eight-day retreat given by a Father

John Marti from the Bombay Seminary. Other activities also kept Ian busy. After only three months he was interceding with the Father Provincial in Melbourne on behalf of Paul Wenisch, SJ. Father Paul had started publishing a paper called Christ Reigns and in Ian's opinion he was in need of a printing machine, the funding for which could be raised in Australia.

Peter Sontag, SJ, was to become a pivotal person for young Ian. When they first met, Father Peter — an American Jesuit who had arrived in India two years earlier — had already begun the Institute of Home Study (IHS) with the aim of explaining Catholic doctrine to non-Christians with no access to higher studies. Sontag saw Ian's potential as a writer and encouraged him. Most likely thanks to Sontag, Ian was to become acquainted with the writings of Catherine de Hueck Doherty, Dorothy Day, Leonard Cheshire, and Boris Simon's book about Henri Marie Groués — better known as Abbé Pierre.[16] These writers, among others, had an important influence on Ian by making him aware of the necessity for Christians to actively help the poor.

Years later, Ian (by then Brother Andrew) met Dorothy Day in Calcutta, and told her how the Catholic Worker movement she had started in 1933 had been an important part of his spiritual journey. During his time in Poona his main concern was an intense spiritual life, a personal spiritual life, unfortunately cut off from the everyday sorrows and struggles of the poor. After all, he had been sent to India to serve the missions of the Society of Jesus. However, while reading The Catholic Worker newspaper, which other Jesuits received regularly, he was reminded of how he had always wanted to do something for the poor, especially in the form of a community to which the poor and lonely could come and experience a sense of hospitality.

In his capacity as a junior Jesuit, he did try to do something for the poor (albeit indirectly), and maybe, as his contemporary Phil Crotty related in an interview, Ian's earlier "betting strategies" now came in handy. In a letter to Father King, Ian expressed an idea he had been pondering: he would send Father King Christmas cards

Part – II: Travers – As a Jesuit in India (1954 – 1966)

made in India. Ian was already selling them for 16 rupees per 100 with envelopes — and about 14½ rupees without envelopes. He even asked Father King to send him Olympic Games cover stamps so that he [Ian] could sell them. Such was the force or charm of Ian's conviction that, after working out important and pertinent details, Father King took up the new enterprise.[17]

Ian was starting to find his niche as a man, as a Jesuit, and a writer. From his letters to the Provincial he seemed to be happy in the Society of Jesus and grateful that he was in India.

> One thing I am very grateful for, Father, is to have been sent to India before Philosophy. And greater ease in learning Hindi. I think there are enormous advantages in meeting Indian scholas.[scholastics], seeing village life and conditions, hearing at De Nobili a great variety of talks by leading men on important local affairs, as well as getting used to the climate and generally settling in.[18]

He was looking forward to his ordination:

> Last week we had the ordination (39 new Fathers) and they were very impressive. It was the first time I have seen the ceremony and I must say it had me counting the years to the Priesthood. Relatives come from all over India, as well as from Europe & America. It was moving to see the parents' tears of joy as they received their sons' first blessings.[19]

Such a scene would have surely moved Ian, given that by now his father was trying to rebuild their relationship:

> Dad has been writing to me much more frequently. He is of course still lonely, but is keeping on very well. He was 77 on Monday, but from all accounts is in A-1 health.[20]

At the same time Ian seemed more at peace with the situation. His father started to approach the sacraments again, and at Easter 1956 Frederick intended attending the Holy Week functions. Holy Week, the most solemn week in the Catholic Church, was also celebrated with great devoutness at De Nobili:

> Now of course, we are in the midst of the Holy Week ceremonies. We have them in the Theologians' chapel and the people are in attendance too. It is wonderful to see them kneeling after a hard day's work in the heat. How God must love them. The Marathi women instead of genuflecting, they prostrate themselves touching the ground with their foreheads and it is certainly a very fervent gesture.[21]

Ian, as ever, was more inspired and touched by the simple, ordinary people than the ceremonies and rites.

With Holy Week over, the major vacation was due. On 19 April 1956, the seminarians were off to Mahabaleshwar, a hill station in the Sahyadri mountain range. Located in one of India's few evergreen forests, during the British Raj it had served as the summer capital of Bombay province. Nature certainly attracted Ian. He was enthralled too by the ruins of the forts of the great Mahratha warrior Shivaji. Beauty also caught his attention. As always, however, he was more captivated by the relationships he could build with others, wondering while on his jungle walks and mountain climbs how he could be of service to a diverse spectrum of people:

> I met quite a few people up there — only the well-off & of course Jesuits, can make it. It is amazing how interested they are to learn something about the Faith. As my little bit of experience here grows, I come to think more and more that our time will be most fruitfully spent with the educated and influential folk. If we can find an attractive presentation that respects the people, I think it would be well received — no easy task, of course.[22]

Then, after his vacation, with the resumption of studies a different focus was required:

> Of course, after a month back at classes it seems years ago. The pressure is on this year, as we are having plenty of classes, but I think we'll survive it all.[23]

Part – II: Travers – As a Jesuit in India (1954 – 1966)

During the minor vacations, he used the time to undertake "a bit of a study of Missiology in a group under Fr [Richard] De Smet and it is very interesting. I have been studying the Dossiers of Père Charles and must say I find these a revelation. Fr De Smet attributes much of Belgium's drive in the last generation in this time to his work."[24]

"Living with Ian was good fun. He was a good companion!"[25] This is how Phil Crotty, now retired, described Ian during their time spent together in Poona: "I think it was Christmas-night Mass, or one of those night Masses, I remember, and we went on cycle, push-bike. So we attended the Mass, and we may have been serving at the altar or something like that. Anyway, after the Mass he was a bit of an adventurous person. He said, 'Let's do a circle of the city!' That means the main part of the city, at 1:30 in the morning. So we went off cycling and we did a circle of the city, we raced around, around, around."[26] What is also interesting is that his companions never called him Ian. To this day, the Jesuits who knew and lived with him all call him, "Travers". Father Crotty described Travers as one who, "was really loved. There was kind of a softness about him. There was a radicalness about him. There was a certain mad streak; that's what I mean with the fun. He had this streak. I think he needed to do what he did, to be his own, this slightly wild streak. He had that wonderfully. That thing I told you about riding around Poona in the middle of the night, that was him. Slightly mad, slightly wild but trying to get in touch with people. Oh, it was really about being in the city, we were locked up in the monastery and here we were riding around on cycles."[27]

THE NIYOGI REPORT

In a letter of 6 September 1956, to Father King, Ian mentioned very briefly that the scholastics in Poona were doing well despite exams and the Niyogi Report. He added that the very same morning, students from four schools had been for a walk and been beaten up. Whether the Niyogi Report and the beating were connected is hard to say, but it is worth mentioning something about that report.

India has always been wary of Christian missionaries, because of their support for the lower castes and the poor. When, in 1885, Fr Constant Lievens started his missionary work particularly amid the Mundaris and Oraons, he discovered that people were suffering due to enforced labour and land spoliation by the *zamindaris* — the landowners. His apostolate among these peoples involved accompanying them to the courts and defending them against deceit and unjust laws favouring the land owners. As a result, a huge conversion movement was set in motion. It is said that at that time Christians numbered over 73,000.

There may have been no direct connection between Father Lievens' activities in the nineteenth century and the 1956 Niyogi Report, but certainly the work started by this venerable Jesuit was not well received by the higher authorities of later times. Just a few years after her independence from British rule, India faced the division of assets between India and Pakistan, along with a huge refugee problem. Estimates are that about 5.5 million non-Muslims moved into India and a very large number of Muslims left India for neighbouring West and East Pakistan. India faced even bigger problems in the long term: the need for economic development; the eradication of poverty; and the imperative to rid the country of centuries-old social injustice, inequality and oppression. And it was in these areas that the Roman Catholic and other Christian Churches were most committed. Fear on the part of the civil authorities led them to establish a committee chaired by M. Bhawani Shankar Niyogi, a retired Chief Justice of the Nagpur High Court, and including five other members. The Niyogi Committee Report on Christian Missionary Activities was eventually issued by the government of Madhya Pradesh in 1956.

Its recommendations included the withdrawal of those foreign missionaries whose primary task was proselytization,

Part – II: Travers – As a Jesuit in India (1954 – 1966)

and the abolition of all medical and other professional services used as a direct means of conversion. The Constitution of India was expected to be amended so that conversion by force or fraud were absolutely prohibited. Also prohibited was any circulation of literature meant as religious propaganda without the approval of the state government.[28]

As expected, the report provoked dispute in India, especially among theologians, Christians and politicians. Its repercussions would be felt almost ten years later when Ian, by that time a Missionaries of Charity Brother, had to register at the foreign office, and young men coming from outside India to join the Congregation would find it difficult to enter and stay for a long period of time.[29]

SITAGARHA — Teachers' Training Institute

March 1958 found Ian finishing his philosophy studies and starting his regency period, the time between philosophy and theology in which the young Jesuit dedicates two or three years to direct ministry. Ian was sent to Sitagarha:

> I shall leave Poona with mixed feelings. It has been a really wonderful time (in spite of Philos.) and I have been very happy here. Still I am looking forward to the next item on the programme — Regency at the ashram in Hazaribagh. This anticipation is probably the blissful ignorance of a fool, since I'll be trying to teach in Hindi — so the need is for the gift of tongues in a hurry. Even so it will be great escape from the books.[30]

On the way to Bihar, Ian together with another student from Patna, broke the journey to visit the Ajanta and Ellora Caves. Before settling in Sitagarha, he spent three months teaching and acting as headmaster in a parish school in Hazaribagh. It was only in June that he finally arrived at the Teachers' Training Institute (TTI) in Sitagarha.

Sitagarha is situated six to seven kilometres from Hazaribagh. Hindi and Santali are the main local languages. In 1958 the

Hazaribagh Jesuit Educational Society established the Teachers' Training Institute to, as the name implies, educate and train young men who wanted to become teachers in village schools. Nowadays, the TTI is known as Primary Teachers Education College and features a two-year diploma course to prepare teachers for primary schools in Jharkhand.

Fathers Joseph de Pypere and Phil Crotty, and Ian were the intended pioneers of the Institute, but just as it was about to open, Crotty received a message from the Provincial, Fr Austin Kelly, to go to teach at University College in Ranchi.[31] This was a blow to Ian for two reasons: Phil knew more Hindi than he, and Phil and Ian were friends and made a good working team. In an article in *Hazaribagh*, Ian wrote:

> It was a wet rainy day in July at the beginning of the monsoon in 1958. The first trainees had ploughed their way through the muddy four miles from Hazaribagh to Sitagarha. And so our mission began a new venture for the training of teachers for village schools.
>
> It would be hard to imagine a more modest beginning. There were seventeen students, three of whom left the next day. The staff consisted of the Principal, Father de Pypere, SJ, a Belgian Jesuit loaned to Hazaribagh by the Ranchi Province, Brother Stanislaus Kerketta, SJ, an Indian lay-brother, and myself — an Australian. The kitchen was not yet built and the cooking was done in converted kerosene tins in the shelter of a rather open verandah.
>
> Since then the number of trainees has grown to over forty, and Rev. John Hurney, SJ, has added much more than his $33^1/_3\%$ numerical increase to the staff.
>
> In the Ranchi and Hazaribagh mission-fields there are more than 900 Catholic schools. Most of which are in the villages. Now, Mahatma Gandhi's idea of education for village India was to fit the children to live a richer and fuller life in their villages and to teach them improved methods in the work

particular to their own locality, whether it be spinning, weaving, agriculture, carpentry, pottery, etc.

In the field of our work most of the people are peasant farmers. So we have chosen Agriculture as our craft. The teachers are trained in the traditional subjects of Child Psychology, Methods of Teaching, School Management, etc., and they also learn new methods of Agriculture in class, as well as doing practical work on the farm we are trying to build up.

This means that they will be able to give the children of the villages an education adapted to their own environment. If their education is solely along the traditional lines, it often happens that for lack of opportunities in the village they flock to the cities for work, with the result that the benefits of education are lost to what is the largest section of the Indian people, namely, the villagers, who make up eighty percent of India's vast population, which is fast approaching the 400 million mark.

It is not an easy task to train teachers, especially when you are trying to cope with subjects like Child Psychology and Poultry-keeping, in a language that you are still struggling to master.

Still, it is a tremendously rewarding and inspiring work when you take time off to realise that the trainees you are trying to form will be teaching in their village for perhaps thirty years, and will have the whole succession of children from their village sitting before them all day for several years, wide open to the influence of a good and upright teacher. It is a very beautiful work and it is not only in the hands of us here at Hazaribagh, but all of you who say a prayer for our Mission and help in so many ways, you have a real share in a work, the fruits of which will not pass away with this life, but will shine for ever in the souls of thousands of Indian children who have found the true life from teachers who have been trained at Sitagarha.[32]

In various letters Ian confessed his inadequacy for such a job, especially when he had to teach courses like pedagogy and child psychology in a language he felt he was not good at. He used to prepare his lessons in English, translate them into Hindi and then read them to his students. As soon as the lesson ended he would leave the classroom so that the students had no opportunity to ask him questions. But Ian was not faint-hearted and whatever he undertook received his full effort (at least in the beginning). Eventually, his dream was to write a textbook in Hindi providing teachers with methods for teaching several classes. Even in adversity he never lost his sense of humour and in a letter to Michael Ryan, SJ, he admitted that his students nearly went on a strike because they could understand neither his classes nor his notes. Was this an exaggeration? It could be. What is worth mentioning is that more than forty years later, the Institute was still using Ian's notes for the curriculum.[33]

The fact that while Fr de Pypere was busy with the building and land management, Ian had the task of feeding the students, represented another challenge:

> They can't pay for their food and my happy task is to run the kitchen at 24/- per month. Some of the students are married with five or six children. So I laugh at myself teaching them Child Psychology.[34]

After visiting Sitagarha, Michael Eather wrote in the *Xavierian News* in 1962:

> Actually I take a couple of subjects in the Teachers' Training Institute and find that very interesting and rewarding as well. I get plenty of practice in Hindi too, as all the teaching there is in that language. We prepare boys with a two-year course for a government exam which qualifies them as primary teachers; they are all tremendously eager to do well, but they all find the theoretical subjects that are taught rather heavy going, as many of them have only studied up to eighth or ninth grade. But they all seem to get up to standard

in two years, and so far, no-one has failed. (This is mainly the work of Ian Travers-Ball who started the place going and laid the foundations for his successors).

But, before being a teacher, Ian was a Jesuit. It was not a job, but a vocation. And it was in relation to his vocation that Ian encountered his biggest hurdle — community life. From the time John Hurney, who had travelled from Australia to India with Ian, arrived, Ian found it very difficult. John himself was going through a vocational crisis, he did not have much Hindi, and on top of that John and Ian were very different. Geoffrey Solomon quoted Ian:

> He and I had been together before and we were very different characters. He was a very generous fellow and had no trouble in accepting me but I had a terrible struggle in living with him, even in being civil and talking nicely to him. It went on all that second year, I behaved very badly and meanly in that little community of three people. I knew I was doing wrong and that my behaviour was not charitable or loving but I just couldn't get over it. It was as if there were some kind of psychological knot tied up inside of me. Once or twice I wrote a letter to the Superior saying that I wanted to leave and go back to Australia, but somehow at the last moment I didn't pursue it.[35]

According to fellow Jesuits, "John Hurney and Travers did not get along very well. John was straightforward and Travers, less straightforward, very perceptive — much quieter than John. John was a straight shooter. Travers was much more benign."[36] For Ian, this was a great humiliation. Were his superiors aware? We will never know the answer. We do know, however, that Ian was called a year earlier than usual (possibly at his own request) to continue his theology studies back in Poona. His contemporaries also see it as plausible that Ian was older than they and so was permitted to continue his studies earlier. At any rate, by March 1960 Ian was back in Poona to start his Theology.

POONA — Theology Studies

Ian's theology studies started about a year after Angelo Giuseppe Roncalli was elected Pope John XXIII and gave notice of his intention to convene the Second Vatican Council. The council sought to revive the central role of Scripture and provide versions of the Bible in the local languages of the faithful. From then on the Mass would be celebrated in the vernacular. Culturally, this was the famous decade known as *The Sixties,* which became synonymous with the new, the radical and the subversive. In fact, the term usually describes an era of irresponsible excess and flamboyance that might also have had an impact on certain religious practices.

Some inside the Roman Catholic Church resisted changes and formed the basis of today's traditionalist Catholic groups; others left the Church for the opposite reasons. They felt that Vatican II's reforms did not go far enough. Most Catholics accepted the changes and it became a time of upheaval, a time of experimentation even within the Church herself. In Ian's own words:

> [I] was ordained a priest in India on 25th March 1963, after seven years of formation, which took place before the Second Vatican Council. That has left me as a sort of in-between creature amid the many ensuing changes in the Church, some good, some, as I see it now, not so good.[37]

About Ian's academic studies we really have nothing. We do not know whether or not he excelled in theology and other subjects. Changes were already taking place at the Papal Athenaeum and the use of Latin was tapering off. The years of philosophy were still in Latin but when the American Jesuits came from around the Jamshedpur and Patna Missions and joined the seminaries in Poona and Kurseong, changes occurred and the use of English increased. In Kurseong, even though lectures were in English, exams were still in Latin, to the shock of one American Jesuit seminarians who refused to sit for such a test. Exams were stopped, meetings were held, and from then on even exams were held in English, much to the seminarians' relief.

VOCATION PROMOTER

As soon as he arrived in Poona, Ian was assigned as a vocation promoter, recruiting young men who showed an interest in religious life within the Society of Jesus.

> Well to come to business — my letter is not so disinterested after all. I am conducting a bit of a campaign from here for vocations from Bombay, Kerala, Madurai, Mangalore, etc. There are a few nibbling and it would help a lot to let them have an occasional copy of "Hazaribagh". I asked Austin [Kelly] — who was just here for visitation — and he is very keen on the idea. Could you send me 25 copies each month? If you have any old copies, they would also be very useful. In fact, I have cut out pictures from old copies and made posters of them which I have sent to schools in the south.
>
> There are real possibilities in this line and I think we could get a good number every year, once we get our name known. Here is the ideal place, as we have got monks from all the vital places and they can put us right in contact.
>
> It's not just a matter of getting vocs [vocations], but we have to make them feel welcome once they come ...
>
> We've got a chance here as five of the boys are in philos. They are outstanding fellows — full of zeal and aware of problems right on their toes.[38]

Ian received the copies, and in a letter to Father King thanked him for sending the magazine each month that in turn was sent on to the boys: "Though I don't write much, I know that I wouldn't even have a ticket to the refectory if it were not for all you are constantly doing."[39]

In March 1961 in a letter sent to Father King from Mangalore, he explained the reason why he was away from his base in Poona. He was going round recruiting in parishes and villages in Mangalore, Kerala and Tamil Nadu. Two Jesuits recruited by Ian in the course of those travels were Fr Francis Lopez, originally from Mumbai and Fr K.A. Sebastian from Kerala. Father Lopez recalls that when he first met Ian and was asked by him whether he (Lopez) was interested in joining the Jesuits in Hazaribagh, he immediately accepted. In those days great stalwarts like Tony de Mello were emerging from Hazaribagh and Sitagarha. Ian was always cautious and prudent. Even though Francis was nineteen at that time, Ian wanted to meet his parents and have their blessing. According to Francis, his father really enjoyed the chat he had with Ian because it was a chance to speak English. Ian left a good impression on Francis' father, who even later kept in contact with him by letter. Francis considered Ian to be a wonderful guide: "I still remember when I went to Patna, Bettiah, for my candidateship, you know he wrote me a nice letter, and the first sentence I still remember, though he is dead and gone and I am so old. 'Resist your first temptation and the next will be easier to overcome.' And that was the trademark of my life."[40] He continued:

> He had a very shy character, very much withdrawn. I don't know very clearly how I came to the conclusion that he was not a community man. He was a community man but mostly because of his spirituality, that sort of spirituality he had already built up. So that would keep him aloof, keep him away from the mob or pretty big crowd. He was very instrumental in promoting, helping, guiding and moulding. Very nice man. You look at him and he had big eyes, and he simply stared in your face and he had that beard ...I must say his face would come close to Jesus Christ, so when I ever looked at him, he almost had me bow down before him. You feel shy, you feel a little scared of such people and they have big eyes and their eyes are so powerful, they immediately attract you towards them.[41]

THE WRITER

The earliest mention of any article written by Ian Travers-Ball, SJ, for an outside magazine or newspaper was in the widely distributed Bombay Diocesan newspaper *The Examiner*. It was an article which dealt with the social issues India was facing:

> Our country and its leaders are wrestling with enormous problems: poverty, hunger, unemployment, a huge population, integration of the varied communities of the land. Can I say I have taken a single step to relieve these problems? And if I haven't, my criticism of anyone is hollow and empty. It is so easy to blame others: the government, Congress, Communists, foreigners, poverty, the clergy, the laity. But I can blame no one else whatever their position, until I have faced up to these social problems, thought about them and taken at least a first step towards doing something.[42]

The first article published outside India, and held in the Missionaries of Charity Brothers' archives, was written by Ian in June 1962 for *The Month*. "The Writer in India Today" dealt with the strengths, weaknesses and opportunities of writers in contemporary India. In the article, Ian demonstrated an understanding of the situation in India not only from a writer's but also a sociologist's perspective. He had a good grasp of the English language and how to convey his ideas, and seemed already to be well-read in Indian literature. From then on, either under his own name or a *nom de plume*, he contributed to a variety of magazines: *The Examiner* in Bombay, *The Month* in England, and in the United States, *America* (a Jesuit periodical) and *Review for Religious*.

Ian was a remarkable and prophetic writer. Two of his writings during this time stand out. One, "No Magic Key" was published in 1963 in *America* magazine. The subtitle indicated what would be one of the tenets of his life: "Success follows only a lot of people doing a lot of little things." Little places, little people, little things — no big institutions, no big important people, no big enterprises are required — a theme which would echo until the end of Ian's life. He was already starting to move from his head to his heart, especially in the second article which would be crucially relevant to his life. "Rich Failure" published in 1963 in Volume 22 of *Review for Religious* explored the routine and mundane life into which a Religious can lapse and how that monotony can result in a sense of failure. Ian described how it is failure that makes a man think. God must always purify the Religious before He accomplishes great things through him. He must be jerked out of his complacency. He must stop taking everything for granted; it is failure of one kind or another that does this, provided failure is received creatively. Three pertinent ideas emerge from the article: God alone can help me, I need to re-examine my life, and finally as a result of this examination, I purify my intentions.

After the death of Father Peter Sontag, Theodore Bowling, SJ, succeeded him at the Institute for Home Studies (IHS) in Poona. The IHS programme consisted of fifty folders called *Know Christ Letters*, designed to explain Roman Catholic doctrine to non-Christians who had undergone less than a university-level education. When Father Bowling was on vacation in the United States, Ian was asked to take over the IHS programme. He promptly produced a series of ten pamphlets entitled *Meet Christ* to replace the old *Know Christ Letters*. According to Phil Crotty, SJ, these letters "in English as well as Hindi and most probably also Marathi were a means to make Christianity known in a simple non-threatening way. He [Ian] did that and he really enjoyed doing that. He was part of a group of people who were interested in dialogue. It was a dialogue magazine really. Dialoguing with Hindus and this is pre-Vatican [Council] II days so you are talking tentative efforts to reach out to other religions. I know he enjoyed doing that. He was also taking a journalism correspondence course but he did not finish. I think he saw that as a kind of vocation career — writing."[43] For some time Ian did in fact consider this idea, but God had other plans for him.

While managing the IHS programme, Ian — under the pseudonym Christanand (Hindi for Joy in Christ) — had begun one of his own publications, *MARG: "A Religious Newsletter for Modern Life."* It was a small (5" x 7"), eight-page monthly publication, and the first issue was produced in September 1964. Ian — by that time already Father Ian — was inspired (even when it came to the colour of ink used) by the English newsletter *Search* edited by Michael de la Bédoyère. The purpose of *MARG* was to show the relevance and meaning of religion in helping modern men and women face up to the problems they meet in daily life. *MARG* was a success, and people started asking Ian to increase the number of pages. This idea was impractical but he did come up with another option. He decided to publish what he called *A Map of Life*, made up of four booklets: *You Are the Driver*, *Points to Ponder*, *Seeing Clearly* and *Facing Hard Facts*.

PRIESTHOOD

A precise and succinct article by Don Collins is difficult not to reproduce in its entirety. It appeared in an issue of the *Xavierian*, [early 1963] and actually dealt with Ian's imminent ordination to the priesthood in India, but certain expressions used give the impression that Don knew Ian fairly well.

> Many Old Xavierians were seen at the recent Ordinations at St Patrick's Cathedral, Melbourne, but how many Old Boys will be present next March at Ranchi, India, when Ian Travers-Ball, SJ, is to be ordained? If you were a "Burke-Hooligan" about the middle thirties no doubt you would remember Ian, a quiet retiring fellow — tall and lean wandering slowly along Studley Park Road to and from his home in Kew. Ten years of schoolboy life amongst the Jesuits must have left their mark for after a few years out in the "world" as an insurance agent, Ian "returned" to the Society in 1951 as a novice; later, one year Juniorate and he was whisked off to India (for the record on the same

ship as Frs Michael Mulhearn, Michael Doyle, Steve Daly and Brother Jim McCormick). When Jesuits arrive on the mission field the first immediate problem is the language (or should we say "languages") so Ian found himself at Language School in Manresa House in the small but rowdy and crowded town of Ranchi. No doubt Ian has some not too fond memories of the blaring microphones spilling out their melodies at all odd hours of the night and morning.

Also on the mission fields as elsewhere the years speed by. 1955 saw him in Philosophy and by 1958 Ian had been "charmed" into a teaching post at the Teachers' Training College which had only just been opened at Sitagarha three miles or so from Hazaribagh. Here "Fr" T. Ball faced his biggest assignment yet for although he had had only a few short months at language school he was expected to lecture in Hindi on such abstruse and complicated subjects as Child Psychology, Pedagogy, Physiology and Botany. Ian however has always been partial to a good gamble — in fact, he can recall early days coming away from the course with only his taxi fare — so he accepted the challenge with his calm demeanour, but with gripping tenacity. What he did was this — he made notes on his subject matter, then wrote out his lectures in Hindi, had them corrected and then delivered the lecture. Later he compiled these notes into a book and today, 1963, these notes form the foundation of all lectures given in these subjects at the Institute—no one has fundamentally improved on them since. The amount of work heaped on his shoulders in those days was so great that Fr [Edmund] O'Connor swears that Ian used to work in his sleep.

Fr T. Ball's particular apostolate however has been in encouraging vocations — this he has fostered not only by his own personality and retreats but also by his writing articles in Indian Social Survey magazines. Indeed in recent years his writings have developed quite a name

Part – II: Travers – As a Jesuit in India (1954 – 1966)

for him — a short time ago one of his articles on the Indian social situation was published in the English Jesuit Intellectual Magazine Thought — a weekly production from Delhi. So prominent has he become in this field that we hear whispers that the Indian Social Institute look upon him with envying eyes.

And so you can see that Fr Ian Travers-Ball is quite a dark horse, he has a deceptive mien and appears to have unfathomable depths of capability which on first acquaintance are not obvious. He is still fundamentally very Australian, but has so well adapted himself to India — an adaptation of the mind more than of the externals; those that know him well say that his secret to success is his imperturbability and finally his sense of humour.

All Old Xavierians congratulate him on reaching that Primary milestone in his Priestly life and wish him every grace and happiness on his Day of Ordination.

We do not know the exact date when Ian returned to Ranchi for his ordination. In the Ranchi Bulletin of St. Mary's Cathedral, the following announcement was published: "We shall rejoice and thank God on the coming 23rd, 24th and 25th of March [1963] at the ORDINATION to the Subdiaconate, Diaconate and Priesthood, at the hands of His Grace in the Ranchi Cathedral, of five Ranchi-originated and four Australian Theologians for our Province proper and our Hazaribagh Region, namely:- Fr. Patrick Kullu (Rengarih), Fr. Marcus Lugun (Torpa), Fr. Thomas Bara (Rengarih), Fr. Placidus Lakra (Tongo), Fr. Deonis Tirkey (Trainser), Fr. Maurice Dullard, Fr. William Dwyer, Fr. John Reilly, Fr. Ian Travers-Ball."[44] It was a blessing to have the presence of the Australian Provincial Fr. Austin Kelly for the Ordination, and various friends and relatives were also present. For our Ian, his brother Brendan and Marie, Brendan's wife travelled to India from Australia. According to Fr. William Dwyer who was ordained with Ian that same day, it was the custom for many years to have Jesuits receive the three ordinations of subdiaconate, diaconate and priesthood on consecutive days. Bill also remembered that Andrew and he "shared a room in Ranchi in March 1963 during the days of the ceremonies. During the three days before ordination, Ian was his usual unflappable self — still waters run deep."[45]

The scene in Ranchi Cathedral was impressive. As His Grace Archbishop Pius Kerketta stretched out his hands to call down the Holy Spirit upon the young Jesuits, the hands of more than sixty priests were raised with his.

Unfortunately joy and sorrow were mingled on that day:

> His Grace Archbishop Kerketta was just giving his final blessing to the four young Australian Jesuits he had ordained Priests in his cathedral in Ranchi when Mother Odille [de Coster], the Ursuline Matron of the Government Hospital, sent an urgent message to the cathedral to say that Father Michael Brady had been brought into the Casualty Ward seriously injured in an accident on his motor bike. As Father O'Connor, our Superior, was still at the altar for the Ordination Ceremony, Father Lou Lachal and I [Fr Austin Kelly] rushed to hospital. We found poor Father Michael in a bad way suffering from loss of blood and from shock, with his right leg severed below the knee.[46]

The following day all the newly-ordained priests moved to Hazaribagh where they were to say their first Masses. These celebrations took place in different places in Hazaribagh; Fr Ian Travers-Ball said his first Mass in the novitiate chapel at Sitagarha. A lot of people wrote to congratulate Ian in letters which Ian's brother Brendan and his wife Marie perhaps brought with them from Australia. He could not answer each one of them personally, and so wrote a public general letter, which was also published in the *Hazaribagh* Issue of August 1963, No. 120:

> I could not possibly write at length to everyone who has written to me for my ordination to the priesthood, so I shall run off a number of copies describing what happened in Ranchi and Hazaribagh in the last month. First of all, however, I want to thank you for writing.

You have no idea what a difference to my understanding of the priesthood it made to receive your greetings and thoughts and prayers. It was by realizing what you thought of the priesthood that I began to realize what was happening to me.

We had an eight-day Retreat here in Poona before leaving for Hazaribagh. It was a wonderful time and God sent me many lights and ideas in those days. Then I set off on the 1200-mile journey from Poona to Ranchi, which meant 48 hours' travel.

In Ranchi we met those who had come from Kurseong for ordination, and received the Sub-diaconate, Deaconate and Priesthood on three consecutive days. There were nine of us, Bill Dwyer, Maurice Dullard and John Reilly from Australia, and five Indian Scholastics from Ranchi itself. Everyone in Ranchi was tremendously kind and we had nothing to do except take ourselves to the Cathedral on time and try to prepare ourselves spiritually for the great occasion. Monday 25th March arrived and big crowds came to the cathedral. My brother, Brendan, and his wife, Marie, had decided at the eleventh hour to come, and after a rush trip arrived in Ranchi with five minutes to spare. Their experiences would make this note into a small book.

The ceremony — three hours of it — went very smoothly. His Grace, Archbishop Kerketta was very calm and kind and the Belgian Jesuits of Ranchi, so tough and hard-working, wore their hearts on their sleeves for the occasion.

I must say I was not carried away by excitement or emotion there in the Ranchi Cathedral at the tremendous thing that was happening to me. But two things struck me very much soon afterwards. When we came out, I heard that Father Brady, an enormously active and successful Australian missionary in Hazaribagh, had been hit by a car on his way to Ranchi for the ordination on his motor cycle. He had lost his leg and at that time was in very grave danger. Thank God he has since pulled through wonderfully. Here when we are so desperately short of men, just as four new priests were being ordained for Hazaribagh, one of our greatest men loses his leg and almost his life. God's plans are amazing, and we know that, He brings undreamt-of fruit out of all that happens. Another thing that struck me greatly on that morning was when an old Belgian Jesuit, Fr De Keyser, who has been working in India for over 50 years from the early pioneering days in Ranchi, knelt down for my blessing — I who have scarcely done anything in the Lord's service.

It is impossible to describe everything that happened that morning. As I said, your wishes and prayers for my ordination impressed me very much with what it means to be a priest; well you had brothers and sisters here in the Catholics of Ranchi, who also showed what they thought of a priest with their wonderful greetings and welcome. Both you and they have driven home to me very forcefully that the priest is for the people and that his life has no meaning at all if it is not lived with the people very much to the fore and as representing them before God — chiefly at the altar each day at Mass.

After lunch we four Australians made the 60-mile journey to Hazaribagh — passing Fr Brady's motor cycle still grimly lying on the roadside. Hazaribagh had its own special welcome and deeply sincere charity. I stayed at St Xavier's School for two weeks where I received hospitality and friendship that I won't even try to describe.

The page is running out and I can't do much more than mention my first Mass on Tuesday at Sitagarha, where I had been teaching for two years. I prayed for you and for all who had so generously wished me well. I know that God will hear those prayers for you — not because of any merit on my part, but because He gave me so much in

Part – II: Travers – As a Jesuit in India (1954 – 1966)

those precious days, and I know that He was in no mood for saying No to anything.

Also it is impossible to describe the joy of saying Mass each day and being able to help people in their needs in the Sacrament of Penance.

Again I thank you for everything. Our work in Hazaribagh is developing wonderfully. There are big difficulties, but enormous opportunities. I repeat that you have helped me to understand what happened to me in Ranchi cathedral. I am really your priest, and my life's work now is to pray to God and offer sacrifice on behalf of the people of India and for you who have helped me so much. I shall pray for you and yours all my life, and I beg you to pray that I may be a real priest of Jesus Christ. I said in my letter I would send you this.

Ian Travers-Ball, SJ.[47]

Ian's ordination card was a print of the Sacred Heart as painted in 1960 by the Indian artist Angelo de Fonseca.[48] Jesus is depicted in red ink against a black background, wearing what looks like traditional Indian dress. On the back was printed the quote from the Letter to the Hebrews (5:1-3) describing the purpose for which any priest is chosen from among his fellow-men. Two themes were emerging in Ian's thinking: A priest is for the people and his life has no meaning if it is not lived with the people. A priest is one with the people because he, like the rest of the humanity, is beset with human weaknesses.

But let us for a short moment leave our Ian in Hazaribagh and move some 400 kilometres away to Calcutta in the neighbouring state of West Bengal. As early as 1962, Mother Teresa (Agnes Bojaxhiu), who had founded the Missionaries of Charity Sisters in 1948, began mentioning that she thought it would be appropriate to have a Society of Missionaries of Charity Brothers. They could, she felt, help with the leprosy work, teach in the Sisters' technical school for young men and do other works more easily undertaken by men. In January

1963, she mentioned this idea to the then Apostolic Internuncio to New Delhi, His Excellency Monsignor James R. Knox. Permission was granted in February 1963 by the Archbishop of Calcutta, the Most Reverend Albert V. D'Souza.[49] Having received the necessary authority and convinced that God wanted the new order for men, at a General Council meeting Mother Teresa decided that the day for initiating the Missionaries of Charity Brothers would be on the Feast of the Annunciation, 25 March 1963, which happened to be the same Monday that our Ian was being ordained in Ranchi Cathedral. The first Brothers were recruited from among the older boys staying in Shishu Bhavan, the Sisters' home for children at 78 Lower Circular Road in Calcutta. It is worth mentioning that the paths of Ian and Mother Teresa had already crossed in February 1962, when the latter gave a talk at the Papal Athenaeum. The two did not speak that day. In Kathryn Spink's *Spirit of Bethlehem*, Ian described his encounter with Mother Teresa:

> It happened in 1962, a year before I was ordained a priest. I met Mother Teresa. For whatever reason (I am not sure whether she then started a house of the Sisters there), she came to Poona and she gave a kind of talk or lecture to the seminarians. That was the first time I saw her, of whom I had heard very little. She was not very well known then, even in India. I still remember my first impression of her, hearing the first words that she said in that address.... I can't remember, though, what the words were. But I remember the very great impression of a person very close to God that came out and that struck me.[50]

After a two-week stay in Hazaribagh, Father Ian returned to Poona to finish his theology studies and at the same time continued the running of the IHS. In December 1963, he wrote his first Christmas letter to family and friends, a practice he would continue until the Christmas before he died. Two major events dominated his life in 1963 — his ordination to the priesthood and the publication of his *Life of Christ*:

The closing year has been a very big one for me — the most important yet — for it saw me ordained a priest in March. I have been preparing for that for so long, and it has been the goal at the end of all the years of study. And I must say that the experience of being a priest is far greater than the expectation. It is something one feels oneself growing into all the time.

There is so much you can do. There is the Mass every day — and somehow it seems a new experience each day. It is there that I am able to bring everything together — work, people in trouble, needs, hopes, and above all my worship of God as one who depends on Him for every breath I take. It is also the wonderful occasion for remembering you before the Lord and of saying a tremendously meaningful prayer for you — and a tremendously powerful prayer where it is enough to say "and for all those I know and want to pray for." Each Sunday, I go out for Mass and Confessions to a parish, a hall or hut where Mass is said....

Another big event this year was the publication of the little "Life of Christ" for Hindus that I had written. It came out in July and, thank God, has been well received. It has been taken up rather extensively by various groups in Bombay, Poona, Madras, Bangalore, etc., who distribute literature about the Christian faith in different ways. One of these groups distribute 400 copies each month.

People are attracted by the personality and teaching of Christ, but there are enormous difficulties for them in following Him, often family problems, their job may be involved and other reasons. That is why it is terribly important to pray for them that God may give them the strength and courage to do whatever He wants from them no matter how difficult it may be. You can be quite sure that no plea for them that you address to the Lord will go without real fruit.[51]

The year 1963 was over and by February 1964, after a major exam he had concluded his theology studies. Ever since he set foot on Indian soil, Ian had been experiencing a nagging feeling of restlessness. He was happy as a Jesuit, he was happy as a priest, he was happy as a writer, and above all he was good at all three. But, there was something missing. There was that growing feeling that he was being called to do something for the poor. As early as 1960 and to some extent even before that, he had pondered the idea of going to live as a Jesuit in a slum area of Delhi. He had spoken to his superior and to his spiritual director and they had both advised him to finish his formation, be ordained as a priest and wait for Tertianship before deciding. They had never discouraged him. With these thoughts in mind, he continued in Poona and in 1964 wrote more and more articles and small booklets and leaflets.

An interesting letter dated much later (when he was almost 70 years old) reflects on one day he spent as a young priest in a juvenile prison:

> For me, this experience of myself as priest of the Mass is a rich and beautiful one. It involves an awareness of the Mass as gathering, and even creating, the community of Christ.
>
> Soon after I was ordained in India I was sent to a juvenile prison for Sunday Mass — a harsh place with about 400 boys, of whom at any one time about 40 would be Catholic.
>
> The authorities gave us a little room with a shaky table and a roof that leaked in the monsoon. When I would arrive Mass was announced and the Catholic boys from the different sections would come to the room. As Mass began around that shaky table of an altar, it was always a striking experience of the Christian community gathering or being gathered around the Mass.[52]

Part – II: Travers – As a Jesuit in India (1954 – 1966)

B.A. SANTAMARIA and SOCIAL ISSUES

In June 1963, Ian wrote "Don't Let Asians Feel Lonely" for the *Messenger*:

> Among the many marvels of our day, air travel has made it commonplace to have breakfast in Sydney or Melbourne and supper in Bombay or Calcutta on the same day. It has also become possible to be a foreign missionary at home.
>
> On buses and trams, in the lunch-time crowds on the city streets, we often see students from foreign lands, either colourful in their bright saris and turbans or else less colourful, but no less clearly foreign in more Arab western dress.
>
> They are part of the 10,000 Asian students studying in Australia to take back to their people the skills they learn in medicine, engineering, nursing, agriculture, science, economics and the rest. When they return big hopes will be placed in them and big jobs will await them.
>
> They will have all the prestige of a foreign degree. They will be a real voice in their country.[53]

Ian knew exactly what was happening in Australia, and possibly the mention of the 10,000 Asian students was no coincidence. He knew what the Jesuits, the Australian government, and the Australian Church, together with the Catholic political activist Bartholomew A. Santamaria, were doing.[54] Much of this will be dealt with later in this book, but it is worth mentioning here the involvement of B. A. Santamaria in the fight against Communism in Australia and his possible influence on Ian both at this time and in the decisions which he would ultimately take in the early '70s.

Santamaria's tactics to try to break the control the Communists had on all the major unions were widely known. Before the war in Indo-China, the colonial empires in Asia were on the verge of collapse and that brought the independence movements.

The question was, who would control these? The Vietnamese Communists were being educated in France and Moscow, the Indonesians in the Netherlands. But where would a non-Communist leadership emerge? Soon the Jesuits and the Church — both organised at an international level — became involved in providing training for non-Communist indigenous leadership. Hence the large number of Asians studying in Australia. Whether or not these tactics were effective is hard to say. Quite a number of Vietnamese, for instance, decided to settle down in Australia and not go back to Vietnam once they had their degrees.

We don't know whether Ian had met B. A. Santamaria prior to 1955 when the latter visited the Australian Jesuits in Poona. Nor do we know whether this was a private visit or whether it had anything to do with Santamaria's anti-Communist work in the South Asian sphere. But after this meeting there was an exchange of letters between the two, of which only one was found. It was written by Santamaria dated July 1956. In it, Santamaria mentioned the brainwave which according to Ian was "vibrating in your subconscious (as you put it) it might interest you to know that we are putting it to the Bishops of Asia to issue a Joint Statement on the social problems of Asia. The idea is to set out, briefly, the main lines of the Church's answer to the Asian revolution based, of course, on Catholic Social teaching.[55] Unfortunately, Ian's introductory letter to the above was not preserved, but Patrick Morgan, author of *B. A. Santamaria, Your Most Obedient Servant (Selected Letters 1938-1996)* and *The Mannix Era,* stated that around June 1955 a temporary committee of an International Secretariat of Catholic Action in Asia was set up with an Indian as president, the same Santamaria as secretary and other members. (It was considered to be the Asian extension of Santamaria's *Movement* supported at that time by the Australian bishops). The "committee drafted a statement opposing colonialism and Communism, and in favour of the family and the rural village unit; the statement was however issued only by the Indian hierarchy (Valerian Cardinal Gracias of Bombay was at this stage a strong supporter)."⁵⁶ Possibly this was the "brainwave" which Ian had proposed to Santamaria.

Ian's articles dealt increasingly with social issues around the world and in July 1963 he published one in *America* magazine entitled "India and the Negro Question." In his articles he even started questioning the role of the Catholic Church in areas where the poor were being discriminated against because of the colour of their skin, something which occurred to some extent in India. "I have never lived in America and I cannot know all that lies behind the race problem. But I have read *America, Commonweal, Time,* and I have read the Indian papers. And today I cannot help wondering at the lack of a loud clear, Catholic voice recently."⁵⁷ For Ian, if President Kennedy, a Catholic mourned in India, had spoken out against racism, or if Pope John XXIII, who was mourned by the Indian press and government, had been "a strong Catholic voice [to] champion the Negro, the impact would have been great, indeed."⁵⁸

The amount of information that Ian could gather and store prior to the existence of the Internet and in a country so far away is impressive. Amazing is the number of authors mentioned in one of his articles, "Challenged to Reconcile," published in *America* in December 1963: Karl Stern and his novel *Through Dooms of Love*, Hendrik Kraemer, the noted Protestant missiologist in *World Cultures and World Religions*; Edward Caldwell Moore, then Professor of Christian Morals at Harvard in his Dale Lectures. Nor were the political situations in Indonesia, Egypt, Uganda, Congo, Cuba, and Chile neglected. In his article "Vocation and Vision", published in the 1964 issue of *Review for Religious*, Ian even mentioned the film *La Dolce Vita* by Federico Fellini. It was a 1960 film and parts of it were condemned by the Vatican newspaper *L'Osservatore Romano* after it was perceived as a parody of the second coming of Jesus. For Ian the film captured vividly "the tragedy of ...modern man's greatest sufferings ...the feeling of meaninglessness in life."⁵⁹

31 JULY 1964

People in Australia who prayed for the Australian missionaries in India were called "co-missionaries". In every issue of *Hazaribagh* co-missionaries were presented with intentions they were invited to pray for during that particular month. In July 1964 co-missionaries were supposed to pray for the intentions of Fr Ian Travers-Ball, in his important post of Regional Director of Vocations. In an article Ian subsequently wrote in the October issue of *Hazaribagh* entitled "Those Deadly Monthly Intentions", he described in a somewhat tragi-comic way his experience of the monthly intentions:

> Actually, it went all right up to 22nd July when I noticed as I walked along or when I got up from a chair, that I felt a bit dizzy. This continued for a couple of days, but I thought it was just the monsoon weather or I was getting a cold in the head or something.
>
> On 25th, I had to lie down a few times, and I couldn't eat anything. On Sunday 26th after struggling through Mass, I spent, the whole day in bed. Same on Monday — and this, dear Co-missionary, is July 1964 when you're supposed to be praying, for me.
>
> Then came Tuesday. When I woke up and tried to lift my head, the bed, walls and ceiling all started to shake furiously. And this happened every time I tried to lift my head. When good Brother Fonteyn, the infirmarian, saw all this he at once decided I was a hospital job. And so by 8.30, after a nice ride on the floor of a small truck, I found that my big month as star of the Mission Intention, had brought me to a bed in a Parsee hospital. Here, however, from the beginning I received wonderful treatment. I began to pick up, but on the evening of 30th, I slid back and felt terrible. In fact, I was quite sure that I would die on 31st July which is the feast of St Ignatius, founder of the Jesuits. Here was my big chance to make everyone realise that they'd been living with a real Man of God all

these years. Wouldn't they sit up and take notice when they saw that he'd been transported to heaven on the feast of St Ignatius?

Well, that little piece didn't quite work out, for I survived the holy day, and on 1st August woke up feeling much better. But please note, all monthly intention devotees, that it was now August. July was over. You were praying for someone else now, and I began to climb up hill fast. In fact, by 5th August I was home, and picked up fast with Ovaltine, bananas and everything that Brother Fonteyn could get into me.

There were certain benefits from that sickness. I'd never been really sick in my life before; and I must confess now that it does provide a real satisfaction to be able to relate the whole story in either the spoken or the written word to anyone who stumbles into asking, "How are you now?"

It also showed me the need to be patient and to put everything in God's hands. After all, He is the Manager, it's His world, and He has an amazing way of bringing good out of evil.

I've noticed, too, since I got better that there are really sick people in the world, who suffer a lot. When I went back to hospital for a check-up, I saw with different eyes a girl waiting with her parents to see the doctor. I realised that she was so weak that she could hardly keep her head up. There was a fat man waiting too. Every movement seemed to cause him pain. I don't think I would have noticed this before. In the bed next to me in the hospital was a man who had five lovely children, who were brought in to see him in turn by their young mother. He was terribly worried by the hospital expenses. He was not earning anything those days, and had to borrow from the money-lender.

When I went to the hospital after a week, he had gone down terribly.

Then to crown everything, on my return home I expected to find my work all backed up and everything in chaos. How could they manage without me? But everything was moving like clockwork — even letters I had not answered for weeks had been answered for me. All very healthy for the humility.

All the same, I'm writing to that editor of "News from India" to say that if he must bring names into his monthly intentions, he should kindly let me know in advance, before he puts me down again. Then I can say a few prayers for myself.

And on reading this over, it struck me that perhaps, if the monthly intention had not got me all those prayers, I just might have pulled off that sensational 31st July, feast of St Ignatius stunt — with, of course, St Peter stopping any nonsense at the pearly gates.

To end this little tale on a note that cannot fail to do good, would you pause in your tracks for a moment to say a small prayer for all those in India who suffer in any way and who are so very dear to God.[60]

Little did he know that he would eventually die thirty-six years later on another great saint's feast day!

TERTIANSHIP — From Sitagarha to Calcutta

By June 1965 Ian was back in Sitagarha, this time at Stanislaus College, a stone's throw from the Teachers' Training College. Tertianship is the final stage in Jesuit formation, the so-called "third stage of probation". Usually it comes after the priest (or Brother) has completed his studies, been ordained and worked for several years. In Ian's case, most probably because he was considered a late vocation, he was allowed to start tertianship earlier than the rest of his *confrères*. Part of tertianship is a thirty-day-long Ignatian retreat, the second after novitiate. While in Sitagarha he was made the Vocation Director

Part – II: Travers – As a Jesuit in India (1954 – 1966)

for the Hazaribagh Region, and he continued to produce *MARG*. By this time, *MARG* had already changed its name to *PremMARG — A Religious Newsletter for Modern Life*, after Father Ian had been instructed that there was already a magazine of that name.[61]

Phil Crotty, SJ, recalled that it was as early as this that Iannes B. Moyersoen, SJ, the tertian instructor, told them that "Mother Teresa was looking for a Jesuit to take care of the Brothers' wing of the Missionaries of Charity. He invited any of the tertians who would be interested in helping Mother Teresa in taking care of the Brothers." The first Jesuits Mother Teresa had wanted to take over the Brothers were Yugoslav Jesuits, Fr Michael Gabric and Fr Robert Antoine who were already living in West Bengal. Gabric was serving as a chaplain in one of her homes for the poor.[62] Carl Dincher, SJ, from the Jamshedpur Province had also been approached by Mother Teresa but had declined.[63]

Two things were unexpected for Ian. In November 1965 he was invited to speak in Delhi at a seminar on "Motivation for Social Work". At the same seminar, Mother Teresa was also asked to give a talk. This was the first time that Ian and Mother spoke to each other. According to Geoffrey Solomon, "an innovation in the year's tertianship allowed each man to spend an 'experimental' month in an activity of his own choosing." Ian decided to go to Calcutta and see the work of the newly erected Pious Union. He had no intention of joining them, only of getting an idea of what and how they were doing:

> A year or so after ordination, I had the opportunity of a month when I could go and work, sort of as a work experience and I heard Mother Teresa had started work. She was not so famous, early '60s, but she was known around India and I thought if I went to work with her for a month, I'll get a few ideas of work with the poor. I went to Calcutta not really knowing anything much about anything there. And the situation I walked into was that she had established and started her congregation of Sisters about 20 years before that had grown and spread and she began to feel that there

should be an Order of Brothers, doing the same sort of work for the poor. And she'd actually started, a few young lads had come along and the Sisters were working, well they were working under the Sisters.[64]

On 1 December 1965 Father Travers-Ball arrived at Nirmal Hriday, the Home for the Dying, and was taken from there to Shishu Bhavan where he joined in the life and work of the Brothers.[65] After spending the day with them he would go back to the Jesuit St Xavier's College on Park Street (a fifteen-minute walk from Shishu Bhavan), and retire there for the night. Ian was very much taken by their simplicity, poverty, and work. Nevertheless, the Brothers' need for a priest to be with them, guide them and form them was obvious to him. At the same time, Mother Teresa was very much aware that the Catholic Church did not allow a woman to be the superior of a male congregation.

> But Mother Teresa was looking for a priest who would take charge of their training, take charge of the whole new group. So I went into, saw that situation and within about ten days, I realized that this was the call... She asked me directly, she had been asking a lot of people to take it over but she hadn't got anybody and somehow it just came together and I decided there that I would go ahead.

> I was staying at the Jesuits' College St Xavier's, and I remember the night I finally made my decision, which would mean leaving the Jesuits and I had been walking up on the roof ...praying about it and finally I decided, "This is it." I came downstairs and almost unbelievably walked around the corner of St Xavier's College in Calcutta and who do I bump into but Father Harold Lalor who was visiting India and who was staying at the College? And I thought to myself, he's the one who got me into the Jesuits and now I have to tell him I'm going to leave them. And I told him that and I didn't know what he'd say. And what he said was, "I think that's wonderful" he said.

And immediately I understood! So it was, all that went quite quickly then.[66]

On 31 December 1965, after receiving the approval of his superior in Hazaribagh, Edmund B. O'Connor, SJ, Fr Ian Travers-Ball wrote to the Superior General of the Jesuits in Rome — Father Pedro Arrupe. On 22 January 1966, the reply came from Rome, from both Pope Paul VI and Father Arrupe, presenting him with three very generous options: he could stay with the Missionaries of Charity Brothers for three years and at the end of that time decide whether or not to renew his stay, or he could return to the Jesuits at any time, or he could leave the Jesuits and join the new society.[67]

Phil Crotty asserted:

> I was against him about leaving the Jesuits. I argued with him quite seriously, we had a very long discussion, saying to him, "Why can't you remain a Jesuit, why do you want to leave the Jesuits?" He could remain part of the Jesuits and still be co-founder of the Brothers. But this is the early days of the Brothers. He was quite clear, he wasn't in any way influenced by what I said, nor could I persuade him for something else. I was coming strongly that his leaving the Jesuits was a mistake and he said, "No, I can't, if I'm going to join them, I'm going to be one with them. And if I am still a Jesuit, I am not one with them. I need to be one with them."[68]

1. Hazaribagh c. 1955.

2. Poona 1956 – Ian with scholastics.

3. Poona c. 1955.

4. Archbishop of Ranchi—Pius Kerketta with the newly ordained priests.
Fr Ian (back row, second from right) – 25 March 1963.

5. Ordination Day – Fr Ian standing at the back.

6. Ordination Day.

Part – II: Travers – As a Jesuit in India (1954 – 1966)

7. *First Mass — Sitagarha — 26 March 1963.*

8. *Sitagarha - Fr. Ian during the construction of the Teachers' Training Institute.*

Endnotes :

[1] Michael Doyle, SJ, born in Jakarta and educated at Kostka, Burke Hall, and Xavier College. He had studied first-year law at Melbourne University and just completed his philosophy at Loyola; Stephen Daly, SJ, was an ordained Jesuit priest when he travelled to India. He taught at St Aloysius College and Campion Hall in Sydney; Michael Mulhearn, SJ, was an ordained priest when he left for India; John Hurney, SJ, born in Balgowlah, Sydney and educated at the Christian Brothers' College and St Aloysius, had just completed his first year of arts at Loyola. He was to become a Jesuit Brother.

[2] From a letter dated 26 October 2000, from Dr Frank Mobbs to Brother Andrew's sister after Andrew's death. Dr Mobbs was born and raised outside Sydney, Australia. His interest in theology and philosophy led him to teach in institutes of higher education in England, Canada, Papua New Guinea and Australia. He died in 2017.

[3] "Passage to India", in *Hazaribagh*, Newsletter of the Australian Jesuits in Northern India, No. 26 January-February 1955.

[4] Constant Lievens, (1856 – 1893). A Belgian Jesuit priest, missionary among the tribal people of Central India, he was regarded as the apostle of the Chota Nagpur area — nowadays Jharkhand and Chhattisgarh.

[5] Children of God: "Harijan" was a term introduced by Mahatma Gandhi to refer to the community of Dalits, previously called "Untouchables".

[6] 19550217 LJ to Harold King, SJ.

[7] Ibid.

[8] 19550414 LJ to Harold King, SJ.

[9] Ibid.

[10] 19560000 AM – Around the Clock in Ranchi.

[11] From a talk given by Brother Andrew circa 1994 or 1995 at Gracewood - God's Farm, Australia.

[12] 19550612 LJ to Father Provincial.

[13] Ibid.

[14] In 1955 the Papal Seminary and the Papal Athenaeum were transferred from Sri Lanka to Poona, in close proximity to De Nobili College, the Jesuit formation house in Ramwadi. The Jesuit Superior of Poona supervised the transfer. Thereafter, the Pontifical Athenaeum, which until then had catered almost exclusively for seminarians of the Papal Seminary, became more broadly open to the students of the Society of Jesus and other religious congregations. In 1972 the Pontifical Athenaeum adopted the Indian name of "Jnana-Deepa Vidyapeeth" (JDV).

[15] Roberto de Nobili, (1577 – 1656). Born in Italy. As a Jesuit, he arrived in Goa, India in1605. In 1606 he moved to Cochin and eventually settled in Tamil Nadu. True to his name, he claimed noble background and approached

Part – II: Travers – As a Jesuit in India (1954 – 1966)   109

> the Hindu priestly caste, adopting their local customs which enabled him to converse with them on Christian themes — a method of adaptation to preach Christianity then seen as innovative. De Nobili was one of the first Europeans to pursue an understanding of both the language and literature of Sanskrit, Tamil and Telugu. He composed a catechism, apologetic works and philosophic dissertations in Tamil, and contributed to the development of modern Tamil prose writing.

[16] Catherine Kolyschkine, (1896 – 1985). Born to wealthy and deeply Russian Christian parents, at the age of fifteen, she married her cousin, Boris de Hueck. When the Russian Revolution destroyed the world they knew, Catherine and Boris fled to England, and then, in 1921, to Canada. In the following years she experienced grinding poverty. "Sell all you possess, and come, follow Me," was Christ's message that inspired her, in the early 1930s, to go and lead a hidden life at one with His poor in the Toronto slums. (http://www.catherinedoherty.org/life/ Web. 6 April 2020.).

Dorothy Day, (1897 – 1980). Born in the US. After a middle-class Republican childhood and a few years as a Communist sympathizer, Dorothy Day converted to Catholicism. An orthodox Catholic, political radical, and a rebel who courted controversy, she attracted three generations of admirers. Day went to jail for challenging the draft and the Vietnam War. She refused to hear any criticism of the pope, but she sparred with American bishops and priests living in well-appointed rectories and tolerating racial segregation in their parishes. (https://www.catholicworker.org/dd-new-bio.html Web. 6 April 2020.).

Geoffrey Leonard Cheshire, (1917 – 1992). Former British RAF pilot Leonard Cheshire took a dying man with nowhere else to go, into his home. With no money, Leonard nursed the man himself at his house, "Le Court" in Hampshire. They became friends and this act of kindness prompted others to turn to Leonard for help. (https://www.leonardcheshire.org/about-us/our-history Web. 6 April 2020.).

Abbé Pierre, OFM Cap, (1912 – 2007). Born in France and was inspired from an early age to follow a religious life he became a priest in Grenoble. In 1942 he joined the Resistance and helped to hide Jewish members of the community from the Nazis. His charity was aimed not only to help the homeless to find shelter but also on affording people the dignity of work. Abbé Pierre appeared to transcend the religious and political differences of the country and was appreciated in a variety of quarters. Admired by Catholics, for presenting the best aspects of a living Catholic faith, he was also appreciated for his strong criticism of the Catholic Church's conservatism. (https://www.biographyonline.net/humanitarian/abbe_pierre.html Web. 6 April 2020.)

[17] 19570517 LJ to Harold King, SJ.

[18] Ibid.

[19] Ibid.

[20] 19560705 LJ to Harold King, SJ.

21. 19560330 LJ to Father Provincial.
22. 19570517 LJ to Harold King, SJ.
23. 19560705 LJ to Harold King, SJ.
24. 19560330 LJ to Father Provincial.
25. 20180320 IJ Phil Crotty, SJ.
26. Ibid.
27. Ibid.
28. https://www.en.m.wikipedia.org Web. 8 April, 2020.
29. In an article for the *Examiner* later in 1963 Ian noted, "The restrictions on the entry of foreign missionaries to India came as a hard blow to the growth of the Indian Church." (Brother Gordon MC, "Missionaries of Charity — Journal," Los Angeles: Unpublished Source, 1978).
30. 19580228 LJ to Fr. Harold King, SJ.
31. 20180320 IJ Phil Crotty, SJ. Fr Crotty, SJ, in Sydney, remembering the Institute, "Now there were no doors or windows in the building, one night we were completely robbed by a gang of thieves. They came and stole our cycles, watches. And Travers and I, I remember, we chased them in the night when we discovered we'd been robbed. I remember we chased them until the police caught up with us."
32. 19600500 AM in *Hazaribagh* No. 84.
33. From an informal chat when the author visited the Primary Teachers Education College, in Sitagarha in 2019. Vincent Hansdak, SJ, the principal and William Dwyer, SJ, both mentioned the college's continued use of Ian's notes till a few years ago.
34. 19580827 LJ to Michael Ryan, SJ.
35. Solomon, Geoffrey D., *Brothers of Mother Teresa,* Homebush NSW: St Paul Publications, 1987.
36. 20180227 IJ Hans Hendriks, SJ.
37. Brother Andrew MC, *What I Met Along the Way,* London, UK: Darton, Longman and Todd Ltd., 1987.
38. 19601027 LJ to Harold King, SJ. Although Father Austin Kelly was behind the work and encouraging Ian, he was still concerned that a scholastic was undertaking it.
39. 19610926 LJ to Harold King, SJ.
40. 20190117 IJ Francis Lopez, SJ, and KA Sebastian, SJ.
41. Ibid.
42. Brother Gordon, MC, "Missionaries of Charity — Journal," Los Angeles: Unpublished Source, 1978.
43. 20180320 IJ to Phil Crotty, SJ.
44. 19639226 AM in *Ranchi Bulletin* No 2/63.
45. 20190701 Email William Dwyer, SJ.

Part – II: Travers – As a Jesuit in India (1954 – 1966)

46 Michael Brady, SJ, survived the accident and in the July 1963 No. 119 issue of *Hazaribagh* there is a photo of him (together with Father G. P. Lawlor) on crutches. He had lost his right leg and was awaiting an artificial one. He was still hoping to go to Bhurkunda where he ran a school for about 600 children.

47 19630800 AM in *Hazaribagh* No. 20.

48 Angelo de Fonseca, (1902 – 1967). Indian painter and pioneer of the Christian cultural renaissance in India whose works can be admired in many places around the sub-continent and at De Nobili College.

49 19920126 LF to Kathryn Spink. Brother Andrew wrote, "I hadn't realised it, but quite probably it was Archbishop Vivian Dyer who was first broached about the Brothers. He died quite soon after his consecration. And by 1963 Albert D'Souza was in place."

50 Spink, Kathryn and González-Balado, José Luis, *Spirit of Bethlehem*, London, UK: SPCK, 1987.

51 19631200 LP on the Jesuit Mission.

52 19970500 LP.

53 19630601 AM *Messenger*.

54 Bartholomew Augustine Santamaria, (1915 – 1998). Australian Roman Catholic anti-Communist political activist and journalist. He also had an influence on the founding of the Democratic Labour Party and was a friend of Fr Harold Lalor, SJ. He was married and had eight children.

55 19560726 LF from B. A. Santamaria — courtesy of Mr Patrick Morgan, editor of B.A. *Santamaria — Your Most Obedient Servant*. The letter is not included in the aforementioned book.

56 Morgan, Patrick ed., B. A. Santamaria — *Your Most Obedient Servant*. (Selected Letters: 1938 - 1996). Australia: The Miegunyah Press in association with The State Library of Victoria, 2007.

57 19630713 AM India and the Negro Question — America, 1963.

58 Ibid.

59 19640000 AM Vocation and Vision – *Review for Religious*, 1964.

60 19641000 AM in *Hazaribagh*, No 133.

61 *PremMARG* continued after Andrew stopped publishing it. The last edition was in 2013, as confirmed by Ted Bowling, SJ (20210128 Email Ted Bowling, SJ).

62 Robert Antoine, well-immersed in Bengali culture was at that time chaplain at Mother Teresa's Home for the Dying. Michael Gabric was a Yugoslavian Jesuit missionary in 24 Parganas who had persuaded Mother Teresa to open centres in rural areas in India. She admired him because like her he saw the immediate needs of the poor and sought to bring Christ to them. His personal practice of poverty was probably appealing to Mother Teresa and when she was still in Albania, Father Gabric's letters about the Calcutta missions had inspired her.

63 From an informal chat with the author in Raiganj, 1998.

64 From a talk given by Brother Andrew circa 1994 or 1995 at Gracewood - God's Farm, Australia.

65 Nirmal Hriday (Pure Heart) also known as the Kalighat Home for Dying Destitute, the first home of the kind opened by Mother Teresa in 1952 in the pilgrims' resting house in Kalighat, close to the Kali Temple in Kolkata; Shishu Bhavan (Home of the Child), at 78 AJC Bose Road (at the time Lower Circular Road), is the home opened by Mother Teresa for abandoned children.

66 From a talk given by Brother Andrew circa 1994 or 1995 at Gracewood – God's Farm, Australia.

67 The Document of Exclaustration of Father Ioannes Travers-Ball, SJ.

Most blessed Father,

Father Ioannes Travers-Ball, a priest of the Society of Jesus professed in the Province of Ranchi, thrown at the most sacred feet of your Holiness implores an *indultum exclustrationis* so that he might better devote himself to the social apostolate among the very poorest of people.

Et Deus etc.

In line with the powers conceded by our Most Holy Lord, the Sacred Congregation placed in charge of the business of the Assisting Religious, the testimony of the Most Reverend P. Proc Gen., SJ, having been considered, kindly grants to the Most Reverend General Superior so that, so long as the narrated matters are true, he may concede, in accordance with his own judgement and conscience, to the requesting party the sought option of exclaustration for no more than three years; and also the suitable dispensation over the rules incompatible with his station, the obligation of shedding the appearance of religious habit having been carried out, and of serving the vows and the other obligations of his professions in line with the canon 639 of the Canon Legal Code. However, the requesting party (will be under the jurisdiction) of the Ordinary of the territory where he will dwell in place of the Superiors of his own order, and is also subject by reason of his vow of obedience and will be held to return at once if, perchance, during the duration of the *Indultum*, he is recalled to claustration by his legitimate Superiors.

Whatever contrary matters not impeding, [Signature]

[Seal]

With the power granted to us, we concede to Fr Joanni Travers-Ball the simple exclaustration of up to three years in line maintained with the parameters of the annexed rescript.

Given at Rome on the 27th day of January 1966

[seal]   [signature Petrus Arrupe, SJ]

I testify that this exemplar concurs with the original.

E. B. O'Connor, SJ

Regional Superior of Hazaribagh

68 20180320 IJ to Phil Crotty, SJ.

PART – III

BROTHER ANDREW MC – CALCUTTA (1966-1972)

PART III

MOTHER AND SONS
CALCUTTA
(1964-67)

*The Jesuits say I have kidnapped
Father Andrew from them.
Our Lady must have done the kidnapping
for she,
being the first Missionary of Charity,
naturally wants the best
for the glory of her Son
and the good of souls.*
– **MOTHER TERESA**

*I loved the Brothers
from the beginning.*
– **BROTHER ANDREW**

Having acquired the necessary permissions from the Holy See and from his Jesuit superiors, Ian still had another hurdle to overcome — his father. Ian worried about him. Frederick was just coming to terms with his son being a Jesuit and so far away in India when a bigger complication presented itself: Ian's leaving the Jesuits. In a letter written to his Provincial, Fr John Rolland Boylan, Ian explained this predicament.

> I think Fr O'Connor has written to you about the step I am taking. Just today V. Rev. Fr [Paolo] Dezza's letter came approving of temporary exclaustration. The Congregation confirmation should follow soon.
>
> It is not an easy step and a very very painful one. I think if one wants to know whether he loves the Society, he should try to leave it. I have not wept for years, but I wept today when the letter came.
>
> When you were in Bombay I spoke to you in general of the desire to work for the very poor. I had been advised to wait

till tertianship by Sp. [Spiritual] Fathers & Fr Superior for about six years now and this year in tertianship has shown me that God wants this. Fr Instructor, Fr Superior and a couple of other experienced SJ's have all advised me and approved the decision — so I feel confident that it is God's will. But the step remains so hard.

Once I am in the new work, I suppose it will be easier. Then there are the explanations. Poor Dad will be very upset — just now when he has accepted the Society. I can only entrust him to God's love — and that is enough.

The work with the new Congregation is full of possibilities. God has blessed the work of Mother Teresa in most extraordinary ways. And those who know her put her in the class of St Ignatius, Francis of Assisi, Teresa [of Avila]. But for myself I feel that I am going to the work with only my inadequacies & weaknesses & failings....

I feel great joy at going to work for the very poor. I feel that for me now that Christ calls me to himself there where He is most needed.

Fr Lalor will be able to give you some details when he returns.

I feel that I must thank the Society and especially the Australian Province. Because whatever I have received — after God — comes from the Society. I don't think I have ever loved & appreciated the Society more than I do now.

I shall pray for you and the Province, Father. And please pray for me because I need God's help so much for every step I take from now on.[1]

Ian signed the letter: "*Your son still in Christ, Ian Travers-Ball, SJ.*"

Possibly the fact that it was a very painful decision for Ian mitigated the effect on poor Frederick. There are no letters in any archives indicating that Ian wrote directly to his father, but the fact that no letter was saved does not mean that he did not

Part – III: Brother Andrew MC – Calcutta (1966-1972)

write. The only one still preserved is to his dear sister Aimée, the closest to him in age:

> I am typing this letter, and am covering all the ground of my story, because I cannot explain the whole story in many letters.
>
> When I came to Tertianship, I asked all the family to pray for me for a special intention that concerned a decision that I realised I had to take during the year. Since 1960, and even before that in a vague way, I have felt that God wanted me to devote my life to the very poor. I was always advised by my Superiors and Spiritual Advisors not to do anything immediate, but to wait for Tertianship, when I would make the 30 days Retreat, and have peace and quiet to reflect and pray about the matter. Well, I did this, and I realised that God wanted me to go ahead with this —without seeing just how or where it would be.
>
> Well, it came down to two possibilities. One was to go alone into the slums of Delhi, and the other was to work with a new group of Brothers forming in Calcutta to work for the poor. When I spent the month with these latter, I saw that this would be the best. I referred the matter to my Superior in Hazaribagh. Then it went to the General of the Jesuits in Rome, and I received their fullest blessing and encouragement. Finally, it was approved by the Holy See.
>
> Now next week, I go to Calcutta to live with the Brothers, and to take charge of them. There will be much to do, as they are not yet properly set up. They will have to officially be formed into a new order, they will have to be trained, and all the time we shall be working amongst the poorest of the poor in the slums of Calcutta. I shall still be a Jesuit, but Rome has released me to live outside the Society for three years, at the end of which I either return to the Society, or I take vows in the new Congregation. It has been worked out in a very wonderful way in Rome, and everything is in my favour — and my Superior here in India has told me

that I can come back at any time if necessary, so there is nothing to worry about on that score. (This was the very hardest decision that I had to make, as never have I loved the Society as I do now.)

The group that I am going to are known as the Missionaries of Charity. Fourteen years age a Loreto nun, a Yukoslav, [Yugoslav] named Mother Teresa, did exactly what I am doing –only with much greater risks. She left the Loreto convent under the same arrangements to work for the very poor, starting her new Congregation. To make a long story short, her work developed in a most extraordinary way. She has been acclaimed by the Pope, she has received very high honours from the Indian government, and has become famous in Europe and America. In fact, it is generally agreed that she will surely be canonized a saint one day. Now the Order for the Brothers is being formed.

For myself, I am terribly happy about it all. I could never have dreamed that it would work out in this way. Since I took the decision, I have experienced very great spiritual joy, and peace and happiness, which I believe is God's way of confirming the decision. Also, the great encouragement I have received from all my Superiors right up to the Holy See, is a great consolation.

But the greatest thing is that I shall be able to work fully for the poor — and Christ Our Lord has said that whatever we do for the poor, we do for Him. And He himself was born homeless, He fled into Egypt as the baby of a refugee family. He showed special care and love for the lepers, the beggars, the sick, and when He died naked on the Cross, His body was laid in the tomb of another man. The word "poor" just doesn't mean the same thing in India as in Australia. It means here that families have nothing — like the one I met recently, who only had a few peanuts in their home. It was all that they had eaten all day. It means families sleeping in the streets, with not even a hovel for shelter.

Part – III: Brother Andrew MC – Calcutta (1966-1972)

> It is like the boy of 17 I saw on Christmas Day, brought into Mother Teresa's homes burning with a fever, having been picked up unconscious on the street, and who died within a few hours of arriving, from starvation.
>
> I had to put it strongly like this, because only in this light can you understand what I am doing. I believe that God has given me a very special grace to do something for what is the most urgent matter in the whole world today.
>
> The work will be hard, it will involve a sacrifice, and I do not have many qualifications, but if I turned away from it after seeing the need, and hearing God's word, I would be the most to be despised in the whole world. You could only be ashamed of me, as I would be of myself. I believe that God is calling me to this, and that He is giving me a tremendous grace in doing so. And if it is God who calls me to it, then he will give me all the help and strength that I need. That is why, in spite of all my faults and weaknesses, I am going with a heart full of confidence and joy. No one can tell how it will all develop, only God knows that, since it is obviously His work (judging from the tremendous amount Mother Teresa has already done, starting from nothing). I know you will pray for me, and you will share also in a very special way in whatever I do for God's poor.
>
> God bless you.
> Ian.[2]

Was the family happy or sad? Did they think he was abandoning the Jesuits and taking a big risk? Did they think he was crazy to leave such a prestigious society for another which was just starting, with all the uncertainties that implied? We do not know what ensued in the family. But thanks to the archives of the Australian Jesuits in Melbourne and to the valuable intuition and foresight of the Jesuits in charge at that time, what we do have is a letter written by Mr Frederick Henry Travers-Ball (a year after Ian's incorporation into the Brothers) to Fr Austin Kelly. There is no need for explanation. It is most fitting to start this part of Ian's journey with the Missionaries of Charity Brothers with such a letter — an act of blessing from the father of their co-founder to the Brothers.

> F. H. TRAVERS-BALL
> 14 FINDON CRESCENT
> KEW E4
> 18th May, 1967
>
> Rev. Father Austin Kelly, SJ,
>
> Hawthorn.
>
> Dear Father Kelly,
>
> Your kind and enlightening article in May Hazaribagh was kindly read to me this morning by my daughter, Lucy. (My sight to read or write has gone, I have cataracts on the eyes).
>
> I want to thank you very much and your society for all that has been done by it to enable Ian to carry on the work now allotted to him.
>
> In a letter dated 25th March he writes, "Here we have received a very big piece of news this week. Our society has been given approbation by the Holy See — and tomorrow the Archbishop is coming to read the decree and then we shall become a new religious congregation. Our name will be the Missionaries of Charity."
>
> I thought you would like to learn Ian's words telling me.
>
> I am 87 years of age and, for the past five years, have been confined to the house and a wheel-chair following an operation of the right femur, and in addition to my lost sight, I am, in God's mercy much disabled.
>
> But please do accept my deep thanks for your interest in my son, Ian.
>
> Very sincerely,
> Frederick Henry Travers-Ball.[3]

CALCUTTA, 1966

When Ian arrived in Calcutta on 19 February 1966, the new Society was made up of thirteen Brothers: Michael, Aloysius, Ignatius, David, Damien, Bernard, John, James, Stanislaus, Dominic, Peter, Paul and finally Andrew. Early that Saturday when he reached Shishu Bhavan he found them all so sick from the previous evening's meal that none of them could get out of bed until later that morning. That same morning, Father Travers-Ball decided to hang a picture. When he began hammering the nail into the wall, a large piece of plaster came down. Mother Teresa was watching. She said nothing but immediately walked out.

Later in the day there was a simple ceremony at which Father Travers-Ball received a small cross from Mother Teresa and took the name of Brother Andrew. The reason for the choice is not now clear. One plausible explanation: Andrew was the first of the two apostles "who became followers of Jesus after hearing what John had said" (Jn 1:40). Andrew was also one of the few apostles who brought people to Jesus: "Early next morning, Andrew met his brother [Simon Peter] and said to him, 'We have found the Messiah'... and he took Simon to Jesus" (Jn 1:41). When Jesus felt sorry for the crowds who had followed him and had no food, it was, "One of his disciples, Andrew, Simon Peter's brother, [who] said, 'Here is a small boy with five barley loaves and two fish'" (Jn 6: 8-9).

The following Monday, Julien Henry, SJ, arrived as usual at Shishu Bhavan to give the Brothers their instruction period.[4] He had been asked at the outset by Mother Teresa to be the Brothers' spiritual director, and he had been visiting twice a day (except Sundays): in the morning to direct their morning prayers and meditation, and in the evening for their forty-five minute recreation period. At times he had also taught them geometry and other subjects he felt would help them to instruct younger boys in employable skills at the Sisters' technical school. In addition, once a week Father Henry used to celebrate Mass for the Brothers at Shishu Bhavan. Later in the week of Brother Andrew's arrival, however, he told Father Henry that from then on he (Brother Andrew) would be taking care of the Brothers' formation, after which Father Henry's visits ceased. Another Jesuit who filled Andrew in on the Brothers' story at this time was Fr Celeste van Exem, who was close to both the Brothers and the Sisters.[5]

Holy Thursday that year fell on 7 April.

A little over a month after I came (it was Holy Thursday) it was very hot weather and I had asked Mother to come for the liturgy on Holy Thursday. Before that the Brothers used to always go to the Mother House, the Sister's novitiate, for big feasts (Christmas, Easter), and they would be on the altar. And I felt we could have the liturgy ourselves and I asked Mother and she agreed to come for the Holy Thursday.

She came a little early and we were talking at the refectory table and I mentioned that some of the Brothers were sleeping on the terrace at night because it was so hot. Mother objected strongly to that and said we can't do that. The Brothers must sleep in the dormitory in the fixed place. I guess I blew up. I suppose it was a big change for me going from the Jesuits to the Brothers and there were a lot of things I was uncomfortable with without realizing it. I said to Mother, "You know, Mother, those things, on those things about whether the Brothers sleep on the terrace or what, I feel that we have to decide that ourselves." And I said, "I personally cannot live in a situation where all those details are fixed." And I said, "I think we have to make this very clear, and on this depends whether I stay or whether I go back to the Jesuits." I forget what Mother replied but I do remember that she went, got up — she went out — she went back to the Sisters' place which was just down the road.

And she did not come back. It was perhaps an hour before the liturgy which I think was to start at five in the evening. She did not come back. I can also remember that that was a

Part – III: Brother Andrew MC – Calcutta (1966-1972)

very distracted liturgy for me. My mind was not very much in what I was saying at all at that time. I didn't know where I stood. I didn't know where anything stood. We met again. I can't remember.

Within a few days I think and I don't remember all the conversation but I remember Mother saying, "I have entrusted the Brothers to you and you do what you want and it will be all right." They were not her exact words. I can't remember them, but that was more or less the gist of it. Mother even came and said, "I will speak to the Brothers and I will tell them." I stayed downstairs. Mother went up. I don't know exactly what she said but it [was] all very short and very brief and she told them Brother Andrew was the superior and that they were to accept him as such.[6]

The opening entry in the Congregation's first journal (it seems that a journal had been kept prior to 1966 when the Brothers were in Shishu Bhavan but eventually lost) is dated 1 May 1966. Started by Brother Andrew in his own handwriting, it describes how it was the Feast of St Joseph the Worker and a Mass was celebrated at Shishu Bhavan for all the workers, followed by breakfast and the opening of the Home for Helpless and Destitute Lepers in Dhapa.[7] After this news comes a list of new assignments of various Brothers in charge of the apostolates and house chores, with Michael as Servant. What is interesting about this list is that from the start the one in charge of the community was not called "Superior" but "Servant".[8] That was one of Brother Andrew's first contributions to the Congregation. Significant also in the first entries he wrote is the fact that on 12 May 1966, when he left to do some work in Bombay, he referred to himself as "Father" and not yet as "Brother". His last entry is dated the first week of June, after which another Brother took over.

Around this time, the Brothers felt the need to move out of Shishu Bhavan to a place of their own. It was Fr Aloysius Hari Vanigasooriyar — the Director of Boys' Town of West Bengal — who offered to rent them part of the house at 16 Koyla Sarak Road in the Kidderpoor section of Calcutta, not far from the dock areas inhabited largely by poor Muslims.[9] The entry in the journal for 2 July 1966 states: "Today is a great joy for our community: we shifted from Shishu Bhavan to Kidderpoor (former Boys' Town house) on the Feast of the Visitation."[10] Because the house on Koyla Sarak was much smaller the Brothers decided not to take their beds with them. Instead, they started sleeping on thin mattresses on the floor and in the morning would roll them up and stack them neatly in a communal area. When Brother Andrew mentioned this to Mother Teresa she was strongly opposed to the idea. Concerned for the Brothers' health, she said they would all fall sick because floors in West Bengal were damp. Brother Andrew later noted that "there was an unpleasantness that ended on that note and I went away."[11]

Until Brother Andrew's arrival the first Brothers had led, under the caring and watchful eyes of Mother Teresa and the Sisters, a life structured in exactly the style of the MC Sisters. As necessary and good as this arrangement may have been initially, it created the problem of Brothers being treated as the Sisters' "little brothers" rather than as men who were fully Missionaries of Charity. Brother Andrew felt the need to change this situation. Having come to the Missionaries of Charity as a Jesuit, he brought with him the strong belief that there was a place for freedom in religious life. He felt the need to form men trusted to have as much freedom as possible to work and live and fulfil the aim of the Congregation out of a deep personal conviction. Behind this decision to make Brothers' life as free as possible (while recognizing fully the need for obedience and authority) lay the faith that the Spirit of God was present in each individual.

Brother Andrew's re-organisation of the Brothers' life did not take place all at once but gradually over a period of several years. Some of the changes ultimately made included the abolition of the system whereby each Brother had his own number marked on all his clothes, dishes, missal and such; doing away with each Brother having his own bucket; no longer using "Joseph" as the first part of their names, for example, Joseph Aloysius; no longer folding their

Part – III: Brother Andrew MC – Calcutta (1966-1972)

table napkins, bed quilts and other things exactly as the Sisters did; going barefoot in the house instead of wearing slippers; no longer wearing the "third dress" (a white shirt and white trousers used only for meditation and Mass in the mornings and changed after breakfast). Other changes included designating Mary, Mother of the Poor patroness of the Society with the feast day on 11 October rather than adopting 22 August in honour of the Immaculate Heart of Mary that was the Sisters' patronal feast day (more on this will be shared later on); and of course, sleeping on the terrace on hot nights and on mattresses placed on the floor rather than on beds. All the time that these and other changes were going on Mother Teresa was able to see what was happening. At times she was afraid and, on several occasions, tackled Brother Andrew about different points, usually expressing strong misgivings. At the end of such discussions, however, she would reveal some of her true greatness, professing not to want to spoil God's work and telling Brother Andrew that she had confidence in him and really had no fear. Without having any particular plan or intention in mind, what Brother Andrew had been doing all this time was trying to establish for the Brothers an identity of their own. An indication of the human element in this whole development, however, is discernible from his remark that part of his reason for seeking to make the independent nature of the new Community clear was his reluctance to be led by a woman:

> The idea of being under a woman and having a woman showing the way I know stuck in my throat at times. There was something of pride in it I'm sure...
>
> But I still feel that whole process was necessary. It's alright to have a woman as founder (and we have a very wonderful woman as foundress and we are very privileged and very fortunate in that)...
>
> But I think we cannot or could not be a congregation of men living as Sisters.[12]

The day after all the Brothers moved to their new rented home, Albert V. D'Souza, the Archbishop of Calcutta visited them. They lost no time before setting to work, according to the journal entry for 4 July 1966: "In the evening, after tea, Brothers went on survey among slums to see their condition."[13] A couple of days later Mother Teresa came to the new house.

Around October 1966 Brother Andrew started writing some "preliminary remarks" on the Sisters' constitutions in an attempt to compile a new set for the Brothers.[14] Young men started to get to know the new Congregation, some of them through the work of the Sisters, others through parish priests who knew Brother Andrew from his time as a Jesuit. At the beginning of November, Brother Andrew wrote an article "A New Indian Congregation" in a Calcutta newspaper. In it he described how the men who have come to the Society and stuck out the hard life and the many uncertainties have become the very generous and solid foundation of the new society. So that now as new Brothers join, they fit into a group of a tradition of dedication and seriousness in work for the poor and in the spiritual life.

Brother Andrew also wrote of the "spirit of generosity, dedication and joy of the young Brothers as the surest sign that the Society's existence is in accordance with the will of God."[15]

Koyla Sarak was by now becoming too small and Boys' Town needed the space back. Brother Andrew started to look round for a larger and a more permanent house. The attempts proved fruitless to the extent that he decided to travel to Delhi and check the possibilities of moving there. On 12 November 1966, back from his ten-day expedition, he announced that most of the Brothers would move to Delhi and manage a city-government night shelter. Two of the Brothers who had finished a course in leprosy training were asked to stay in Calcutta to continue the leprosy work. All other works would be transferred to the Sisters or stopped altogether. On Saturday, 26 November 1966 the community of Brothers in Koyla Sarak celebrated the feast of St Andrew — the namesake of the founder. The occasion was also a farewell for the Brothers leaving for Delhi. Next day, however, after Sunday Mass, a phone call from the Mother House announced the postponement and later the cancellation of the

Part – III: Brother Andrew MC – Calcutta (1966-1972)   127

move to Delhi owing to government regulations applicable to the night shelter. The Brothers would not have been fully free to run the shelter, and the Archbishop of Delhi had not agreed to these regulations set by the Delhi Corporation.

On Monday, 28th, while Brother Andrew and Mother Teresa were at the Archbishop's Office in Calcutta, a disagreement ensued. From the letter which Mother Teresa wrote to Brother Andrew after the incident it seems to have been about an aspect of the work in Nirmal Hriday, the home for the dying. Various Brothers who joined the Congregation at that time confirmed that the Sisters running Nirmal Hriday were treating them as their workers. Brothers even remembered doing night duty in pairs on a regular basis, and then in the morning being expected to follow the routine of the novitiate. After their apparent altercation, Mother Teresa expressed her displeasure in what seems quite a strong letter:

Dear Father Andrew,

These are the few points I am putting on paper — which I think will help solve some of our problems.

1. In future — do not discuss anything of the Brothers with me or with any other Sister.
2. Let not the Brothers work in Nirmal Hriday as regular workers — only on occasions when you wish to send them.
3. We shall take care of Dappa [Dhapa] home — and Kalighat Lepers.
4. Re. the house you go round and decide for yourself what you wish — I need not see it. It may be better that we keep Park St. [the Sisters House on Park Street] as it is for the Sisters.

Every year — you can have from the Leprosy fund Rs 15,000/- for the year to meet all the Leprosy work expenses as the money we raise is for the work of all the

Lepers that are under us — as I had told you before, His Grace is Your Superior — all permissions, etc., must be given to him — there is not even necessary to tell me anything. I only want—that the Poor be served.

I hope soon the erection comes — then many things will become very simple for you.

I am very sorry that some of the Sisters had not treated the Brothers properly — I am leaving for Bombay & Goa tomorrow evening —

Take care of the Brothers & yourself — for you all have a beautiful work to do for God and His Poor.

Pray for me.

Yours in Jesus.
M. Teresa MC.[16]

Mother's greatness and humility is apparent from her second letter to Andrew.[17] Less formal than the first which she had directed to "Father Andrew", in this second she called him "Brother". Also, in the first she signed herself, "M. Teresa MC" and in the second just "Mother". Maybe Mother Teresa realised that she had possibly written the first letter out of frustration at seeing the Congregation she had started and loved, moving away from certain practices. It could also be that she was not happy with Brother Andrew's plan to take the Brothers to Delhi, or with his stand in defence of the Brothers. We will never know all these details. What we do know is that both Andrew and Mother were stubborn and opinionated; at the same time both knew that the work was not theirs but God's, and what they were trying to accomplish was not for their glory but for the good of the poorest of the poor.

Dear Brother,
By now you must have received my letter — it must have surprised you but you know the reason — I want you to be completely free — "The work" must remain His. I do not want to be an obstacle. Each time something like this

Part – III: Brother Andrew MC – Calcutta (1966-1972)

happens, Our Lord proofs [sic] it difficult — for example, the house. I hope you will be happy with what Jesus is giving you — I told B. to accept & make all arrangements as it is vacant — you can get in by the 15th when I hope to be back — it is like Park St. & it is much less than what we were giving Fr Van [Vanigasooriyar — it is really a gift of God. So please contact B. & tell him to prepare everything in the Missionaries of Charity (Brothers) as you have the Bank A/C. Once it is erected — we will get the society registered also & exempted of all taxes — we will pay everything from Shanti Nagar. Then we could pay back — I am so happy & you bringing the young Jude just cleared everything. I am glad you brought him. Let Sr Gertrude see him, start treating him he seemed such a holy child. Many more will come — you will grow & bring much fruit. Only never, not even in your thoughts think that the work is yours. It is His — B. will do all the legal work & he is doing it for the love of God — God wanted us both to have that humiliation in front of His Grace — thank God we both took it with a smile. Some of the people told that you are not looking well — please take care of yourself we must not spoil this work through our own faults —

Pray for me —

God bless you
Mother.[18]

Brother Andrew's first Christmas letter to friends and benefactors as a Missionaries of Charity Brother spoke about the beginnings of the new group and the work undertaken by Mother Teresa. However, at the heart of the letter stood the poor. For Andrew, the poor (or poverty) were not an abstract concept but a collection of persons, each with all his or her dignity. For him, the poor woman or man had a face and a name:

Last year I wrote to you from the peace and beauty of the monastery at Sitagarha, surrounded by lovely mountains, trees and jungle. It is a very different world from Calcutta which is crushed under the misery, chaos and poverty of a very dark period of its history. I think I asked you to pray that I may do whatever God wanted from me in a desire that I had long felt to work for the poorest of the poor. Well it has all worked out in a most unexpected way. About 15 years ago a very remarkable nun in Calcutta started a new congregation to work for the poor in the slums. Her work met with quick and remarkable success, and now Mother Teresa has about 250 sisters and 20 houses in India and South America working for the poor.

She saw the need for a similar society of Brothers and a few young men came together for this work. They were all youngsters and there was need of someone a bit older to take charge. And to make short a long and rather extraordinary story, that is where I came in last February. Now if anywhere in the world there is a person struggling with a job several hundred times too big for him, I am the one. For what is needed here at this stage is a superior to guide the new religious Congregation, to plan the work for the poor, to be the spiritual director of the Brothers, in a word, to establish a new order spiritually and materially.

Perhaps it is just as well that there is little time to stop and think, because if I grasped where I really stand, I would surely sink like Peter walking on the water. But it is God's work — and He seems to make a habit of choosing the ridiculously inadequate to do His work.

There are, however, signs to show that God wants the new society. To me the clearest and most encouraging of these is the spirit of generosity and cheerfulness of the young Brothers in doing work for lepers, slum dwellers, those dying on the streets, work that is not pleasant by any natural standards. I have never seen one of them grumble or complain at anything they have been asked to do for the poor and destitute sick. What tremendous lessons they teach me who am supposed to be their teacher and guide!

We are sixteen Brothers. Most are young, many of them have not completed high school, but all the same, we are treating about 2000 lepers, We have opened a little T.B. clinic for unemployed workers in the docks, some schools in the slums, we also take a small box of elementary medicines to the slums where the people do not otherwise get any medical care.

We have a few little guests in our own house — a crippled boy who has been abandoned by his family, a little boy who is a bit mad (and who is nearly driving me mad while I'm trying to write this letter) but he makes us laugh a lot with all the songs and dances he learned when he was begging. There are four other urchins whom we found begging on the railway stations and who are accomplished little pickpockets. And then there is Christopher, a refugee from Pakistan who lost both his legs in a train accident after coming to India. We don't have much room in the house, which is not our own, but these guests — in spite of all their noise — bring us a very wonderful blessing, for they are a real presence of Christ in our midst.[19]

MANSATALA ROW

On 15 January 1967 Andrew and his young Brothers moved to a large three-storey house at 7 Mansatala Row, a fifteen-minute walk from Koyla Sarak in the same Kidderpoor area.[20] Staying in the same neighbourhood was a major advantage since the Brothers could continue the apostolate they had already started.

> We have been very fortunate in getting a place of our own this last week — or at least we have our name on the title deed beside the one who has loaned us the money. We really need

it, as we were 35 living in a house for six in the old place.

But this place seems to be filling up fast as the Brothers have brought home quite a few homeless boys from the streets since we came here. One of these boys, about 11 years old was supporting his little sister, age two, on the station. Their parents had died. He wouldn't agree to come with us until he first saw her settled with the Sisters. It is astounding to find beautiful qualities among these children of the streets.

Please pray for us, as we are all hopelessly inadequate for the work we are doing. And please pray that more generous young men may join us.[21]

Next day a thanksgiving Mass was celebrated with Mother Teresa and Sister Agnes, MC.[22] A few Loreto nuns were also present.

Along with the new house came great news. On 22 March of that same year, Albert D'Souza — Archbishop of Calcutta — visited the Brothers to announce that the Society of Brothers had received Rome's recognition. Thus four days later, on Easter Sunday, "the Solemn Proclamation of the Decree of Approval was announced by His Grace, Archbishop Albert D'Souza at 6:30 pm in the presence of a large gathering of lay people, nuns and priests, including Msgr Eric Barber, Vicar General and Jesuit Provincial of Calcutta; Fr Henry who had been Spiritual Director of the Brothers for a long time from the beginning; Mother Teresa, and many of her Sisters and some Sisters of Loreto and of the Apostolic Carmel. Benediction from the Archbishop with the 'Te Deum' followed the proclamation of the Decree which His Grace then handed over to the Superior."[23]

Brother Andrew was happy with how the new Congregation was progressing, and one of the first persons to whom he expressed this joy was his former Jesuit Provincial:

V. Rev. and Dear Father Boylan,

There is no limit to your thoughtfulness in giving so much of your time on Easter Sunday to visiting Dad and then sitting down to write a long letter to me. I can imagine how thrilled Dad must have been.

Father, Easter Sunday was a big day for us as the Archbhp. [archbishop] having received permission from Rome, came here and read his decree constituting us as a Religious Congregation. So it has come. I can still scarcely believe it. You can really see how God has brought it along one step at a time. We got this house in January and it is a real blessing. It is near the old one — so we can continue our work in the slums. It has room enough for our future growth.

We are now 20 Brothers — and they do very well. It is truly a great privilege to be with them. More inquiries are coming in. We begin our noviceship on 8th April — and I become a novice once more — this time, however, with the novel turn that I shall be Mag. Nov. [Novice Master]. Certainly one would never sit down and plan things that way. And what a glorious lack of experience and everything else for such a job at such a stage of our history.

But it is all God's work and He will have to make up for everything. I feel much more secure and steady in this new vocation these days — and I don't think much about the future. The amount of work the Brothers are doing has increased greatly in the last six months. We shall do quite a bit of work even in the noviceship.[24]

On 14 May 1967 Mansatala's Journal recorded, "The superior general of the Little Brothers of Jesus, Rev. Father René Voillaume came from Bangkok. By evening he flew to Madras."[25] René Voillaume would be the first of a number of distinguished guests to visit Mansatala and Brother Andrew in particular. Among them were Dorothy Day and Brother Roger of Taizé. Over the years another guest would be Jean Vanier with whom Andrew would strike up a friendship, especially since their philosophy of life, spirituality and their commitment to the poor were extremely similar.[26] Brother Andrew's Jesuit confrères were still very much in touch, writing and visiting him. His former tertian director, Father Moyersoen, paid him a visit on his way to Mangalore, while Father Austin Kelly was still helping him financially by channelling funds from donors, especially after writing an article in *Hazaribagh May 1967, No. 161.*

2 June 1967, the Feast of the Sacred Heart of Jesus for that year, was a special day for the young Congregation. The first novitiate was inaugurated with thirteen novices. Margaret Costigan was an Australian lay missionary living with Mother Teresa at Lower Circular Road in 1967. At that time, Mother had told her that she did not have lay missionaries but if Margaret would come and adopt the exact lifestyle of the Missionaries of Charity without necessarily becoming a professed member of the Congregation, that would be fine. Whilst there, she wore the habit, adopted the name Sister John of the Cross and lived exactly like the Sisters. It was while Margaret was living at Lower Circular Road that she met Brother Andrew. Margaret recalled Brother Andrew saying to her, probably on the day the novitiate was started: "Today I am a novice, the novice-master and the co-founder and superior of the Missionary Brothers of Charity." To this Margaret — she herself being Australian — replied flippantly, "Don't let it go to your head."[27]

As novice master, Brother Andrew was pretty strict. A number of Brothers confirmed this, especially when it came to silence, wasting food and the care of material things. "One morning at breakfast, the previous day's *chapattis,* flat breads, were brought to the table. They were cold and dry and nobody found an appetite for them. Brother Andrew, having noticed our rejection, got up from the table and removed all the bread from the table and ordered us to eat those chapattis. Not another word was said. We all ate them in silence including him. He was a strict disciplinarian. I remember when we went to Noorpur for our eight-day retreat before we entered novitiate, in his first meeting, he gave us the instructions not to destroy nature and not to chase the birds."[28] "One day the

Part – III: Brother Andrew MC – Calcutta (1966-1972)   135

bell rang for lunch, and all ten of us novices came to the refectory. There were pieces of rubbish on the floor and nobody picked them up, so Andrew was moving things and he started sweeping, and he said, 'Yes Brothers, it is easy to sit and watch the general cleaning and washing and sweeping the floor. You are standing there and watching. There will be no recreation for one week.'"[29] "How many times did we break a glass or something and for three days we were allowed no recreation. And so we were waiting for that day when he breaks a glass. So one day it happened. He was coming to the refectory with a glass and a plate and his glass fell and broke. We were all laughing. By the time he came back from cleaning up, I had already put another glass for him."[30] "Once I was scolded by Andrew because after breakfast I was sitting down talking, and he came and said, 'Today long time in the refectory, no?'"[31] "Poverty was very important to him. During candidacy and novitiate time, if you had torn clothes, you will have to show them to Andrew, he will check them and then he will give you one slip of paper, to get underpants, second-hand underpants we got. And then you show the slip of paper to the Brother in charge and he then gives you what is needed. Two pairs only we were allowed. That was the poverty that time."[32]

19 October 1967 marked the opening of the second house of the Missionaries of Charity Brothers. Some Brothers had gone for a picnic around Dum Dum Cantonment and while there were, providentially, offered a house at 16 Hari Mohan Dutta Road. Manning this second house was not a problem for Brother Andrew; he decided to separate the come-and-sees from the novices.[33] Thus Brother Felix, who was himself a come-and-see but somewhat older than the others, became the local Servant. In fact, Brother Andrew forbade the novices to even visit the Dum Dum house for the duration of their novitiate.

A couple of months after the opening of the house in Dutta Road, Father D. Martin, a Salesian priest working in Hong Kong, stayed with the Brothers in Mansatala. He and Brother Andrew discussed the idea of the MC Brothers opening a house in Hong

Kong. This was the first time a real possibility arose of the Brothers beginning work outside India. Brother Andrew wrote about it to Bishop Lorenzo Bianchi of Hong Kong. The Vicar General, Auxiliary Bishop Francis Hsu, replied but he did not seem very eager, claiming that learning the local languages was quite difficult. But he also said that Brother Andrew was always welcome to visit. Later in the year, Brother Andrew did make plans to visit but in the end did not. With not a single Brother having taken temporary vows, wasn't it too early to even consider such a possibility?

Instead, around November that same year, he went on a tour of the parishes in the Ranchi Archdiocese looking for possible vocations. His target of the Far East was still there, however, and there to stay. Evidently Brother Andrew had enquired of the Jesuits. In a letter from the General of the Society of Jesus, Pedro Arrupe, dealing with the dispensation from vows in the Society of Jesus, he [Arrupe] mentioned, "The Assistant for East Asia is of the opinion that Djakarta is the city in the Far East where there is the best chance of working in the poorest surroundings, though there are very poor areas in Thailand, Laos, Cambodia and Vietnam. Djakarta is a Jesuit Archdiocese and you will probably find there guidance and help, provided you go there with the necessary credentials from the Calcutta religious and ecclesiastical authorities."[34]

Christmas 1967 brought with it the now usual letter to friends and benefactors. The growth in number of Brothers, inmates and houses was the main topic.

> Last year at this time we were sixteen Brothers; now we are thirty-three. We had five abandoned little boys with us; now we have thirty, and others are in boarding schools. Last year we had with us one man, a legless refugee; this year there are fifteen homeless, bed-ridden men... God is wonderfully blessing our work.[35]

With Christmas over, Brother Andrew took Brother Marcel and again went around Ranchi to meet some of the young men. This time, the circuit coincided with the transport of foodstuffs from

Part – III: Brother Andrew MC – Calcutta (1966-1972)

Calcutta to Ranchi. Without "passengers" the truck would have come back empty to Calcutta. In the words of Br Anima Prasad, "Eventually, the truck became synonymous with Andrew's craziness and impulsiveness, and at times an occasion of derision for those Brothers who are still in the Congregation and who had been 'picked up' by the famous truck."[36] The same Brother Anima who boarded the truck at Noatoli that 18 January 1968 recounted,

> I am a truck vocation. It is a part of my life story, a precious and unforgettable story. Brother Andrew frequently used this story in his talks. It was not because he wanted to make us laugh. Sadly, many of us failed to grasp what he was trying to tell us through this story. Of course, none of us were qualified or had any degrees or professional status. We were all from very simple and ordinary families. The famous MC truck had run twice to Konvir Noatoli Parish in the district and Diocese of Gumla [about 88 km from Ranchi]. That day we were thirty who came back by truck. Then a year later, the truck went again to the same parish and brought back twenty-four boys.

> This funny truck vocation story started right in our school run by the St Gabriel Brothers and in our parish. A Belgian Jesuit was the parish priest at that time, and somehow knew the little group of MC Brothers. He started to contact some of the schoolboys as future MC candidates, but he never told any of them to go to MC. None of those boys had any knowledge of MC. He was very friendly with me and used to give me some spiritual books to read. He encouraged me to pray and to visit the Blessed Sacrament before going to school. He even encouraged me to either go to the diocesan seminary or to join a religious society, but that was beyond my ability. When he had already gathered a number of students, he invited Brother Andrew to his parish. It was in the beginning of 1967 that Brother Andrew visited and he personally met with each of the boys.

> One day during class, the parish priest called me over. When

I arrived he introduced me to Brother Andrew as a guest priest from Calcutta. But, what to talk about? I did not know. I saw a tall and thick-bearded man. I was nervous and felt to run away from the room. He greeted me and he gave me a chair to sit on. He himself sat down on his bed (there was only one chair). I saw he was uncomfortable on the bed and so I gave the chair back to him and I sat down on the floor. He immediately got up from his bed and lifted me up and put me on the chair. Later he introduced himself. He said, "I am Brother Andrew, we have newly started a congregation. There are a few Brothers and we are working for the poor people." What Brother Andrew told me did not reach to my little heart. But what I felt and what touched me was his humbleness and his simplicity....

Within a few months, Brother Andrew wrote me another letter saying that he would be coming soon to the parish and would inform the parish priest of the date. It was 18 February 1968, when I came to the parish with my few little things. There were other boys who had come and I saw a truck parked in the parish compound. One of my companions commented that most probably we will be going with that truck. When I heard this I was not so pleased. After some time, Brother Andrew arrived and confirmed that we would be going with that truck. He said to keep our things on one side of the truck and to get inside. Twenty-nine of us got in and in Ranchi we picked up one more to become thirty, a full truck. The next day we reached Mansatala. I can say this is the way God brought us. This is the way we met Brother Andrew and this is the way we came by truck.[37]

Twenty-five years after this event of the (in)famous truck event, in his Christmas letter, Brother Andrew recalled,

> Many young men threw in their lives for this work. They came mostly from remote interior areas where limited opportunities for education existed and their families were

Part – III: Brother Andrew MC – Calcutta (1966-1972)

poor. But God found them and called them.

They came in numbers: and several times, we made the journey to Calcutta together as a batch of recruits in a truck. The "Truck" became a part of our history — spoken of for a while with a deep warm smile. But gradually it became an embarrassment: "A truck is not the way to recruit vocations." And so the "Truck" gave way to more respectable ways — and ultimately to fewer recruits.

But with the truck came many wonderful young people whose lives have touched people all over the world. For myself, I have to confess that I remain an unrepentant advocate of the "Truck".

I believe that "the Truck" comes out of the Gospels: the shepherds on Christmas night, Joseph, the fishermen of Galilee, the lepers, the beggars, the possessed, the publicans, tax collectors, the sinners, Mary His Mother. These were the community of Jesus. They were "Truck" people rather than successful, self-reliant people.[38]

With Missionaries of Charity vows approaching, Brother Andrew had to be released from his vows in the Society of Jesus and so, on 5 March 1968, he wrote to the Regional Superior of the Jesuits, Fr E.B. O'Connor:

Most Reverend Father,

Further to our recent correspondence and your reply of 23rd February, I now formally request you to arrange for me to be dispensed from my vows in the Society, so that I may make my profession in the new congregation of the Missionary Brothers of Charity. This I hope to do on 2nd June 1968, and I would be grateful if the date of my dispensation could take force on the day before that.

I should like to include in this request an attempt to express my deep gratitude to the Society of Jesus for all that it has done for me. I may be founding this new congregation, and naturally have a deep affection for it, but I can say in all sincerity, that I have no less affection for the Society, which I shall always consider my mother. And I pray that I may always remain a real son of so great and loving a mother.

My gratitude to you, to all my superiors and brothers in the Society. I ask for forgiveness for my many many infidelities in my years in the Society, and I beg to remain in the prayers and holy desires of you all. I shall always pray for the Society.

Your affectionate son in Christ.[39]

Another such letter was written to the Archbishop of Calcutta. Both the Jesuit Superior and the Archbishop of Calcutta had gone through the necessary canonical formalities, and an answer was received from Rome through the Archbishop of Calcutta:

Sacra Congregatio pro Gentium
Evangelizatione seu de Propaganda Fide
Prot. 2204/68
Rome – 24 April 1968

Your Grace,

I am in receipt of your two letters, Nos. 542/68, and 543/68 dated 13th April, with which you requested for Brother Andrew a dispensation from the impediment to make his profession in the Diocesan Congregation of the Missionary Brothers of Charity, which arises from his having been a professed member of the Society of Jesus, and, at the same time, permission to make his profession of vows with the first group of novices on 2nd June next.

In this regard, I am pleased to inform Your Grace that the Sacred Congregation, with the present letter, grants both the dispensation and the permission which you have requested.

With renewed sentiments of personal esteem and every best wish, I remain.

Sincerely yours in Christ,
G.P. Card. Agagianian
Pref.
Edward Pescais
Undersecr.

On 2 June 1968 Brothers Andrew, Aloysius, Damien, George, Benedict and Sebastian became the first to make their first profession as Missionaries of Charity Brothers, and did so on the terrace of 7 Mansatala Row. By this ceremony Brother Andrew automatically ceased to be a Jesuit.[40] Had he remained in the Society of Jesus, he would have made his final profession as a Jesuit at about this time. His first profession as a Missionary of Charity was, therefore, in the form of final vows.[41] As well as being the General Servant, Brother Andrew remained the novice master. To Austin Kelly he wrote:

> On 2nd June, the first group of our novices will make their profession. It is a great day for us. I too shall be making my profession with them. It will be with very mixed feelings, as this involves ceasing to be a Jesuit. However, I don't think I shall feel very different, for it is the Society that has gone so deep into my formation and life that I will always be a Jesuit at heart — at least I hope and pray so. You, Father, have had such a part in the whole direction that my life has taken — and this in this new congregation also — that I must take this occasion to express my deep gratitude to you.
>
> Please pray for me, Father. As the congregation grows, the responsibility grows — and I feel so inadequate. But I trust in God. Yours devotedly in Christ.
>
> Andrew MC.[42]

Only a year and a half had passed since the day Brother Andrew set foot in the City of Joy, but he soon became well known in certain circles. In fact, he would be asked to give talks on *The Responsibility of the Church in India Today*, at a regional seminar on the situation of the Church in India. Andrew also attended joint meetings of the voluntary organisations conducted by the Calcutta Junior Chamber and presided over by the Mayor of Calcutta, Mr Gobinda Chandra Dey. At times he was asked to address them. He was even elected delegate for the priests in the region.

It is also worth noting that between June and December 1968, Brother Nicholas Prinster, OCSO, who had been a Trappist monk for nineteen years at the Abbey of Our Lady of the Holy Trinity of Utah, United States of America, was a come-and-see at Mansatala Row.[43] Brother Nicholas did not survive as an MC Brother. Life as a come-and-see in India was hard for him. Andrew and Brother Nick were almost the same age, however, and a deep spiritual friendship developed between them. When Brother Nick returned to Utah, he kept up a constant active link with young American men aspiring to join the Congregation, and even with one of Andrew's sisters.

Before the year 1968 ended the Rev. Dr James R. Knox, Archbishop of Melbourne, visited Mansatala Row and Brother Andrew took the opportunity to ask him to call on his father who was rather sick. As it transpired, Frederick Henry Travers-Ball died on 23 December of that same year, at the age of eighty-nine. A house was also rented on Dr Sudhir Basu Road with the original intention of using it as a haven for women wishing to escape the environment of prostitution. The Archbishop of Calcutta dissuaded Brother Andrew and ultimately the house became a place for street boys. In an article that appeared in *Age* in Melbourne a few years later in October 1971, "Brother Andrew — Man of Mercy," Max Beattie wrote:

> One of Br Andrew's pet projects, one which must wait, is the establishment of a sort of holiday home for prostitutes, run by girls who have left the professions permanently or temporarily. It would not be a place where the girls would come to be lectured on the error of their ways, simply a

place to stay for a while, to think, to try to work out some other way of survival. Of course, if they did decide to leave the brothels permanently the Missionary Brothers would be pleased. But if not, then there would be no strings. Because he is Calcutta wise (and that is very wise, for this is a savage city), Br Andrew was amused at the idea of persuasively rescuing them from their present employers. "You'd end up in the river," he said.[44]

SOMETHING BEAUTIFUL FOR GOD, 1969

The year 1969 launched Mother Teresa to fame through Malcom Muggeridge's BBC (British Broadcasting Corporation) documentary *Something Beautiful for God*.[45] Brother Andrew was also interviewed for the film at the Dum Dum community. When asked about the point of taking care of twenty-five boys in a city with millions of people in need, Brother Andrew did not hesitate to talk about the appreciation and the importance of the small ones:

> Once you look at the problem as a problem, then it's ridiculous, but, you have to look at those twenty-five individual boys and I think there is a value — we have to see the value in each one of the little mental…. There is a funny little boy here — a little bit mental, crippled and that boy fulfils a tremendous purpose here. When new boys come, often from the station, a little nervous, they keep very near to the gate, ready to run away when they see anyone coming towards them, and this little boy with his little tricks and jokes…. It's wonderful how he welcomes them in his own way.[46]

He stressed the idea that the Brothers tended to keep the number of people they accept in their homes to not more than twenty or twenty-five, in order to preserve the family spirit. "Up to twenty the boys form a little bit of a family: the bigger ones help the small ones, the handicapped ones, it does a lot of good for everybody."[47]

That same year various Brothers were ordained as priests. Unfortunately, this new development created problems, most probably those other congregations of Brothers with a few ordained priests would have faced. Whether the newly-ordained Brothers felt superior to the non-ordained, or whether the regular Brothers felt inferior and inadequate is open to discussion. The fact remains that it created tensions which the Brothers had to tackle and discuss. While Brother Andrew was in Bangalore for the national seminar on The Church in India Today, the Brothers sat down, prayerfully to share their ideas on the subject. When Andrew came back, he had further discussion sessions with all the Brothers, pointing strongly to the fact that priests and non-priests must look upon each other as brothers. Still it was a topic of concern which he raised in a letter to James Robert Cardinal Knox on a separate issue:

> I would be grateful for a prayer for our Congregation. We are just going through a bit of crisis about having priests in the Congregation. It's alright about me, but there's a bit of tension about the younger Brothers going to the seminary. Please God, it will be settled. Everything has come out fully into the open in frank discussion. So now we all have to try to settle it. The little bit of time I've had here has taught me that we shall never be able to say, 'Now it's all settled.' For we always have to struggle with our tensions and selves. This seems to run through the whole of Church History.[48]

The topic was again raised with the priests of the diocese in whose parishes some of the Brothers were working. Brother Andrew had to send a letter to them and to the archbishop, explaining the role and work of the priests in the Brothers' communities — they were committed to service of the poor alongside the other brothers.

Brother Andrew's Christmas letter for the year 1969 was tinged with unrest and chaos. He perceived a wave of revolution following the pattern of China or Vietnam. He confessed not to know what would be best, given the great hardship and suffering was on the horizon. At the same time, he wrote of the benefits:

> But somehow it is good to be in Calcutta today. There is terrible chaos and uncertainty, but there is also very great vitality. One can feel alive here. Bengal is going through this great social upheaval....
>
> Recently, I had to travel a little in other parts of India which were quieter and more peaceful. Before I went I was looking forward to getting away. But I must confess that I was glad to get back into the crowds of the rush hour in the evening.
>
> You adjust to chaos. You come to live in it. In fact, it becomes your life, and it would be hard to live elsewhere. There are great spiritual benefits also. For you come to realise that there is not much security in the things that you grew up to think provided security. In a chaotic situation, one lives close to danger, death and disruption — close to struggle, conflict, human degradation. These things are basic. They are real. And reality does lead one to life.
>
> Disorder, danger and the presence of great misery prevent one from settling down too much; they remind one in their own way that one is a pilgrim in this world, and is not here forever, and that we have to try to make the best of it especially for those who are poor and suffering.[49]

Still Andrew saw hope and found that the joys of working with the suffering poor were many and deep:

> There is the joy of seeing people relieved of at least a little of their suffering, of the sick cured, of families finding employment for a breadwinner, of children of the streets finding a home and responding as loved and loving human beings, of alcoholics and drug addicts overcoming their difficulties.
>
> There is the joy of seeing a little one-legged boy from the railway station playing happily in the room as I write this. Now he finds shelter, a home, food and a little love. It is

worthwhile to have lived for this moment alone, where one has been able to share in some way in such a story. For us here seeing these things directly, it is much easier, for such sights and experiences are a great encouragement and happiness. I think the faith and love of those from afar who share in this work is much greater — for they do not have the consolation of seeing the light in young eyes or hearing the laughter and singing.[50]

THE BANGLADESH WAR

Around February 1971 Brother Andrew was feeling the need for a holiday. He decided to visit Australia, having not been back there since the day he first set foot on Indian soil in 1954. But on 26 March East Pakistan declared its independence — becoming Bangladesh — and a multitude of refugees flocked to West Bengal. His planned trip had to be postponed. On 16 April 1971, together with Mother Teresa, Brothers Philip and Dipchandra, two MC Sisters and two Sisters of Loreto, he made his first visit to a refugee camp near Kaliyaganj (some 400 kilometres north of Calcutta) to help with relief work.

Following the influx of thousands of refugees from Bangladesh, mostly to West Bengal, Indira Gandhi, Prime Minister of India, declared war on West Pakistan. Late in 1971, Pakistan surrendered and in Bangladesh people rejoiced. Pakistan claimed that 26,000 people died in the Indo-Pakistani war; India and Bangladesh made the unsubstantiated assertion that the figure was three million. It is more likely to have been around one million. Still, eight million seems to be the generally accepted number for refugees entering India.[51]

Like other Religious, Brother Andrew did not spend long stretches of time working at the East Pakistani refugee camp. He would go for a short while and then touch base in Calcutta. In a letter, he described the suffering of the people in the camps:

Part – III: Brother Andrew MC – Calcutta (1966-1972)

This is to thank you for your very kind gift for our work here with the refugees from East Pakistan. It came just at the right time, for we are doing a lot of work in different camps and areas. The condition of the people is unbelievable. They have come walking long distances, they arrive exhausted and often sick, they have nothing except what they can carry themselves. And now they find themselves in another country without any roots and no chance to get jobs or land. They don't know what their future will be, and there is nothing for them to do all day except to line up for their ration of food. So you imagine how demoralizing it is for people.

And there are so many. Already 7½ million have come, and still they are crossing in thousands. There are reports of a huge wave of people trying to get through to the border, but looking for a way through the military action.

The Brothers are working in four places, the largest of these being a camp of 60,000 people where 7 Brothers with a Muslim doctor who is himself a refugee are the only medical team, with cholera and gastro-enteritis still prevalent. To add to the trouble now there is a terrible flood in that area, and no supplies can get through.

The whole situation is so complicated, and it is impossible to see where it will all end. And it is ordinary people who suffer so much. Like a woman I met the other day in the camp. One child had died 3 weeks before, a second just a few days before and the third was dying. She said, 'I walked for days with swollen legs and through the dangers of the firing to save these children only, and now they are finished, and I am alone in a strange land.'

It is really hard to imagine the suffering. All we can do is to try to relieve some of the suffering and the hunger, and to offer a little concern. And that is what you have done through your gift. Things are very, very bad. The threat of war is great — and you can or can't (I can't) imagine what that would bring. It is possible to think of Calcutta with all supply lines in chaos. The strife goes on from within and without. In Dum Dum they hear bombs every night.

I just don't know what is going to happen.

Thanks again, and keep this staggering part of the world in your prayers. It is about all any of us can do very effectively at this stage.[52]

This particular period of turbulence also affected life in Calcutta. The war between India and Pakistan and the arrival of refugees contributed to the increase of people with mental instabilities roaming the city's streets. In response to this alarming situation, together Dr Satrujit Dasgupta, Dr R.B. Davis, Mr P.M. John, Mother Teresa, Brother Andrew and a few others founded the Antara Society on 13 September 1971. The organisation's primary objective was to provide care, treatment and rehabilitation for the destitute and very poor suffering from mental disorders, including drug addiction and alcoholism. Most of those involved were connected with the Mar Thoma Syrian Church, founded in 1967 in the Park Street area. By 18 October 1971, they had already opened an outpatient mental clinic in the church. Brother Andrew's involvement might have come about because he had been open to the idea of having weekly Alcoholics Anonymous and Neurotics Anonymous meetings in Mansatala which he at times attended and which may have been run by Dr Dasgupta and Dr Davis.[53]

INCULTURATION and INDIANISATION

Amongst the many visitors who would spend some time with the Brothers in Mansatala was Fr Garry McLoughlin, an Australian priest.[54] In fact, he had arrived when Andrew was with the East Pakistani refugees near Radikapur in Uttar Dinajpur. While Father Garry was in Calcutta he kept a fairly detailed and very compelling diary on the situation of Calcutta and the Brothers during the early 1970s. It also reveals important insights into Brother Andrew.

Part – III: Brother Andrew MC – Calcutta (1966-1972)

In an entry dated 1 May 1971, Father Garry wrote, "Andrew said an 'Indian Mass' this morning because of the 'St Joseph the Worker' feast — incense, Indian music and flowers strewn." During an "Indian Mass" the priest usually sits on the floor either on a cushion or a stool at a low altar, and all the participants will be similarly seated on the floor around the altar. The celebrant does not wear the traditional western-style vestments of alb, stole, cincture and chasuble, but simply puts on a shawl. Other small rituals like *aarti*, in which light in the form of a flame and songs are offered to God take place before the actual Mass. Andrew celebrated this 'Indian' Mass usually on Sundays and feast days. He would always make sure that during the offering there was the customary *prasad* — an offering of sweets — which would then be distributed to the people, especially to any non-Catholics present.

At that specific time great disputes were going on in the Indian Church. One school of thought maintained that this Indianisation of the liturgy was in accordance with Vatican II and should therefore be undertaken as much as possible; the other alleged that this was actually Hinduisation of the liturgy and that the Church was losing its identity and character. Andrew was of the first school, believing that Indianisation of the liturgy would definitely help Christians, especially in villages.

It could have been a year or two earlier that Andrew attended a retreat given by Fr Samuel Rayan, an Indian Jesuit priest and a pioneer of theology with an Asian perspective. Fr Sebastian Vazhakala, who was a young Brother at the time, confirmed that after that retreat Brother Andrew started adopting the Indian way of celebrating the Mass.[55]

On 13 May 1971 Father Garry wrote: "Tonight I went with Andrew to a meeting of a few friends — a couple of Indian laymen, Fr [Robert] Antoine, a Jesuit keen on Indianisation and teaching at Calcutta University and another Flemish priest who was a student of Personalist philosophy. We talked, at Andrew's suggestion, about the priesthood. Can a layperson be appointed to consecrate the

Eucharist? We thought yes. (Andrew has in mind the community of Brothers — why put a bloke through seven years of special study just to say Mass for the others. Why not just appoint one of the Brothers to do the job?) The discussion was open, the atmosphere relaxed. Perhaps we have thought too much of the priesthood in terms of a share in the episcopal power rather than as an expression and embodiment of the priesthood of the church."[56] Unfortunately in no other writings, letters or talks, was this philosophy ever mentioned or developed by Brother Andrew.

At this point in the history of the Missionaries of Charity Brothers, it would be difficult not to notice the openness and variety of experiences to which the Brothers were exposed as part of their growth and formation. For instance, Christmas night Mass in Mansatala was open to Co-Workers and friends of the community. Annie Joseph recalled attending Brother Andrew's Christmas Mass every year with her parents and her other seven siblings. As a young girl she remembered him as a compassionate, caring, holy man with a beautiful smile and joyful simplicity. After Mass there would be a piece of cake and two balloons for the children.[57] Also, daily Mass at Mansatala was open to whoever wished to attend – * Christians and Hindus alike — and Andrew wouldn't hesitate to distribute communion to all.[58] During another Christmas, the Brothers organised food distribution for the people living on the streets around Mansatala. Most were Hindus and before the distribution they offered their pujas and sacrifices. At times, novitiate classes were also taught by Anglican priests with Night Points on Sundar Singh, a convert from Sikhism to Christianity.[59]

IN AUSTRALIA

By late July 1972 Brother Andrew had again decided that the time had come for his home visit to Australia. After a council of four Brothers had been appointed with Br Ferdinand Tigga, MC, as its head and thus Vicar General of the Congregation, Andrew wrote a last letter before leaving:[60]

Part – III: Brother Andrew MC – Calcutta (1966-1972)

Dear Brothers,

This is a simple letter before I leave for Australia. I have visited all your houses and seen all of you in the last week. So there is not much to be said now. It is good that I am going away — good, for me and good for the Society, because we must learn to live in all circumstances, and you will learn many things in my absence. And many things that I have been doing you will have to learn.

You have elected a good council and a good Brother as your Vicar. He will do well, and I am very happy with your choice. Remember that he has all the authority that I have when I am here, and he is the one in full charge of the Society. I know that you will give him your full support and co-operation.

You will pass through difficulties in the next few months, and there will be crises. That will happen whether I am here or not. Remember that it is by facing difficulties and crises that we grow if we accept them in the correct spirit of faith...

And I ask you all sincerely to 1) Love and serve the poor, 2) Love and serve each other, 3) Love and serve God in Christ.[61]

On 2 August 1972 Brother Andrew left Calcutta for Australia, aware that he might not return to his former role in India. A few Brothers, who were already professed at that time, admitted when interviewed that they had feared even then that Brother Andrew might not return. A former MC Brother, recalled, "When I went to join him in Saigon, he [Andrew] told me he was already disappointed because he thought the Brothers wanted to run things themselves. That was quite a disappointment for him. In fact he even mentioned that he felt like he had lost his faith and he was going back to Australia to decide what he wanted to do, and then he realised after being so long away from Australia that he couldn't settle back there, and from there he decided to go to Saigon. This was a complete revelation for me."[62] It is really not a shock or surprise considering that Andrew in 1972 was forty-four — the perfect age for an existential mid-life crisis.

By now, all his brothers and sisters were married and already had small children. Jim and Gregory, Lucy's children had been five and one respectively when Ian left for India, so Jim's first memory of Uncle Ian comes from when he was already in his early twenties: "I remember in the 1970s, which is probably one of the first times when Ian came back to Australia, taking him to the football at the Suburban Hawthorn Ground. I remember at that time I had a little green MG and so Ian and I headed off to the football ground. I remember we went in and stood and watched the football and I think they won and he was delighted. He was happy to do all those sorts of things."[63]

Aimée's son, Julian was born two years before Uncle Ian sailed for India and his sister Anne was born in the same year, 1954. So they awaited his return with curiosity because their only memoirs of their "mysterious" Uncle Ian were connected with their visiting the Jesuit provincial house at Christmas and awaiting a phone call from a relative who lived in a faraway country — a call courtesy of the Jesuits in Australia for those young Jesuits who had gone to the missions in India.[64]

We know only a few facts about Andrew's vacation in Australia. Kevin King, SJ, on the office staff of the Australian Jesuit Mission in India based at Power House in Hawthorn, organised a meeting at Newman College, Parkville, on 6 October 1972, at which Brother Andrew celebrated Mass and after which people met with him personally. The other poignant meeting was with Filomena Cuni — Mother Teresa's cousin — and her family. Mother Teresa's mother, Drana Marko, was Filomena's father's sister. Filomena was married to Luca Cuni seen in a photo with Brother Andrew. Unfortunately, Luca was killed on 21 May 1980.[65]

One person who really admired Brother Andrew at this time was Moira Dynon. She had first met him in Calcutta in 1969. Whilst there she wrote to her husband: "Brother Andrew is doing

Part – III: Brother Andrew MC – Calcutta (1966-1972)   153

wonderful work — at his Home I gave undernourished children milk and New Zealand milk powder biscuits and fed a baby with a bottle of milk."[66] From then on Moira started sending milk for the children:

> Yesterday we received the shipping papers for the milk that you have sent. And it was a very pleasant surprise. It will be a very great help in our distribution for the babies and children. It is especially valuable at this time, since the supplies of milk powder from America have stopped, and we just don't know what will happen. It is wonderful how something unexpected comes along just when it is needed.
>
> Calcutta is in an awful mess at present. With all the uncertainty supplies, jobs, etc., are also uncertain. And it is the really poor people who are the first to suffer. So your gift will be of help to people who really need it.
>
> Kindly thank all those who have a part in this gift for us. With all best wishes and a prayer for you all.
>
> Yours sincerely.
> Andrew MC.[67]

Something was on Andrew's mind: Vietnam. In a letter dated 12 November 1972 to Brother Nicholas at Holy Trinity Abbey in Utah, Brother Andrew wrote:

> Your letter was a great help where you mention the need of starting somewhere outside India. I have been thinking about this a lot since coming here. The Brothers seem to have done very well in my absence of nearly 4 months. That seems to leave me free to move about more. The only question is the holding together of the community and the Spirit. But then God does not depend on me.
>
> I am thinking of Vietnam at present. Please pray about this and if you have any ideas please let me know.[68]

*1. Br Andrew (first right at the back)
with first group of Brothers in Mansatala Row 1967.*

2. Br Andrew with a group of Brothers c. 1967.

Part – III: Brother Andrew MC – Calcutta (1966-1972)

3. Br Andrew 1969 on Mansatala Row (courtesy Val Noone).

4. Br Andrew 1970 – Mansatala Row.

5. Br Andrew possibly with Bangladeshi Refugees c. 1971.

6. Br Andrew with orphan boys.

Part – III: Brother Andrew MC – Calcutta (1966-1972)

7. At Mar Thoma Church c. 1971.

8. Earliest photo of Brother Andrew and Mother Teresa.

Endnotes:

1. 19660118 LJ to John Rolland Boylan, SJ.
2. 19660209 LR to Aimée.
3. 19679518 LR Frederick Henry Travers-Ball to Fr Austin Kelly.
4. Julien Henry, SJ, (1901– 1979). Born in Belgium, he was one of the first Jesuits to support Mother Teresa's work. Ordained as a Jesuit in 1931, he arrived in India in 1938 and worked in St Teresa's parish. He was the Sisters' spiritual director from 1949 until his death.
5. Celeste van Exem, SJ, (1908 – 1993). A Belgian Jesuit priest who, shortly after his arrival in India in 1938, met Mother Teresa while she was still a Loreto nun. Van Exem became a major influence on the formation and running of the Missionaries of Charity Sisters. It was to him that Mother Teresa wrote most of her letters describing the progress of the Congregation and her spiritual struggles and doubts.
6. 19770816 Brother Andrew talk to the Brothers, 16 August 1977.
7. Dhapa, on the edge of East Kolkata was notorious for criminal activity such as the running of illegal drugs, liquor and other contraband material by the mafia and gangs.
8. Superiors at all levels — local, regional and general — are called "servants" in the Congregation of the Missionaries of Charity Brothers.
9. Kidderpoor or Khidirpur is a neighbourhood of metropolitan Kolkata bounded by Alipore to the east, Mominpur to the south, Hastings in the north and the Hooghly River in the west. It has a number of notable, especially Christian and Moslem, educational institutions.
10. Until 1969 the Feast of the Visitation was celebrated on 2 July.
11. 19770816 TB at Cambria Street.
12. Ibid.
13. Mansatala's Journal (1966 – 1972) Calcutta: Unpublished source.
14. From a talk given by Brother Andrew to the Brothers in Los Angeles in 1977: "Perhaps I should say something on the Constitutions. I wrote the Constitutions. Not all of it, much of the Constitutions are quotations. They are taken from various other sources... large tracts of the Constitutions are taken from the Decrees of the Second Vatican Council especially on the vows, profession, religious life. Some are taken from the Jesuits. Some constitutions rules — some are taken even one here from the Benedictine Rule. Some are taken from the original rules of the Sisters. Some are taken from canon law; are required for all religious congregations. But I alone, I am not boasting, I alone prepared them or compiled them or whatever it was. Some I wrote myself, some rules. There are some rules of the Constitutions that from the beginning... from the time we had a novitiate practically (1967, '68) some parts we have not been following, not been implementing." The Constitutions of the Missionaries of Charity Brothers were revised after a commission of

Part – III: Brother Andrew MC – Calcutta (1966-1972)

Brothers was formed in 1992. The new Constitutions were approved by the Fifth General Chapter in 1998.

[15] Brother Gordon, MC, "Missionaries of Charity — Journal," Los Angeles: Unpublished Source, 1978.

[16] 19661128 LS from Mother Teresa.

[17] This second letter is undated but must have been written between 28 November 1966 when the incident happened and her first letter was written and 15 January 1967 when the Brothers moved into 7 Mansatala Row.

[18] 00000001 LS from Mother Teresa (for archival purposes, since this letter does not have a date, it is referred to as 00000001 — even though it was written between 28 November 1966 and 15 January 1967)

[19] 19661200 LP Christmas 1966.

[20] For the purposes of this book the term "Mansatala" is used to refer to the generalate house of the Missionaries of Charity Brothers to avoid confusion with "Mother House" which is the generalate house of the Missionaries of Charity Sisters. The Brothers universally call their generalate house "Mansatala".

[21] 19670122 LF to Tom Stuart.

[22] Sister Agnes, MC, (1929 – 1997). Born Subashini Das in Calcutta, she was the first young girl to join Mother Teresa as an MC nun in 1949.

[23] Mansatala's Journal (1966 - 1972) Calcutta: Unpublished source.

[24] 19670331 LJ to John Rolland Boylan, SJ.

[25] René Voillaume, (1905 – 2003). French priest and the founder of the Little Brothers of Jesus and the Little Brothers of the Gospel whose spirituality is inspired by the life and writings of Charles de Foucauld.

[26] Frère Roger Schutz, (1915 – 2005). Swiss Christian leader and monastic Brother, founder in 1940 of the Taizé Community— an ecumenical monastic community in Burgundy, France. He served as its first prior until his murder in 2005;

Jean Vanier, (1928 – 2019). Catholic philosopher and theologian who in 1964 founded L'Arche — an international federation of communities spread all over the world for people with developmental disabilities and their assistants. From Jean's interview about Brother Andrew: "I was deeply touched by his person. I sensed that he had one way of looking at the Brothers, a different way from Mother Teresa. He wanted to live with people; and I say live with people and not just do things for people. The Sisters do things for people and then they live separately. I have the impression that he was a deeply holy man., and I dare say, a saint. I really believe that. He was very different from Mother Teresa who had succeeded. His holiness is in his poverty, and I always felt that there was a poverty, a fragility with him. But I think that's why I loved him so much. I felt close to him, and we corresponded a little when he was back in Australia. I felt a deep friendship with him and when I heard that he had to leave, misunderstanding or whatever it is, it happened and I can see how it could be difficult for the new superior to have somebody like

Andrew, who was the founder with his fragility. I can understand that, but I can understand the immense pain in Andrew." (20180409 IF Jean Vanier.)

27 20190226 Email Michael Costigan.
28 20190508 IB Abraham Ellickal, MC.
29 20191113 IO Sebastian Vazhakala, MCC.
30 Ibid.
31 20180516 IB Anima Prasad, MC.
32 20180127 IB PT Thomas, MC.
33 Come-and-See is the first part of the MC formation, after which the come-and-see enters novitiate. After two years, the novice professes the four vows — poverty, chastity, obedience, and whole-hearted and free service to the poorest of the poor — for one year. As a junior, the young Brother renews his vows for another five years, when he enters an intense preparation time known as tertianship before making his final life profession.
34 19680223 LJ from Pedro Arrupe, SJ.
35 19671200 LP Christmas 1967.
36 At the time of writing, the truck is still preserved at Shanti Dan, Tangra (Kolkata).
37 20180516 IB Anima Prasad, MC.
38 19921200 LP Christmas.
39 19680305 LJ to E. B. O'Connor, SJ.
40 For this reason, Brother Andrew again wrote his will, "bequeath[ing] and appoint[ing] all my moveable and immoveable property whatsoever and wheresoever which I actually possess or may subsequently possess unto the General Servant of the Missionary Brothers of Charity." In 2016, when Mother Teresa's will was submitted for probate, it was suggested that the same should be done for Brother Andrew. It then became known that in 2000 he had written a new will, with his nephew Julian Millership as sole executor and bequeathing his property to the Missionaries of Charity Sisters in Australia and Aid to the Church in Need in Sydney, Australia.
41 Brother Andrew's vow formula reads: "Heavenly Father, Creator and Lord, I, Brother Andrew, vow and promise to you in this Eucharistic Sacrifice through, with and in Jesus Christ, Your Son, in the unity of the Holy Spirit, and with the help of Mary Mother of the Poor, poverty, chastity, obedience and also to devote myself to work among the poor, according to the Constitutions of the Congregation of the Missionary Brothers of Charity for life. In making this whole offering of my life back to You, its source, I am keenly aware of my own utter helplessness to live it generously and perseveringly. So with great confidence in the promises of Your Son, Jesus Christ, I rely fully on the support of Your boundless love and mercy. Made at Calcutta on the Feast of Pentecost, this 2nd day of June, 1968. Andrew, MC, Signed by Rev. Eric Barber Vicar General and witnessed by Br Benedict, MC, and Damien, MC."

Part – III: Brother Andrew MC – Calcutta (1966-1972)   161

42   19680514 LJ to Austin Kelly, SJ.
43   Brother Nicholas Prinster, OCSO, was too old and sickly to be interviewed. He died peacefully on Monday, 18 June 2018. (From an email to the author by Dom Casimir Bernas, OCSO dated 25 June 2018).
44   Brother Gordon, Missionaries of Charity — Journal, Los Angeles: Unpublished Source, 1978.
45   Malcolm Muggeridge, (1903 – 1990). As a young British lad he was attracted to Communism but after living in the Soviet Union became staunchly anti-Communist. He converted to Christianity in the 1960s.
46   19690413 IF by Malcolm Muggeridge.
47   Ibid.
48   19690509 LO to Cardinal Knox.
49   19691200 LP Christmas 1969.
50   19701200 LP Christmas 1970.
51   After India's independence from British rule in 1947, two nations were formed: India and Pakistan which was made up of West and East Pakistan, with more than 2,000 kilometres separating the two and with Karachi in the western part as its capital. The idea behind Partition was that Muslims and Hindus could not live peacefully together. Pakistan was thus the first modern-state founded on religion since although India had a Hindu majority its peoples were of a variety of faiths including Islam, Sikhism, and Christianity. When, therefore, East Bengal (prior to Partition part of India) became East Pakistan, many considered the decision a grave mistake, especially when East Pakistan tried to impose Urdu as the official language when the vast majority spoke Bangla. An opposition movement arose and violence spread throughout the county. On 26 March 1971 the first announcement by radio of the declaration of independence of East Pakistan, thenceforward to be called Bangladesh was made. Further tensions arose, political events gathered momentum, and clashes were frequent between the Pakistan Army and the insurgents, giving rise to war. The Bangladeshi minorities, including the Bengali intelligentsia, were considered the main instigators of nationalism and were the Pakistani army's prime targets — particularly Hindu males who were killed and Hindu women who were raped. (https://www.newworldencyclopedia.org/entry/Bangladesh_ War of Independence Web. May 15, 2020.
52   19710811 LP East Pakistan Refugees.
53   Alcoholics Anonymous (AA): a fellowship of men and women who help each other with their shared problem of alcoholism. Other fellowships emerged from AA, one of which is Neurotics Anonymous.
54   Garry McLoughlin, (1942). An Australian diocesan priest in the Archdiocese of Melbourne at the time of his stay in Calcutta. In 1971, he took a year's leave from the diocese and spent several months in Asia, including three months in India. He left the priesthood in 1973.

55 20191113 IB Sebastian Vazhakala, MCC.
56 Garry McLoughlin, "Calcutta Diary," Melbourne: Unpublished Source 1971.
57 20190711 IF Annie Joseph. Founder and director of Ankur Kala, an NGO helping women at risk to generate their own income through artisan works.
58 20200630 IB Michael Batley.
59 Night Points is a practice in some religious congregations whereby a member of the community imparts spiritual and practical points relating to the next day's Gospel readings for the Mass.
60 The duty of the councillors is to help the servants in matters of government and administration and give a vote of consent or advice when necessary. The First Councillor is the Assistant General, also called the Vicar, who assists the General Servant with the entire governance of the Congregation.
61 Brother Gordon, MC, "Missionaries of Charity — Journal," Los Angeles: Unpublished Source, 1978.
62 20200630 IB Michael Batley. Asked by the author which Brothers Andrew had considered wanted to run things on their own, Michael Batley said Andrew did not specify. This appeared contradictory in light of Andrew's intention that Brothers should take the leadership of the Congregation. However, knowing that a couple of years earlier there had been tensions between the ordained and non-ordained Brothers, Andrew may well have had in mind the possibility of ordained Brothers wanting to assume the authority of the Congregation.
63 20180305 IR Anne and Julian Millership, Jim Smith. James (Jim) Smith is married to Gabrielle. They have five children: Thomas Harry, Matthew, Kate, Andrew and Edward. James' brother Gregory is unmarried.
64 20180305 IR Anne and Julian Millership, Jim Smith. Julian, Anne and David are the children of Aimée Millership née Travers-Ball, the youngest of the three sisters.
65 Luca Cuni, (1911 -1980). Albanian community leader. During his secondary schooling he improved his knowledge of Albania's history, literature and language. He later studied classical Greek, graduated from the faculty of philosophy in Skopje, Yugoslavia, and is reputed to have become a professor at that institution. 1 July 1936 he married Filomena Marko (d.1979) in Skopje. With his wife, son and daughter, Cuni sought refuge in Austria (1944 - 45) and Italy (1945 - 49) where they lived in refugee camps before sailing for Australia and arriving in Melbourne on 27 March 1950. A talented linguist who spoke eight languages, he helped newly-arrived immigrants; as an interpreter, he worked for the police, in the law courts and in prisons; as a devout Catholic, he preached and conducted funeral services. Shortly before his death, he broadcast on the topic of law and order, and spoke of the pointlessness of vengeance and the virtue of forgiving one's enemies. 21 May 1980, while working as an interpreter at the Supreme Court, Melbourne, Luca Cuni, with four others, was shot by a man who had threatened to kill anyone associated with a particular hearing. Survived by his daughter and son, he died next day

Part – III: Brother Andrew MC – Calcutta (1966-1972)

in Royal Melbourne Hospital and was buried in Footscray cemetery. http://adb.anu.edu.au/biography/cuni-Luca-9877 Web. 18 May 2020.

[66] From unpublished memoirs of Moira Dynon, courtesy of her daughter Jacinta Efthim.

[67] 19701125 LF to Moira Dynon.

[68] Brother Gordon, MC, "Missionaries of Charity — Journal," Los Angeles: Unpublished Source, 1978.

INTERLUDE – I

THE VIETNAM-CAMBODIA PERIOD
(1973 – 1975)

This year has been heart-breaking.
We lost five houses in Vietnam, and Cambodia.
The buildings don't matter. But to be separated so finally from all the people that one came to know and love is so unbelievably painful
I shall never be the same again after this,
and I know and hope that I shall have an ache in my heart for them till the day I die.

– BROTHER ANDREW

An entry in the journal compiled by Brother Gordon in the late 1970s reads like this: "Late Nov., 1972, in Australia — Brother Andrew decides to stop in South Vietnam to see the situation there on the way back to India and he hurriedly changes his return ticket to include a short stay there." In fact, on 24 November he left Perth, arrived in Singapore, and the next day was at Tan Sun Nhut airport in Saigon, South Vietnam. There he stayed with the Jesuits, went about the streets of the city to get a feel for the needs of the people, and on 26 November 1972 was cordially received by Archbishop Paul Nguyen Van Binh. Even though nothing was fixed at that point, Brother Andrew left the meeting with the impression that there would be no difficulty from the Archbishop's side. Next he met Father Huynh Van Nghi, the Director of Caritas, Saigon, and on 29 November 1972, he was back in Calcutta.

What triggered Andrew to decide to stop in Vietnam? Former MC Brother, Jeremy Hollinger, reflected:

> I think that when Andrew went to Saigon he was questioning if there was really a place for him in MC in its most traditional form. I suspect he went there because he could not live the daily life as it had been formalized and

established in India. He did need the excitement of crisis, and needed to be starting new ventures and taking risks. In short, Andrew's initial going to Vietnam reflected his own doubts and contradictions about MC, being General Servant, and perhaps even what he wanted for his life going forward. He would never share this with the Brothers in India, as he did realize how this would shake them. He needed to live on the edge.[1]

Andrew himself alluded to this incongruity in his last Night Points to the Brothers in 1999:

> There has to be development and I recognize again in myself, I would say, I am a person for beginnings. When things become more developed I don't fit in so well. Even as a Jesuit I didn't work very long with them before I left. Most of the years were formation years but there were two or three works that I did as a Jesuit in Hazaribagh, which was very much — back then in the '50s and '60s — was very undeveloped, a very new area and everything was being sort of started from nothing.
>
> Two or three things that I was involved in there and also in Poona in the writing sphere, I had a part in the beginning and I could handle that. I fitted in well where things were a bit rough and ready and not too highly organised and where improvisation and risk taking were very much part of it — and that was the Brothers in the beginning. Very small, a lot of uncertainties, not much depth in terms of training and development and expertise, and all our affairs were sort of a bit like that. I must say that's the sort of situation in which I feel at home.
>
> When things become bigger and larger and more settled, and need more an administrative care and management and organization, there I'm afraid the Lord hasn't, I don't think, endowed me too much. So I think again God works everything in a wonderful way. For those beginning years I think the qualities and the attitudes I had might have played

Interlude – I: The Vietnam – Cambodia Period (1973-1975)

a part. They would not have played a part as the times and changing conditions called for, for more development. Just the growth and the increase in numbers calls for something different and I don't think I had that. In those years I always had one... from very early on I had an understanding of my role as General Servant, Co-founder or whatever. I didn't share it with anybody. You must remember in all those years there was a great difference... in the age and the development of the Brothers and myself. I was older, much older. I was a priest. I had a formation. The Brothers were young, at the beginning of their formation and inexperienced. And so there was the Jesuit on the one hand I suppose and the young Brothers on the other. So there was a big difference and there were a lot of things I was not really able to share, personal things, with anyone.

But I realized as time went on that I was consciously working towards the day when the young Brothers would come up and take over and I would move out. A sort of a John the Baptist role. John the Baptist, his role was to announce the coming of the Lord and to prepare for it and to do what he had to do and then when the Lord came John the Baptist backed out and moved on. He was beheaded in that whole manoeuvre. But that was an understanding I had from the very beginning, even when we went to start the Society in the first start outside India in Vietnam.

As I mentioned the other day, one of the reasons for that start was to accommodate the non-Indian vocations. There were applications coming from people outside India and they could not enter India because of the visa restrictions. And so that was the purpose in making that stand. And that I can tell you was a very lonely decision. Nobody really understood. The Brothers were upset and disturbed — which was in 1972, 73. The Brothers were upset and disturbed that I was going to be off the scene. Mother Teresa did not approve of that. In one way she saw — but

> she thought the strongest pull, the strongest claim was that I should be with the Brothers. This is 1972 so it's not a very old congregation. There's no one who's been there for a long time.
>
> So I went to Vietnam. I'd come back every two or three months and stay for a little while and then go and always there was this pressure. You should be back in India where the majority... and there was a logic to that. As I say Mother was pretty pressing in that.[2]

As with most of the decisions that Andrew made in his life, there was that "moment of destiny". He would contemplate something for some time until a moment occurred when he realised it was time to act, to move or change, causing him to make what appeared to be a rushed decision. It was the Australian Archbishop Hilton Deakin who coined this term:

> I suspect that our lives have a particular trajectory that, if we are reflective, we discern slowly and often obliquely, and then only in retrospect. We all have what I would call "moments of destiny" in our lives. In these brief times we sense that our life's journey, often experienced as chaotic, has a direction. When we look back we can, if we are lucky, discern how life's disparate elements form part of a meaningful whole. The experience is momentary, for soon daily life closes in on us again, and we find ourselves back on the familiar track, with only a memory to encourage and guide us. However, we store such memories and they help us see new significance in what we do, and thus regenerate hope within us.[3]

Without going into elaborate detail about a very complicated situation, it is worth delving a little into what was happening during this period and earlier in Vietnam and also trying to understand the relationship between Vietnam and Australia.

THE WAR IN VIETNAM

As decolonization took place in Asia, Laos and Cambodia obtained their complete independence. Vietnam, however, was still occupied by the French who had chosen to stay. As a result, the Viet Minh — a national independence coalition formed by Ho Chi Minh in the northern part of Vietnam — started an insurgency against the French. By the beginning of 1950, Vietnam was embroiled in the Cold War, with China and the USSR recognizing Minh's Democratic Republic of Vietnam based in Hanoi as the legitimate government of Vietnam. A month later, in February 1950, the United States and Great Britain acknowledged the French-backed State of Vietnam in Saigon. The first Indo-China War began and by 7 May 1954 the French were trounced by Ho Chi Minh and his army. This defeat led to the Geneva Conference, where amongst other issues decided, Vietnam's division was set at the 17th parallel until 1956 when democratic elections would take place with international supervision. All agreed except the United States and South Vietnam. Some provisions were made: a three-mile demilitarized zone, French Union Forces to regroup in the South and the Viet Minh in the North, and free movement of the population for 300 days. Canada, Poland, and India would monitor the ceasefire. On 9 October 1954, the French flag was lowered at Hanoi Citadel.

After the end of hostilities some 900,000 people heading southward were processed through official refugee stations. (Journalists reported as many as two million people fleeing from Viet Minh soldiers who frequently beat and sometimes killed them.) These were mainly Catholics, intellectuals, business people, landowners, anti-Communists, and members of the middle-class. About 52,000 Viet Minh and their families fled from the South to the North.

The then Prime Minister Ngo Dinh Diem — a Roman Catholic — was backed by the United States. Since neither the United States nor South Vietnam had signed the Geneva Accords, Diem refused to hold elections in 1956. For its part, North Vietnam had also violated the agreement by not withdrawing all troops from the South and hindering the movement of those North Vietnamese who chose to seek refuge in South Vietnam.

On 1 November 1955 the Vietnam War started and went on until 29 March 1973, when the United States withdrew from Vietnam. The Viet Cong continued their advance from the North with the fighting lasting until 30 April 1975. With the North Vietnamese victory the Communists took over and North and South Vietnam were reunified into the Socialist Republic of Vietnam. The United States and Australia had many mutual interests but one in particular was the mutual fear of the spread of Communism.

AUSTRALIA and VIETNAM RELATIONS

Between 2 and 9 September 1957, Prime Minister Ngo Dinh Diem visited Australia. At that time Sir Robert Menzies was the country's leader. Everywhere Diem was honoured as a man of courage, faith and vision. It should be noted that Diem was a member of Vietnam's minority Catholic Church and his brother, Pierre Martin Ngo Dinh Thuc was an archbishop. Both the Australian Catholic leadership and the media were more than happy with his presence.[4]

Two main figures emerged during this visit: B. A. Santamaria — unofficial leader of the Democratic Labour Party and a staunch anti-Communist, who particularly praised Diem's achievements — and Fr Harold Lalor, a leading confidant of Santamaria and a colleague of Archbishop Thuc since their seminary studies in Rome. Diem was also accompanied by his priest-nephew Francis Xavier Nguyen Van Thuan.[5] B. A. Santamaria and Van Thuan became very good friends and from then on Vietnam became Santamaria's main focus. How and where could a non-Communist leadership emerge to counter the effect of the Communist infiltration Australia so feared? As an international organisation already present in Vietnam, the Jesuits provided the answer. Thus, after Diem's visit, Asian Catholic students were brought to Australia with the intention of

Interlude – I: The Vietnam – Cambodia Period (1973-1975)

forming Catholic leaders. Was the Communist threat a real one? Did Santamaria and Lalor miss the whole point? It is not the intention here to evaluate the success or failure of such an endeavour. What is relevant is the timing, the geographical setting, the organisations and the people involved, especially Brother Andrew, a former Australian Jesuit (still with strong ties to the Society). Meeting Santamaria and Lalor during their "educational programme against Communism" would surely have had a significant impact on him.

It is no surprise, therefore, that after his four-month stay in Australia, Brother Andrew decided to stop over in Vietnam and get a feel for the situation. But an interesting entry occurs in the previously-mentioned journal edited by Brother Gordon. Dated October 1972, it says: "Brother Andrew reads an article by Victor Zorza in *The Australian* newspaper in which the author states that even if a cease-fire occurs in Vietnam there will still be poverty in the country and he relates how he remembers packs of children roaming about in Europe after World War II."[6] Without disregarding the political and sociological reasons for Andrew going to Vietnam, what always moved him to undertake a new venture in life were the poor; their hardship, their lifestyle and their suffering.

When, on 29 November, he returned to Calcutta, Andrew found that the Brothers had managed well and so he refrained from re-involving himself in many of his previous activities. During his annual retreat in the house in Nurpur, it became obvious to him that if he had to start new communities outside India on his own, they must be small oases of love. Nothing big. As a result of this insight, he drafted some notes entitled "For a House Outside India." According to Andrew, such communities should from the beginning be manned by local people and not depend on foreign personnel. They would thus be communities in harmony with the culture of the people around them, even in their poverty. Poverty and simplicity should be real — both based on Gospel values. Above all "the foreigners must have great respect for the local people & especially for the local young men who join the community."[7] It is very telling that Andrew just says "the foreigners" and not "the foreign Brothers". Was he already intending to have an open community with Brothers, volunteers and the poor living together?

On 14 February of that same year, Brother Andrew held a council meeting to explain what he was doing and the reasons for it. He announced that he intended to start in Saigon, but that if that failed, there were other possibilities such as Laos, Hanoi (because there was a slight possibility of being accepted as a priest), and lastly Manila (because Bishop Jaime Lachica Sin of Iloilo in the Philippines had requested that the Brothers come to serve the poor there). Before leaving he wrote a general letter to the Brothers:

> You have noticed that I have been thinking a lot since I returned from Australia. When I went away I was anxious to see how the Society continued in my absence. I went to Vietnam on my return to see if there was work there. When I returned to Calcutta I saw that you had all done well.
>
> I decided then that I would go to Vietnam, but there have been many doubts whether I am doing the right thing. At any rate, I now have a return ticket to Saigon, leaving Calcutta on 28th February.
>
> I don't know what God wants exactly. There are many uncertainties. So far I have a Visa as far as Bangkok. I don't know if I shall be accepted in Vietnam by the government or the Church.
>
> In my retreat at Nurpur, it seemed clear that I am to go. I shall try to go to Saigon. But I leave it to God to choose the place: Vietnam, Laos, Cambodia, Manila . . . or nowhere.
>
> I shall try to start a little community of the abandoned, the misfits, the hopeless ones wherever it may be. It may or may not be exactly the same as the MC Brothers, but it will be in the same line and in the same spirit. It will be determined by whom God calls and sends.

Interlude – I: The Vietnam – Cambodia Period (1973-1975)

But what about you Brothers in India? I have a Return Visa for three months. I may come back in May for a visit. But the point is that now you have to continue yourselves as the Society. You are the Society. And the Spirit of God is with you.

We have so many good trustworthy Brothers. The Society has grown in an extraordinary way in just 10 years. It is not our work, certainly not my work. It is God's. He has started. It is only your unfaithfulness or lack of confidence in Him that can stop the Spirit from continuing his work of love for the poor and suffering through you.

My only advice to you is that:

1. You look to God in prayer for His guidance and strength,
2. You keep a very simple way of living and working. Beware of adding things in your houses for your own comfort. And don't try to build up efficient dispensaries, schools, hospitals, etc.
3. You look always for the poorest and most needy people.[8]

THE INTERLUDE BEGINS

Brother Andrew left Calcutta on 28 February 1973 fully trusting the Brothers, but at the same time wondering whether he was doing the right thing. Was it right to leave them to manage on their own even though they could be trusted? Was it right to attempt to start work in Vietnam in such a difficult situation? But then Andrew was not a faint-hearted man and never feared risk or failure. Difficulties were never a hindrance to doing the work God had entrusted to him because he always maintained hope in God who had sent him and who would not abandon him and his Brothers. After a few days in Bangkok where he applied for and was granted a one-month visa for South Vietnam, on 3 March 1973 Andrew landed in Saigon and went to stay with the Jesuit community. In a letter to Brother Nicholas in Utah, he wrote that he hoped to "start a small and very simple community of needy ones of any description. I would try to rent a little place among the people, and would hope that it would be a little community of love, of hope, peace, of reconciliation. It would be like Nazareth.... The place would not set out to 'do' anything special, like dispensary, rehabilitation, etc., but just 'be' a little home and sign of love & hope."[9]

A couple of weeks later, on 17 March 1973, Brother Andrew met Nguyen Thi Kim, a Vietnamese widow with three children, who quickly understood the essential idea of what he was trying to do and was eager to help. The search thus began for a house to rent. Geoffrey Solomon quotes a letter in which Andrew described how he met his new helper:

> I've rented a couple of rooms and in fact have the use of the whole house [on 102/33 Cong Quynh] where a family lives who don't mind how many people stay in the house.... The story of how I got here is a bit like a novel. I was looking for a helper who'd speak Vietnamese and be able to do things I couldn't. After a number of blind alleys I met a girl who'd been working in a "Girlie Bar" with all that means. Six years ago her husband was killed on his motorcycle by an Australian who was drunk and was himself killed in the crash. She had three small children and got no compensation. So she had to go to work in a bar, where there was good money.... She jumped at the offer I made her, seems to understand what the idea is and is capable.[10]

Nguyen Thi Kim or Ba Kim (Ba is the Vietnamese title for a married woman) helped him to manage the house once people in need started moving in and continued to assist Brother Andrew throughout his stay in Vietnam. Without her, the Brothers' work in Saigon might never have been possible. With a place to stay and Andrew's official residence papers signed by Archbishop Binh, he and Kim were ready to start work. What is amazing is that it took them no time to start accepting people (perhaps people already known to Kim) at Cong Quynh. On 23 March 1973, when writing to Val Noone, Mary

Interlude – I: The Vietnam – Cambodia Period (1973-1975)

Doyle, Garry McLoughlin and members of a group who ran a house of hospitality for homeless people in Fitzroy, Andrew outlined the Saigon project.[11] He also drew comparisons and contrasts with the Fitzroy group whom he had visited in 1972, in particular regarding hospitality but also expressing disagreement with what some of them wrote about Vietnam in *Retrieval*, a current affairs magazine:

> I've been thinking of you all quite often since I came here early this month because you think a lot about this country. I've come here to see if I can be of any use. I don't think it's possible at least for now — to get the Brothers' thing going.
>
> What it looks like being is the House of Hospitality approach. I've rented an apartment and am seeing how it develops. There doesn't seem to be the same massive poverty as in India. But there are crying needs. And it seems a much easier place to work than India in many ways.
>
> The place I am in would make your hair stand on end (well probably not Gore Street hair). To make it brief they've all been in the girl business — which incidentally is one of the biggest businesses in Asia too — India included. The picture you had in Retrieval recently could have been taken many times around the corner in Kidderpore.
>
> Well, I seem to be headed in this direction, at the moment. Plenty of these girls around here. Things are bad now. The Yanks have gone — the girlie bars are mostly closed. And they are used to a lot of money — and have families (old parents, brothers & sisters & their own children) to support. I don't see the way yet. Maybe one need is the support & education (in a broad sense) of their kids. They have very moving stories.
>
> At the same time, there is the old person who has no one — the widow with children — the maimed soldiers & civilians. So at present we are open to anyone. We have a widow & her son and three neglected kids here at the moment. And there's a girl who has had enough of the old game, who is

sort of General Everything. She is really taking to the idea and giving the thing a direction.

So there it is. Of course, the future is terribly uncertain (the last 7 years in Cal. [Calcutta]) were a good novitiate for this. It's so complicated here — especially when you look at it all from the ground level of the ordinary people — say the girls. If the North come, they'd be for it, to say nothing of myself among them! Apart from them it's complicated. I feel that you've got it down in Retrieval too much in terms of black and white. Incidentally, keep sending Retrieval to India — not here. I'll catch up when I get there.

All for now. It would be good to have yarn. I think I'd be more for cleaning up the shit for people who can't make it to the jakes [Australian slang for toilets] — than for the political bit, which so often seems to mean just a reshuffle of bastards who want the power — or go "gag-ga" when they get it. Whatever it is, there's plenty of need for work with the little ones who've been trampled on, especially when you don't know what the score is in the political arena.

I wonder if you met Leon [Allen].* He is a great guy — and a tremendous support.

All for now.
Love to everybody.[12]

In April he wrote a letter to his sister, Mary Ennis:

I was so happy when I received your letter that on the way home I shouted myself to a beer in a little bar and read it.... We have twelve children and two widows staying here. They are very kind and it is wonderful how they all accept me. But their stories would be best-sellers in some of the magazines that nice people shouldn't read!... I have been terribly fortunate in the girl who is assistant-cum-interpreter. She has really made it possible for things to get going...

Two nights ago we had a bit of excitement. Quite late there was a sudden explosion in the house at the back of us —

Interlude – I: The Vietnam – Cambodia Period (1973-1975) 179

> five or six yards away. A soldier home on leave found his wife had left him for someone else. She was in her family's home next to us. He threw a grenade into the house killing himself and one other person and seriously wounding three others... Our children were upstairs asleep and at the sound of the explosion came running down the stairs to where we were. The smallest, half asleep, fell on the stairs and had a terrible gash over his eye so we had to take him to hospital for stitching. It was already after curfew and I was wondering just when we were going to get a bullet in the back of the neck. Especially as we went on a motorcycle, with the girl holding the little boy on the back, and blood everywhere. So there is the element of excitement in the game. And now the little boy is all right.[13]

On 21 May, as promised before he left for Vietnam, Andrew returned to Calcutta. His stay coincided with Brother Bernard and Brother Sebastian's final profession and the first profession of new Brothers in Mansatala. There he announced, "Now we have started a community of love in Saigon."[14] When, after three weeks, he went back to Saigon, Br Michael Batley, an Englishman who had been in Mansatala, accompanied him. While in Calcutta, Andrew had also met Don Cowan — an Anglican priest attached to an Anglican Franciscan community from Australia — who was spending some time with the Brothers in Mansatala. Andrew encouraged Father Cowan to follow him to Vietnam and Cowan did so on 19 June. He was thus the fourth member of the community at Cong Quynh, living with the Brothers in Saigon between June 1973 and June

---

* The question about Leon Allen is probably a slip of memory on Andrew's part. Leon had been among those helping with the open house for homeless people in Fitzroy led by Mary Doyle and Brian Noone. In October 1969 Val Noone shared with Leon the tape recording of his 29 January1969 interview with Andrew (Appendix II), then in January 1970 Mary Doyle and Leon Allen both Andrew in Calcutta. Leon then joined the Brothers in Calcutta and later Saigon and Cambodia.

of the following year. Cowan recalled that during that year, Brother Andrew's headquarters were always Cong Quynh, though for a time he lived in the other two Saigon houses and in Phnom Penh, all of which were opened later that same year:

> In my year in Saigon ... we occasionally received visitors at Cong Quynh, eg., Fr Nghi (supportive Parish Priest), assorted government officials wondering who we were and what we were doing. They seemed to approve, but most seemed puzzled, having never before seen any establishments such as ours. Few Westerners ventured into our slum districts. Saigon was a demanding place in which to live.
>
> The American, Australian and New Zealander troops had left by the time of our arrival, yet the war continued around the city, not within. One could be shot if seen in the streets after the midnight curfew. An infra-red guard plane droned in a circle all night every night over the city, watching for any mass movement on the ground.
>
> The Viet Cong had infiltrated anyway and communicated to us via local people the fact that our work was acceptable for the time being but would be unnecessary once they took charge. Then we would have had to leave.
>
> [Brother Andrew used to celebrate] daily Mass there at the dining room table around which we all sat in our community room. There was no space for a chapel. It was our "everything room." Andrew, Michael and I slept on the floor ...
>
> Brother Leon usually slept in the adjacent room, a very cramped store room. If there was a visitor one of us would sleep under the table, the chairs piled on top of it for the night. The house became very crowded with mothers and children and children without parents at all.
>
> Andrew shared in life exactly as we all did. He never "pulled rank" as General Servant. I experienced him as precisely that: our "general servant". I cannot recall his ever having

Interlude – I: The Vietnam – Cambodia Period (1973-1975)

an argument with any of us, or anyone else; he never raised his voice. He could be very funny.[15]

Interestingly, it seems that Andrew was open to accepting into this first community in Saigon anybody prepared to share the poverty and simple life of the local poor and who had a desire to live in a praying community.

Before he returned to Saigon, Brother Andrew wrote to his friend Sr Margaret Ryan — a nurse/midwife — whom he had met on his trip to Australia some months earlier. Andrew had invited her to go to Vietnam with him, but at that time she had declined the offer. She was a newly professed nun and being younger than Andrew, most probably respected and admired him:

> Which brings me to a complaint about your letters: the admiration and praise of Br Andrew makes me squirm. If only you knew the reality of what lies underneath that smooth surface. You are not the only one. And it is a terrible burden to have the esteem of such good and loving people, when you know what you really are. I do nothing except run around, get other people to do the dirty work, with the help of other people's money.... It is unknown Brothers and donors who are the real heroes. I have been here three weeks and return to Vietnam on Thursday.
>
> The Brothers do well, and it has been good to be with them, though it has been hard to be away from Saigon at this point when they are struggling. I don't know where it will all end there. That country has suffered so much, and it seems that there is still much to be gone through there. It doesn't seem to matter much what we do, except perhaps to try to make the opportunity for a little love and happiness to flower. Knowing all the time that any flower will probably not last long, but will be trampled in the mud and blood. It is painful to think of when you come to love the people and children who are with you. I don't think I have ever felt that tragedy of our human situation so much. I still don't understand what is happening there, nor what I am doing there.

But I have experienced a richness of life there that is almost too much to bear, and I feel somehow crushed and shattered. Maybe Br Andrew is dying there, and someone new is being born. But that is for God to sort out. I just don't see anything further than Thursday when a plane will land me there. I find myself going one day at a time now, with the only certainty that God is the God of love, of compassion, of happiness and of life. I pray that I may never lose this precious grace. For with this, one can endure the anguish that is caused by loving relationships with other wonderful people. It is all just a bit too much.[16]

To Brother Nicholas, on 21 June 1973, Andrew wrote,

We must try to build [the Saigon community] up with Vietnamese rather than foreigners. Which leaves us again with the problem of the youngsters from the West. It really looks as if the only thing is for communities to be started in places like the US, Australia, England. For it seems to be improper to overload things in Asia or elsewhere with outsiders, when it is so vital that things grow in local soil and in their own way. Our task may be to attempt a start but to move on as soon as possible. Otherwise we can prevent things from growing as they should.[17]

With Andrew at the helm, the small Saigon community moved quite fast. In fact, in June of 1973, Father Huynh Van Nghi (the director of Caritas) talked to Brother Andrew about the possibility of running their two-storey house in Phu Lam — a section of the capital on the outskirts of the city — as a night shelter for travellers.[18] Andrew agreed and the Brothers took over the running of the Phu Lam house on 8 August 1973. At the same time the purchase of the entire building at 102/33 Cong Quynh was concluded. Now, thanks to the generosity of an Australian benefactor, the Brothers owned the whole house. In a letter to his sister, Mary Ennis, Andrew wrote:

The work goes on well and is getting a bit known. We've had two young mothers come in with 15-day-old babies. Both had been left behind by the fathers. One left this morning to go back to her mother in the country. At first she had wanted to give the baby to us. She couldn't stand the sight of it, as it reminded her of the father. We tried to talk her into keeping him and finally she realised she had come to love him, started feeding him and could not let him go. So that was all beautiful — though we are all a bit sad the baby's gone. He was lovely. But the second mother is here and may stay on and work, as we need someone else now. We have over 25 children. It is sad that her baby was born with club feet but we'll see if something can be done… There is a lovely atmosphere in the house. It is a very happy place and that is wonderful. There are problems of course but it would be funny if there weren't.[19]

Less than a month after the acquisition of Cong Quynh, Brother Andrew was given the opportunity to buy a small plot of land about twelve miles from Saigon. He saw it as a possible farm-type home for destitute families with no place to stay in the capital. Obstacles soon arose, however and nothing really ever came of the idea.

By 24 July 1973, with more than fifty people living in the Cong Quynh house, and with things most probably getting a bit out of hand, Brother Andrew wrote a paper called "Aim at 102/33." Divided into two parts, with the first defining the situation of the people being given shelter in the house, and the second defining who the Brothers were and what their mission was, it made one thing clear: that the "community (Brothers, adults, children) should be a *gathering*. And should be the salt of the earth, the light of the world, the yeast in the dough."[20] This was not a task reserved just for the Brothers but for all — Vietnamese or foreigners, Catholics or Buddhists. Andrew reminded the Brothers that at the same time, "we Brothers may be more aware of this task through our background. And this should help us to give direction to the life of the community as a whole. But we should aim at sharing this awareness — without of course any narrow evangelism."[21] He ended by affirming that, "It will finally be that what this house is, is more important than what it *does*."[22]

With the opening of the Phu Lam house, one of the women who had been staying in the Cong Quynh house, My Le, and her three children moved in to manage the place. Brother Andrew started spending his nights there until he left for the United States.

The trip to North America was organised by Eileen Egan. She had inquired of Brother Nicholas, OCSO, whether Brother Andrew would be willing to address the National Catholic Laity Convention in the United Sates in October. Brother Andrew agreed and left for the United States on 1 October. Before doing so, he wrote a circular to his family and friends. Dated August 1973, it was probably his first public letter since his arrival in Saigon. He admitted to having doubts about whether it was the right decision to leave the Brothers on their own in India and whether it was right to attempt to work in Vietnam.[23] But, he maintained, "One thing is sure, coming here and the things that have happened have been extraordinarily rich experiences for myself. Coming into a new culture, without the language, at an uncertain time and alone all force one into the depths of one's own weakness and emptiness, where the awareness of one's basic need of God's help is deeply felt."[24] Having spent a few months in Saigon, he confessed, "The drama and tragedy in so many lives is just overwhelming."[25] But this was not a deterrent for Andrew. He ended this letter with a beautiful statement: "The people win your heart immediately."[26]

When Brother Andrew arrived in Los Angeles on 1 October 1973, he was met by Mr and Mrs Lloyd Tevis (who had corresponded with him since his time as a Jesuit seminarian), and Fr Don Kribs, Chairman of the Co-Workers of Mother Teresa on the West Coast.[27] Mother Teresa was also invited and she stayed at the Maryvale Convent of the Daughters of Charity. Sr Estela Morales, who managed to take a photo of Mother and Brother Andrew together, remembered mostly her excitement and awe at meeting Mother Teresa for the first time: "Brother Andrew came across as a quiet and humble person, definitely

Interlude – I: The Vietnam – Cambodia Period (1973-1975) 185

overshadowed by Mother's presence!"[28] On 3 October 1973 both Andrew and Mother spoke at the annual luncheon of the Ladies of Charity at the Beverly Hilton in Beverly Hills, California. Mother Teresa was there to receive the Louise de Marillac award. The following is a transcript of Brother Andrew's address:

> Dear friends in God's love, on Monday morning I set out from the new beginning of the Missionaries of Charity in Saigon, a small house in a very overcrowded part of the city, and as I left, the people in that house, some widows, their children, some old people, some girls left with their new babies, I received a loving farewell from them. That was Monday and now, on Wednesday, I find myself here, having been given a loving welcome at the airport by Father Kribs, Mr and Mrs Tevis, and now by you here.
>
> And somehow there is a meaning in that bridge between the poor people and yourselves here, who, in many ways, have been so favoured — all of us from more affluent parts of the world. But somehow God makes a bridge and we are all working with the hope that more love and more peace will come among people. And this gathering here today, this beautiful gathering, is so full of meaning in what God is doing in His world of people.
>
> We remember this morning those people who have brought us together like this, that give us this rich opportunity of meeting each other in the atmosphere and love that you can feel here today. It is the poor people who give us so much for they are the ones who have brought us together, and we remember them. We are not helping them only; they help us so much. They are people, great people, and they teach us so much.
>
> I would like just to tell you the story of one of the people in our house in Saigon, a young woman named My Le. She is 34 years of age. When she was 19 her husband was killed, her Vietnamese husband was killed in the war. Circumstances forced her into a terrible situation and

today she has 3 children. The first a little girl, Trung — 6 years old whose father is an American, the second a boy — Phuong is 4 years old, his father an Australian, the third child, a little girl — Dung, 3 years old whose father is a Japanese. She came to us a few months ago really at the end of her tether. She had not heard from any of the fathers of her children for more than 2 years. She had gone around from house to house, from friend to friend and relatives, staying with the children as long as they could support her, but she had to move on. And finally the list of her friends and relatives was at an end, and a rickshaw driver told her somehow about our place. And she arrived with her suitcase with the few clothes and belongings for herself and her children, and a few cooking vessels that she had managed to keep together. She arrived, really at the end of her tether. My Le has been through a lot. She causes trouble also, but the point I would like to make is the greatness of that woman in the way in which she has held together her little family, how she struggled, her sense of responsibility and duty and dedication. My Le is a great person. My Le teaches all of us so much. She is poor and she is one of the great ones who offer us the privilege and the rich grace of coming together and of loving. When we think of the poor we must be so very humble.

For the poor are the loved ones of God, they have a courage, they have a spirit, that is so wonderful. So it seems to me full of meaning here today that we are united together in our efforts to love and serve, and we are brothers and sisters of the poor and suffering ones all over the world. And we thank God for His goodness and love, and we remember in our gratitude that it is the poor who make us rich.

Thank you all very much.[29]

Andrew was a storyteller and he could get right to people's hearts by recounting tales of the poor and the suffering.

Interlude – I: The Vietnam – Cambodia Period (1973-1975)   187

From Los Angeles, Andrew and Father Kribs left for Washington, D.C. From that evening until the morning of 7 October, he participated in the Pax Christi conference in the nation's capital, after which the two flew up to New York City to visit the MC Sisters. From there, Brother Andrew went to Philadelphia to meet John Hollinger, FSC.[30] Minneapolis was his next stop where he met Mrs Patty Kump, national chairperson of the Co-Workers of Mother Teresa in America.[31] In St Louis, Missouri he met Brian Walch who later, in June 1974, joined the MC community in Saigon. The National Convention of Catholic Laity in New Orleans began on 14 October and when it ended five days later Andrew travelled to Holy Trinity Abbey in Huntsville, Utah to see Nicholas Prinster, OCSO. Also staying at the abbey at that time was Gary Richardson:

> I first met Andrew in the fall of 1973, at a Trappist abbey in Utah. He was kind, gentle, articulate, and I was drawn to his sense of humour. We took long walks together in the abbey grounds, and he related to me his thoughts about the Brothers, and described the community in Vietnam, and what he felt was being asked of the Brothers in such a situation. This thrilled me.... This was what I had been moving towards since an experience I had in a small city in Nicaragua two years previous. It was a rebirth for me on those cold days of that year in the colour of the changing seasons.[32]

By 4 November he had arrived in New York where he celebrated Mass at the Catholic Worker. Next day Eileen Egan accompanied him to meet Rev. Msgr Barry at the New York Chancery about the possibility of starting the MC Brothers in New York. Brother Andrew believed there was much work to be done in America among such people as drug addicts and alcoholics. He left that same day for London (where he was met by Br Michael Batley's parents) with the idea of possibly starting the Society in the United States within six months'. By 9 November Brother Andrew had arrived back in Calcutta, completely exhausted. Yet within a week, he was off to Saigon.

Confronted with a number of problems in Saigon, Brother Andrew felt unwilling to leave Brothers Leon and Michael and Fr

Don Cowan to face them alone. At the beginning of February 1974, therefore, he wrote to Gary Richardson suggesting that the four young Americans — John Hollinger, Paul DeMartini, Ray Riddick and Gary — whom he had previously talked to in the United States, join him in Saigon. In the letter Andrew explained:

> Here the type of work we are doing presents a difficulty. There would not be a great deal of work immediately at hand. For we have arranged it so that the work is done by the people themselves who have come here in their need. More, of course, would open up as we learn to speak Vietnamese. I find myself that there is more emphasis on the contemplative aspect of our life. There is great meaning in the midst of all the confusion, suffering, division everywhere of trying to be a small community where people try to be good, to be loving, to be at peace, to pray and make intercession.[33]

On the evening of 7 February 1974, a few days after Brother Andrew sent this letter, he received a cable New York, from Fr Robert Charlebois, Director of Southeast Asian Catholic Relief Services (CRS), asking the MC Brothers to go to Cambodia and help with the refugee problems there.[34] Not even a week passed and Andrew was off. The day before he left, he wrote to Sr Margaret Ryan:

> Thanks for your letters, and I just feel like writing to you today, which is the best way to write letters. What you say about religious communities is interesting. I think I've come to believe more that size does not matter. It's important that there be little oases of people amid all the strife and suffering who are trying to be good, loving and to pray. Our problems are just too big for me to even dream of working at. That's all we have here — just a house of people finding a little of the relief and love that they need and some of us try to pray and make intercession …
>
> We've been asked to work with the refugees in Phnom Penh, and I'm supposed to be going tomorrow morning. There are only three planes a week, and I have to go to the

Interlude – I: The Vietnam – Cambodia Period (1973-1975)

airport to "standby" for a seat. To be honest with what's been happening there in the last week, I think I hope there won't be a seat. Air Vietnam have cut their services down to DC planes. The problem may be to get back as there is heavy evacuation. But it's salutary. The condition of the refugees seems to be very bad. According to yesterday's news, "acres of houses" were destroyed making more people homeless. It's only 150 miles from here.

Things are not much more certain here as regards the future. The threat is as much from the economic as from the military. Things are really bad. Four of our children's mothers are in jail for hawking drugs. For the type of people we are working with, the only alternative really is selling drugs or prostitution. The only things there is any money in. All the same we are in the process of buying another house, as this one is more than full. And the amount of life that has been lived in this house since last March makes the investment well worth it already. We can count on the Lord looking after his people.[35]

On arriving at Phnom Penh's Pochentong Airport he barely had ten minutes to talk to Father Charlebois because Andrew's airplane had been delayed in Bangkok, and Father Charlebois was boarding the same flight out of the country. After a few days, Brother Andrew flew back to Saigon via Thailand and from there tried to call Brother Ferdinand in Calcutta to ask him to send four Brothers to initiate the work in Cambodia. International calls proved impossible to make, however, and so Brother Andrew wrote. Before Brother Ferdinand received the letter, a cable had arrived from CRS in Delhi with the same request. But there was no mention of Brother Andrew and Brother Ferdinand was too worried to act independently. He went to Mother Teresa who, having a few months previously visited the country and decided against opening a community, expressed her concern for the Brothers' safety. At the same time she suggested that Brother Ferdinand start preparing the paperwork, passports and visas, for the possible candidates. Eventually four Brothers —

George, Amrit, Clement and P.T. Thomas — were chosen, but the latter was denied a passport. So an American guest, Frank Barone volunteered to go instead.

Meanwhile in Saigon Brother Andrew bought a third house, a two-storey building in a section of the city called Khanh Hoi. His original intention was to use it as a home for women recently discharged from prison. But on 5 April 1974 an article entitled "Halfway House for Ex-Women Prisoners' Kids", appeared in the English-language newspaper, *Saigon Times*, explaining the aims of the house. As a consequence, an official from the Ministry of Interior Department of Corrections came to Cong Quynh to tell Brother Andrew that the Ministry could not approve the plan to use the Khanh Hoi house for female ex-prisoners because the Brother's security status was deemed uncertain. The house already held some families from Cong Quynh, and soon filled up with more women and children with no place to stay — many of them also suffering physically or mentally.

At this point Brother Andrew was in a dilemma. Was it feasible, and in the long run sustainable, to have men from the West coming to Saigon for their formation as MC Brothers? In a letter he had sent on 27 February to an interested American, he confessed:

> I too, have been scared of the prospect, but this response [of John, Paul, Ray, Gary and Mike] has given me the courage to feel that it is something that God is doing. And I think it may be that he has a plan for Indo-China that goes beyond our limited and fearful vision. If you should decide, however, not to come to Saigon, there is certainly a tremendous work for you to do with the young people in the States. And I believe that the needs and suffering in the affluent countries are as great as anything found in the Third World.[36]

Ultimately the style of formation adopted by Andrew for the Brothers outside India, would be an Exodus-type of formation — an allusion to the *Book of Exodus* in the Bible that describes the Israelites' deliverance from the slavery they endured under the

Interlude – I: The Vietnam – Cambodia Period (1973-1975)

Egyptians. For Andrew, Egypt symbolised an oppressive situation in which people became "unfree". Egypt extended beyond a particular geographical area to the whole world and encompassed the lives of those same Brothers. What is poignant in the *Book of Exodus* is that the Israelites were not extracted from their surroundings and placed in a formal "school." Instead, it was their forty-year journey through the desert to the land promised by Yahweh which formed them into His Chosen People.

The idea of Andrew's Exodus formation was that the young MC Brothers — especially those outside India, in places where a proper organised style of formation was impossible — were to be formed through the direct and simple way of relating to, living, and sharing their lives with the poor. For John Hollinger (former Brother Jeremy), as quoted by Solomon:

> The formation in Saigon was extremely unorthodox but intense and profound. The whole country was going through this experience of destruction and doubt and we shared in that. We had no choice. We would meet with Andrew two or three times a week for an afternoon. Two sessions each time and then Mass and a meal together. The rest of the week we might come in [to Cong Quynh] for something but we were pretty much on our own, yet it was all one of the most profound experiences. You just had to surrender and realise how dependent you were, totally dependent. For me it was a very contemplative year.[37]

On 4 March 1974, Brother Andrew had returned to Phnom Penh from Saigon to get a better understanding of the situation in Cambodia while helping CRS as best as he could on his own. In his General Letter of April, 1974, he wrote:

> It is terrible to see what is happening there, to see from a helicopter an endless line of families with their few belongings on a buffalo cart, moving on, crossing streams like a scene from [the movie] The Ten Commandments. Terrible to lie in bed at night and hear the rockets and hear everything beneath you tremble. Terrible to drive

30 miles along Highway 4 out of Phnom Penh and see not a village or a building that is not in ruins. Terrible to realise that it is not just the buildings of the village that are destroyed, but the whole village with its life and structures. Terrible to see people flung into refugee camps or strung out along roadside or riverside by the clash of political theories which they probably do not grasp and none of which are worth the cost these people are paying.[38]

Dith Pran, in *Children of Cambodia's Killing Fields (Memoirs by Survivors)* published in Thailand by Silkworm Books in 1997, related how much suffering had come about. By the mid-1950s the French had left and Cambodia was free and neutral. Prince Sihanouk's pride was short-lived, however, because the North Vietnamese army extended itself and started moving inwards along the Cambodian border, dragging Cambodia into a war not of its making. In March 1969 US President Nixon ordered secret bombings in Cambodia, killing many civilians and pushing the Communists deeper and deeper into the country. The North Vietnamese troops began training a Communist guerrilla group calling themselves Khmer Rouge and soon, with Chinese and Soviet weaponry, this group gained territory, exploiting the corrupt Lon Nol government and the destructive bombing.

While Brother Andrew was still on his pilot mission in Cambodia, Mike Geilenfeld and Gary Richardson arrived in Saigon. Within a few days the three were in Phnom Penh. They started familiarizing themselves with Cambodia and going with CRS medical teams to the refugee camp at Kampong Speu and the nearby *wats* (Buddhist temples and their associated buildings and land). They could provide very simple aid such as helping to keep order in the lines or wrapping pills for distribution.

About this time Joel Blondiaux — a French doctor and at the time a Taizé Brother — who had been working with the MC Brothers in Calcutta, arrived in Saigon. Even though his stay in Indo-China was rather short-lived, his testimony is very valuable:

Interlude – I: The Vietnam – Cambodia Period (1973-1975)

> In Saigon, Andrew welcomed me as a brother. The experience of the spartan life alongside the ex-companions of GIs [American soldiers] and their babies, the sharing of commodities, and the monastic life in one room with Andrew and the guests of passage, for three weeks, in the expectation of a Cambodian visa, was a very strong moment. Added, food poisoning, a dramatic allergy after shrimps' consumption, during which Andrew gave me all the necessary care and kind attention. So I left for Phnom Penh with the promise to see him coming soon with two of Kidderpoor's main Brothers, with no details about modalities of installation and dates. In the meantime I was accommodated at the Hotel de la Poste and CRS contacted me for a possible collaboration. I confess to having, besides solitude, poorly supported the atmosphere of the NGO CRS at the time and its compromise displayed with the US administration and military network, the hostility of the French present at the hotel who looked rather badly at this collaboration of a French with an American NGO, so when Andrew came alone and for a few days only, without the expected Kidderpoor Brothers, I told him that I preferred to return to France.[39]

Was Brother Andrew aware of the possible political implications and complications Joel mentions, for a Frenchman volunteering with an American NGO in a war-torn Communist country? It might be plausible to assume that Andrew made decisions without first evaluating the possible consequences, and that at times he expected of others the same kind and degree of commitment mixed with excitement and risk-taking as were characteristic of him. One thing is, nonetheless, sure: Andrew took care of his Brothers when he noticed that things were getting out of hand and too difficult for them — a trait which we will encounter later on in the year when Brothers had to leave both countries.

The yearly public letter supposed to be written for Christmas 1973, found its way into the mail some five months later. In it he described the three communities in Saigon and the opening of the house in Phnom Penh. He ended by stating:

> Writing this letter makes me reflect on the value of all of us being loosely united around this work — you by your interest and concern, the Brothers in India, Vietnam, Cambodia, and of course, the poor, the suffering and wounded ones who in God's love, give such richness to our lives which have been so privileged in many ways. There is hope in the midst of confusion, division, injustice, in just a few people across the world who at least desire to be good and loving and peaceful, who want to pray, to make intercession and offer something of their lives to the God of love and to their brothers and sisters who suffer.
>
> There is hope. There is joy — for there is goodness and beauty and life in the depths of man's misery and suffering. The cross rises from the lives of all men. And our mystery is that through our suffering we grow into new life.[40]

On 28 April 1974, George, Amrit and Clement (the three Kidderpoor Brothers) and Frank Barone arrived in Phnom Penh. Frank would soon begin working with the children — giving them hot milk, vitamins, bread and rice — while at the same time learning Khmer (the language of the Cambodian people) from them. The number of children being cared for gradually increased.

On 18 May while in Cambodia on his way to Calcutta for the First General Chapter, Brother Andrew wrote that since there were many Chinese Catholics in Southeast Asia it "would be wonderful to have a Chinese branch [of the Society since] it would open up so many possibilities."[41] Realism or just enthusiasm on his part? How could one expect to have a Chinese branch of the Society by being in just two war-ravaged countries? Was Andrew thinking along the lines of a proper religious congregation or just a fluid sort of group with a lot of goings and comings, which would be an offshoot of the "proper one" in India? Brother Gordon remembered that during a visit in Saigon in 1974 John Harte SJ discussed similar questions with the Brothers.[42]

Interlude – I: The Vietnam – Cambodia Period (1973-1975)

On 26 May 1974 Brother Andrew was elected to continue as General Servant. Among the many topics discussed at this General Chapter, one that is of interest for this book is the expansion of the Congregation. The Brothers gathered in Calcutta were aware that for expansion to happen, the General Servant needed sufficient freedom to travel, especially around Southeast Asia to establish the Society there. At the same time he was expected to pay regular, more or less quarterly visits to the Mother House (Mansatala) in India. For this reason, the Brothers in India were to assume full responsibility for the Society there in India including the expansion of the work. Calcutta would remain the Society's centre, to which the Brothers looked for inspiration and example. But while preserving the aim and spirit of the Congregation and its dedication to the poorest of the poor, as the Brother's journal recorded, "We shall preserve our unity in our diversity. In view of this we shall try to adapt the dress, lifestyle, etc., of the place as far as possible so that the Society is duly incarnate in the soil, that is to say, shall achieve a local expression of one and the same Society, for instance, a Vietnamese expression, a Chinese expression, etc., in the same way as we have an Indian expression of our Society here."[43]

With the General Chapter over and with its blessing to go on expanding the Society in Southeast Asia, on 5 June 1974 Brother Andrew left India for Phnom Penh and then Saigon via Bangkok. Sometime before leaving India, however, he invited Brian Walch, (the American in Calcutta whom he had met in St Louis), and Anton van Don, (a Dutchman who had also come to visit the Brothers in Calcutta), to come to Saigon to help with the work.

Anton van Don, who would become Brother Anton, MC, had just arrived as a volunteer in Mansatala when he met Brother Andrew for the first time:

> There were a lot of Brothers gathered in the refectory and he was talking about his experiences of what he was doing in Cambodia and in Vietnam. And he mentioned among others that he needed people who spoke French, and people

that had some nursing experience. And that was like it was addressed to me.

At that time I was already worried about how much longer I could stay since I only had a three-month visa — the maximum time I could apply for as a tourist. My idea was to go to neighbouring Nepal and apply for another visa and come back to Calcutta. But then listening to Brother Andrew, I thought I could go to Vietnam. After all I spoke French and had experience as a nurse. But, he had talked about refugee camps, the war and all that, and I had no experience in that field.

Soon after, there was the General Chapter. Brian [Walch] and I were sent to the community in Antara. When the chapter was over, immediately there was the first profession on 2nd of June, 1974. Brian was to leave very soon after that and so I was already planning on going to Nepal.

But, in the middle of the festivities of profession, with the house full, so many relatives, and very solemn... and in the middle of that, Andrew just met me and he said, "Don't you like to sit a bit away, we can talk now?" And we sat on the veranda next to his room. It seemed that he also needed a break from the feast. He talked and then I explained my situation.

He then said that he was going to Vietnam, to Saigon, and that there are people from America, and an Australian I think. And so he proposed that I maybe go to Vietnam.

So there I was left, Andrew left, and he was in touch somehow. With Brian he had already set a date that Brian would fly to Thailand and then to Saigon, and it was then that Andrew suggested that we travel together.

So there I made my decision to give it a try.[44]

In less than two weeks both Anton and Brian arrived in Saigon. After spending a few days in Cong Quynh, they moved to the Phu Lam house, thereby making it a full-time residence of an MC community for the first time.

Interlude – I: The Vietnam – Cambodia Period (1973-1975)

At the same time John Hollinger, whom Brother Andrew had met in Philadelphia, Gordon Wineman, and Bernie Walsh from Chicago arrived in Saigon. Hollinger recalled:

> When I arrived in Saigon, Vietnam in 1974, I had met Andrew only once, during a speaking tour of the US. He came to Philadelphia where I was living as a Christian Brother, while attending University to get my Bachelor's degree. He had a charisma that was immediately evident to all who met him, and at that time he indicated I should wait until the following summer to join the community, as they were planning a house in New York.
>
> Little did I know... that a few months later, I'd be planning a trip to Vietnam instead. Brother Nick, the Trappist, arranged for three of us to travel by steamer in June 1974, arriving 22 days later in Saigon. The Indo-China Excursion as Geoffrey Solomon called it, was in full bloom, and Andrew was living in Saigon along with Leon and Michael, who both left within a few months of our arrival.
>
> In this small house in Cong Quynh district, three Brothers were living among many women and their half Vietnamese, half American children, in addition to taking on two other houses that were opened to provide shelter for even more mothers and their mixed-race children who were considered outcasts in Vietnamese culture. After Michael and Leon left, Andrew, Gordon, Anton and I were left to manage these houses. And in those same months three Indian Brothers arrived and went on to Cambodia to work, along with three American come-and-sees, Gary, Michael and Brian.
>
> I share this, only because it highlights that this was the MC we came into. There was nothing of normal or traditional religious life in these communities, and yet we were very much formed by the crucible of these countries. We did pray, we did have Mass together, and Andrew did spend

most afternoons teaching us about the Congregation, its spirit, its rules, its history and all that in the context of the crucifixion we witnessed each day in these countries torn apart by war, in the minds of the people, "the American war". For all the formality and tradition this formation lacked, it was made up for in intensity of lived experience.[45]

Adjusting to a new culture, a new type of life, while getting to know each other and trying to live together was not easy for the young Americans and Indians in Cambodia. The community was frequently divided. To add to this tension, one fine June day in 1974, a Cambodian military general visited the Brothers and decided that the house where they were staying in Kampong Thom (which had just had electricity and plumbing put in) should be given to some of his officers. The Brothers were obliged to move to "the bungalow," an old war-scarred, French hotel where the CRS medical teams were lodging.

Life was hectic and hard both for the young Brothers and for Andrew, and yet he would not have traded the experience for any other. He sensed that it would not last forever but, as always, he was taken by the people, the individuals. To his sister Mary he wrote:

> I thought life in India is rich, but here it is just too much. I don't know exactly what it is. I guess it is the people who are so wonderful. But I don't think I'll ever recover from Vietnam. It would be awful to try to live anywhere else. It is sad to think of what will be the future. That is so uncertain. They say things have never been so bad for the people as now, with the state of the economy, and all the war money and aid at an end. It is always the little guy who pays the price. The big ones still get enough.... I was at the home of a prostitute that we are helping a bit the other day. She had three children and her old mother. The landlord had taken away the fan because she was behind with the rent. She no longer has any new clothes and looks a bit scruffy. There is no chance of another job, and so poor, poor mum has

to go out and walk the streets at night and bring the men home, where her own kids see the comings and goings. It's strange, but somehow I always feel in places like that I am on sacred ground. It all just shatters so many of your ideas. If that woman is not close to God in the way she keeps on battling for her family, then I don't even know the name of the game.⁴⁶

While on a visit to Phnom Penh on 17 July Brother Andrew was interviewed by a *New York Times* reporter. In the article, which appeared in the 19 July edition, he was quoted as saying of the street children of Phnom Penh:

The important thing is to give them friendship and love and some laughter and joy to relieve their immediate needs. But the door has to be open at all times so that they are not confined because the freedom of the street has become very much a part of them. They come with one tremendous asset, the ability to survive. If we soften them up and take away that ability, I don't think we've done them a service. Their lives are going to continue to be rough regardless of what we do.⁴⁷

It was only in July of that same year, that the Phu Lam house in Saigon, received its first resident patients (as opposed to transitory night travellers). Eventually, the house would become a home for some old people, several blind and/or crippled boys, some street boys, and small families that just had nowhere else to stay. It also served as a night shelter for poor travellers. A few months later, after almost a year and a half of unceasing help to Brother Andrew and all the other Brothers, Ba Kim took a three-month vacation (she returned in November).

Again, problems arose in Phnom Penh. The Brothers moved from École Miche to a two-storey house of their own at 83 Hem Cheav. The first floor was used as a night shelter and classroom area for the seventy to seventy-five street children who came every afternoon for activities. The second floor was for the Brothers' use. But the move could not resolve their serious disagreements. They also felt caught up in a difference of opinion between the local Catholic Church and CRS: on the one hand, Archbishop George Ramousse thought the Brothers should be living among the people and learning their language instead of helping with CRS distribution projects and working with street children; on the other, CRS said it had a lot of food needed for the refugee camps' soup kitchens that was starting to spoil because it was not being moved fast enough. Some of the Brothers thought that they should stop working in Kampong Thom, even though CRS had already started building a house for them near the camps. These outside pressures exacerbated tensions inside the community. At the end of the meetings to resolve these problems, Brother Andrew expressed the view that the Brothers should put more emphasis on getting food, clothing, medicine and such things into the hands of those needing them. He was in favour of keeping the work in Kampong Thom going, in the hope that somehow the Brothers could be a source of mediation between the local Church and CRS.

These conflicts weighed on Brother Andrew and the situation seemed dreary and drab:

> It's good when someone reflects on what is happening, as you seem to do, and not just let it all drift into oblivion. Somehow that seems to help dispose us to recognise things that God brings up to us at times and that are really his calls. I was just thinking yesterday that I have never really planned any step or move in my life that eventually was a little fruitful. It has always been something that came up to me, and just demanded a bit of a gamble at the time — in faith I suppose.

> One day something has to be exploded — and that is the Brother Andrew myth. It all just boils down to being present to a very favourable set of circumstances at the right time. And so I said, the readiness to take a risk. It is God's work and the hard, generous work of hidden people. It is truly wonderful from that angle. When we meet, ask me to expound on that a bit.

> It is the secret to poor old Br A. [Andrew]. In a sort of stagnation recently, I was wondering why doesn't God make us brilliant, decisive and all the rest, so that we could really set things up well and effectively. And then I realised that that wouldn't be anywhere near as precious as the fruits of our stumbling, feeble, unfaithful ways. There is something beautiful in what comes out of our clumsiness and failures. It is terrible to say, but it seems that God has to really break us before we even begin to sense the mystery of our lives, much less the mystery of God. And it is so terrible the way he breaks us. If some cruel persecutor did the job at least we could claim heroism. But when it is our own thoughtlessness and unfaithfulness, when we can blame no one else but ourselves, it is awful.
>
> But it is the wonderful truth. Really it is the truth that sets us free. Then you don't have to worry any more — except that you just hope that you haven't hurt and harmed others too much. But even that thought shows there is still much to grasp, for the God of love and goodness brings others to life even through what we inflict on them. Well that got a bit out of hand, so I had better bring this to an end.[48]

Late 1974 was still bleak. Andrew's Christmas greetings for that year testified to this desolation:

> As I try to put these words together on a Sunday afternoon in mid-November, it doesn't look as if we are due for the happiest Christmas ever or the most prosperous New Year on record. . . . There is plenty of cause to weep and mourn if we want to. Just this morning I was thinking of all the forebodings and fears for the future and of what to say in this letter.[49]

But the ever-hopeful Andrew managed to perceive the beauty in just a little event:

> And then one of the little girls in the house here skipped down the stairs with a happy smile on her lips. And that little

girl would have plenty of reason to be worried and anxious if she sat down to consider her history and her prospects ...

You can thank that little girl singing her steps down the stairs this morning for saving you from more of that kind of heavy thoughts [that] have been plaguing me for this year's letter. She really asks me: What are you here for? Are you here to work out your own problems or are you here for us? And that is where she is like Jesus at Christmas: He didn't come at Christmas to work out his own problems or for his own personal fulfilment. He just came for us people, to show us the way of caring for and loving each other in faith and simplicity.[50]

Around mid-December 1974, Brother Leon asked to be dispensed from his vows and returned home to Australia. Christmas brought joy and pain in the Cong Quynh house. A woman came with her four-day-old baby, seeking shelter. While at the house, however, she almost completely ignored the child and after about four days she left the infant behind and went back to selling candy near a movie theatre. She never came back. In the end Ba Kim adopted the baby as one of her own.

The year 1975 did not start on a good note. On 6 January the Viet Cong staged a rocket attack on the radar station near the Brothers' Phu Lam house. The building was severely shaken but no damage was done and no one was injured, although some of the people staying in the house were very frightened. Brother Anton recalled that even though there were these random onslaughts, the city was still fairly quiet, unlike in the countryside where attacks like these were rife.[51]

A couple of days after this shelling, Brother Andrew called a meeting to consider the Brothers' situation in Saigon in the light of what was happening in Indo-China and economic conditions in the world at large. It was clear to all the Brothers that things were much worse politically, economically and militarily in Vietnam than they had been six months earlier. Nevertheless, the new Brothers

Interlude – I: The Vietnam – Cambodia Period (1973-1975)

expressed their desire to remain in Vietnam to keep the work going for long as God would allow.

After a ten-day stay in India, on 29 January 1975, Brother Andrew left Calcutta for Phnom Penh but only got as far as Bangkok. Phnom Penh airport was closed because of heavy Khmer Rouge shelling. Not until five days later was he finally able to fly into Phnom Penh. Before leaving Cambodia, he arranged for the Brothers there to be able to go to Saigon for a week's rest. Things were so unstable and unsure. Yet Brother Andrew wrote in a letter to Brother Nicholas in Utah, "We are getting passports for 3 more Indians to come ... and if they come here [to Cambodia], the Americans [Mike, Brian and Paul] could possibly come to Saigon, where we can be together more for formation. But it changes so fast, I don't seriously consider things one month away."[52] He managed to leave Phnom Penh thanks to a helicopter that took him back to Saigon.

On 8 February 1975, Brother George, Brother Clement, Mike, Brian and Paul arrived in Saigon for a week's vacation. (Brother Amrit remained in Phnom Penh to keep the street children's night shelter running during their absence). While the group was there, Brother Andrew held a meeting with (practically) all the Brothers of the Congregation present in Indo-China. The situation was becoming too tense and dangerous. What should the Brothers do? Should they leave both Cambodia and Vietnam when the United States embassies decide to evacuate their personnel? All had to discern between two conflicting possibilities: by staying on, the Brothers could be endangering people's lives since Communist reprisals against those who had associated with foreigners seemed likely; at the same time, it was argued, they would be more fully identifying with the poorest of the poor who had few, if any, means of escaping whatever happened. Another pressing consideration was that if the Brothers did stay they might be unable to receive any funds, but all felt that this could not be a reason for leaving. The performance of acts of love could not be linked to the availability of money. Brother Andrew respected his Brothers' desires and thoughts, and refrained from issuing a blanket order as to whether or not they should leave Cambodia and Vietnam in the event of an evacuation. The general consensus, however, was that the Brothers should stay or leave as a community.

During this time several pregnant women staying in the Brothers' house gave birth and other mothers came with their new babies. There was talk among the Brothers in Saigon of opening another house for such mothers and their infants. Brother Andrew began gathering money in the bank to purchase a fourth house. Wasn't it unreasonable to buy houses and land in a war-ravaged country with so many uncertainties and insecurities about the future, especially after the meeting to decide whether or not to stay? Or was it a matter of answering to an immediate call, a direct need? In a letter dated 6 March to Brother Nicholas, Andrew acknowledged the complexity of the decision:

> It's been hard to decide whether to stay on or to go. There's the need of the people and there's the lives of the Brothers. We could offer our lives, I suppose. But I don't think that offering would be backed up by a sufficient reason as we would not be able to do much for anyone — not that 'doing' is the most important thing as we have said before.[53]

Andrew was torn between the needs of the local people and the danger that his Brothers would be facing.

A few days later, on 9 March, while in Phnom Penh, he wrote to the Brothers in Calcutta:

> This is to bring you some news from Cambodia. The Brothers here are all well and doing wonderful work in a very dangerous situation. The war is very bad and very close to where we are. It seems that it will not continue very much longer and the Brothers will be evacuated. It will be very hard to leave the people who will continue to suffer much.
>
> I came here from Saigon on 4th March, and will return before long. It is rather frightening at times, when the

Interlude – I: The Vietnam – Cambodia Period (1973-1975)

rockets fall. They fall in the city streets and the market and many people are killed — many innocent civilians. Sometimes on the streets you can feel that everyone is afraid.

I am so impressed with the spirit of the Brothers here. They are joyful and cheerful. I do not think there is a happier community of MC's anywhere. They do not think about their own lives or safety, but are caring for the people in such a dedicated way. This is such a grace and blessing for our whole Society. And they do their work in such a quiet peaceful way.

Surely your prayers are helping so much in this way. Keep on praying for them: 1. That they will do their work with the love of God and 2. That when there is an evacuation, they will be safe.

In such circumstances, you realise what is important and what is not important. We have only our life to give — and that is already given to us.... The Brothers in Saigon are well.... Maybe Mother Teresa will be visiting us soon. She should not try to come to Cambodia. I hope that I shall be back in Saigon when she comes there. If not the Novices will take care of her. All for now. We pray for you all in India in our Mass & prayer here.

Love and prayers.
Andrew.[54]

Brother Andrew got back to Saigon from Phnom Penh the day after the crucial battle of Ban Me Thout. The loss of this city to the Communists marked the "beginning of the end" of the war, which happened on 10 March 1975.

Andrew felt that it would be demoralising both for the Brothers in Cambodia and for the people they served if any of the MCs had to leave before CRS. In fact, all the Brothers, with the possible exception of Brian, were in favour of leaving Cambodia whenever CRS was evacuated. CRS departed on the 19th of the same month, when Brother Amrit, Brother Clement and Mike also left for Saigon.

Mike brought with him Brian's fairly long letter to Brother Andrew and the other Brothers explaining why he felt he must remain in Cambodia. After reading the letter, Brother Andrew described it as "irrefutable". He was, nevertheless, unhappy that Brian had decided to stay. He sincerely hoped that Brother George, who had remained behind to straighten out the last-minute details, would be able to convince Brian to leave with him. Worried about Brian, Brother Andrew sent him a telegram saying, "Hoping and praying that you leave." But Brian was adamant. His decision to stay was his own free choice, not an act of disobedience because, as a come-and-see, he was not bound by a vow of obedience.

On 18 March Brother Anton's mother arrived in Saigon to spend a couple of weeks with her son on her way to visiting relatives in Indonesia.[55] As soon as she arrived, Brother Anton went to inform the Dutch Embassy of her presence in the country. At the embassy he was asked if the two should be placed on the evacuation list. Later that morning while at Cong Quynh, he told Brother Andrew about the list. This prompted Andrew to suggest that the American Brothers go to their embassy and ask about any evacuation plans, Jeremy and Mike found out that, together with Gordon, they were eligible for evacuation if the need arose. Reassured by this news, Brother Andrew asked Jeremy, Mike and Gordon whether they wanted to leave before a general evacuation since the large number of Americans still in Vietnam would be sure to create such chaos that some of the Brothers might not be able to get out of the country in time. When Brothers Clement and Amrit found out that their Indian Consulate had no evacuation plans, Brother Andrew decided they should return to Calcutta as soon as possible. Around the same time, Andrew went to see Father Nghi, to ask him if he thought the Brothers would be an embarrassment to the Vietnamese Church if they stayed on after the fall of the capital. Father Nghi told him that if they were to remain it would be a big help but that it would involve a great sacrifice on their part. By that time South Vietnam had already lost or abandoned the northern two-thirds of the country. The Viet Cong were thus closer to Saigon and its fall was imminent.

Interlude – I: The Vietnam – Cambodia Period (1973-1975)

Brother Andrew wrote another letter to the Brothers in India on 21 March, asking for prayers for Brian. While he acknowledged that Brian's decision to stay in Phnom Penh was generous, he also believed that it could cause the local people trouble and put them in danger if they had to look after him. Brian's choice could even cost him his life.

Did the Brothers speak openly about what was happening in the country? Were they afraid of the Communists? According to Brother Anton:

> Andrew was afraid, that he would be associated with Communism; we would be arrested, and the work would stop. But we knew that here and there were possibly fellows that were Communists.... There was one fellow, an ice-cream vendor, Herviet, I think his name; I remember that we suspected him.... And others were saying, no, he was a very nice fellow. It could well be that we had some Communists sheltered in the night. We didn't get into politics but Andrew certainly was not for the rights of the Communists. No way. That's true. And also he had this fear that if the government had any suspicion that we were somehow Communists, we would be arrested. And that was his issue with the red bag.[56]

A mischievous smile crossed Brother Anton's face when prompted to say a little more about *the red bag*:

> I had found somewhere in donations a little cotton red bag which was easy and light to carry especially on the bicycle. But it was a red, fiery red, and Andrew said, "*You cannot use it.*" But I had nothing else, I only had a big backpack and I was not going to carry that. Andrew had this idea about Communism, and the colour red was Communist. I tried to argue with him that it was just a bag. But Andrew was adamant about the red bag. It was years later that he softened up about it![57]

It was to his sister Mary Ennis and his friend Pat O'Sullivan, SJ, that Brother Andrew expressed himself freely and sincerely about the fear he felt in Saigon and Phnom Penh. At the same time, he was convinced he was where he should be at that precise moment, being present to the poor and suffering, irrespective of the possible consequences:

21.3.1975.

Dear Mary,

Yours of 12th arrived safely yesterday. So good to hear from you. Good to know you are all well. Am glad you met Leon. He is great really.

When I got back from Phnom Penh I wrote to Phyl and asked her to ring you to say I was back safely. It looks as if that will be my last trip there. Hard to see it going on much longer. It is a terrible thing a City about to fall. And there are the rockets that hit anywhere. And I'll tell you about getting in and out of the airport sometime.

And now it's wild here in Vietnam. The speed of the developments in the last week has left everyone gasping. They feel the bottom has fallen out of everything. People in the country are all packed and ready to move. It is just an awful feeling.

Three of our Brothers came in from Phnom Penh two days ago, and they feel pretty bad about leaving it. And they haven't realized yet that the rockets aren't coming. We have two men there still.

It's worrying me having people who totally depend on us. The women with their children who are healthy will have to manage, but there are the old, the disabled, the mental ones, the babies, the expectant mothers. And what is so hard you can't see the details of how things will eventuate, and so you can't plan.

If I didn't believe in God as the Lord of History, it would be awful. But with faith, you can accept whatever will happen and the loss of everything. And strangely you can do this with a very real joy. So we are in good spirits really.

Interlude – I: The Vietnam – Cambodia Period (1973-1975)

When I was last in Phnom Penh that was the striking thing. Everything there was so awful — and you could feel the fear and grimness everywhere. And yet there was this tremendous spirit of joy and cheerfulness among the Brothers. It is harder for them now that they have left.

So there is nothing to worry about. For myself I have been ready for anything. I have had such a rich life. But I was worrying about the young Brothers, but I see that they too have the same tremendous fulfilment and purpose. So, dear, we are alright. There is no present danger in Saigon.

Love to all with prayers.
Ian.[58]

Brother Andrew was ready for whatever might happen to him in Saigon, much as Brian Walch was ready for anything, even to die in the midst of the poor suffering Cambodians in Phnom Penh.

28th Mar. 1975. Good Friday.

Dear Pat,

P.C. [Pax Christi]

I thought about you often, and still do. I can imagine that you are up to your neck in it back home....

The rest of this letter may be a bit dramatic. It's not really, and I'd be glad if you could pass on what follows to my family and the Brothers in India if anything happens to me. I don't want them to worry now, and there is only a remote chance.

Things are happening so fast around here. The awful question is to stay or to leave? We are still in the middle of that in Cambodia with half the men here and half still in there. But we have decided to evacuate there before the end. In a way the decision is easier there, as we don't have people totally dependent on us. Here it is different. Many of the people could take their place in the line along the road with the rest of the populace. But we have some who are disabled, too old, too tiny, etc. And it would be hard to leave them.

Of course, it's almost ridiculous to talk about it, because you just can't decide anything till things happen, and you have a few facts to work on.

So what I am saying now may never happen. But I can see us bringing all the disabled ones into one house, and one or two Brothers (Probably one staying on) and that could be myself. From that point on what would happen is guesswork at this stage. If I'm off the scene in any way, I'd just like the wonderful people to know that it's what I wanted to do. Maybe it's right, maybe not. I think I've learned that most of our decisions are really ambiguous. But that doesn't matter because we see God still brings good out of whatever mess we seem to make.

I — and no one else — should have any regrets if Bro. A [Andrew]'s run ends. It has been such a rich life I sometimes wonder if I am not just sated with this richness of God's giving. A spell in a prison or a rocket on the nose would be truly right, just, salutary and good.

There is nothing heroic in this. Living with the rockets in Phnom Penh of late, and the awful atmosphere there of a city about to fall gave me an understanding of fear that I did not have before.

Well that's enough of that. We shall probably see the day when we shall laugh about this letter as we consider spiritual things in our time-honoured way. And I hope that we may still have another session right in Saigon.

This has been a tremendous Lent. A real stripping down.

I don't have illusions about life under the Comms. [Communists], the bit I have seen and read shows that they don't allow any independent, organised, active, group life to operate. How are you to be Church in such circs

Interlude – I: The Vietnam – Cambodia Period (1973-1975)

[circumstances]? Maybe I'm jumpy, Pat, but I'd give you 3 to 15 years in Australia, before you're there. When the framework goes, the important thing seems to be a faith-direction.

What struck me about our men in Phnom Penh this time was their tremendous spirit of joy and cheerfulness. And I suppose it's true what Jesus said: I am with you right to the consummation of the world — and that's enough.

Love, Pat, and prayers
Andrew.[59]

One interesting fact: The letter sent to Father Patrick was an aerogramme; on the outside Andrew had scribbled a last note, "St. J. did a good job in Cambodia." We do not know what that good job was but, according to Father Patrick, this was a reference to the small metal statue of St. Joseph he had given to Andrew some years earlier. Those who knew and lived with Brother Andrew in later years mention that he always carried this small statue in his pocket, tied to his handkerchief.[60]

Meanwhile in Cambodia, on 1 April 1975 Lon Nol stepped down as head of the Cambodian government and left the country. Next day the strategic port city of Neak Luong fell to the Khmer Rouge.[61] On 3 April Brother Andrew received a telegram (probably sent 1 April) from Father Gehrig, the Director of CRS in Cambodia, inviting the Brothers to come back. Because the telegram was sent before the fall of Neak Luong, Brother Andrew decided against this idea. On that same day, in the afternoon, a meeting was held in Cong Quynh, at which it was concluded that Brother Anton should leave immediately. He had been informed by the Dutch embassy that an evacuation plane would be flying out next day for Bangkok. After the meeting Brother Andrew prepared several papers to be delivered to the Brothers in India. Exhorting them all to pray for the Brothers in Saigon and Phnom Penh, he also urged them not to criticise any political leaders and never to get involved with any political activity: "Our MC aim is much more radical. It goes to the hungry, suffering man directly. And the poor man or woman is Christ."⁶²

Evacuations started on 5 April, with Brother Anton leaving for Holland, followed by Brothers Amrit and Clement for Calcutta. Brother George left around 7 April on a flight to Bangkok and then Calcutta. Before Brother George left Phnom Penh he told Brian that he could not continue to stay in the Brothers' house because his presence could endanger people's lives. Brian went to the Cathedral steps where he read his Bible during the day and slept at night. Père Robert Venet, the French priest who had been CRS's representative in Kampong Thom, obliged him to go to the nearby archbishop's house, but during the night Brian sneaked downstairs to the kitchen, took some food, and went into hiding behind the Cathedral. He stayed there until the Khmer Rouge took the city on 18 April. Père Venet last saw Brian being led off at gun-point by the Khmer Rouge. No further news of him was ever heard. It is assumed he was either executed or died soon after his capture in the forced exodus of Phnom Penh's residents which saw more than two million people driven into the countryside to a life unknown.⁶³

Mike could not wait for evacuation by the US embassy because his thirty-day visa was due to expire, so a flight to Calcutta was booked for him for 12 April. The same evening on which the ticket was purchased, however, Brother Andrew heard a radio announcement asking for US citizens with valid exit visas to escort orphan children being flown to the United States. Brother Andrew asked Mike if he wanted to go on it. Mike would rather have gone straight to Calcutta but agreed to telephone the announced number. Calling from a phone at a nearby hotel, he volunteered to be an escort and learned that the plane was scheduled to leave the next day. Because his thirty-day tourist visa for Vietnam (provided in Cambodia) had not yet run out he did not need an exit visa. The plan was for Mike to escort the children to the United States, visit Brother Nicholas at Holy Trinity Abbey, see his family for about a month, and then leave New York for Calcutta. On 11 April he left Saigon aboard the "baby flight" and landed at Lark Air Force Base

Interlude – I: The Vietnam – Cambodia Period (1973-1975)

in the Philippines. Upon boarding the plane for America, he was recognised by five Cambodian children who had stayed at the night shelter in Phnom Penh. When the people in charge of the operation realised that Mike spoke Khmer (Cambodian) he was put in charge of the forty Cambodian children on the plane.

In Saigon the threat of siege was imminent and the situation seemed to be getting tougher. Brother Andrew sent Jeremy and Gordon to the immigration office to get their exit visas on 12 April. Up to this point the idea had been that, after leaving Vietnam, the Brothers would just try to stay together. If they were to be evacuated to Bangkok, the Philippines, Guam or Hong Kong they should not go back to the United States but stay together. Perhaps Brother Andrew could try to start again elsewhere in Asia. The Brothers in India had been considering opening a house in Bangladesh in June. That was, therefore, a possibility for Western Brothers (hampered as they were by the inability to get visas to remain in India). Later on the same day, 12 April, Brother Andrew discussed with the two remaining Brothers the option of their going to the United States. They could try to rent an apartment together until something more permanent could be established. They would not even call themselves Religious, but just live together, seeking out people in need and possibly getting jobs in a hospital to support themselves. Somewhere on the West Coast would be near Brother Nicholas, Mr and Mrs Lloyd Tevis and Fr Kribs. Following the discussion Brother Andrew wrote up a "Charter" for them:

> This morning in the uncertain & fearful time a remark of John led a little later to the thought of starting a house in the U.S. with John, Gordon & Mike. The way they would all be together is so strange — and the formation of this past year in Indo-China is extraordinary ...

> They could perhaps live together and do very simple work with the unwanted, the lonely, the old, the disabled, in county hospitals.

They are young and there would be a danger of others putting pressure on them to be or do something foreign to our spirit. There would also be the danger of 'wild' young men joining them who would disrupt the group.

I would have great confidence in their combined spirit. To counteract these dangers of influence, it would be good to start in a very simple hidden way — not even calling the group a 'religious' group in the strict sense. As to young candidates, they could accept men for a definite period, say one or two months — after which they would go away. And then the group could either invite them back or tell them not to come. Would need to be careful of [people] who would want the group to be something different or would be too difficult to handle. In a word, they would have to try to discern after two months whether a man had the spirit of the group or not. And courageously tell him.

Would be necessary to foresee that the Co-Workers, in their love, did not overwhelm the group. In the States, etc., social welfare is heavily organised. There is no need of a new group to do complicated work. But it can often by-pass the personal need of the lonely or sad individual. So it would not matter how simple & personal our work: talking, visiting, maybe sheltering. Should be no pressure to doing things or to having results to show.

The essentials of the community would be:
1. a community of men
2. trying to be good
3. trying to be loving
4. trying to pray a little
5. living in simplicity & poverty
6. working in a simple style
7. with the Gospel & Eucharist at the heart of their lives.

There would be so many reasons against such an attempt; it would be young novices running it, I may be stuck in Vietnam, etc. But much unexpected things have happened & developed in the past year that we can have hope — if God wants it. It would be an Easter rising out of the passion of Vietnam and Cambodia.

I have explained this to Br Ferdinand in India and asked them to give you the chance to do it. If this is God's idea, He will bless it. With a prayer.
Andrew

P.S. Anton should be invited. It may be the way for him to start in Holland after a little experience with the experiment in the U.S.[64]

During this time there were rumours that the banks would be raided. Andrew had joined the queues and withdrawn all funds on the day the doors closed. It was money set apart for buying the fourth house. The amount, which he predicted could last all the houses for two or three months, created a problem. Where could so much money be kept safely? His bed was a mattress on top of boxes of tinned milk powder provided by CRS, and that's where the money ended up.

It was only on 21 April that Jeremy and Gordon left Saigon for India. As an Australian citizen Brother Andrew believed he would not be as much of a danger to the people as Americans. Three days later, at about four in the morning, rockets landed near the Cong Quynh house. The resulting fire was extinguished shortly before it could do any damage to 102/33. Andrew scrambled for the tins of milk powder: "I went for the money. I thought whatever happens to this house we've got two others. If we've got the money we can make a go of it. If we haven't got the money the whole show's finished. So I went and dug out the milk and put the money in a bag."[65] Later the same day Brother Andrew wrote to the Brothers in India:

The 3 houses are in good spirit. We really have the poor & helpless ones. And it is so good to be here with them. There is not much work for me. But the presence is so important.

> How God transforms our nothingness into something fruitful. People up and down the lane who have never smiled now seem so happy when they see me.
>
> The Church is marvellous. The banks, airlines, embassies have all gone, but so many Brothers, Sisters, priests, bishops stay on. There is a lot wrong with the Church everywhere, but there is so much love and goodness.
>
> No one knows what will happen. Surely we shall not be allowed to work. Probably the foreigners will be arrested and later sent out. But it could be worse. But that is all right. How better could an MC give his life than with the poor? It would be such a grace. And if God has a plan for the future here, then being here makes that possible. Whatever happens let us rejoice in the Lord.
>
> The people suffer so much: families separated, always running, the rockets and the fires. It is so awful for the sick & helpless ones. We can just entrust them to God's love. And if we MCs share in the suffering of the people, it is a small thing among so many. But such a grace.
>
> Love & prayers.
> Andrew.[66]

Rockets continued to strike quite close to the Cong Quynh house for a few more days. After two places around the city were bombed a twenty-four-hour curfew was declared. On the night of 29 April, after Brother Andrew learned from one of the women in the house that the United States had ordered the long-expected evacuation to begin, all the lights in Cong Quynh went out and two rockets exploded very near to the house.

30 APRIL 1975 – FALL OF SAIGON and AFTERMATH

Saigon surrendered. Below is a copy of the entry 30 April 1975 in Brother Andrew's journal:

After the awful attack of 8 p.m. last night, things grew quiet till a rocket hit close at 4 a.m., and a stone hit My Le. But again we survived the night. God takes care of His poor. Maybe we have one of the few happy houses here with the children playing and the adults OK. . . .

The radio says the Americans have gone, but V.C. [Viet Cong] refuse peace talks; they want total surrender; we can expect a few more terrible days. News of looting of American houses, and Vung Tau has been taken. A lot of shelling in the morning. But you grow accustomed to it. In quiet prayer was able before God to see something of the value of God's final plan for us. Through all this suffering He brings us to Himself. The faithfulness in continuing to look to Him is the value. Then a heavy shelling. And then the surrender. People in our lane in dazed groups. Thank God the shelling is finished. Now I suppose we wait for what happens, wait for that final meeting with the new rulers however it takes place. After lunch the new forces moved along Tran Hung Dao Street. There was no shooting or terror. People and soldiers waved back. And people collected furniture and things from the big houses and offices. Hondas, cars, cycles, rickshaws raced along as they were passed by tanks, armoured cars, etc. Boys threw their rifles over the factory wall in the lane. There were tense moments, but these passed. Plenty of shots in the air and crackers. The three houses have survived to this point: rockets, looting, chaos. And so God takes care. Will have to see how and when to report my presence. Too tired and drained tonight to think. It will be good to sleep tonight without rockets. Can only pray for Holy Spirit to guide my decisions — He has up to now. Tomorrow is the feast of St Joseph the Worker.[67]

Two days after the fall of Saigon, Ba Kim returned to visit Cong Quynh, having left her children and siblings with her father at Vung Tau. She did not lodge at 102/33 but in one of her aunt's houses nearby. After a while she began a cycle of staying near Cong Quynh to help Brother Andrew and returning to Vung Tau for two to three weeks at a time, until the new government finally forced all the residents of 102/33 out.

An entry in Brother Andrew's journal (as printed for his 1975 Christmas letter) reads as follows:

15 May 1975

One thing is clear: there is a value in being here in helplessness and powerlessness and uncertainty, with a complete dependence on Providence and God to show what He wants in the decisions of others. There is something of the Kingdom in this: Need to reflect and pray on this.

There are the three houses open (one would be enough). NEED TO BE OPEN TO GOD AND WHAT HE WANTS — not to have any predilection to stay or to go. There is a tremendous meaning in it right now — today. Try to live this. Be open to God coming in people who come for shelter, to talk, etc.

WHAT WOULD JESUS BE IN THIS SITUATION? He would be faithful in His love for the Father and others. Would be faithful to truth. Would be trying to do the will of Father. I am in a totally different order — the folly and power of the Gospel. Christ is alive and present and active in my being here. MUST LET HIM DO AND BE AND EFFECT WHAT HE WANTS. He will do this if I let Him. I must wait and be open. IN THIS SITUATION JESUS WOULD BE LOVING.[68]

On 16 May 1975, when it was announced that all foreigners must register with the new government, Brother Andrew did so. According to the Italian journalist Tiziano Terziani in his book *Giai Phong! The Fall and Liberation of Saigon*, registration began on 10 May and foreigners were assured that, "all those who work honestly, do not oppose the Vietnamese people or the policy of the Revolution, and who respect the laws and customs of the country

Interlude – I: The Vietnam – Cambodia Period (1973-1975)

will be able to continue their normal activities," at the same time no foreigner could leave Saigon and surrounding areas without a special permit from the revolutionary authorities.[69]

For 18 May 1975 Brother Andrew recorded the following in his journal:

> After Mass it struck me that maybe the form of government a people has is not the most important thing. Maybe, like suffering in human life, it shows there is something beyond — the great Beyond that calls us from within. Under any form of government, people live out their lives with great joys and great tragedies. They have their insoluble pains and sufferings — whatever the government. These are not taken away in Christ, but they are given a life-giving, redemptive value.
>
> Here people will go on living their lives. They will have their pain as before. But they will live and breathe. And the Spirit of God will be present and active.
>
> Maybe I should not be concerned about the form of government or party that rules wherever I am. There is something more radical. The form of government touches the surface of people's lives, but there is something deeper, where God comes into peoples' lives.
>
> Every day they will go on living, they will have to work, they will have something to eat, their minds and their children's minds will be influenced by the culture around them. For me it may be a temptation to think of coming out of this with a message about the political or economic conditions. This is in the realm of accidentals.
>
> What is the message? See how people must go on living their lives, facing the new events and circumstances that come to them. They will only be able to grow in real life through how they accept these things. Reflecting on the tragedy in human lives: the refugees fleeing in terror, the separations, rockets, corruption, ruthless advance, wounded, broken

lives, as well as what is to follow... Does it not all point to the great need of redemption, of a very deep liberation? The Message speaks as much to one single, broken or unfree life, as to the many. IT TELLS THE GOOD NEWS OF THE SECRET OF GOD'S LOVE IN CHRIST. How can we help suffering to come to Easter, to new life—to become redemptive, liberating, life-giving? It involves a looking beyond the personal sufferings, the suffering of a people.[70]

Taking advantage of a reporter who was leaving Saigon, two days later he wrote a letter to the Brothers in India and a similar one to his family addressed to his sister, Mary Ennis:

Dear Mary & All,

Well here we are again — it feels like 5 years since I wrote. I am safe and well and surely it is all the prayers that have done the trick. I have thought about you all so often and could imagine you worrying, and lots of people asking. I do hope you are all well.

There has been no way of writing. Still no letters can go and a reporter is taking this — he hopes to leave tomorrow on the first plane. He very decently arranged a news item through Reuters which may get in the media in Australia.

It has all been a tremendous experience and it is good that I stayed for many reasons. All the Houses are still open and able to help many people — and still are. I've had my moments, and I think I'll take the tight-rope act in the circus later, but there is no danger any more. The poor people have been marvellous and they have taken care of me.

Everything is very uncertain — it is a totally different country now. I don't know how long I shall be here, it depends entirely on the government. At present there are no planes or ships out. I don't know if I'll be able to get money. Don't send until you hear.

The problem is if I leave I won't be able to return and that's the end. At the same time there are difficulties in India, and

Interlude – I: The Vietnam – Cambodia Period (1973-1975)

I should visit there, but at the moment there is no possibility of going anywhere — so that settles that. It will all work out. It has all done up to now in a most unexpectedly wonderful way, and it looks as if God has something going. He must surely want me still in business because I could have sold out many times and in a great variety of ways in the past months.

The hard thing is not being able to plan future moves. I miss having the open road in front of me — I don't think I'll ever be able to sit still again for five minutes — but that will pass.

There have been so many very beautiful moments even though it has been and still is such a hard time for the people. The new government has a lot to do organising itself, and it's too soon to say how things will eventuate. Everyone is sitting and waiting and living on whatever they have with them. It's important in such circumstances to remain open to whatever opportunities arise and wait for the chips to fall. If God has something for me here for the future He will show it in the fall of events, so pray for the gift of patience for me.

We've had all five babies born in the last month and they are all well, but it was worrying for the mothers. I saw Fr Dargan and he is well, and will leave as soon as there is a plane or ship. The other Jesuits are well but share in the great uncertainty. It's hard to imagine the total change in everything — it's as if the Americans were never here. If you can write through the ordinary mail do not make any reference to the government or conditions here. I do not know when the mail will open up.

It seems there are 3 Australians in Saigon, the newsman has been very decent to me. The real story has not yet come out and by the time it can probably no-one will be interested any more. It has been an unbelievable experience living through it all and I don't think I'll ever be the same again — I don't think I could ever see anything as being very permanent again. It was something to see the final evacuation, the helicopters coming in and going out all the afternoon, and the feeling of knowing that was the last way out.

And then the next day to see the North Vietnamese tanks and armoured cars racing along the road from our terrace, in all the uncertainty of not knowing how they would act. Well each plane came and we survived. My God, survival can be a miracle. You go to bed at night and you thank God that you've survived that day, and you wonder if you'll survive the night and the rockets, and the same thing over again in the morning. Happily there were not too many days like that, and you could finally say that you've survived, but though there were only a few days like that they seemed like years. Thank God there was no prolonged battle for the city, one is so helpless in a crowded city. There's nowhere to run, and it's best to stay right home. I used to look at those few-day-old babies sleeping so peacefully when the rockets were coming, and it was good to contemplate.

If I do have to leave I'll go to Calcutta and see things there where they are having difficulties — there's a lot waiting. There are 4 of the men who were here with me and they can only stay in India for a few months visa, and then we'll have to start somewhere else. I have a feeling I'll be going through the whole wonderful, but nightmare of a story somewhere else [another] day.

All for now, love to you all. The thought of you all and your prayers has been a very great support and consolation.

Love and prayers,
Andrew.[71]

By 24 May 1975, Andrew was distressed. In his journal he wrote: "It is clear that the new government will not allow me to stay or the houses to continue. It's a hard thing to walk out of a house that

Interlude – I: The Vietnam – Cambodia Period (1973-1975)

you've loved, and leave everything and everyone forever."[72] It seems that around this time, Brother Andrew sent his journal about Saigon to Brother Nicholas, OCSO, for safe-keeping. On 30 May Brother Nicholas wrote to Brothers Jeremy (John) and Gordon in India: "Father Andrew's journal is a spiritual one. Of course, there is so much about the work. He said he wanted me to read it, but I've only read about a quarter. He said I should communicate his decision to remain in Vietnam to his friends. I hope to get a letter out this week now that we know he's there & alive. His sister wrote me that a communication was in the Australian papers that on 23 May he was listed as alive & well. More later. Love and prayers always. Nick."[73] (What happened to this journal? It remains a mystery. One possibility is that Brother Nicholas returned it to Andrew once he was in a more stable community.)

Sadness, insecurity and uncertainty about what was God's plan for him are echoed in the entry for 1 June 1975. Leaving was already a fact. There were no doubts about that. The only thing unsure was the "when":

> A wet, quiet Sunday afternoon at Cong Quynh. One month has passed since liberation, and today begins a new week and a new month. My position and that of the people in the house is a strange temporary thing. Life goes on fairly normally, but it can't last. Government policy has not been stated and the money will run out. One thing: we have continued through May — and that is a big and surprising thing. It is your Providence, Lord.
>
> WHAT IS THE CALL NOW? A month ago it was to keep things going and remain open to developments. What is it You ask now? The same I suppose. But is there something more?
>
> Should I be trying to arrange for the people? And yet none of them has anywhere to go or any resources. No group is open to take anyone — not even any Sisters or Caritas. I suppose we continue while there are resources, and trust in Your loving Providence to care for these people (the widows, children, etc.) at your radical level of divine

love and their eternal welfare. (The lot of many of those who fled the country, those who died on the road or in boats, those hopelessly separated from loved ones across national borders and curtains, people in Cambodia, India, Bangladesh.) Leads to thanks for all You have done and the hope that You will come again.

We can continue through June financially and a bit beyond. Perhaps that is far enough to look ahead — especially in these circumstances.

For my work in India with the new Brothers, I can leave that to God. It seems clear still that I STAY HERE AS LONG AS THE HOUSES CAN CONTINUE. All the other work I can entrust to Your Providence. YOUR PLAN IS SO OFTEN THE UNEXPECTED. So openness to Your coming in events.

As for all the people in the houses here, I must be thankful for all that You have done up to now. And as I contemplate the impermanence and dispersion I am forced as never before to the mystery of Your coming again.

When I go away from here with tears and sorrow, it must also be a waiting in joyful hope for the coming of Your son, our true Saviour.

At that time You will gather all together in joy and peace and love: the people of these houses, the lepers, the refugees, the Cambodians, the street boys, the bar girls, Tuyet, Kim, Loan and their babies, the old, the mental, the hunted. You will bring them all together in Your love. THIS IS THE COMPLETION OF THE MYSTERY OF SUFFERING.[74]

On 4 June he wrote a letter to the Brothers in India which he also sent to Brother Nicholas "and Friends":

It is good to be able to write to you through someone who is leaving here. The Post Office is not handling international mail.

Interlude – I: The Vietnam – Cambodia Period (1973-1975)

I am very well and things have gone far better than I imagined. There were moments, but we suffered no harm. Our three houses are open — one is a bit shaky, but nothing serious. And it has been good that we have been able to help the people thru these days. There is real need and new people are coming regularly. I don't know how long we can keep going. No prospect of being able to get money in and I have enough for a good two months. And then??? ... So I suppose it calls for waiting on God to show the opening. The new government here has a lot on its hands and hasn't got around to our people or me yet — though we have registered.

The economy is running on whatever people carried over with them from before — and of course, that is running out fast for a lot of people. And many are without work. Nothing drastic seems to have happened to people though you feel constrained in many ways. And there is the awful waiting for people as they wait for the new form of life to open up.

I am glad I stayed on for many reasons. There were some pretty frightening moments, but happily they passed fairly quickly. It has been a tremendous experience. It has been extraordinary to see such a total change of power. There is not a trace of the old order or power. And all this has been effected in a surprisingly smooth way. But it can't go on like this for too long. People will have to be given work and that will involve a lot of movement. It will mean a tremendous change for many people.

The style and behaviour of the North Vietnamese soldiers has been impressive. They are disciplined, respectful, friendly, honest, not a trace of looting. They have been amazed by the standard of life they have found in Saigon. The one big question mark is freedom. And that is the great fear already felt.

I could come out of this with lots to say on the military or political or diplomatic aspects of it all. But it seems that much more important is a reflection on the spiritual meaning of it all. There is the total collapse of tremendous military & economic might, the suffering of people, the prospect of continuing conflict that will involve the lives of many and the futility of power to solve the human problem, be that power economic, military, political....

It's nice to philosophize about, but it's hard for people. It's hard for those who need our homes. They are happy to be here now, but we all know it can't go on. And none of the 140 people has any place to go. So there is a need to trust in Providence.

Now that the excitement has died down and the thrill of having survived has died down, the waiting gets a bit dreary. But that's wrong because there is a lot happening in the houses.

It's not easy writing letters, I find. The general atmosphere makes you a little guarded in what you manifest — and though this letter will go without censorship, I feel a bit uneasy putting thoughts in writing.... But at this point what I have written is better unpublished.

...I expect to have to leave somewhere between August & Christmas. But God may have some other plan — and while I am here, it's open this side.

I remember you all in my lonely Mass here.

Love and prayers to all.
Andrew.[75]

On 14 June 1975 Brother Andrew announced to the many people staying in the Phu Lam house that it would have to close in two weeks' time. A week later, a military patrol came to 102/33 Cong Quynh asking such questions as, "Where does the money come from?" and "Why is Brother Andrew doing this work?" On 26 June Brother Andrew was arrested in the street and held for interrogation for a couple of hours, during which he was asked for the information on the registration form that he, as a foreigner, had

Interlude – I: The Vietnam – Cambodia Period (1973-1975)

to carry with him but which he sometimes failed to do. Knowing that his departure must be imminent, on 27 June 1975 he went to the immigration office to apply for his exit visa. He tried to be careful to avoid being picked up again. Neil Frame, a journalist from Los Angeles, described in what circumstances he came to know Andrew in Saigon:

> I met him in Vietnam in the summer of 1974. He and Brother Jeremy came to the office of an American friend of mine, Dick Hughes, who founded a project for street children in Saigon and Danang called the "Shoeshine Boys Project." Dick was an actor who decided to go to Vietnam on his own to see how he could do humanitarian work. The Missionaries of Charity Brothers were working with the poor not far from Dick's office. Jeremy either heard about Dick from a hometown newspaper (Pittsburgh, Pennsylvania), where Dick was also from, or from his work with the bui doi (dust of life) boys. Dick initially went to Vietnam around 1968-69 as a journalist and left about a year-and-a-half after the 1975 communist takeover. It was in this period that Dick had more contact with Andrew, who also decided to stay. The new government pretty much left them alone. However, Andrew apparently had a penchant for not carrying his government identification and was marched at gunpoint to the local police station, which was in the same building as Dick's office on Vo Thanh St., across from a Catholic church in downtown Saigon. As Dick usually left his door open, a few times Andrew would wave to him and joke about leaving his papers at home... again... as he walked by, hands over his head. It was not a tense situation, more like a running joke with them.[76]

Things were becoming more restrictive, however. On 28 June a Communist officer came to the Cong Quynh house with several soldiers and asked the people in the house about Brother Andrew. The officer told one old woman who had often been the cause of trouble there that what Brother Andrew was doing might appear good on the outside but on the inside he was evil. "You can do what you want with me," the woman retorted, "but I say he's good on the inside too." The officer informed Brother Andrew that the new government would take care of the people but that he could stay at the house until his plane left. A month passed, and Brother Andrew had no more contact with the house in Khanh Hoi, but then there were only three women and their children left by this time.

On 10 July an important statement was issued concerning foreigners' possessions in general:

- every foreigner authorized to leave the Republic of South Vietnam must obey the laws and policies of the PRG (Provisional Revolutionary Government) if he wants to take objects in his possession with him;
- foreigners are forbidden to sell, give, or otherwise transfer personal property or real estate in their possession, if this disturbs order and public safety;
- in order to protect the legitimate rights of the state and people, every Vietnamese citizen must have special permission from the proper authority to receive, in the form of a transfer or gift or simply to manage, buildings, land and any other kind of real estate or personal property belonging to persons of foreign nationalities.[77]

By 29 July 1975, although Andrew had not been expelled from the country, the houses had all been taken over by the government and soldiers had moved in. Moreover, he had not received permission to start any new work. All his Vietnamese money had been given out to the people in the house before they were forced to leave. He had burned all his travellers cheques because the government was collecting all currency at the airport, and closed the Cong Quynh house, turning over the keys to a Communist officer. Brother Andrew found temporary refuge with the Jesuits, but this was risky for them since he was not registered with the government to be in their house.

Interlude – I: The Vietnam – Cambodia Period (1973-1975)

Ba Kim returned to Vung Tau. Of all the leave-takings this was the most painful for Brother Andrew. Fr John Boyd-Turner recalled his visit to Saigon and the relationship between Andrew and Kim in particular:

> I stayed with Andrew twice, in the house in Saigon. I came from Bangkok, got there about 10.30 at night. Andrew was in his sleeping bag on the floor on the third floor of the house and he gave me a sleeping bag and he went to sleep on the veranda. So I am resting there, and then this Vietnamese lady around thirty came. Andrew was sleeping on the floor with a pillow. She just sat, and they talked together. I'm not sure which language it was. And then there was silence and she was just sitting there with him, clearly a great love was flowing between them, which was delightful. It was one of those rare occasion where you'd see *cor ad cor loquitor* two hearts talking. That was about some months before the April 75 when the whole thing changed.[78]

Andrew's family members were worried, and it was a relief for them when they knew that he had been granted an exit visa out of Saigon. On 18 August Mary Ennis wrote to Brother Nicholas:

> Dear Nick,
>
> I have been waiting all this time to answer your letter in case I had further news for you of Andrew, but the weeks just passed and grew into over two months of complete silence — then about a week ago I got a phone call from a Mr Dagg, who was the only other Australian left in Saigon as well as Andrew, to say that he had just flown in from Saigon. He and Andrew had been granted exit visas, and his turn had come up first and he was flown out through Laos to Bangkok by the V.C.s. He said there were only about two planes a week being allowed to fly out and Andrew had to go to the authorities every day to see if his name was on the board and when it was he would be flown out at once. Mr Dagg said it would probably be in a few weeks, but he

couldn't say. He said the V.C.s were phasing out Andrew's people, and that Andrew could see the way things were going and that there would be nothing for him to do, so he has closed his houses....

In the meantime, it is absolutely wonderful to know he is all right and will be out before too long. I know how very sad he will be about having to leave there, but he has done good whilst he was there, and that is everything, isn't it Nick? I believe he is well, but don't know what his plans are. We hope he will come home first for a rest before he starts off again, but will have to be patient and wait and see. I am sorry for being longwinded, but I had nothing to tell you, and hope this makes you happy. Brother Ferdinand told me that four Americans have gone to USA on Andrew's instructions, and hope all is well with them...

love,

Mary Ennis.[79]

LAST NIGHT IN SAIGON

19 August 1975 was to be Andrew's last night in Saigon. He struggled to describe the pain felt:

> Then twilight in the coconut trees on my last night in Vietnam. I remembered Jesus' last night (I so different), but I can make the same prayer that the Spirit may come and be with these people. I felt the enormity of this final separation. I can't grasp it. My tears catch it a little. But the terrible finality of it. What are these people left to? And we'll never know. Strange that there should be a full moon tonight. When I put the light out before sleeping, I looked out into the night and said farewell to all in Saigon, in Vietnam, to the people so dispersed — and asked God to be with them, to give them life.
>
> And I thanked God.[80]

Interlude – I: The Vietnam – Cambodia Period (1973-1975)

Brother Andrew left Saigon on 20 August for Bangkok. His intention was to stay with the Jesuits there for a few days to recuperate and also regain communication with his family, Brothers and friends. He was in need of foreign money, but encountered difficulty in getting his travellers cheques reissued.

The first person Brother Andrew wrote to was former Brother Leon:

NEW FUJI, 299
SURIWONG ROAD,
BANGKOK, Thailand
23.8.75

Dear Leon,

Here we are again, and now it's all over for us in VN. I shouldn't be writing letters yet. It is all so terribly heart-breaking.

It was possible to keep the houses going for a while, but one by one they were confiscated and all are now barracks for North Vietnamese soldiers. And the people are dispersed. Some went to someone they could claim in the country — some have been taken to the country to start some sort of commune (incl. Tuyet) and some ? ? 102/33 held out till the end of July. Then I was out. They took me in (courageously) at Yen Do [Jesuit community] — for a foreigner that doesn't fit is dangerous to have under the roof.

The air is oppression, fear, suspicion, resentment. The lack of freedom. I think I've learnt that hunger is not the worst thing. It is to lose freedom. The colour has gone from Saigon + the dash & the style. And the grip gets tighter & tighter.

Kim came & went to & from Vung Tau several times. She is in a terribly vulnerable position — as are so many others.

Well I shouldn't be writing letters....

Finally getting out was not easy. But there's a French plane making 5 trips a week now. The messages I've smuggled out are tragic. The man who used to sponsor our visas is having it hard, and I have to go to Hong Kong for him on Monday. It's as if we are in the James Bond business now. What else is left?

I used to ask myself if it would have been better if we'd never have gone to VN. Certainly these are terrible pages in the story. But there is a lot that has been very wonderful and I think it will last a number of lives.

102/33 was alive to the end. And it was just about the end of the lane when it closed.

When I asked Ferdinand about Brian this morning, twice he replied: "I cannot answer that. George will tell you when you come." — whatever that may mean.

Well, Leon, you surely didn't need this letter but you had to get it. I wonder how things go with you. Your name is spoken in the lane still. In fact one of the VC ladies, now on the job for the govt. was asking about you. By the way, Ba San (blind) was planted in the house to report on us. She gave a good report.

Much love and warmth, Leon.
Andrew.[81]

Another person to whom Andrew wrote was B. A. Santamaria. Patrick Morgan, in *B. A. Santamaria, Your Most Obedient Servant*, reproduced a letter from Santamaria dated 27 August 1975. In it he thanked Brother Andrew for his most welcome letter of 22 of that month. Since Santamaria had strong ties with Vietnam and its people, he was worried about the people he knew personally, among them Archbishops Van Thuan and Binh, Father Thanh, and the Buddhist leader Thich Tri Quang. According to Morgan, "Brother Andrew replied from Bangkok on 31 August that the Catholic Church in Vietnam was still functioning, although a progressive minority was active and privileged; some Jesuit priests

Interlude – I: The Vietnam – Cambodia Period (1973-1975)

had been expelled; people were being moved from Saigon into the countryside; and resistance to the regime was strong in the delta."[82]

After a few days Brother Andrew managed to get the travellers cheques reissued and was off to Hong Kong to continue "carrying out commissions for people who had done the same for him during the past months."[83] On 6 September 1975 he landed in Calcutta. "The excursion to Indo-China had ended."[84] In that year's Christmas letter written while visiting the newly founded community in Los Angeles, he described the suffering but also the beauty of what had transpired:

> I am writing after a year — a year in which so much has happened. It is Christmas again, that tremendous reminder of where our true and only hope lies — in that helpless little Babe which is how God's love & almighty power comes to us. There is no hope in anything or anyone else.
>
> This year has been heart-breaking. We lost five houses in Vietnam, and Cambodia. The buildings don't matter. But to be separated so finally from all the people that one came to know and love is so unbelievably painful. I shall never be the same again after this, and I know and hope that I shall have an ache in my heart for them till the day I die.
>
> The full story of the fall of Saigon and the change-over will never be told. The journalists who stayed on lived mostly in the downtown hotels. They did not penetrate the alleys and lanes of the overcrowded parts of the city. They did not really have the chance to share the feelings and pain of the poor and middle-class. I have not been able to recognize the feelings of the people I knew in Saigon in the reports of the media or in the general idea that people outside Vietnam have of what has been happening there.
>
> The story remains untold — and it will remain untold — perhaps until the voice of some Vietnamese Solzhenitsyn is heard. But if that ever happens, it will be after many years. As for myself, I don't have the heart to even attempt the telling.

And so Vietnam and Cambodia is a closed book for me and the Brothers. And what unfolds there in the lives of the voiceless many in the coming years will not be known to us.

When we were all finally dispersed a woman who had done much in the building up of our houses of hospitality, remarked amid all the tears, "Now we are being separated. But one day we shall all be together again." And she pointed to the heavens. In the meantime there is only love and tears and Jesus to hold us together. And that is the story of so many refugee families divided by continents.

And as I write I wonder where is that little girl who went singing down the stairs as I wrote last year's Christmas letter.

Out of the tragedy of Vietnam and Cambodia, we now have a beautiful little community of Brothers in Los Angeles working on Skid Row. They had come to be Brothers in Indo-China from America and Europe. They are a wonderful group and already penetrate the dark alleys and hotel rooms of the broken men and women swept up, it seems, by a giant broom into the Skid Row of this vast city....

Misery and joyful hope, darkness and light, painful sorrow and joy ...the strange mixture in the lives of us all.

And so we come to Christmas, the celebration of a newborn Baby, so wrinkled and red and weak. It is Jesus, God's gift of life.[85]

Interlude – I: The Vietnam – Cambodia Period (1973-1975)   235

*1. Melbourne 1972 – Br Andrew with Luca Cuni
(before his trip to Vietnam).*

2. Saigon – c. 1973 - Ba Kim with three orphaned children.

3. Saigon – Br Andrew with children at Cong Quynh.

*4. Phnom Penh - Br Andrew with CRS workers,
MC Brothers and Bishop Ramousse (4th from left).*

Interlude – I: The Vietnam – Cambodia Period (1973-1975)

5. *Los Angeles October 1973. Br Andrew and Mother Teresa at Maryvale (courtesy Sr Estela Morales DC).*

6. *Saigon 1975 – Andrew, Gordon and Anton (standing) Jeremy and Michael (kneeling).*

Endnotes:

1. 20120902 Email Jeremy Hollinger.
2. 19991024 Brother Andrew "Night Points," Kalyani (Calcutta): Unpublished Source 1999.
3. Deakin, Hilton, with Jim and Therese D'Orsa, *Bonded Through Tragedy, United in Hope: The Catholic Church and East Timor's Struggle for Independence. A Memoir*, Victoria, Australia: Garratt Publishing, 2017.
4. All this media coverage would later have a negative impact on Australians when news of Diem's autocratic style and religious bias with policies favouring the Catholic Church such as military and civil services promotions for Roman Catholics and the restriction of the construction of Buddhist temples, became known. The Buddhist crisis escalated in 1963 with the iconic self-immolation of Thich Quang Duc —a Buddhist monk — on a busy Saigon road.
5. In 1967, Van Thuan was appointed bishop in Nha Trang, and six days before the fall of Saigon on 24 April 1975 he became the co-adjutor archbishop of Saigon. When the Communists arrived, he was told to return to Nha Trang. He refused and was arrested. His mother — Diem's sister — had managed to escape to Australia. After 13 years in a re-education camp, nine of them in solitary confinement, he was released in 1988 and allowed to visit his parents in Australia. In 2001 he was made cardinal and died a year later. He was named Venerable in 2017 by Pope Francis.
6. We do not know whether Brother Andrew was aware of who Victor Zorza was. Born Israel Wermuth in 1925 and Polish by birth, he was a journalist who, after spending time in Soviet work camps, helped the West to better understanding of the Soviet Union. After evacuation to the United Kingdom he joined the British Broadcasting Corporation (BBC). In 1977 his daughter Jane died of cancer, aged 25. In an earlier visit to India, Jane had challenged her father to leave the world of international relations and draw attention to the struggles of the poor in the developing world. He left everything and moved to a remote village — Lakhamandal — in Northern India while writing a regular column in The Guardian. He died in 1996.
7. Brother Gordon, MC, "Missionaries of Charity — Journal," Los Angeles: Unpublished Source, 1978.
8. 19730213 LG.
9. Brother Gordon, MC, "Missionaries of Charity — Journal," Los Angeles: Unpublished Source, 1978.
10. Solomon, Geoff D., *Brothers of Mother Teresa*, Homebush NSW: St. Paul Publications, 1987.
11. Val Noone was a priest of the Melbourne Archdiocese who was laicised in 1974 and married Mary Doyle. They live in Fitzroy, Melbourne.
12. 19730323 LF to Val Noone.

Interlude – I: The Vietnam – Cambodia Period (1973-1975)

13. Solomon, Geoffrey D., *Brothers of Mother Teresa,* Homebush NSW: St Paul Publications, 1987. (Unfortunately some of the original letters to his sister no longer exist, but thanks to Solomon who reproduced some of them, we still have copies.)
14. Brother Gordon, MC, "Missionaries of Charity — Journal," Los Angeles: Unpublished Source, 1978.
15. 20190315 IF Don Cowan; Fr Don Cowan, (1936 Australia) was a priest of the Anglican Communion. He was received into the full communion of the Catholic Church in 1997 and has been based in New Zealand since 1975.
16. 19730611 LF Margaret Ryan, RSM, quoted from a letter to Br Geoff Brown, MC. 20001105.
17. Brother Gordon, MC, "Missionaries of Charity — Journal," Los Angeles: Unpublished Source, 1978.
18. Caritas shares the mission of the Catholic Church to serve the poor and to promote charity and justice throughout the world.
19. Solomon, Geoffrey D., *Brothers of Mother Teresa,* Homebush NSW: St Paul Publications, 1987.
20. Brother Gordon, MC, "Missionaries of Charity — Journal," Los Angeles: Unpublished Source, 1978.
21. Ibid.
22. Ibid.
23. 19730800 LP.
24. Ibid.
25. Ibid.
26. Ibid.
27. Lloyd Tevis, (1920 – 1990). An American law professor at the Jesuit Loyola University, he married Grace in 1945. (1921 - 2016);
Fr Don Kribs, (1934 – 2015). Born in America, he was ordained priest in 1961. Meeting Mother Teresa in 1975 changed his life. He accepted the position of vice-chair of the Co-Workers of Mother Teresa and represented her in the Western region of the US. He devoted the remainder of his life to the sick poor, working on Skid Row in downtown Los Angeles, while serving as Catholic chaplain at LA County hospitals. His presence at the beginning of the MC Brothers' Los Angeles community would be invaluable.
28. 20190806 Email Estela Morales, DC.
29. Brother Gordon, MC, "Missionaries of Charity — Journal," Los Angeles: Unpublished Source, 1978.
30. John Hollinger eventually joined the Brothers in Saigon in June 1974, taking the name of Jeremy.
31. In 1960, after reading about Mother Teresa and the poor in Calcutta, Patricia

Kump decided to write to her. That was the first of hundreds of letters they exchanged and sparked a friendship of more than thirty years. After meeting Mother Teresa, Patricia Kump established the U.S. Chapter of the Co-Workers of Mother Teresa. She died on 8 March 2009.

[32] 20201130 Email Gary Richardson; Gary Richardson helped start the new MC community in Cambodia in March 1974 and subsequently those in the United States and Central America.

[33] 19740205 LB to Gary Richardson.

[34] CRS — Catholic Relief Services was founded in 1943 by the Catholic bishops of the United States to serve World War II survivors in Europe. It expanded across all the continents. Working in the spirit of Catholic social teaching to promote the sacredness of human life and the dignity of the human person, regardless of race, religion, or ethnicity, its mission has always been to assist impoverished and disadvantaged people.

[35] 19740212 LF Margaret Ryan, RSM, quoted from a letter to Br Geoff Brown, MC 20001105.

[36] Brother Gordon, MC, "Missionaries of Charity — Journal," Los Angeles: Unpublished Source, 1978.

[37] Solomon, Geoffrey D., *Brothers of Mother Teresa*, Homebush NSW: St Paul Publications, 1987.

[38] 19740400 LP news from Saigon.

[39] 20190831 Email Joel Blondiaux; Joel Blondiaux, M.D. Ph.D., works as a medical doctor in France. His ending up in Cambodia was nothing short of serendipitous. While living in Calcutta as a young Taizé Brother (cf. endnote 161). Brother and doctor, he worked in the Kalighat Home for the Dying. Most of those admitted to Kalighat having tuberculosis, he wanted to give them sputum exams, radiographs, and proper treatment, and medicine. After some incomprehension between Mother Teresa and him, Mother Teresa decided not to support his visa extension and asked Brother Roger, Prior of Taizé for Brother Joel to be sent to Cambodia where Brother Andrew had started a new foundation. Reluctantly Joel went.

[40] 19740400 LP News from Saigon.

[41] Brother Gordon, MC, "Missionaries of Charity — Journal," Los Angeles: Unpublished Source, 1978.

[42] Brother Gordon, MC, "Missionaries of Charity — Journal," Los Angeles: Unpublished Source, 1978; Fr John Harte, is an Australian Jesuit and companion of Brother Andrew since their novitiate. At the time of the writing, he resides at Campion Hall, Melbourne, Australia.

[43] Brother Gordon, MC, "Missionaries of Charity — Journal," Los Angeles: Unpublished Source, 1978.

[44] 20190314 IB Anton van Don, MC.

Interlude – I: The Vietnam – Cambodia Period (1973-1975)

45 20120902 Email Jeremy Hollinger.
46 Solomon, Geoffrey D., *Brothers of Mother Teresa,* Homebush NSW: St Paul Publications, 1987.
47 Brother Gordon, MC, "Missionaries of Charity — Journal," Los Angeles: Unpublished Source, 1978.
48 19740923 LF Margaret Ryan, RSM, quoted from a letter to Br Geoff Brown, MC 20001105.
49 19741200 LP.
50 Ibid.
51 20190314 IB Anton van Don, MC.
52 Brother Gordon, MC, "Missionaries of Charity — Journal," Los Angeles: Unpublished Source, 1978.
53 Ibid.
54 Ibid.
55 20190314 IB Anton van Don, MC.
56 Ibid.
57 Ibid.
58 19750321 LR to Mary Ennis.
59 19750328 LJ to Patrick O'Sullivan, SJ.
60 This statuette was with Andrew until his death, when it was given to Brother Geoff, MC, during his visit for Andrew's funeral. Unfortunately, Brother Geoff lost it. On 1 November 2020 while the author was making an inventory of all Brother Andrew's possessions, he came across an empty black shoulder bag. Inside he saw a small, zippered compartment on the side of the lining. He opened it, and lo and behold there he found the small metal statue of St Joseph — which had been lost for more than twenty years!
61 Neak Luong, located about 61 kilometres south east of Phnom Penh on the east bank of the Mekong River was and still is at an intersection of important trade and transport since it is on 6 August 1973, the US mistakenly dropped a twenty-ton bomb load, killing about 137 Cambodians and wounding hundreds of others. This incident was depicted in the film The Killing Fields.
62 Brother Gordon, MC, "Missionaries of Charity — Journal," Los Angeles: Unpublished Source, 1978.
63 In 2012, when the local Bishop of Phnom Penh visited the MC Brothers' house in that city, he was intrigued by a photo of Brian Walch on a wall and wondered whether Brian could be added to the list of people martyred by the Khmer Rouge being prepared by the Catholic Church in Cambodia. The MC Congregation consequently researched Brian Walch's life, contact was made with his family, and after a thorough dialogue between them and the MC Congregation about Brian's intentions and reasons for staying, his name

was not put on the list. (20161029 Brian Walch by Marc Daniel Delapeyre, MC, Unpublished article on Milan).

64. Brother Gordon, MC, "Missionaries of Charity — Journal," Los Angeles: Unpublished Source, 1978.
65. Ibid.
66. Ibid.
67. 19750430 LG From a Saigon Journal.
68. Ibid.
69. Terzani, Tiziano, *Giai Phong! The Fall and Liberation of Saigon*, New York: St Martin's Press, 1976.
70. 19750430 LG From a Saigon Journal.
71. 19750522 LR to Mary and All.
72. 19750430 LG From a Saigon Journal.
73. Brother Gordon, MC, "Missionaries of Charity — Journal," Los Angeles: Unpublished Source, 1978.
74. 19750430 LG From a Saigon Journal.
75. 19750604 LB to Brothers in India as quoted in Brother Gordon, MC, "Missionaries of Charity — Journal," Los Angeles: Unpublished Source, 1978.
76. 20180521 Email Neil Frame.
77. Terzani, Tiziano, *Giai Phong! The Fall and Liberation of Saigon*, New York: St Martin's Press, 1976.
78. 20180408 IF Fr John Boyd-Turner. Fr John Boyd-Turner visited the Jesuits in India for the first time in 1964 after obtaining a degree in agriculture. He helped the Jesuits and local people by taking seeds and fertilizers to the villages to increase crop production after the great famine. In the mid-1970s he visited Andrew in Vietnam. In 2005 he was ordained a priest with the Community of Sant'Egidio. He was 77 at the time of the 2018 interview.
79. Brother Gordon, MC, "Missionaries of Charity — Journal," Los Angeles: Unpublished Source, 1978.
80. Ibid.
81. 19750823 LB to Leon Allen.
82. Morgan, Patrick ed., *B. A. Santamaria — Your Most Obedient Servant* (Selected Letters: 1938-1996). Australia: The Miegunyah Press in association with The State Library of Victoria, 2007.
83. Solomon, Geoffrey D., *Brothers of Mother Teresa*, Homebush NSW: St Paul Publications, 1987.
84. From a talk given in 1991 Br Andrew: "The house in Vietnam was in a very poor area off the main road, the people were very poor. . . . The day Saigon fell, I will never forget it, and the people were the same, they were in the streets. They had guns and revolvers and God knows what and these things

Interlude – I: The Vietnam – Cambodia Period (1973-1975)

they were being thrown over fences, they couldn't get them past. . . . And the girls with all their long hair and their fashion, and you would see afterwards all their long hair was being cut, and it was lying in the garbage in the street, free of any sign of any connection with anything. . . . There was all that fear but then the tanks came in and there was the takeover, and it was immediately clear there wasn't going to be a bloodbath, and everybody wasn't going to be rounded up and then the people who got into the American stores . . . and they got the cigarettes and Johnny Walker whisky — all this stuff was going up — and it was being sold on the black market. It was Mardi Gras really. And that went on, I stayed pretty low in those days, I was the only one who looked like an American in the home, so I stayed at home but . . . in the area everybody knew I was there, but what was interesting, it was about ten days and there was almost like a cloud came down, and here the people in the slum suddenly realised that they lost something — that they no longer had any say in where they went and what they did. I kept contact with the Jesuits who had a students' hostel and a university centre. What was interesting was, it took the poor in the slums ten days to realise they had lost their freedom, it took the students in the university three months that they had lost something — they eventually realised — they were all gung-ho on all the slogans and the liberation and then they realised too that they had lost their freedom." 1991 — Audio BP - The Noticeable Anger in the Developing World.

[85] 19751200 LP.

PART – IV

FROM GENERAL TO TROUBADOUR (1976 – 1986)

*The work of the Brothers grew and spread and it was a
tremendous joy and a most thrilling thing to be part of that.
We grew and spread throughout the world and
I even looked forward to the day when the young Brothers
would be able to take over the leadership of the Congregation.*

− BROTHER ANDREW

The year 1976 and the following decade brought many changes to Brother Andrew's life. The return from Indo-China was tinged with brokenness and pain. Noting that the Brothers in India were capable of managing without his continuous presence in and around Calcutta, he opted to make his base in Hong Kong, while at the same time, opening houses around the Far East and later on giving permissions to start communities in Latin America and Africa (not to mention nurturing the continued growth in India). Two major events during these years were the starting of the Chain of Charity and Little Nest in South Korea, and the publication of his book *What I Met Along the Way*.

He was moving from one community to another, from one country to another, always expanding the reach of the Brothers, but all at a great cost to himself. Loneliness and the increasing use of alcohol would ultimately lead to confrontation and his eventual departure from the Society.

LEAVING VIETNAM

Having to leave Vietnam — broken-hearted — was excruciating. Andrew loved the country and her people, especially the poor he was living with. Leaving them shattered him, and the fall of Saigon in particular brought about his emotional fall. "It has been an unbelievable experience living through it all and I don't think I'll ever be the same again."[1]

He did try to keep in touch through letters with Kim but after a few years received no response. As he wrote to Leon Allen:

> No news from Vietnam. I have written several times to Kim, but no reply. And I hesitate to write again for fear the arrival of these letters may be an embarrassment for her. But I'm all right flitting about and the whole deal. There's you and Kim and others who don't have the same distraction. Thank God I still have the firm faith in Good Friday leading to Easter. Without that I couldn't go on.[2]

Around the same time, Andrew received news from Nguyen Minh Loan, a young girl living in Cong Quynh. Loan had been raped and had given birth to a child after the fall of Saigon. Distress runs through her letter: "Father! In the present, my life is as the same as the one when I lived with you at Cong Quynh in Vietnam, but many times, getting troubles more and more ... Father, writing this, I feel very hurt, I do not know how to express to you to understand my life, but I hope you do, you know now how my life is! So I need not to let you know more ... Thuy my daughter is getting 2 years old. She is cute and lovely more than the other children at the Cong Quynh."[3]

Twelve years passed and a memory impelled Andrew to write again to Leon:

> It was not your letter but an amazing memory a few nights ago that moves me to write. Do you remember in Cong Quynh a woman who lived a few doors up the lane with 3 or 4 children who came for meals to our place? None of them stayed with us. Well on the night of Saigon's capture her husband came in to see me. He'd been a deserter or objector or something and had to stay in hiding. He simply said, "Thank you for feeding my family. If I'd had to go out of hiding, I'd have been killed." So there's a few gems in the slops. Amazing that the memory came to me.[4]

It is as if Leon were the only one who would and could understand what they both went through in Vietnam.

Part – IV: From General to Troubadour (1976 – 1986)

OPENING OF HOUSES

This stage in Brother Andrew's life was marked by an exponential growth in communities. At the beginning of 1976 the Congregation had fourteen houses, while by 1986 there were over ninety communities. In a letter to Leon Allen, he admitted, "The stupidest thing is opening new houses — it's all so terrible, but someone seems to want it."[5] Did he really think it was the stupidest thing to do? Who was the "someone" — himself, Brothers or God?

It is also fair to say that the Brothers — both Indian and non-Indian — were enthusiastic and ready to go to great lengths, and at the same time deeply touched by Andrew's trust in them. Marcos Antonio Sutuj Boc, MC, from Guatemala recounted the beginnings of the community of Las Escobas, Guatemala, where the Brothers had to start their four-hour walk downhill in the middle of the night in order to be able to catch the only pick-up truck to take them to the city and from there to buy their supplies for the month.[6] James Besra, MC, recalled the day Brother Andrew sent him together with two young Brothers to start a village community anywhere around the States of Orissa and Bihar.[7] No planning was done. "Andrew told us to go and start a village community anywhere. The instruction was not to disturb the Religious or priests who were already living in the area, to go on our own where God wanted us to go and start there. He blessed us and he gave us the Eucharist in a container. We moved to two villages, Pakur and Sahibganj. I was only twenty-two or twenty-four years old that time. Dilip was my age and Barnabas was between twenty-five and thirty years old. But both were juniors to me in vows. But since Barnabas was the eldest in age he was our superior. So when we came to a good place, we built a bamboo and grass roof house and slept on the floor on a mattress. When Brother Andrew came to visit us, he was very happy with us. He had great trust in us."[8] Afterwards Andrew wrote:

> You may have heard that last June we formed a community to work in the remote and interior villages among the Santal Tribals. The Brothers went around for over two

months and finally have a small place among the people. They aim at living with the people, being present with them, without having any big institutional type of work. They gather the children, bathe them, have some class, do a little medical work as they visit the families, they quietly help a needy family here and there. They have had all kinds of experiences.

They have had the experience of being rejected by both extremes of the rich people and the Marxists. They have met with superstitious fears, etc. But slowly they are being accepted by the people they live with. Their housing and food and living style are very simple. And the three Brothers are keen to continue this work. It is truly work with the poorest of the poor in the villages. I am interested to know if other bros [Brothers] are interested in similar communities and work. If so please send me your name.[9]

At the beginning of 1982 he reported to Peter Murmu:

I have been all around Latin America (Brazil, Guatemala, El Salvador, Haiti, Dominican Republic — before all that France). It is an enormous trip. And I am glad to be staying here in L.A. for 4 weeks without a plane ride. Tomorrow I am going to a Benedictine Monastery for my own retreat. I leave here on 20th March for Tokyo. [One Brother] makes his first vows on 22nd March. And I'll go to Korea on 26th March.
Andrew
P.S. I'll be in Calcutta early May.[10]

At this point it is worth mentioning Andrew's meeting with Msgr Oscar Romero, Archbishop of El Salvador, even though it definitely took place prior to the writing of the above-mentioned letter. Andrew gave the date 23 September but no year.[11]

At my last meeting with Archbishop Oscar Romero who was soon after shot down at Mass in El Salvador, I rather clumsily praised him for his courageous stand. He replied: "It's not me. It's the prayers of lowly people who make the pastor."[12]

Part – IV: From General to Troubadour (1976 – 1986)

It is interesting that he remembered Archbishop Romero's words because often he did not recall what was said at a meeting but rather the impact made on him when a person started talking.[13]

Andrew went or sent Brothers to a country or place to "open a house, a community" and not to "found a community". Founding gives the impression of setting up something with a very solid, permanent base. Andrew wanted to open a community of Brothers who were simultaneously open to the community of people around. He wanted a small, discreet group of Brothers who would respect the culture and traditions of the natives, and not be a threat to their stability. He preferred the culture of the local people to seep into the MC culture as much as possible, without losing the spirit of a religious community.

Los Angeles

By November 1975 the American Brothers who had been evacuated from Vietnam and Cambodia had already established a community in downtown Los Angeles.[14] From the start Andrew liked the less-structured setting of Los Angeles, maybe because it reminded him of the setting of the houses in Saigon.

Perhaps it was because the Brothers in the United States were better at archiving and keeping the correspondence that Andrew used to send to those communities, but the number of letters that still exist from those early years is amazing. It could also be that Andrew was happy with the way things were moving in Los Angeles (and later in Santa Ana). With the Brothers in Los Angeles he could be himself with no titles attached. He was "Andrew" for them and not "Father Andrew", and that was something he liked and he enjoyed.

> It is good to think of you as I write this — and to thank you for all the love you gave me these two months and for all your goodness.[15]

After just two weeks he wrote to them again:

> I think of you all a lot. I think of you often ... It will be good to get news of you all. It seems years since I left — and it's only 17 days ... It is good just to think of you all.[16]
>
> It was a strange visit with you due to events, but it had its own beauty. You are all a very wonderful group of men. My great regret is not to have gone to Sta. Ana.[17]

When a new group of come-and-sees joined the community he took the time to write them a long letter, welcoming them to the MCs and informing them how much the Congregation, the poor, the Church and the world needed them. He ended by telling them:

> These are tremendous days in L.A. I would love to be with you for it all. But I guess God feels He doesn't need me there. So brothers, again I sincerely welcome you — and those who will follow you soon. And I thank God for each one of you. Pray much and realise that it is all God's work. It is his plan, His future and the "doing" must really be His — or it is nothing. Part of me is with you.[18]

After less than a month he again wrote to the community: "I pray for you all & think of you — and feel the loss of being separated. But we are together."[19]

When in April 1976 he was on vacation in Australia, "I do think of you all often and pray for you. I'd rather be in LA than here."[20] While in Seoul, South Korea trying to open a house there, he penned the following: "I am beginning to look forward to being with you in L.A. In fact, I'd like to come right now."[21]

But then, all this praising and wanting to be with them is quite baffling because at the same time to former Brother Leon Allen he wrote, "L.A. (sorry Los Angeles) is promising. But there's nothing to it — and they drive each other mad in their little wooden semi-detached."[22] By 1979 the Brothers in Los Angeles were feeling the need to be able to verbalise the scope and nature of their work with the poorest as different from work in the Indian context. The L.A. group also began asking for a decentralisation process in the Congregation.[23] It is a little difficult to understand what the North American Brothers meant by decentralisation when the Generalate

Part – IV: From General to Troubadour (1976 – 1986)

was in Calcutta run by the Vicar, while the General Servant was based in Hong Kong but travelling all over the globe.

As early as 1979, Brother Andrew perceived the dangers that a religious community in a city like Los Angeles could face. It was then that he wrote to all the Brothers in the United States about the dangers of rushing and individualism in community life. He also questioned some of the new trends and secular fashions being adopted by Religious and priests, and warned the Brothers not to fall into such tendencies:

> This has happened before: a letter to the communities in the U.S. Unfortunately, I don't have a copy of that letter, for I feel that I am going to say something similar again. That letter was a 'slow-down' letter, and it was written because I felt that I'd picked up from letters an excessive rushing at things and work in particular. Well, whether I was right or wrong that time, I get the same sort of vibes at this time. So here goes again.
>
> Actually that opening paragraph just about says all that I need to say. Maybe you need to be reminded that you do live in one of the crazier, chaotic sectors of the world in L.A. It is a frenetic sort of place by anyone's standards. Of the places I visit, the only city that comes near it is Hong Kong. And unfortunately, here no one even realises it. But being 'in it' as you are, does create the danger of your breathing the air so long that you don't notice it so much.
>
> In the midst of the rush, chaos and 'anything goes' sort of situation, it seems important that there are men who are sufficiently out of it to be able to be a little centre of sanity and peace. If we are rushing about at the same crazy pace as the others, then there is not too much need for us …
>
> We must remember who we are, what we are and where we come from? I think the answers to these questions would have Missionaries of Charity and Mother Teresa in big letters. I know I've done all sorts of things with those two

answers. And it's been coming home to me as we prepare for the G.C. [General Chapter] that we have to stick by what we are. Or else we become 250 different societies ...

Very much at the heart of the MC growth and witness is a discipline that is certainly not the spirit of the world today, certainly not the spirit of L.A., and I'd say certainly not the spirit of a large and very vocal sector of the Church today in the U.S. and Europe.

I ask myself more and more these days: Have the losses that resulted from priests & Religious lining up with the fashionable opinions of the secular world in recent times been justified?

In going along with the permissiveness, the liberality, the subjective conscience-making of our times, have we not fashioned a God of our own making, that is now lashing out in all directions, including our house with a terrible destructiveness?

I fear that we may allow the destruction of our own MC if we follow that path. It is not that path that has built us up for better or for worse.[24]

Former Brother Jeremy wrote, "There is a wonderful irony in the way Andrew would castigate the Western Brothers for being too individualistic, and not as communal as he perceived the Indian and other Third World cultures. There was much truth in that, we could never be the simple Brothers he extolled in talks. The irony being, that is what Andrew was also. He could not be that [communal] and his very Jesuit training and education made that even more pronounced. Jesuits were not naturally communal, but intellectuals and individualists, the very thing he did not want us to be."[25]

It was also during the late 1970s that Brother Sebastian Vazhakala was sent to Los Angeles to be the first novice master. "He had been the novice master in Calcutta, a priest who had very definite ideas about MC spirituality, religious life, discipline that seemed more attuned to the MC Sisters and Mother than to even

Part – IV: From General to Troubadour (1976 – 1986)

what the Brothers in India lived. So he was now thrown into Los Angeles. Added to that was the fact that five of us who formed the first professed Brothers there, all came out of Indochina and the experience of Andrew and MC there. For two years we all tried to make it work but there was constant friction in the community."[26] Ultimately Brother Sebastian left the Brothers to start the Missionaries of Charity Contemplative Brothers.[27]

Tensions between some of the Brothers in Los Angeles and Brother Andrew worsened in the 1980s. Most probably the situation should be considered in the "context of the larger issues taking place". Former Brother Jeremy continued:

> Brother Sebastian and his new Congregation, in alignment with some MC Sisters like Sister Priscilla and Sister Frederick, really wanted the Brothers to be more like the Sisters. I would go as far as to say, they wanted to take MC Brothers back into a hard-line pre-Vatican II form of life, prayer, and spirituality. Sister Priscilla had been the Regional Superior in New York for many years, and her contempt for the Brothers was well known. Then with Brother Sebastian's group, and some of our Brothers going to be with him and then the founding of the Missionary Fathers of Charity [in 1984] also, perhaps one can see how the Brothers in Los Angeles were identified as the "unfaithful ones," the ones who did not have Mother's spirit, etc."[28]

Some of the Brothers in the United States at that time felt that even Andrew was now moving towards that more restrictive way. By the mid-1980s the situation between Andrew and some of the Brothers in L.A. had deteriorated further and this disharmony "served" also as a prelude to what transpired in the General Chapter of 1986 and subsequent events.

Hong Kong

As early as 1967 the idea of starting an MC community in Hong Kong had already been on Andrew's agenda after a visiting priest stayed in Mansatala. So when in 1976 the first effort to start a community in Taiwan failed, he looked again to Hong Kong. After more than a month in Los Angeles and a few days with Brother Nicholas at his Abbey in Utah, he was back in Calcutta for just three weeks, during which he managed to spend a few hours with Mother Teresa at Mother House:

> After the meeting I was telling Mother how stretched we are. She said I have been asking the Sisters, to find me 3 professed Sisters for two days for some place — and they haven't found them yet. She was saying, we must let ourselves be pulled like this now. This is the time God is asking the MCs to go into new places. In 10 years, she said, He may have someone else for the work. But now He is asking us. She said there's so much new life in places where just 4 Sisters or Brothers are. And this is true. We have enormous weaknesses and things going wrong. But there is this amazing coming to God through the MCs. But it is all terribly exhausting and you can't help quaking. But we can really go ahead with a lot of confidence.[29]

He was coincidentally to meet Mother again in the airport on 18 February 1976, the day he was leaving for Bangkok. Their meeting was different but intense:

> This letter mentions our weakness. It has grown on me more in the last few weeks. This seems to be a growing mark of the MCs — this terrifying awareness of our own shakiness. As I was leaving the airport for Bangkok, Mother Teresa was leaving for an internal flight — as we parted we were both almost shaking. I could feel in her as we took each other's hands and in her urgent pressing plea for prayers that she feels even more terribly the same fragility of it all.[30]

Of the Brothers who were close to him at that time, all seem to agree on the reason for opening houses in that part of the world. Brother Andrew's ultimate aim was easy access to China once

Part – IV: From General to Troubadour (1976 – 1986)

Communism fell. Thus he aimed for Taiwan, Korea and Japan. On 28 February 1976, he wrote to the Brothers in L.A. sounding optimistic and enthusiastic. For Andrew, this was the *kairos* — the time of God: "I felt God almost shouting that we should start there." His excitement was palpable. He experienced the waiting as painful even though he knew that something good would ultimately come:

> These days are rich & full & thrilling. But there are the many days of dull waiting for us all when nothing seems to be happening and we are just painfully waiting. But the waiting times are the gestation period — which are more significant even than the unfolding.[31]

Andrew was impressed by the beauty of the Far East countries he had visited but above all appreciative and overwhelmed by the welcome he had received from Sou-Hwan Cardinal Kim of South Korea. Difficulties were many especially in the area of language. For this reason he did not envision big structures or big works. "The first work will be very small — maybe a house with about ten disabled or needy people, and at the same time a novitiate."[32] Patience was needed. He also saw the future Brothers' work as enabling a group of Chinese, Japanese and Koreans to find the spirit of the MCs, so that eventually these local Brothers would undertake the real work. Both staggering possibilities and enormous difficulties lay ahead.

After about six weeks in Australia with his family and another six in Calcutta he was off again to the Far East. The Councillors had agreed that he start communities there. As usual, before departing he wrote an encouraging but realistic letter, once more to all Brothers:

> This time I am going away at a very important time for our Society. We have grown very much. There are now 14 houses in India. And we are much stretched out. And we have many weaknesses. It is a little frightening.
>
> We have a big number of novices. And our experienced novice master is going to start a new novitiate in America.

We have young Brothers in many houses. It is a time of testing. Bro. Ferdinand has a very heavy burden.

And so Brothers, I ask you all to try very hard, and especially to help and support each other — especially your local servants. If we do this we shall be all right. Let us all support each other and try to understand the difficulties that we are all working with. Our weakness itself is our great claim on God's help, and He will help us if we turn to Him.

We are truly walking on the water like Peter. That is frightening. We must not look down at our own feet, or we shall go down in the water like Peter when he forgot Jesus. But if we keep looking to Jesus, we shall keep walking.

We also have much to be thankful for. Our Society is growing. All our houses are fruitful and much appreciated in each place.

There is one question that we have to ask ourselves, and that question is the greatest test of whether we live as real MCs. It is the following:

Can I look within myself and my community and see the real life and fruitfulness which is the presence and life and action of God within us?

If I can't see this, then it doesn't matter how much "success" or "results" there may seem to be. For that will all collapse quickly. The secret of the whole MC thing is not our cleverness or efficiency. IT IS ONE THING ALONE: GOD'S LIVING, LOVING, ACTIVE PRESENCE IN US.

We must be very watchful of our "successes". Failure is much safer in the story of Jesus. For Him success and life came out of failure and death. With Christ the world's ideas are turned upside down. And the foolishness of God becomes wiser than the wisdom of men.

And so we can go ahead with confidence. It is God's work. And He will be with us. Let us all pray for each other, especially

Part – IV: From General to Troubadour (1976 – 1986)

> for our new novices, our Vicar, our distant houses, our new novitiate in Los Angeles, our new start in the Far East.
>
> Our greatest poverty in this Society is not the food we eat or the clothes we wear. It is ourselves. We have great poverty in our General Servant, our Vicar, our Novice Master, our local Servants, our Brothers. Our poverty is deep in ourselves. But this is our greatest claim on God.
>
> Let us all pray much for each other.
>
> Love and prayers,
> Andrew.[33]

Taiwan was his first stop and from there he sent two similar letters to the group in Los Angeles and to his sister Lucy. In them he listed in order the immediate needs to start a community: "Permission of Archbishop, Visa, a Chinese helper, a house, the poor who give us life & show the way, one or two professed brothers and candidates, and above all God's grace."[34] In both letters he opened up to them about "the awful loneliness and near despair"[35] he was feeling. "It is lonely & rather desolate in a new country with the task seeming impossible at moments."[36] A few days after these letters, he confided in his friend Leon: "And how long can I go on this 'lonely trip of new starts?' But you can't stop the bloody thing. I suppose we just let it go. But it's awful at times."[37]

After a fruitless week, waiting for his permanent visa in Taiwan, he wrote:

> So I'm going from here to Hong Kong to see the chances of making our Chinese start there. I'll stay for a week. Then try to get to Taiwan on a tourist visa to collect mail and a case I foolishly left there. Then I'll go to India to visit all the distant houses. Early October I hope to go to L.A. for a month. And then I'll try to start again in Hong Kong & Korea. In the meantime we'll try for visas for Korea — which will take time.[38]

He had Brothers in India being prepared to be sent from Calcutta to Hong Kong immediately, but it was only on 27 February 1977 that the first four founding Brothers arrived in Hong Kong: one professed Brother, two novices and a Swiss candidate. They had accommodation with the Salesians in Tang King Po School in Kowloon. After a few weeks Brother Andrew found an eighth-floor apartment in crowded Mong Kok and, with the help of Swiss Co-Workers, they were able to pay the high rent typical of Hong Kong. At the same time Geoff Brown, an Australian candidate, arrived from Calcutta, but he was soon sent to help to start in Korea.

From now on Hong Kong was to be the base of operation for Brother Andrew. This had two advantages in that he could be closer to the newly-started communities in the Far East and have greater ease of movement to start new ones. Hong Kong also removed the difficulty of obtaining a more permanent visa to stay in India (see the Niyogi Report). Whether this was an excuse by Brother Andrew or embraced by him as providential in order to be outside India is not clear.[39]

It was providential that his nephew Jim, an employee of a multinational company, was living in Hong Kong with his family at that time. Uncle Ian's visits might not have been as frequent as they would have liked, but they were always pleasant, especially for the children. Jim was working hard, and so by 10 o'clock on week nights he would already be in bed, but Jim's wife, Gabrielle and Uncle Ian would stay up well into the night. Deep conversations ensued and Gabrielle would recall that as a young mother retained what he said, especially on topics like inculturation and theology. Jim believed that, "Ian was always independent. And he did what he thought was right. He wasn't really a follower of other people. He actually worked out what God wanted him to do and he did it."[40] Even though Jim considers Ian conservative in his views, he does not think that "he was caught up in laws and rules. But, he understood the spirit of God in many diverse places. He wasn't a tight Catholic, he was a man of the world, and he could see God everywhere. And it's not a theory. I thought he became more conservative at the end of his

Part – IV: From General to Troubadour (1976 – 1986)

life, but what I now believe is that he became wiser, he understood a lot more from having lived through so many different experiences and understanding human personality."[41]

Korea and the Chain of Charity

Whilst trying to start an MC community in Taiwan, in 1976, Brother Andrew saw the possibility of opening in Korea. In the 1960s and 1970s South Korea was still fairly poor but it was entering a period of industrial and economic growth. This was also the time of the "conversion boom" in the Catholic and Protestant Churches. Br Peter Murmu and Brother Geoff Brown, who was in Hong Kong as a first-year novice at that point, were selected to start the community in Korea. They arrived on 5 July 1977, and stayed first at the Jesuit Sogang University for two weeks. Everybody was advising the two young Brothers to go to language school but Andrew was adamantly against the idea. As Brother Geoff narrated:

> Everyone was telling us, "Go to language school, go to language school, go to language school," and Br Andrew said, "You don't go to language school." And Brother Peter and I were looking at one another. Anyway, he had his ticket booked two weeks later, not a problem for him. We were having sort of a night prayer in his room each night, after a few days he said. "I believe God will bring us someone who would solve our problem of language."

> Within a few days, an ex-army fellow semi-paralyzed by a stroke, who could walk with crutches and was abandoned by his wife, was looking for a place to stay. He had learnt English while he was a Korean soldier in Vietnam, and was speaking English and Korean. So he was the obvious answer to the prayer. "See I told you," said Andrew. And by the time he left we had a house and we moved out of the university.

> Certainly, that would show again his past of gambling, of taking the risk, go to a country for two weeks, a place where

no one speaks English, with a novice and a junior Brother — that's a bit of a gamble — there was a certain confidence in God in some way that He's part of the show.⁴²

Four months later, a novitiate for the Korean candidates and Brother Geoff was established with Brother Peter officially the novice master:

> This was Exodus novitiate — certainly it was a formative experience — but in the long term those Brothers left. There were many houses in Korea, most of them closed because most of the Brothers who joined left. Within eight months, I was out of Korea, and that one junior Indian Brother was left on his own.
>
> The foundation in Korea boomed for a little while and then busted. Certainly it was successful in the short term and MC Brothers were famous in Korea for doing something no one else had done — there were magazines and interviews and all sorts of things, doing those sorts of things which we don't usually do. You don't come to a country, start a novitiate with no one speaking Korean and accept all these candidates.
>
> You just don't do that.⁴³

Why did the Koreans love Andrew from the very beginning, when he spoke not a word of Korean? Brother Geoff believed that Koreans revered Brother Andrew because, "he had a charm despite the language difficulty. Personality I guess and genuineness I suppose and that work we started with people on the streets, no one had done that before though."⁴⁴ Some Korean women even compared Andrew to Jesus in his facial features.⁴⁵

After over five years of the Brothers' presence, in a letter dated 11 October 1983 Brother Andrew announced to the whole Congregation that since there were four communities with eight professed Brothers and sixteen novices, Korea was to become a region on its own — separating itself from the existing houses and communities in the Far East region — with Seoul as the regional centre. Quite a daring premature move!

Brother Peter remembered how one day when he and Andrew were walking on the streets of Seoul, Andrew did not hesitate to pick up one disabled lady who was begging. "I wouldn't have picked her up because there were already two or three men with us. He just brought her. It was normal for him. We kept her for two days, and then the news somehow spread. Andrew left a great impression since he was General of the Society, with no language, a foreigner, and a man."[46]

Lazaro Sung was probably still a come-and-see when one day he was invited to share his experience as a Brother with a group of the Legion of Mary.[47] Hwang Kum Soo was present. She was a young woman, who had recently been baptized as a Catholic and had taken the name of Liduvina. Liduvina was captivated by his talk, and after the meeting went to speak with him. She confided that her one desire in life was to be a religious but that due to her physical condition no congregation would take her. Brother Lazaro invited her to visit the Brothers and to talk to Andrew: "It was like the blind man in the Gospels and he heard about Jesus, and when he met Jesus he started to see. It was the same for me when I first met Brother Andrew."[48]

Another woman was interested in living a life of prayer but, like Liduvina she was confined to a wheelchair. She and Liduvina would talk together about their desire to be Religious. Thus, through the intervention and encouragement of Brother Andrew, the Chain of Charity was born. Father Park Mun Su, who was and still is the spiritual director of the Chain of Charity as per Cardinal Kim's request, recalled the beginnings:

> They joined together before they met Andrew. They wanted some official status and they were in touch with the Brothers of Charity. They contacted Cardinal Kim, Ordinary of the Diocese. They needed a director, and since they were influenced by the Brothers of Charity and also by Mother Teresa, and since Andrew was coming frequently to South Korea, he [Andrew] agreed to it when he was invited to be their intermediary.

> So when he visited Cardinal Kim, the latter was very impressed with this idea of the Chain of Charity, and he gave permission to Andrew to be their founder and thus they were given official status as a devotional group of laity.[49]

Most people with disabilities in Korea at that time felt very much rejected by society and by their own families. Many had suffered horrendously. "The monthly meetings of the Chain of Charity were focused on the love of God, and that led to sharing about their experiences. Many disabled women began to blossom with these monthly meetings and prayers and so for about four years they had a rapid expansion."[50] Unfortunately, after some time the healthiest member among them who was a very fast moving and dynamic person, split from the rest of the group.

Andrew's involvement with the group, apart from being considered the founder-member, included giving the annual eight-day retreat to members living in the community and a further three-day annual retreat for all members including those living in their families. He would give the retreat in English and Fr Park Mun Su would translate it into Korean.

> As I said, their spirituality had a big impact, at first because disabled persons were so alienated in Korean society at that time; there was a lot of superstition involved, the handicap is a punishment, the family was suffering punishment, the family couldn't make economic progress because of the disabled person, so they were blamed.

> One extreme case is the original member who had paralysis — infantile paralysis — her father was a professor at a university, but he was so embarrassed about his handicapped child that she had been kept in a closed room and when there would be a family event, a marriage or something, she would be put in the room and not allowed to come out. So she was completely rejected. She began to awaken spiritually with Chain of Charity, she began to write poems, simple poems and as it turned out I think she published up to six

or seven volumes and became known nationally. Her poems were very simple, but expressing the pain of rejection or sense of God discovered in small things ...

Chain of Charity had miraculous events taking place.[51]

As with the Brothers, the Chain of Charity followed "Andrew's pattern" of rapid expansion. This might have been a mistake. They were soon asked to open houses in Incheon, Busan, Kwangju and even Jeju Island. They had five communities with at most twenty-four community members. In each city they would also have a number of members who lived at home. Like the MC Brothers, they grew quickly in a short time, but then began to decrease in number. Again, it was because of a lack of preparation and clear identity: Who were they and what were they about?[52] Fr Park Mun Su was inclined to believe that Andrew really had no idea whether they were supposed to be Religious or a kind of Religious, or just a group of people with disabilities living together in community in the diocese and connected with the charity works of the diocese. In a way, Andrew should more accurately be considered another spiritual advisor who had a most profound influence on them — but still members of the Chain of Charity look upon him their founder.

Koreans are very sentimental people, forming relationships based more on sentiment than on common goals. This was also a characteristic of Andrew: "He could deal with people heart to heart. So his sentimental connection with the Korean people was very real and close. So that went beyond language. He was very easy to perceive, say, from his facial expressions, very peaceful and at the same time vulnerable. A vulnerable person, it shows on his face that he was not pushy, not dominant in any way, he knew what suffering was, and he knew how to be close to those who suffered. That has great appeal here in Korea."[53] Of course, there was also his identification with the poor which came from the heart: "He had no ulterior motives, so it's not hard to understand why he was accepted and admired. It's his person and it's his personal commitment and his sentiment and ability to connect people on the heart-to-heart level. That was the source of his influence here."⁵⁴ The converse was also true. Andrew loved Korea and her people, and he appreciated that there was a lot of scope for the Missionaries of Charity to be there. It is also worth noting that one of the pioneers of the Korean Brothers in Korea was Brother Lazaro, a very inspiring person, who was himself suffering from polio. One of his legs was not very stable, and yet Andrew accepted him. The Chain of Charity is now almost extinct. Liduvina is the only survivor who still considers herself a community member while in Naju there are three outside members.

Another group which Andrew helped initiate was the Little Nest run by Jo Young Sim, a flight attendant known by her baptismal name of Alexia. English speaking, she was able to act as an interpreter between Brother Andrew and those attending Mass, homilies and talks. Alexia soon felt inspired by the Brothers' work and service to start her own home and mission, taking care of older women. Andrew encouraged her. The Little Nest eventually started in a small family home but soon, with the help of a benefactor, larger premises were built. At that time in Mangmi-dong the Brothers also had a house for elderly women that was becoming quite difficult to maintain. Alexia came into the picture and eventually started to manage the house herself. Andrew was happy with the arrangement and would take Brothers visiting Korea to see the Little Nest and Alexia. But again, Andrew spoke no Korean; he did not understand the local people's idiosyncrasies. He would come, spend a few weeks, and then leave the Brothers to face the sometimes conflicting situations he had "helped" to create. Tensions arose between the Brothers and Alexia and ties were eventually severed.⁵⁵

With the Brothers in India

All the time spent between Hong Kong and communities in the Far East and other regions might suggest that Andrew was neglecting those in India. This was not the case. Even though his base was Hong Kong, he would visit India at least three or four times a year, especially for the profession of vows. Br Prem Anand Naduvathette

Part – IV: From General to Troubadour (1976 – 1986)

shared what most experienced of Andrew: "In those days there were two things which we waited for. One was Brother Andrew's general letter. We read it alone, we read it as a community, during Adoration, or during spiritual reading. It was something which we really looked for. Second were his visits. We always awaited his visits. Whenever he came back from a trip, we would all come around him, have a cup of tea, and then he will share incidents and news of what happened in each place with the Brothers — mostly the beauty part of it."[56] The day Andrew arrived from one of his journeys would be a holiday for the novices in Mansatala. They had no classes. Brothers from communities around Mansatala would come and listen attentively to him regaling then with anecdotes and stories of his travels while at the same time bringing news, letters and small tokens from Brothers living "abroad". Br Abraham Ellickal recalled Andrew as a "very sensitive man to the Brothers. Whenever he came back from any trip he made sure to bring me the Time or Newsweek magazine because he knew I liked reading. Whereas to the Local Servant in Mansatala he always brought something funny to make him happy."[57]

The great majority of senior Brothers still present and active in the Missionaries of Charity arrived during this period. Brother Andrew was in his early fifties and most of the Brothers were younger. They looked up to him because he was a foreigner, a former Jesuit and the co-founder of the Congregation. He never took advantage of this, however. On the contrary, he felt one with them. Many remembered him as a father-figure — showing them great love, trust and encouragement but at times coming across as strong, stubborn and angry. Br Peter Murmu recalled witnessing Andrew angry: "Twice I saw him very angry. One time when during a retreat we were talking and that he could not accept. The other time during a profession. He insisted that professions would be simple and at this particular profession there were a lot of people, some invited and some not. There were some parishioners, and he started sending them away. We were a little bit embarrassed."[58]

Trust was a hallmark of Brother Andrew. Unfortunately, the trust he had in the Brothers in India was at times taken to extremes. A case in point occurred in relation to the same Peter Murmu, whom Andrew loved and esteemed. At that time, Peter, who was twenty-eight years old, was living in the Far East region, when he received a letter from Brother Andrew informing him of decisions taken in Calcutta (while Andrew was on a visit for the General Council meeting), about which Peter had not even been consulted.

I hope the letter reaches you before the General Letter with the changes. There's lots of news for you. Jeremy is here and we have had Gen. Council meeting. Now the news:

1. Christdas resigned from the General Council and you have been voted as General Councillor. (Congratulations)
2. You have been appointed L.S. [Local Servant] of Barrackpore. You continue as R.S. [Regional Servant] for the Far East and will have to visit the houses.
3. It would be good if you can come to India as soon as possible. And good if you can visit all the F.E. [Far East] houses (incl. Philippines) on the way to India.[59]

This meant that while Brother Peter was to be the superior of the community in Barrackpore, which at the time was (and still is) managing Gandhiji Prem Nivas Centre for leprosy patients in Titagarh, he was also to retain his position as the Regional Servant for the Far East — thousands of miles away.[60] Thus he was to oversee the Brothers living in Korea, Philippines, Macau, Hong Kong and Taiwan. And, if that were not enough, he was also chosen to be one of the General Councillors of the whole Congregation, and all this without his even being asked. Was it trust? Could it also have been the case of a lack of Brothers with leadership skills?

Brother Andrew might have been impulsive with some of his judgements but he was also humble enough to accept that, at times, his decisions were wrongly and quickly taken. That was the experience of another Brother, who while living in a community outside Calcutta, had to go there often to collect the monthly quota of money for the community. Some Brothers complained to Andrew that this Brother had arrived in Calcutta earlier than necessary and stayed at some friend's home. When Brother Andrew found out, a strong scolding followed. But later Andrew was quick to offer an apology when the Brother produced a bus ticket with the date of his actual arrival.[61]

Brother Andrew gave the impression of having a good awareness of who his Brothers were. He knew when to be strict and when to encourage and help them overcome situations that were burdening them. Br Michael Soreng remembered the day when he collected Andrew from the airport: "When I was Servant in one community, someone, (most probably one of the Brothers), had stolen a thousand rupees from the *almirah* [cupboard] to which only I had the key. I was in distress and when a few days later, I went to pick up Brother Andrew from the airport, he noticed how gloomy and sad I was. I explained what had happened and when he saw how worried I was, he said, "Don't worry man, don't worry, put everything in the Hand of God."[62]

One Brother recalled once coming to Calcutta very disturbed. In his perception the Local Servant was acting unfairly towards him. He had already talked with the Regional Servant and was ready to leave the Congregation. But before the final decision, he wanted to talk to Andrew and share his turmoil: "Brother Andrew had just come from abroad so I asked the Regional to go and talk to him. I came to Calcutta, I reached early morning. By that time Andrew was getting ready to go to Kalighat to celebrate Mass."[63] Even though Andrew was in rather a hurry, he welcomed the Brother and quickly went down to the kitchen and brought him a freshly-brewed cup of tea. Andrew — the tea lover — took the opportunity to have one too! "So we drank together and due to my desperation and confusion, I said, 'Brother I would like to see you.' His reply was, 'Don't worry man. Take rest. You travelled the whole night, you take rest. I'm going to Kalighat for Mass, and after that we will meet.'"[64] When around 10 o'clock, Andrew came back from Kalighat, the Brother again approached Brother Andrew, but Andrew suggested he take a walk around Calcutta and maybe watch a nice movie. "So, I went out, and by dinner I was back in the community. After dinner, during recreation time, he was moving around in the veranda, and I again insisted, 'Brother?' And he again said, 'Don't worry, you take rest, let us meet tomorrow.' It took him three days to meet me! So by that time, I had already cooled down, and I didn't know what to speak to him about. My intention completely changed because of his calm behaviour towards me. Then, on the third day, after breakfast, he asked me whether I was free to talk! After meeting him for say ten or fifteen minutes, he just said, 'Brother, I know the superior very well. Be calm and pray, you know, we are all in the sinking boat. Try to survive. You go and you do your work.' After that, I became really happy and calm."[65]

It's as if he had a way of calming the Brothers and others, thanks to his own composure and level-headedness. Maybe it was also because he understood their cultural heritage and background. After all, he had spent all his religious life and formation in India. A very telling and curious letter dates from 1983. A benefactor from Gaya, one of the main cities in the State of Bihar, was asking for a property he had donated to the Brothers to be returned because in his opinion they had not used it as intended as a hospital for the poor. Brother Andrew's reply demonstrates an understanding of the Indian mentality. He used language that the recipient would have understood and at the same time showed an astuteness and a capacity subtly to manipulate with the authority of a man of God, who would receive the necessary and due respect to which Indian culture is predisposed. "We constructed a building for this purpose," Andrew explained, "but there was the action of some violent people who damaged the building and made it impossible to keep the patients there."[66] He made it clear that he did not want to enter into a legal proceedings. Rather he implored the donor in the presence of almighty God: "I can see that you donated this land as a Gift of Love to God for His poor and neglected children. This action is God Himself alive and working in your good self. It was an action that brought you salvation (*Mukti*). A beautiful action."[67] Andrew believed that there might be other parties who were influencing the benefactor and "that this influence that changed your good deed has come from *Shaitan* [devil]. And that is a great danger, because it can only bring evil and death. I hope and pray that this matter can be settled in the Desire of God. Then there will be life and peace and beauty for you, for those other parties and for the poor people. Because God gives life and peace. *Shaitan* brings hatred, greed, jealousy and death."[68]

Questions about Alcohol

Andrew appeared to thrive on excitement. Maybe he still needed the adrenaline rush he used to have from gambling. (It is important to note that there is no evidence that Andrew, while under the vow of poverty, ever used the Jesuits' and/or the Missionaries of Charity Brothers' money to gamble.) Now he was gambling with opening houses, sending young Brothers into communities in remote and at times obscure places. His old passports would have given us an idea of his extensive goings and comings; unfortunately, neither the MC Brothers nor his family members kept them. The sheer extent of these displacements could also indicate that Brother Andrew was running away from something or someone. Was he, by any chance, running away from his very self? Was it related to the pain of leaving Saigon? Answers are hard to come by. He probably did not even have them himself!

Perhaps it was during this decade that Brother Andrew's alcohol consumption increased. Various Brothers — living outside of India — saw him drinking too much:

> During the time I was in Haiti, Brother Andrew came for a visit around 1985 or 1986 when he was still the General Servant. In those days when a brother in authority came to visit us, one day we wouldn't cook, and we'd go to a restaurant. That time, I observed what I had already heard about him. We Brothers maybe had one or two beers, but he finished nine or ten cans, *bapre bap!* Wow! So much he

took. And when he finished he was saying, "Give me some more, give me some more." Then he got a little drunk and he started making jokes. I was laughing because it was the first time hearing him speaking in Hindi, funny things, good things but pure Hindi, *gay dudh deti hay* [Cow gives milk]. And then we went back home and he took some more cans to the community, "I would like to take some more," he said.[69]

Another Brother living in Finland remembered him, "talking a lot after drinking in a restaurant. Not serious talk. I always wanted to go to an Indian restaurant, I didn't even know what the meaning of restaurant was. So once, when Brother Andrew came to visit us, he took us to eat in a restaurant. The regional of that time was saying that they had found him somewhere in Hong Kong drunk. I remember the [Western] Brothers were sharing something in front of us Indian brothers, about Brother Andrew's second time they had found him drunk in the sacristy in Hong Kong drinking the Mass wine."[70] Two Brothers who were both living in Los Angeles, "during the mid-1980's witnessed Brother Andrew tipsy from too much wine at Ingraham in Los Angeles."[71] "I saw the drinking, and Brothers and Co-Workers enabling it."[72]

Br Robi Gut, who lived with Andrew in Hong Kong, related:

The community ... was very austere. Our meals were very frugal, because in the beginning Andrew said, "Do not buy fruits." So the impression could be, because the subject of drinking comes often in Hong Kong, that the community was always a drinking mess. It wasn't. I would say, it was basically a sober, extremely simple community, and if we had alcohol on the table perhaps maximum once a year. I remember once, that was in the later stage, Brother Andrew thought that for Christmas we had to give some beer for the poor we had invited, otherwise they would not come. He did it only once. He put it on the table, and afterwards, we realised it was not the right thing.

> I remember ... for my first vows [one group] had brought two bottles of alcohol. So normally really, there was nowhere, never alcohol on the table. (Brother Andrew used to smoke, and eventually stopped for a while.) For those who know about alcoholism they know about binge drinking. With Andrew, it was always hidden, it was not on the table and it was normally late in the day and rarely in the morning, because in the morning, we had Holy Mass together. There was no mess; no, it was all hidden.[73]

Apparently it was all hidden from outsiders but not from the two Brothers who were living with Andrew in Hong Kong. His drinking at times turned into blackouts and he would not remember the consequences of such incidents. One particular instance prompted Brother Robi, who at that time was the only other member of the community, to ask for help from superiors because he did not know how to handle a situation complicated by the fact that Brother Andrew was the highest authority in the Congregation.

> I've been stricken with a disability, i.e., if I drink, it takes too much out of me the next day — and I get a blurred head. So I do it much less.[74]

It is very telling that after this letter to his friend Fr Patrick O'Sullivan, SJ, Brother Andrew started writing to the Brothers about the problem of alcohol in the communities.

> Your prayers are asked for a Brother who has developed the sickness of alcoholism. He has been drinking heavily on visits to communities and it is out of control. Unfortunately at this point he is not willing to admit that he is an alcoholic and so it is very difficult to help him. Please pray for him. It is a warning to us that we can easily develop into an alcoholic from a mere liking for drink. Some communities celebrate with alcohol too easily. I personally am criticised for allowing/encouraging this, especially in communities outside India. I accept blame for this, with sorrow. And I am trying to change. Let us pray that the damage may be repaired.[75]

Andrew pinpointed the problem of alcohol consumption in the communities but the only solution he offered was Holy Hours, prayers, and the banning of alcohol from any community function. It is a little disconcerting that he only once during these years mentioned the Twelve Steps of Alcoholics Anonymous (AA), and never seemed to encourage Brothers to attend AA meetings, especially given that in the early years of the Congregation there were regular AA meetings at Mansatala. His letters also suggest that the solution was to prohibit any alcohol without trying to understand why a Brother was drinking:

> ALCOHOL & DRINKING: We have recently had the sad loss of one or two vocations that were affected by drinking. Many of us, myself included, must share responsibility for such losses by our example and encouragement.
>
> So I am now asking that in future there should never be any alcohol at any community meal or celebration. It is a useful subject for us to reflect on prayerfully:
>
> a) It is a big problem in many religious communities and for priests all over the world. b) It is an extremely expensive item, and the huge sums spent on alcohol by priests and religious clearly offends against poverty and the poor. c) We work with alcoholics in many of our communities. We see the evils of alcohol, and we give a counter-witness if we Brothers are drinking. d) We can and should give a witness to a joy and fellowship that is not built on alcohol. We can make a reparation and sacrificial intercession for the victims of alcohol by our abstinence. This will win graces for many of the victims of the commercial exploitation by the alcohol industry.[76]

ANDREW AND THE MC BROTHERS' IDENTITY

The way Brother Andrew came across and the way he wanted the Brothers to be were congruent — fully human. If there was one thing he was sure of, it was the fact that he did not want any mystery or supernatural aura surrounding the Brothers just because they were founded by Mother Teresa.

Brother Andrew would often use the Hindi phrase *kachara samaj* to describe the MC Congregation. *Kachara samaj* literally translates as a "rubbish congregation" — not a very complimentary description of a group of people trying to live their values and vows as best they could. The phrase was not intended to be disrespectful, however. A dumpster is not pleasant to see. It is not usually found in the middle of a city but in some secluded place outside the city walls. It is a place where crows lurk, rummaging for rotten pieces of food. Rich people never go around dumpsters or garbage areas. Only the poorest of the poor scavenge there, hoping to find useful things that they can recycle or use themselves. Scavengers look for rotten things whereas the poor will look for "valuable" things which might bring them a few coins. The same dumpster has no "awareness" of what can lie within. If their own co-founder compared the Brothers to a *kachara samaj* it was for a reason. They might not be aware of the richness within them. Brother Andrew was convinced that inside the *kachara samaj* there was a treasure which only the poorest of the poor could discover. For him it was always the poor who could extract the goodness inside him and inside his Brothers.

When between the 1986 General Chapter and that of 1992, the First Constitutions were being revised, in Article 1.23 the Brothers wrote, "Brother Andrew spoke of 'the Four Essentials' as a way of emphasizing certain characteristic aspects of our way of living our consecration." It is not clear when or whether Brother Andrew actually coined the term "Four Essentials", because we have no writings in which he specifically uses that phrase — "My only advice to you is that: 1) You look to God in prayer for His guidance and strength. 2) Keep a very simple way of living and working. Beware of adding things in your own houses for your own comfort. And don't try to build efficient dispensaries, schools, hospitals, etc. 3) You look always for the poorest and most needy people. God will be with you as long as you do this."[77] It seems that the first time he specifically encouraged the Brothers to keep up "four points: UNITY, SIMPLICITY, CARE FOR THE POOREST AND PRAYER," was in a general letter written on 17 January 1979. But in the foreword by Ann Blaikie to Kathryn Spink's *Spirit of Bethlehem*, she wrote, "He [Brother Andrew] also stresses that there are four essentials for his Brothers — to live in community, to pray, to work with the poorest of the poor and to live a life of poverty."[78] In the same book, Spink mentions Brother Andrew stating, "The fourth essential is that we ourselves, in the community, live in a poor and simple style."[79]

Simplicity

He spoke and urged the Brothers to stay simple in all aspects of their lives. Simplicity was needed even in the way the Brothers dressed, adorned their chapels and their houses:

> As I was visiting the houses, I saw that most houses have too much furniture. Let us try to give away some items of tables, chairs, almirahs, etc., from each house. Also we must be careful not to bring in anything that is not necessary. Clocks, electrical fittings, etc., should be very simple, in the spirit of M.C. poverty. The same applies to our clothes. Brothers should not wear costly shirts, and should keep to the number allowed. We must not buy *Illustrated Weekly* or such.[80]

This call to simplicity extended even to education which is still considered the biggest contradiction in the community's life.

> I hear Brothers talking about training. I think we must come to a clearer understanding on this. I hope you will discuss the question openly in your preparation, and you have

every freedom to do so. I shall state here my thinking on it clearly: I am fully opposed to the idea that Brothers need further training. There may be a very rare exception to this, to meet some special need. For us there is another standard.

What is the difference between an unschooled Brother washing and bathing a poor patient in Kalighat and schooled General Servant giving big talks in America? There is only one way to judge: the LOVE with which it is done. Let us be real revolutionaries in refusing to judge people by any false standard, but judge by something that is of value.[81]

Brothers still struggle with the fact that he was obstinate in not allowing higher studies when he himself was well-versed, educationally well-prepared, and continued to write books. A major discussion erupted in January 1985 during a formators' meeting in Korea when the subject of further education came up. He was upset, he was angry, he stopped the meeting and sent the Brothers to reflect for the remainder of the day. Were they to reflect so that they would come back agreeing with him? What amounted almost to a dread of higher education seemed to be, "rather inconsistent with his stated desire for his Brothers. He said that he wanted the Brothers to grow in freedom, to live and work out of a deep personal conviction in the spirit of the congregation, and yet he did not want them to grow in their intellectual capacity to make such choices. It is true that to do MC simple and direct work, you do not need university degrees; but then both he and Mother had already obtained a good, solid academic and spiritual education."[82]

Brother Andrew thought that too much study made one complex and unsuited for the backdrop of simplicity suggested by the MC Constitutions. If higher studies were asked of the Brothers joining the Congregation, it would have gone against Mother Teresa's unconscious intention: that of giving to the poor and the underprivileged the opportunity to enter and join her Congregation and thus share in her work for the poorest of the poor:

> Many of the Sisters, the first Sisters of Mother Teresa didn't have much education and wouldn't be accepted by other congregations. It is the same with the Brothers, I don't know why. That's how we grew and spread, particularly in India.
>
> This particular parish we [visited], each year, we were getting a few vocations from there, it was. . . not a very developed place at all, this lad came, finally I said to him, "You know we are getting a number of vocations from here" and he said, "Yes, you know the reason is that we have a school here, and it used to be run by some religious but they pulled out and the school still goes on, but now the teachers they drink a lot and we. . . we don't get good results, we can't get in the seminary, the Jesuits run a tight ship, we cannot enter the university college, so we come to you."
>
> I think he was dead right! I don't know why he put his finger on something real that really has been at the heart of the growth of both the Sisters of Mother Teresa, particularly in the early years and of the Brothers.[83]

If the service of the poor was kept simple, personal, direct and small, there was no need for higher education. Maybe too, the question should be seen in the context of the bigger picture. Brother Andrew was not for large institutions with many residents or inmates. He thrived in and loved the village communities in which *being* was (and still is) more important than *doing*. In such conditions, no higher studies are needed and one can really be who one is, a true brother to the people around. He even justified his philosophy in one of his letters:

> We often hear that "so many MC Brothers are leaving because of poor formation." Let us be clear: We do not have more Brothers leaving than other Congregations. And there are some Congregations that have many more leaving than we do — some of them with many years of formation.[84]

"Whatever the reason, the greatness of Andrew lay in the fact that, highly intelligent, well-prepared and well-versed as he was, he could nonetheless reach out to the humblest and poorest of suffering persons, and at the same time, that suffering person felt understood and welcomed by him."[85] Andrew's conviction was that after God, the main agents of formation were the poor, and not educational studies.

Prayer and Community Life

Prayer was another cornerstone for Andrew:

> Unless we continue to grow in prayer and union with God, we shall lose our spirit. And then our vocation is finished. Let us always remember: A BROTHER WHO DOES NOT CARE FOR THE SPIRITUAL LIFE AND PRAYER IS NOT A BROTHER OF THIS SOCIETY. HE IS SOMETHING ELSE. And he cannot be happy in this life.[86]

Community life and good relationships with one another were of utmost importance to Andrew. He knew and accepted the fact that community life was difficult, but it was also precious. He believed that community was vital and insisted on that bond, that link:

> Let us try to have great love and acceptance of each other. I think our problems will be much easier if we have this love. All of us are weak, imperfect men. But we get angry with each other because of the disagreements we have and our mistakes. Let us try to understand each other's behaviour. My Brother is struggling with his character just as I am. And when he says or does something that hurts me, I must try to understand and forgive. If we can do this, we shall make a great progress. This is not easy. We must pray for this gift from God. Let us often pray for greater love among Brothers in all the houses.[87]

Love and Service of the Poor

Love and service of the poor were imperative for Andrew. There was no greater school for Andrew and "for MCs [than] the poor man who comes to us with his simple immediate need and prayerful reflection on the Gospel."[88] For Andrew, the duty and obligation of an MC Brother was not only to give food to a hungry man, attend to the medical needs of a poor woman, or help to distribute material items during relief work:

> We are also called to work to make people new men. We have to reach out not only to the bodies of men, but their hearts and minds also. We have to try to be instruments by which the poor understand more the value and beauty of their human lives and destiny. We have to help the seeds of God's word to come to life and grow in the people and in their bustees. This we must do by bringing the love and the light and life of Jesus wherever we go. If we forget this part of our work, we are leaving undone what is most important, and what people are most hungry for — more hungry for than for bread.[89]

It is plausible to say that — for Andrew — love of and identification with the poor, work for the poor, simplicity, community life and prayer were all interrelated and interdependent, and he never advocated one over the other. When in 1982 he visited a community in the Calcutta area and saw what he considered to be a "strong and extravagant building," surrounded by an "enormous compound wall and gate" and guarded by a "fiercely barking dog," he was, by his own account, livid. He was angry not only because the house seemed to be the best in the road but, more importantly, because the Brothers were giving out the wrong Gospel message. Furthermore, he was worried that people, the political parties and the poor would start considering the Brothers to be big *zamindars*.[90]

MOTHER TERESA, BROTHER ANDREW and OTHER MALE BRANCHES

It was on 10 September 1946, while Mother Teresa, then a Loreto nun, was travelling on a train between Calcutta and Darjeeling for her annual retreat, that she received her "call within a call". The call was hers, a personal call from God relating to a specific mission. She was more than convinced of what Jesus was asking of her. It is well known that Mother never liked to talk about herself, "her" call or "her" work. She deemed herself to be only a pencil in the hand of God — nothing else, only an instrument. But, one question arises: how did she convey her call, the mission, the spirit, the spirituality of the Congregation to Brother Andrew? There is almost nothing archived, nothing written or said in any talk either by Mother or by him. Only a letter to a friend of his, "She [Mother Teresa] & I never really went into her 2nd call — beyond what she would say to anyone. We didn't much share our spiritual journey in great depth. I was not a personal spiritual guide for her though I think we did encourage each other spiritually at a personal level."[91] Sisters, who lived and worked in the Mother House in the 1970s and 1980s, however, all recall having seen Mother and Andrew sitting down and talking for long hours.[92]

Mother Teresa and Andrew were both practical, endowed with common sense and direct in their response to the needs of the poor. Maybe, without their even knowing it, they were very alike in character, personality, and in what they believed to be essential to the MCs. When Mother was faced with a situation in war-torn Beirut in the 1980s and wanted to transfer some physically and mentally challenged children from a dangerous part of the city to a safer place, she informed the authorities that she would go and take them, "one by one". The same spirit was manifest in Andrew when he was asked by Malcolm Muggeridge in *Something Beautiful for God* what the point was of taking care of only twenty-five boys, when the needs in Calcutta were so great. Andrew answered, "Once you look at the problem as a problem, then it's ridiculous, but, you have to look at those twenty-five individual boys and I think there is a value we have to see in each one."[93] Both were stubborn and not to be deterred when the poor were at stake.

Their love for Mary, Mother of Jesus was more than evident. Whether their particular devotion was to the Immaculate Heart of Mary or to Mary, Mother of the Poor was not important. Titles were just titles. In both Mother and Andrew a growth occurred in their theological understanding that the very Jesus being touched in the poor was the same Jesus adored and received in the Holy Eucharist.

Whereas Mother Teresa insisted on poverty, Andrew spoke more about simplicity. Theirs were two apparently different philosophies but with the same ends: a freedom and detachment from material things for a greater identification with the poorest of the poor and with Jesus. Another basic tenet held by both Mother and Andrew was that of "being present with the poor", rather than just "doing and working for the poor". It might not be very apparent in Mother who seemed to favour large homes for the poor and destitute. But from the very beginning, Mother Teresa had a deep sense of enculturation with Bengali customs and way of life, an enculturation not with the middle or upper echelons of Bengali society but with the poor of Calcutta. The poor did not need another white-European memsahib to work for them. They needed someone who was one with them. The poor would never have accepted her if she had not been one of them. Andrew's desire was identical — total identification with the poor. In fact, before he ever met the Congregation he was already considering going to live in a slum in Delhi.

According to Eileen Egan, the courage that sustained Mother was of a transcendent nature.[94] The same can be said of Andrew. The courage to leave prestigious Societies such as Loreto and the Jesuits, required faith — a faith in what they both believed was God's will and a spiritual conviction that they were following His wishes. There was definitely a risk involved. They never feared risk! There might have been fear of ridicule from other members of the Congregations they were leaving; what if the whole "thing" collapsed? There was definitely a fear of the unknown, but at the same time, there was a peace and a conviction which could only have come from their deep trust and surrender. Maybe their greatest fear was that they might fail to follow God's call.

In both Mother Teresa and Brother Andrew this radical option for the poorest of the poor, this awareness of the suffering of the poor around them, and the compassion they both felt for the broken, the unloved and the wounded, mingled with the "success" and "fame" they both experienced, had its price. It brought a sense of loneliness in the case of Andrew and a sense of abandonment by God in the case of Mother. In both cases, it was an internal movement that kept them humble.

In a letter to Kathryn Spink, Brother Andrew asserted that Mother Teresa was the closest he had been to a great saint. He acknowledged a richness, beauty and meaning which came to his life through her. But at the same time he could recognise faults in her. Andrew admitted that at various times he got on Mother's nerves, because of his ego and conceit, which according to him collided with traces of the same in her, "daughter of Eve" that she was. The beauty of Mother, as explained by Andrew, was that she gave him total freedom — entrusting to him the co-founding of the Congregation of the Brothers — even when she disagreed with him (although at the same time she could be annoyed and upset with him and show it). According to Andrew, however, this was a sign of her being fully human and it would be awfully petty to deny her this right.[95]

Eileen Egan wrote of how Brother Andrew's emotions were nearer the surface than Mother Teresa's: "I was with him once in New York when he came upon a strange Cambodian-type cross made by refugees in Phnom Penh. They had made thousands of such crosses from scraps of wood and tin expertly tooled. His eyes filled with tears and he stopped dead, covering his face with his hands. Brother Andrew was more vulnerable than Mother Teresa and more open in admitting to vulnerability."[96] This could explain why others found him so accessible:

> Just since I started to write this, a very young first-year novice, plucked up the courage to come in to the great GS, and said he is sad and lonely and thinking a lot of his family at home who are very poor. He said that when he

goes to the slums he thinks of his own family who are in the same condition of poverty. And so there is always the beauty and the pain.[97]

A young, first-year Indian novice approaching the foreign General Superior of the Congregation in the India of 1977 was surely not a common occurrence. What did that novice see and perceive that enabled him to pluck up courage and open up to Andrew? There is a similarity with the Apostle Andrew, the first disciple of Jesus. What did the disciple see in Jesus that first day that made him go and stay with Him for the whole day without having ever met or talked to Jesus?

Love for the Congregation was a hallmark of both General Superiors. Brother Andrew acknowledged that his love of the Brothers was implanted from his very first encounter with the initial group, a love which Mother Teresa shared.

It is a real pity that the only correspondence between Mother and Andrew kept in the archives of both the MC Sisters and Brothers speaks mostly of their differences. They wrote to each other whenever they were at variance or a difficulty arose. As already indicated, these divergences occurred over small mundane issues, such as financial matters and other very practical considerations. They were never arguments over the spirit and charism of the Congregation.

One of the biggest written disputes between Andrew and Mother, which ironically demonstrates the love she had for the Brothers, originated after he wrote a letter to the Brothers to clarify their relationship with the Sisters. At the time when the Brothers as a Congregation were still financially reliant on the Sisters but wanted nonetheless to be independent, the men felt there were times when some Sisters were interfering with the day-to-day running of their work. To the Brothers, Andrew wrote:

> I want to clarify a few points in the relationship between M.C. Sisters and Brothers. We are really brothers & sisters of one family — after God it is Mother Teresa who has

founded both Congregations. But in fact we are two distinct Congregations. M.C. Brothers is a separate Congregation of the Church with its own superiors. But still we receive so much from the Sisters in many ways. In fact we depend very heavily on the Sisters for our financial support, especially in India. It is good to be aware of this. In India, we Brothers could not continue our work without the financial support of the Sisters.

This should lead us to a feeling of gratitude to Mother and the Sisters — a prayerful gratitude. This awareness should also make us very humble in realising our dependence. It should make us realise that we do not have much security. We could easily have a situation in the future of a Sister in charge who does not approve of us and does not want to support the work of the Brothers. We have already experienced this in individual cases. This insecurity and uncertainty regarding future support is very good for us. It is a very real and very healthy poverty. We must be happy with it.

But there is still one more point that seems a contradiction. We are dependent on the Sisters for financial help, but we must remain independent as regards interference. There has been a case recently where the Brothers have been drawing their money from the Sisters. And the Sister in charge was not happy about the expenses (with reason perhaps). She called for our account books, reported it to Mother. We must not allow this. I have told the Brothers there that we will try to find some other way to support that house.

Another case is where Sisters are helping very generously with materials in starting one of our new houses, but the superior is telling the Brothers what and how they must do the work. Again this is wrong. We can accept the help of the Sisters, but we must remain free and independent. And if necessary feel the lack of material help. There are times too when we are not able to accept the patients and children the Sisters send, if our work does not allow it.

This interference comes from their love and interest. But it is not healthy for us. And while we keep a relationship of love, respect and co-operation in serving the poorest of the poor, let us be careful to keep a prudent distance in all matters. And if one day for any reason we lose the financial support of Sisters, then we shall be able to rejoice in being truly poor with Christ and His poor.[98]

Andrew then wrote to Mother Teresa, attaching the above previously written letter. Mother was upset. She wrote back quoting his same letter:

Dear Brother Andrew,

Thank you for your letter and the enclosed — I wish you had spoken to me before you put it on paper. I don't think it was necessary to hurt like this.

I am sorry that the Brothers are made to feel so bad "Remain independent as regards interference."

I spoke to the Brothers as I have done so often whenever I have spoken to them re-Poverty. You feel I should not have done so. "We must not allow this. We must remain free and independent." What do you mean? You are creating some unChrist feelings — I promise you I will never again advise any Brother, do not be afraid — If you are afraid as I see from your letter of you losing your freedom, that the Sisters are interfering with the work in any way — Kindly let me know and I will speak with the Sisters and prevent any further hurt. In future let the money be given only from the M.H. [Mother House] & then you can send to your houses as you decide — The money does not belong either to the Sisters or the Brothers — it belongs to the Poor for whom people have given — If you take the money directly from here — you will not need to fear — of interference or making you feel bad.[99]

Part – IV: From General to Troubadour (1976 – 1986)

Mother Teresa was definitely hurt. It is, however, as if she regained her strength and resilience, eventually disarming Andrew by ending her letter, "Brother Andrew, do not be afraid of losing your freedom nor your authority — Sisters & myself we will keep away — I will not keep any contact if you so wish, but the love for the Brothers you will not be able to break."[100]

Other MC Male Branches

There is a very telling adage in the Spanish language, *Cuando el río suena piedras trae*, which loosely translates as, "There is no smoke without fire." This was the case in 1977:

> You have passed on to me the rumours about the Sisters in N.Y. [New York] starting the Brothers of the Word. I sincerely hope they are only rumours, and would find it very amazing and distasteful if they have taken such a step without a word to us. So our attitude should be that we do not know anything about it, and we are in no position to be involved in any way. I would like you all to be quite clear about this.[101]

Even though a month later he wrote directing the Brothers to calm down, Andrew was upset. Mother Teresa had started a new male group of Brothers without informing, let alone consulting him. In an undated letter to Brother Nicholas, as quoted by Solomon, Andrew stated:

> I'm glad you saw the funny side of the Brothers of the Word. You just have to. I had the story right but the wrong continent. It's not N.Y. [New York]. It's Rome. And it's M.T. [Mother Teresa]. There's Cardinal Protectors and all in the act. And M.T. has really kept me out of it. I only got the pieces together after she left Calcutta this time but I wrote pretty strongly to her. So there's a bomb between us and neither of us has defused it. Now we can't meet again before October. I feel it's a pretty bad show and full of dangers. But I still don't have all the facts. So I'm trying to keep cool. And after all with saints

etc. I have a gut feeling that she's probably right — but, boy, I'll go in with my hand on the holster!¹⁰²

We might never know what he wrote to her, but we do have her response to him:

> Dear Brother Andrew,
>
> In the name of Jesus I ask you to forgive me for hurting you. There was not a thought nor desire to do anything like that. I wish we could have talked it over—but please Brother — do not think those 'bad' thoughts of disappearing from the MCs. This thought was not in anybody's mind — still less in mine — You are not the obstacle — please Brother — don't write like this — it is not true.
>
> I am sorry that we could not have talked this over together — but I am sure — has nothing to do with you & me
>
> Pray for me as I do for you
>
> Yours in Jesus
> M Teresa MC¹⁰³

Was the issue settled? Hard to know because three months later, another came up, this time regarding another branch of Brothers — the Contemplative Branch. This time it hit home harder because Brother Sebastian Vazhakala, an ordained MC, who had been the novice master in both Mansatala and Los Angeles, was asking to leave the MC Brothers to join the contemplative branch and help found it. But there are deeper considerations in the letter that Mother Teresa subsequently wrote. She wanted the newly founded Congregation of Contemplative Brothers to be an actual branch of the MC Brothers and for those Brothers to take vows within the Congregation of the MC Brothers — something which Andrew would not and in fact did not accept.

> Dear Brother Andrew,
>
> I have been waiting and praying for a line from you after that painful letter — Mother love is always greater than the pain inflicted — by the one she loves.

I was very happy to be with the Brothers but I missed you — much — They are really the gift of God—so good—so all for Jesus. It was a grace for me to be with them —

Re — the contemplative branch of MC — when you & I and all the rest of the Brothers & Sisters become unable to go to the Poor — we will need to spend our lives in adoration, silence and contemplation — also there are religious & others who want this kind of life — of deeper contemplation & silence with just the two hours daily contact with individual Poor — to pray — whether in their home or hospital or street — what we have in N.Y. now is "MC Contemplative" — There will be no new congregation — just a part of the MC Society — That is why you should be grateful and happy — that the good God is giving the Brothers the gift of Contemp. MC

After years of work for Jesus — we need to get apart alone as Jesus did — I ask you Brother in the name of Our Lord do not refuse the gift of God — to the Brothers — You too will be happy to have a place in the MC Contemp. where you can spend your last days with Him alone. It was a very great surprise to me — when Br Sebastian spoke to me of his long desire — of which he had spoken to you — To me it was a sign of approval of the need the Brothers have — of this branch — I leave it to you to decide fully — as re - Br Sebastian — and the acceptance of the Branch Contemplative being a living branch of the MC Brothers You pray fervently and with humility — and let me know I will be in Rome by the 15th or 16th —

Do not be afraid — that I want to claim the Brothers in any way — God gave them to me and with great love, joy and trust I gave them to you — and never in all these years I have doubted or been unhappy about the giving. God has done great things in you and through you — to the Brothers and the Poor. I have never felt even a thought of distrust in you or doing — my heart & conscience is in perfect peace regarding this — so let us not allow anything else to come in now and spoil God's work. What about Br Angelo [Scolizzi] for the Br. in Rome?

With much love & joy. Pray for me

God bless you
M Teresa MC[104]

In a letter to Brother Gordon, Andrew wrote,

> Please pray for me in Calcutta. Things are pretty rough between MT and me. Angelo has flown there from Rome, wanting to make his profession with us, because Rome is asking for this, as he can't be left swinging without a congregation. M. [Mother] seems to want this, and they may have done it by time I get there. Either way it's going to be rough. I feel there's something pretty big here for what may be in the future ... Everyone's in on the act now, from Cardinal someone of the Congregation for Religious in Rome who writes to me asking for the above course, [Lawrence] Cardinal Picachy* and God knows who else. The hard thing is that no one understands the point — if there is one.[105]

Eventually Angelo Scolizzi did not take vows within the MC Brothers but, according to a website, he was ordained a priest and founded the Universal Fraternity of the Word Missionaries of Charity Third Order, M.C. III O.[106] It was only in the middle of 1978 that things started to settle down between Andrew and Mother. In an undated letter quoted by Solomon to Brother Nicholas, OCSO, Brother Andrew wrote:

> And staggeringly a German priest in charge of what M.T. [Mother Teresa] has set up in Rome turned up last Sunday. A fine guy who was sensitive to what was bugging me. And I find that has helped me to accept the situation — which I was struggling to do. Though I don't know what will happen ... "[107]

---

* Lawrence Trevor Picachy (1916 – 1976). Indian Jesuit, spiritual guide to Mother Teresa, Archbishop of Calcutta and elevated to Cardinal in 1976.

Part – IV: From General to Troubadour (1976 – 1986)

The outcome appears to have been conciliatory:

> Dear Brother Andrew,
>
> You don't know how happy I feel at having talked [about] the Brothers of the Word with you. Fr Mariangelo having been with you & now going to Rome is also another great proof that Jesus is at work in this new Seed of love. So let us thank Jesus for all His love for us all. May I ask you to help the Brothers especially the tertians to deepen their love for Our Lady — I am ready to send you 9 Rosaries for them — made by our Novices. The Brothers belong to Our Lady in a special way — She will protect & be with them always.
>
> Pray for me as I do for you.
>
> God bless you
> M Teresa MC[108]

In 1985, after the MC Brothers had raised questions about the various branches, Brother Andrew felt the need to clarify the distinctions between all the male groups. After describing them, he admonished and exhorted the Brothers to "please read what I have written here again carefully. I have written each word carefully, and I don't want Brothers running around saying Br Andrew wrote this or that — when it was not what I wrote at all. (You see, I know MC Brothers!)" He then ended the letter by asking the Brothers to "file this letter carefully. It will make very interesting reading after 10 years. Someone is then likely to look very stupid — probably me!"[109] Thirty-five years have passed since that letter was written. Nobody looked stupid. Rather it was a necessary dose of prudence at the time of writing to enable all the groups involved to develop and deepen their identity within the MC family.

In a letter to his friend Kathryn Spink in 1992, Andrew reminisced:

> Funny how time and mellowing change one's answers — here regarding the founding of MC Contemplative Brs & MC Fathers. I'd say M.T. [Mother Teresa] was wanting a male branch of MC that was closer to the Sisters in details of

prayer life, discipline and sort of general tidiness than what I was producing with the Brothers. As for me, I can see now that I was peeved that she went ahead without me on both these ventures — male pride stung. It was her directness in going after her goals that avoided getting bogged down in diplomacy or Anglo-Saxon politeness with me — which would have produced nothing worthwhile and would have hindered the whole development. I was by-passed — rightly & happily so.[110]

AUSTRALIANNESS

Amid difficulties, suffering or stress, Andrew never lost his sense of humour. In a letter he sent to Brother Gordon, after mentioning tensions he was having with Mother Teresa, he added:

> But I'm so damned mad and stung that it may just be my pride. Just pray that I can keep somehow cool, and not blow the whole bloody thing ... So it's going to be an interesting Christmas. I could end up in a stable somewhere myself, which wouldn't be a bad thing.[111]

In another letter to Brother Jeremy, the typographical errors in the original letter were more than evident:

> At last here are these certificates. I'm sure they're wrong. As I was typing the stupid things I got madder and madder, and the typewriter started to jump more spaces. I can imagine what headaches you have over the visas.[112]

It is what Australians call a "larrikin" sense of humour — with apparent disregard for social or political conventions.[113] "Calcutta is really hot. I write this with everything wet with sweat: clothes, fingers, even the paper. Just wonderful climate for all the decisions and crises."[114] His humour was at times dry, satirical. To one Brother he would send Peanuts comic strip cuttings from the newspaper. But he particularly loved the Australian cartoonist, Michael Leunig, and occasionally he would send one of Leunig's comic strips to his friend Gerard Monaghan.[115]

Part – IV: From General to Troubadour (1976 – 1986)

> What about this for breaking taboos?
>
> It seems that you are keeping the International CLC [Christian Life Community] going from Rome. I hope to God you're doing that better than I am with MC Bros from Calcutta. I can't ever go to Rome. It would really be testing Providence too much. Our existence is ignored by them. But one day some Msgr [monsignor] is going to wake up and ask where has this huge bloody Congregation of Brothers come from?[116]

We could speculate as to what might have happened if an American Jesuit from the Jamshedpur Province — or a Belgian Jesuit from the Calcutta Province or a Maltese Jesuit from the Dumka Province or an Indian diocesan priest or bishop — had taken over the administration, the leadership and formation of the new congregation of the Missionaries of Charity Brothers. The fact is that Andrew was an Australian with all the characteristics typical of his countrymen.

Australians are egalitarian and do not like to think they are better than anybody else. Andrew called the Brothers by name, no titles used. With the poor he was one of them. He did not want to be put in a separate or higher category. He did not want to be given different treatment. Many Brothers recounted how when they arrived at the Congregation's generalate house on Mansatala Row to join for the first time, they did not know they were being welcomed by the General Superior. As soon as these young men arrived, he would quickly go to the kitchen on the ground floor to fetch tea and biscuits for them. He would talk to them in Hindi if they were not fluent in English.

There was an informality about his human relations. MC village communities in Andrew's days were still very frugal and austere in their set-up. Like the people in the villages around them, the Brothers had no toilet facilities inside or outside their mud houses. Thus it was not uncommon to see Andrew, while visiting such communities, pick up his water container and walk out into the open fields to relieve himself in the early morning. No doubt the locals were intrigued to find this tall sahib walking with them for his morning rituals!

Andrew loved authenticity and sincerity. He could be compassionate with the one who accepted he had erred, but intolerant with the one who denied making a mistake. He never tried to attract attention to his academic or other achievements or gave the impression that he was better than anyone else. "While waiting to get a train ticket from a vending machine in Japan, a local man came up to him and instructed him on how to get the ticket. This man did not know that it was not Andrew's first time using the vending machine with Japanese instructions. Andrew did not want to embarrass the man and so patiently let him explain and then thanked him."[117]

Australians are shy of formality in dress. The early Australian scholastics and Jesuit priests who arrived in Ranchi in the early 1950s were appalled to find that they had to wear the European-style cassock all the time, even while riding a bicycle or going to the bathroom from their room. Andrew had been taken aback in Shishu Bhavan in 1966, when he found the young Brothers using a white shirt and white trousers for prayers, meditation and Mass, and changing afterwards for work. Thus when Mother Teresa sent a bolt of fabric to the Brothers for them to make habits, he promptly sent it back to Mother House. For Andrew, informality of dress made the Brothers more approachable to the poor and also helped them to identify with the poor they served. He always wore a simple shirt and pyjama (loose, lightweight trousers).

"No worries mate," was a phrase he frequently used and one often heard in Australia indicating a laid-back attitude. At the same time, he was direct and would not mince words, getting down to business with a minimum amount of small talk. Above all, Australians place a high value on relationships: it was not unusual for him to go down to the docks in Kidderpoor for a cold beer with fellow Australian Jesuits when they popped in for a visit.

Part – IV: From General to Troubadour (1976 – 1986)

According to Eileen Egan, Brother Andrew smiled frequently and was down-to-earth even though his face was that of an ascetic — withdrawn from the world.[118] In one of his retreats while talking about miracles, this down-to-earth quality and common sense come out very clearly:

> If you want a miracle you've got to be really helpless, they don't happen as long as you're able to do it yourself. It wouldn't make any sense. God has given our brains and our intelligence and our faculties to do this for yourself and he expects us to use them. Miracles don't happen at that point. He is not going to multiply the loaves and fishes there as long as you've got stuff in the cupboards, in the pantry, in the fridge and all that. Just go and open the fridge and cook your dinner, with the hands He gave you.[119]

Again, in one of his letters to the community in Los Angeles, referring to the problem of finding a suitable house and the possibility of being offered a big place he wrote:

> You spoke of the possible convent. We will never get the ideal place. Even a "lavish" convent need not worry us too much. I think the building matters less than how we live in it. You can store all the unnecessary things in one room — and fit out the rest of the place very simply. It can be part of poverty to accept what is offered. So I would be slow to refuse a place that is offered. It does not matter if it is big for now. When we moved into Mansatala there were less than 20 Brothers. And maybe later we could have hospitality for the poor in the place. For me the main question is whether the location is convenient. It would be a strange 'poverty' that would lead us to refuse a house that is offered freely, and then have to pay $300 a month rent for a "poor" place. As I said, you can roll up the carpets etc. & put them in one room and live simply in the rest. If God offers us a big place now, it may be that he will have lots of people to put in it by the end of the year. What I am saying is, Don't be too quick to refuse

whatever Bishop offers. And we shouldn't put standards that would exclude any place he might have.[120]

Brother Andrew was direct in his approach if the situation asked for it:

> Professed Brothers should be fully occupied both morning and afternoon. There should be a continuing search for the poorest of the poor that we are not yet reaching. We must remember our work is to go out to the people in the spirit of the Good Shepherd, rather than to be working at home.[121]

There was no need for pretence with him:

> We are a Congregation that is made up of the Brothers that we have and are. The present Brothers are this Congregation. We are not as highly trained and qualified as others. Therefore, we will not do our work in the same way as others. We should understand this and accept ourselves and our Brothers as we are in reality.[122]

He accepted that there was corruption in the society but at the same time, he claimed:

> Brothers, you may well ask: What about you, Brother Andrew, You are making us look into the darkness of our lives? I can answer by telling you that I am finding the same corruption in myself, much worse than in you. I can see it more clearly now. And that is a beginning. I do not yet find the strength to turn away from it. But I feel that God is beginning a new work of purification in me, and I trust that He will complete this work in me.[123]

He was tougher when it came to waste, not for the sake of wastage itself but for the sake of the poor who lacked basic needs while the Brothers had all their needs met and more:

> It is strange to hear complaints about food from MCs who live and work with the poorest of the poor. I have heard of several houses where Brothers want and have mutton, and are not willing to have beef. In India mutton is the

food of the rich. Please note that beef is to be used instead of mutton. The Local Servants have the responsibility for immediately correcting this.

In India we have plenty of *lungis* available from Titagarh.** And I have heard of Brothers insisting on buying costly *lungis* from the market. Let these costly *lungis* be given immediately to the patients; and the Brothers use the Titagarh ones. I would consider a Brother who continued in this way unfit for final profession. There is waste in our houses in allowing electric light to burn in rooms where no one is present, in letting soap get spoiled in containers with water, etc.

These are small things, but let us see that careless waste is very bad. Once a reporter asked Mother Teresa if she got angry when she saw how the rich live. She replied that this did not make her angry, but that she was always angry to see things wasted.[124]

Material waste was not the only abuse Brother Andrew recognised. He also remarked on excessive leave-taking and visiting:

I am sorry to say that there are many abuses in this, especially in India, to a point where it is out of control and strong action has to be taken. It is hard to find a community these days without finding some member absent with his family or elsewhere. There has been a great increase in the number of such visits. Parents seem to be seriously ill and dying several times over. And these illnesses multiply at Christmas, Easter and the holiday season. Family marriages, arranging jobs and education of family members, law cases are all used for visits and absence from one's community. Sad to say it has come to a point where it is very difficult to judge which are genuine cases and which are not.[125]

** A piece of woven cloth about 115 cm in height and 200 cm in length, usually tied around the lower waist by men.

VISITS TO AUSTRALIA

We have very little information about Andrew's visits to his family in Australia, other than what we can glean from reading between the lines in some of his letters. His first visit was in 1976 after returning from Vietnam and he was busy with various engagements. We do not know what most of them were but one was a meeting at Genazzano Convent in Melbourne. Val Noone, whose different views on Vietnam, caused tensions between him and Brother Andrew, recalled:

> Andrew gave a public talk to a couple of hundred people at Genazzano, portraying himself as the doer of good works who had been unjustly treated by the incoming Communist rulers of Vietnam. That the independent patriotic and Communist party-led Vietnamese government should be suspicious of an Australian priest who was closely associated with the Jesuits of Yen Do Street and with Bob Santamaria, (who were known as supporters of the American war), seemed logical to me. I challenged some of Andrew's views but he was not fazed by that.[126]

Although happy to meet his family and friends, Andrew felt out of place in his native Australia. "But I'll be glad to get out of Australia. It's not my scene. It must be the closest thing to the moon on this planet — unreal. But they do fatten you up."[127] A few weeks later he again wrote to the Brothers in Los Angeles, this time lamenting the changes happening in the land of his birth:

> You may be interested in a criticism I have run into here — also in Japan. It is that our work of charity delays the day of fundamental social change. It has been bitter in places — and I find it sad. But there is really no conflict. While some work to change political & social structures, there are people lying battered at the roadside and they cannot wait for the system to change and that is the work we MC's profess to do.[128]

During his second visit to Australia in early 1981 his brother Brendan died. There is nothing archived about this sad event which occurred on 12 March. Brendan was the brother who had attended Ian's ordination in Ranchi in 1963. (His other brother Leo was to die on 16 October 1985.) Leo's daughter Leone recalled: "The brothers Brendan and Leo and Ian, all called each other Joe. I don't know why particularly Leo and Brendan, but then they extended it to Ian, and when Ian and my father were here together, honestly I don't know what they would have said but they'd be roaring with laughter and my father's eyebrows used to pop when he was really amused, and Ian would be reminding him of different things. They had a wonderful time."[129] But then Andrew was an easy person and he had a good time even with his three sisters, with whom he used to stay when he visited Melbourne. They loved him!

In January 1986 he again visited Australia. It is not known whether he went for his usual home visit or specifically for a meeting to which he had been invited — the Marist Brothers' youth festival at Kilmore. Other speakers were Bishop Eamon Casey of Galway, Ireland, President of the Irish Catholic Relief agency, and Val Noone who spoke about nuclear disarmament. To his friend Kathryn Spink he afterwards wrote:

> Interestingly I spoke of this gambling addiction to a large group of young people on this trip to Australia — the Youth Festival that brought me here this trip. And it was interesting that the young people seemed to appreciate my saying that and could identify more with me. And accepted what I had to say.[130]

In 1987 he returned to Australia:

> My 2½ months in Australia had me on the move at a fairly brisk pace. And so there was not much chance to write and thank you for much kindness and warmth.
>
> This letter tries to say Thank You; and it offers the chance to share a thought or two.

> The visit started in Melbourne in July. There were lovely days with family sprinkled in between retreats, talks, etc. And there were lovely walks in the bush, on beaches and the beautiful suburban streets in Australian cities with their amazing trees and solitude.
>
> Work started with an 8 days' retreat at the Passionists' monastery at Temple Stowe with a rich group of lay people, religious and priests.
>
> Similar retreats in Sydney, Goulburn and Rockhampton were highlights of the visit. There were weekend retreats and days of prayer with others who didn't have the luxury of a longer time. There were meetings, days of prayer and sharing with groups of struggling broken people, the handicapped and the troubled. A few days with Aborigines and remote farmers in Central Queensland added a wonderful variety and brought me to a real thankfulness for this whole privilege.
>
> It is always good to come back to one's roots. And for all our problems and ills, Australia remains a very beautiful and privileged land.[131]

Jane Simons, Leone's daughter and thus Brother Andrew's grandniece recalled his visits to their home in Sydney:

> Sports. He loved sports, Australian football, cricket and just stuff like that he was right into. The other memory I have is when I moved out into a shared house at university. The house was full of friends of mine, and it was pretty terrible, pretty murphy and we were not very good at cleaning up. And, he came up when we invited him over for a curry. He said Mass, and afterwards we were all crammed into this tiny little kitchen and he didn't care, he was enjoying it. There would have been about twenty people in there. We were all young students and everyone was drinking beer, not him, but he didn't mind any of that, and I remember him just carrying on about this curry which my friend had

cooked for him, that he made everyone feel good. 'This is the best,' he was saying. And the guy lives in India right? So probably he had a million curries, but he was going on and on, that it was the best curry he'd ever had.

Oh he was so funny, and everybody was asking him about Mother Teresa. Oh, it was really a nice time. I just remembered it very well. That would have been 1987. That's probably my strongest adult memories because I would have been 19 then. Well, I remember this particular curry night, yeah, people were asking him all sorts of questions, and I was a bit worried that it was too much for him — all those students questioning him, but he just handled it, he knew exactly what the questions were and just handled it in a really simple but reflecting, in a really Jesuit way.[132]

There are a few things which both Julian and Anne remembered most about their uncle during his Australian visits. His love and knack for betting was one. Gifting somebody with a betting slip for a small sum is a very normal part of Australian culture: "Uncle Ian always produced a little ticket for you. Just a five-dollar penny ticket for someone to win the football premier, or the Brownlow Medal which was for the best player in the competition. About the gambling, there was one [story] of Ian's winning before he died, he got 400 dollars for the Brownlow Medal. He certainly won a lot of his bets on them, because he used to say, 'I had a bit of a win on Saturday.' And I remember sometimes he'd come over to Kew and it was all delivered — the food, he'd organised. He'd get Chinese, on his winnings."[133]

WHAT I MET ALONG THE WAY

During this decade a few books were written and published about the Missionaries of Charity Brothers with a special emphasis on the role of Brother Andrew in their founding and forming. *Apuesta por Cristo en los Pobres* was written by José Luis González-Balado and his wife Janet Playfoot, and published in Spanish in 1985 by Paulinas. It was translated into Italian, and also into French under the title *Pari sur Dieu*. In 1987 Kathryn Spink, together with José Luis González-Balado published *Spirit of Bethlehem* with the SPCK (Society for Promoting Christian Knowledge), which could be considered the English version of *Apuesta por Cristo en los Pobres* but was by no means a direct translation. In the same year, St Pauls Publications in Australia published *Brothers of Mother Teresa* written by Geoffrey D. Solomon.

Of much interest is the book Brother Andrew himself wrote. *What I Met Along the Way* was published by Darton, Longman and Todd (London) in 1987. In his introduction Malcolm Muggeridge thanks God that, "there is a book ... giving an account of his [Andrew's] travels during 1984, when he journeyed round the world visiting communities set up by the Missionary Brothers of Charity in many countries. Yet the book is not so much about these communities as about the people he met, what he saw and thought ... He meets and studies people rather than observing scenery. What he cares about is the spiritual dimension of people's lives, the active, loving presence alive in the depths of living."[134]

It was a pilgrimage which started in Hong Kong and Korea and took him to the African Continent: Nigeria, Ghana, Madagascar, Nairobi. From there he journeyed over to Europe: Sweden and Paris (where the Brothers had recently opened communities), and then to Latin America including Brazil, Bolivia, Lima in Peru, Colombia, Haiti, Guatemala, El Salvador and Mexico. Finally Brother Andrew travelled back to Tokyo and Korea via Los Angeles in the United States.

A few things in particular might catch the readers' attention. The first story that Andrew narrated was of a shy withdrawn Korean girl who on a weekly basis visited one of the Brothers' communities for homeless and helpless men in South Korea. She never spoke to anybody but instead would bring flowers, arrange them in the chapel, then leave and return the following Saturday. As time went by, she began to stay a little longer and later started interacting with everyone. She took to sharing a meal and sometimes also cooked one. Because she was able to bring beauty to others around her her life changed. "Small people doing little things in obscurity may be the world's great saviours."[135]

Towards the middle of the book, Brother Andrew inserted an autobiographical essay entitled 'The Weakened Spine'. By his own account it was written in the late '70s or early '80s and never published. After describing the Church events following his ordination in 1963, he confessed: "After a number of years, however, it struck me that I had been attacked by some kind of wasting, decaying disease that had softened up my spiritual and moral backbone, and which led me to crash heavily and frequently."[136] Faithfully he continued to follow the timetable of the community but that was not enough:

> My vow of poverty did not stop me from having money for myself and using it for my own purposes. My vow of chastity did not prevent me from taking the commandment of God fairly lightly, while my vow of obedience presented no problem. My superiors seldom, if ever, confronted me with an order to do this and that ...
>
> If I ask myself now as I write these lines, "Where did it begin to change?" I realize that the first thing I remember dropping was the daily Rosary which was an obligatory practice for us ... Later would follow the religious dress, the Office, the bells, the regular prayer and so on. Gradually I came to the point where I suited myself in everything ... I began to give first place to my own self. I became my own god ...
>
> It is the hard-to-believe story of an unfaithful man used by God, the story of God's love, mercy and forgiveness being immeasurably stronger than his justice ...[137]

It was a laughter-inducing experience that first awoke him to the fact that something was not right. A friend from India happened to be in Los Angeles with his wife at the same time as Andrew. They wanted to go to Disneyland and they took him along:

> We bought books of tickets for the various attractions and started with the guided tour led by a girl dressed in appropriate Disneyland garb. She had us in a group of twenty, all adults, and gave us this little talk to start with about how we were to keep together, keep wearing our blue cards, not get lost, not wander away, etc ... As she went on I found myself getting more and more irritated until I felt quite angry.
>
> And then waiting on the platform for the wonderland train in Disneyland, it suddenly hit me as this pretty girl warbled on, telling me what to do and what not to do. I realized that for ten years at least, no one had told me what to do or what not to do. In those years I had come to have authority over a lot of people. I had told them what to do, but no one told me. And here in Disneyland on this fine morning when this young tour guide was telling me what to do, I didn't like it. Soon the Disney train came, and by the time I had obediently fallen into line, passed through the gate, not lost my blue card, done everything I was told and was nicely seated, by that time I was able to laugh at myself. And that was a healthy laugh, even though it didn't repair my spinal column.[138]

By his own admission, it would take another two years before he began to realize that something was wrong with his spine.

Years later, reminiscing about *What I Met Along the Way*, Brother Andrew remembered that he was not very enthusiastic about giving interviews or talks to launch and promote the book. He was afraid that the media would distort his intentions. Teresa de Bertodano, commissioning editor at Darton, Longmann and Todd finally convinced him: "She said, 'the media can distort anything except holiness. There is a great power in the sacred.'"[139] He agreed to an interview on British television aired live on 29 April 1987. It turned out to be a "success," and being Andrew, he turned a situation charged with extreme emotions into a humorous one:

Part – IV: From General to Troubadour (1976 – 1986)

I was interviewed in England on the Terry Wogan programme of the BBC — prime time about 7.00 o'clock because of that book that I wrote ... The publishers were very surprised I got on it — Margaret Thatcher and Lulu got on it—Lulu was on the night before ...

So I got on and it's live — they say anything between seven and nine million people watch that programme. The only reason I got on that programme was not because I worked in Calcutta or Mother Teresa — the reason was, here was this fellow who was a gambler, he lost all his money and turned a priest or something or other. And I came out. Derek Nimmo was the one before me and I waited in the wing and then I sat down and you never see him beforehand, and you don't meet him. So I came in and sat down and Wogan looks at me and says, "Br Andrew, that's a nice shirt you're wearing tonight, would you tell us about the day you lost your shirt at the races?" Several million people were watching. It was a wonderful interview, he and Nimmo got into a ... Nimmo tried to be smug, they went into detail, but for me he gave me a wonderful run.

Well ... when I stay in London, I stay in Kilburn, which is not a very nice part of London where all the down-and-out Irish, sort of Skid Row, and the Sisters of Mother Teresa have a soup kitchen and have a place for about twelve men who can stay and some of their helpers. The BBC picked me up in a tremendous limousine to take me. They said, "We do that," the driver told me, "So that they can know if you are stuck in the traffic".

Well, afterwards they drove me home, dropped me at this sort of down-and-out place in Kilburn and it was still quite early and I was really high after all the adrenaline going. I went in and I either wanted to talk about it or I didn't — just to be on my own. No one was around, so I went into the kitchen and made myself a cup of tea and this chap Patrick who was staying there I think he was from Western Australia — he came from a Christian Brother orphanage in Perth and he was a chronic alcoholic. Patrick had broken out that night and he'd gone to the pub. So I made a cup of tea and in comes Patrick and Patrick as drunk as he was, he was down in the pub and the TV was on and he had seen this thing on the TV. So he comes back and he says, "Well, you know I'm drunk, and I've always been drunk, and I drank too much," and then he says quietly, "But I never gambled!"[140]

SPIRITUALITY OF BROTHER ANDREW (1976 – 1987)

On the subject of spirituality, a few premises should be taken into consideration. In the Catholic Church spirituality is the practice of living out a personal act of faith following the acceptance of such faith. Although Catholics are expected to pray together during the Celebration of the Eucharist, many different forms of spirituality and private prayer have developed over the years. We talk of Ignatian spirituality or Benedictine or Augustinian or MC spirituality. When it comes to describing a person, it is hard to pinpoint with any precision what his or her spirituality was or is because it is his or her own way of approaching God in prayer and living out the Gospel — a personal way of relating to the Divine. What goes on in the heart of the person in front of God is another way of looking at spirituality. Nobody can be considered an authority on the spirituality of any other person or saint. We can only catch glimpses from the way he or she lived out the message of Jesus in words and actions. In the case of Brother Andrew we find clues in the way he dealt with his fellow MC Brothers and especially the poor.

Another premise is that the basic tenets in one's life remain unaltered, unchangeable whereas the way a person sees things when he or she is twenty, or forty, or sixty years old can change over time: some aspects may grow, others are left behind, even as others are purified. Consequently we might see a slight shift in Brother

Andrew's ways of perceiving and practising the Gospel between the decade of 1976 to 1987, and the years 1988 to 2000.

Andrew's Mysticism

Andrew's spirituality could be considered mystical. He was not the kind of mystic who would experience visions, locutions, ecstasies, raptures and the like. Harvey D. Egan describes mysticism as being "beyond the normal workings of the intellect and senses. The genuine mystic is united and one with God and from this loving union flows a special knowledge, a 'secret wisdom' which stupefies the intellect and short-circuits the memory."[141] All the mystic wants is a deep relationship with God or better still, just God, because simplicity and mysticism go hand in hand. The only thing that matters is love of God — expressed in the love of others, because a mystic is never selfish, neither consumed with self-interest nor personal happiness. Mystics often describe their journey in life as a battle, a pilgrimage, a quest, a lonely search. By wanting and seeing God in everything around them, mystics are attuned to both beauty and pain at the same time. This was Andrew. His mysticism did not confine him to an ascetic hermitical life but, on the contrary, opened him more and more to those who suffered.

Like that of Ignatius of Loyola, Brother Andrew's mysticism emphasized beauty that is revealed and apparent. In this way God is seen through a kaleidoscope of colour, song and complexity: "a multiplicity of images and ideas all intertwine mutually illuminating one another while celebrating the richness of beauty experienced in diversity."[142] There is an example of this type of mysticism in one of Andrew's most beautiful letters. The year was 1971, and in the third week of November while on his annual eight-day retreat in the newly-opened community in Picnic Gardens, he decided to spend a night of prayer in Howrah Railway Station.[143] Thousands of people pass through this station every day and hundreds (if not thousands) had made their "home" on the platforms, especially after the East Pakistan War.

In November I made my annual retreat, and I spent a night of prayer — a sort of vigil — on the Howrah Railway Station, the main station of Calcutta. So much happened, but I'd like to share with you a glimpse I had into a little family, who came to sleep after the trains stopped about midnight. There were another four children from eleven years to five. The mother was a funny little thing in a thin white cotton sari on a winter's night, and she had hair closely cropped for a woman. She had some tins or mugs, a few bits of cloth and some pieces of bread. They were beggars. The station was their home.

The children, three girls and the youngest a boy were full of life, and at that hour of night they all sat down on the station with so many other families and lone people sleeping all around and they had their "evening" meal of dry bread — perhaps the leftovers from some vendor sold cheaply at the end of the day to meet a beggar's purse. But it was not a sad meal. They talked and laughed and joked so much. It would be hard in fact to find a happier family gathering. And when the meal was over they went to a public hydrant and washed their tins and mouths and drank water. Then they spread out their rags to sleep on and a bit of a sheet to cover themselves. And then it was that the little boy did something wonderful. He danced a little dance. He skipped and jumped and laughed and sang. Such a dance, at such an hour, in such utter deprivation. I had my vigil, more than enough for any man's meditation. And the words of the song became real:

Dance, then, wherever you may be
I am the Lord of the Dance, said He
And I'll lead you all wherever you may be,
And I'll lead you all in the Dance, said He.

We think we do much for the poor. But it is they who make us rich. We are in debt to them. There is a really big question: What does the hungry man ask?

What does that funny little mother and her four children ask of me? Bread? Money? Yes, but something more. Something more that is not easy to discover. Money, Plans, Projects, Politics, Aid are all needed, but they're not enough. They've been tried, they've done something, but still leave many people hungry.

Whatever it is that the hungry man asks, I think, it touches us personally — in the depths of our own lives. We, the people of the same world have to change, to become different — or nothing will change.

That little mother asks more than our bread and money. Perhaps she asks us to become her brothers and sisters — to share something with her. Perhaps just the pain we feel at not knowing what to do.

The hungry man seems to put our whole life and its meaning into question. He is my brother and maybe I need him more than he needs me. In the bewilderment that I feel in the face of the hunger of my brothers by the million, I approach the mystery of Christmas, of that dark homeless night long ago, when a poor couple brought their poor child into the darkness of the night. And that child became the light that enlightened every man.[144]

Surrounded by the squalor of Howrah railway station teeming with poor people, amidst the pain, the suffering and the misery of humankind, the mystic is able to perceive beauty, to glimpse the joy in the sheer simplicity of the dance of a small boy — to perceive the Divine in the purely human.

I said: What about my eyes?
He said: Keep them on the road.
I said: What about my passion?

He said: Keep it burning.
I said: What about my heart?
He said: Tell me what you hold inside it.
I said: Pain and sorrow.
He said: Stay with it.
The wound is the place where the Light enters you.
Rumi.

There is no mention of Rumi or any other Sufi mystic in Brother Andrew's writings but the above quote describes his mysticism in a nutshell.[145] It is the merging, the fusion of *beauty* and *pain*. For this reason Andrew's mysticism also approached that of St John of the Cross with its emphasis on a glory that remains concealed, hidden from view. Both John of the Cross and Brother Andrew "came to God" as they were. There was no need to "clean up the mess of their life" and their "disordered feelings", or in modern terms, "defects of character" before coming in front of God. "Rather than dressing the wounds with analyses and excuses John [and Andrew] would have us locate the wound and without explanation stand in it, hold it, before God."[146]

Andrew's compulsions were his need for God. They were not an obstacle to his prayers and to love. At the same time "the wound" drew him closer to those who suffer as the German theologian Dorothee Sölle would say: the capacity for love is strongest where it grows out of suffering. His life was a fairly comfortable one (especially his childhood and teen years in Australia) and yet he was always sensitive to the pain and suffering of the poor, of the broken people he met. He did not run away from the pain because he knew that beauty and suffering go hand in hand:

> Your letter was again that vital combination of the beauty and the pain that runs through everything. I find it more and more terrible to contemplate the stark price that so many of us are paying in the depths of our beings. It is

almost unbearable — probably the contemplation of it more so than the thing itself. Such an intensity of life. One can scarcely stand it.[147]

He called "it" a vital combination of beauty and pain. There were both. One could not live without the other.

Brother Andrew's being in touch with his own raw suffering and with the misery and anguish of the poor, while serving as the General Servant of a new Congregation, with its limits, cost him heavily: physical and psychic exhaustion, darkness, tremendous pain and eventually the cross. His letter to the Brothers after the General Chapter of 1986 gave the impression that he only saw and experienced suffering around:

> At present it is a song about the suffering of our poor people (and our own also) and the life-giving power that Christ gives to their suffering. But so often they do not know about it. World problems today are so enormous: poverty, disease, breakdown, mental illness, regional and racial tensions. Politics, economics, education, psychology, medicine, revolution are only band aids that can effect temporary repairs.[148]

The term "suffering" appeared often in his letters. But it was not a cry of despair. It was one of hope. Andrew believed that Christ did not take away suffering, but gave it a supernatural meaning:

> This is the first song I am singing now as a liberated General. It is the song of life-giving suffering in Christ ... This song is one of joyful hope for our poor people — and for the whole suffering world though their suffering offered with Christ crucified.[149]

Amidst all this apparent suffering, the mystic experienced the deep and numerous joys of being and working with the poor:

> There is the joy of seeing people relieved of at least a little of their suffering, of the sick cured, of families finding employment for a breadwinner, of children of the streets finding a home and responding as loved and loving human

beings, of alcoholics and drug addicts overcoming their difficulties. There is the joy in seeing a little one-legged boy from the railway station playing happily in the room as I write this. Now he finds shelter, a home, food and a little love. It is worthwhile to have lived for this story, where one has been able to share in some way in such a story. For us here seeing these things directly, it is easier, for such sights and experiences are a great encouragement and happiness. I think the faith and love of those from afar who share in this work is much greater — for they do not have the consolation of seeing the light in young eyes or hearing the laughter and singing.

Misery and joy seem to be the strange contradictions of our world and life. It would be a terrible state, except for the fact that the joy so often grows out of the misery.[150]

In Andrew's writings, misery is evident but it definitely runs parallel with beauty. He was a lover of beauty. He wonderfully described one of the houses in Guatemala where he experienced great peace and beauty on Christmas Eve:

Our house is high up next to the small village church and overlooks a deep valley that changes colour every hour as the moving sun gives a different light and shade. It overlooks several ranges of mountains including a volcano of perfect symmetry ... Beauty ran through it all. Beauty can save us, and maybe it's not necessary to go as far as those Guatemalan mountains to experience it — though a pilgrimage can make one more receptive to it. There is beauty everywhere: the beauty of God's creation and the beauty of his people. This beauty is found in every parish, village, family, country. Yet sometimes it's hidden and we have to look for it.[151]

While talking during a retreat about destruction and the culture of death which was being felt all over the world, Brother Andrew also spoke about the destruction of beauty through the force of the evil one constantly working for death and destruction. Andrew's

Part – IV: From General to Troubadour (1976 – 1986)

sensitivity to beauty was due to the belief that where there is beauty there is goodness:

> Even in our own music and our art, our poetry. So much is sheer ugliness ... the fashion of wearing black, everything black. No colour. No life. Things are connected. There was once a young fellow who'd been in the drug world and [led a] pretty miserable life ... And he had a spiritual awakening and I met him a few times over two or three years and he was telling me that he was out of drugs, but he was still totally depressed. He came on a retreat all dressed in black, jumper ... everything in black so I told him, why don't you get a shirt with some pattern, that black is so depressing. And there were some friends around and the next morning he came with a jumper with some colour — had some blue, but at least it wasn't black. I met him again after a year and he had made a tremendous difference just wearing clothes with some colour. It is such a depressing fashion nowadays for young people to wear black. And we wonder why everybody is depressed and gloomy. And that fashion comes from something — something is taken away — the beauty of colour.
>
> Beautiful music, nowadays it's all screaming, and blood curdling noises coming out of the radio. Where is beauty? Art — so much of modern art, stark and ugly. Dostoevsky said that in the end the world will be saved by beauty. Beauty is of God. Beauty is something created, it comes from a Creator. The devil cannot make beauty. He can only produce ugliness. His reign is to propagate the ugly.[152]

Lover of the Church

> Writing this letter makes me reflect on the value of all of us being totally united around this work — you by your interest and concern, the Brothers in India, Vietnam and Cambodia and of course the poor, the suffering, and wounded ones, who in God's love, give such richness to our lives.[153]

This is the Church Brother Andrew believed in. It is a Church where, everybody, rich and poor alike, is related. This is the Church he belonged to — a Church maintained by little people doing little things for little people. His love for the Church and her sacraments came out in his deep devotion and reverence for the Mass. He once wrote of how if everything were to go away, the Mass would stay. In his book *What I Met Along the Way*, he wrote too about the joy and enthusiasm experienced when he celebrated Mass on one of his trips to Madagascar. Br George Dev, who lived in Madagascar, testified to such experience,

> Eventually, one of the "ladies" became very sick and she was dying. So we arranged for the transport and took her and admitted her in hospital. So the other women became very friendly with us, and from then onwards, any problem they had, they would come to us. We wanted to bring them together for prayer. They used to come once a week. So when Andrew came, we proposed Andrew to celebrate a Mass with them. He agreed immediately. And so in one of the slums we had Mass with the prostitutes. And he wrote in that book about the Mass with prostitutes in Madagascar. The women were sitting and crying during the Mass.[154]

The suffering Church for Andrew extended beyond the small sphere of the Missionaries of Charity. His sense of the universality of the Church was exemplified in a general letter sent from Hong Kong and dated 30 August 1985, in which he urged the Brothers to write a brief message of encouragement to prisoners in Czechoslovakia under trial and persecution for their faith:

> I am giving the names of some people in Czechoslovakia.... They may already be in prison. If you wish you can write a small letter to encourage them and to offer your prayers. It will be a great support for them, and it may help them as the authorities may not deal with them unjustly if they know that their story is known to people outside the country. But do not make any criticism of the government or any political comments. Just personal and spiritual.

> Iva and Zdenik Kotria and Petr Kozanek Palackeho. These are husband and wife. She is 36, has 3 children. She writes religious poems. Her house has been raided by police and they have been abused and called to police many times. Zdenik the husband is handicapped. Petr was found with some copies of Iva's poems. He was charged and faces up to three years sentence. Fr Ladislav Trojan O.F.M. is a 70-year-old Franciscan priest, who has been in and out of prison for many years. His house was raided last November and they found Mass items. He is under sentence in prison. Karel and Jindriska Korinek are husband & wife, Seventh Day Adventists. They have been in psychiatric hospital for their religious faith, and are threatened with this again now.
>
> But do pray for them, and for many others suffering for their faith.[155]

From India to Madagascar, from Guatemala to Manila, from Hong Kong to Czechoslovakia, his deep love for and loyalty to the Church remained steadfast. He likewise urged the Brothers to:

> be careful to follow the Church. We belong to a Congregation that is growing and expanding at a time when many congregations are standing still or dying. It is not by chance that Mother Teresa has taken her stand very strongly in the Church and with these three essentials: Blessed Sacrament, Mary, the Pope. These are very much part of our MC life. And if a Brother is away from these, he is surely a dead or dying branch that will break off before long.[156]

He was steadfastly rooted in the Church, and the same words he uttered about Mother can be easily applied to him:

> And if there is one thing that the spirit of Mother Teresa is not, it is not doing my own thing. She is rooted very much in the Church, in the teaching of the Church in the life of the Church.[157]

Life with Content for Others

During the years that followed Brother Andrew's departure from Vietnam, he was increasingly struck by one aspect of the MC work that he felt might be most essential: the meaning of the presence of a community of love, prayer and simplicity, the great importance of what the Brothers meant to people (not just the poor but also Co-Workers, neighbours, government workers, etc.) as distinct from what they did. During his November 1975 to January 1976 stay with the Brothers in Los Angeles he read the comment by former United Nations General Secretary Dag Hammarskjöld that a saint was one whose life had content for others. He was very struck by how much that remark had to say about who the Missionaries of Charity were and who Mother Teresa was.[158]

In a world where meaninglessness was becoming the order of the day, Andrew's life definitely had content and provided meaning for others. He was somebody for each person he met. He was somebody for the Jesuits, for the young man who through him joined the Society of Jesus, or who through his teachings became a school teacher at Sitagarha. He was somebody for Mother Teresa. He was somebody for that novice who found the courage to open up to the General Superior. He was somebody for Ba Thi, the twenty-nine-year-old mother who died in the Brothers' house in Cong Quynh, for Ba Kim who knew what he wanted to do in Saigon from the moment she met him. He was somebody for that little one-legged boy hopping around him while he wrote the Christmas letter. (He would be somebody for all those people he would eventually meet in the later stage of his life in Australia.)

But at the same time and above all, these small people's lives had content for Brother Andrew. Being a "brother" to these people, the awareness of being a "son" of the same Father, made him one with the poor, and they became his teachers. They were the people with true content for him:

I think of Odilia, a young girl in Korea who has been coming to our house in Seoul for nearly three years almost every evening after her work to help with the cooking, and who always has time for a bright word and a smile for the most overlooked of the old and disabled men living with us.

I think of our ambulance driver in Calcutta who in his old age still works to support his family who should really be supporting him now, and who has a devotion and a faithfulness that shame most of us Brothers. One of the most satisfying things I was able to do in this past year was to help him financially to pay off a little land from which he can feed his family …

One night in May I was returning to Calcutta from Ranchi. While I was waiting on the platform another train pulled in, and a crowd of poor tribal people clambered out carrying heavy bundles of fire wood to sell — men, women, old and young. They cut the wood in the mountains, carry it to their villages, cut it to size, tie it, and carry it again a long way to the nearest railway station. Then they battle into the crowded train with it. It is hard and heavy work. They are harassed by forest guards, police, the railways. Finally they sell it in the city for next to nothing. After arriving at the Ranchi station they sleep for the night on the platform and sell their wood in the morning to the merchants.

You would expect such people to be sad and oppressed. But on that hot summer's night, as they climbed up from the tracks on to the platform with their heavy bundles, as they lay down tired for the night, or ate the food of the poor, or smoked a cigarette, there was a laughter, a joking, a contentment, a fellowship that the richer ones of the world may well envy and that might make the reformers and revolutionaries pause to reflect on what they might transform these people into.[159]

In Brother Andrew's eyes these were the true saints. Small and poor as they were, they were the ones who amidst their poverty and suffering, were truly thankful to God.

> One hot Friday evening in April, I was offering Mass in a parish church in a poor barrio in Manila. I noticed an old woman in the second or third row. She was poor, wore a thin faded dress and cheap plastic sandals. She was toothless, and the poverty and difficulty of her life were written all over her. But what struck me strongly was her attitude of prayer as she stood there. Her hands were modestly extended, her head raised a little, her eyes often closed. She was really praying. And I felt so humble and small before her — I, the priest celebrating the Mass. Our seminars and studies on prayer and spirituality have much to learn from simple folk in the parishes and shrines.
>
> The previous night I'd gone for Mass in a desperately poor corner of this squatters' barrio where our MC Brothers were working. Before Mass a very poor family living there asked me to offer the Mass for their intention, which was simply: "In thanksgiving for God's goodness." If they can say Thank You living in such circumstances where are the rest of us?[160]

He would approach everyone, rich or poor, with reverence and respect, but because his life brought him closer to the poor, there was almost devotion in his dealings with them. A beautiful extract from a letter to Brother Nicholas, described the death of the young woman, Ba Thi. Maybe it is Andrew's literary expertise or poetic skill, but these are surely the words of a man who had a deep reverence and passion and who was definitely at one with this "unimportant" sick young mother:

> A week ago in Saigon a most beautiful & moving thing happened. A young (29) mother died in our house leaving a little baby. She'd come a month ago — had TB. Nobody realized that she was as sick as she was. And she died

haemorrhaging most terribly. But there was something in her death & dying, that I can only call a sharing in the Passion & Death of Christ. It was a tremendous grace to be with her as she died. And I think she found in that last month a little of God's love & care in the house. I think we have a saint now in Thi; and I feel that the venture in Vietnam has all been worth it, if it were just to have Thi die in Cong Quynh. That's where it is Christ in the poor who is everything for us.[161]

Was Andrew aware that the Jesuit James Hawkins had uttered almost the same words back in 1971 when he described Andrew and his relationship with Xavier College?

Mary, Mother of the Poor

October 1970 would be the first time that the designation "Mary, Mother of the Poor" was mentioned in the journal of the Mansatala community. Yet Brother Andrew had already included "Mary, Mother of the Poor" in the first Constitutions written in 1967, and in the vows formula of 1968. In an article in the MC Brothers newsletter *Milan* in 1993, he claimed that it was out of human vanity and pride that he had chosen "Mary, Mother of the Poor" instead of the Immaculate Heart of Mary, who is considered the Patroness of the MC Sisters (and subsequently of the other MC branches). The suggestion, however, that the choice of the title, "Mary, Mother of the Poor" was in order to be different from the Sisters might not be the complete story. For sure, he was aware of the devotion to Our Lady under the title "Virgin of the Poor". In 1933 Our Lady had appeared on eight occasions to a young girl in the town of Banneux in Belgium. This devotion was not widely known, although the Belgian Jesuits in India had doubtless spoken of it to Mother Teresa. In fact, a copy of the statue in the Banneux shrine had been installed in the outside corner of the Sister's Mother House in Calcutta well before 1965 when Andrew first came to the city.

In 1985, during a meeting of Regionals and General Councillors in Kathmandu, Nepal, it was decided that the Brothers would start conducting a daily Holy Hour in their communities throughout the world. This came about through the "direct" or "indirect" intercession of Mary, Virgin of the Poor:

> One of the Brothers had brought to the meeting some little prayer cards of the Virgin of the Poor. Mother Teresa last year brought a large and beautiful statue of the Virgin of the Poor to Mansatala. I [Brother Andrew] had found a small pamphlet on this apparition of Our Lady to a simple girl in Belgium. It is one of the apparitions where Mary said very little. And often she repeats the one simple central message: "Pray a lot." It seems to come to us at this point as a special message from Mary. The Daily Holy Hour may be one response from us.[162]

In his article "Mary Mother of the Poor", Brother Ben MC could well be echoing Brother Andrew's insights when he stated that, "Mary is Mother of the Poor not as someone who gives gifts to the poor out of her own wealth and greatness, but as a small, poor person herself, one who shares the self-emptying love of Jesus to the point of giving birth to Him in a stable, walking the weary roads with Him, and standing beside Him in the moment when everything is taken from Him, even His life. And she is Mother of the poor also because she walks with us poor Brothers and stands by us as we try to be faithful to the vocation Jesus has given us."[163]

Weakness, Woundedness and Fragility

As with St Paul, fragility was the cornerstone of Andrew's spirituality: "So I shall be very happy to make my weaknesses my special boasts so that the power of Christ may stay over me, and that is why I am quite content with my weaknesses" (2 Cor 12:10). Why such emphasis and insistence on one's woundedness and fragility? Why is this idea so central to Andrew's spirituality?

Part – IV: From General to Troubadour (1976 – 1986)

Lack of power, prestige or name — being helpless also means not being able to do it on my own. I am not the one in charge.

> One thing is clear; there is value in being here in helplessness and powerlessness and uncertainty, with a complete dependence on Providence and God to show what He wants in the decision of others.[164]

Fragility also implies brokenness. St Paul states that we have to carry this treasure in earthen vessels so that the excellence of the power may be of God and not of us. As human beings we are imperfect. Once we recognise this, we can stop pretending to be strong and perfect.

> Few understand the human weaknesses on which the Missionaries of Charity are built. We are for the most part incredibly unlikely men and my own years as a Missionary Brother have brought with them the daily renewed consciousness of my smallness and frailty in which the need of God's help is deeply felt. The surprising thing is that He is able to use people such as we are to carry out his life-giving work in the world. To me that speaks of power and greatness of God in His ways.[165]

This is the core of Brother Andrew's spirituality of weakness — through our admission of weakness and woundedness we are closer to the poor we serve, and totally dependent on a God who loves us, not despite our faults and sins but from that exact spot where we hurt most.

> My spiritual journey has been lived in very tumultuous years of the '50s, '60s, '70s, '80s, and '90s. It's such a tumultuous era and the changes in pace and in thinking and the impact of many ideologies and culture is quite breath-taking. I've been affected by that. As I mentioned, my earlier years were lived — growing up and after my ordination as a priest in 1963 — in slower times, more secure times. There were problems of course but there was a greater security and peace about life.

And then the 60s and 70s, 80s burst upon us. I think I was affected in the 60s and 70s by a sort of loss of discipline in the Church and in the culture and I let a lot of things go, took things easy. I look back now and I see a sort of miracle that I survived because I didn't live completely to priesthood and religious life as many of my companions and other people, contemporaries did in those years. How I stayed on and didn't lose myself completely, is a gift of God. But these things I am more and more aware of it. I took things easy, my conscience a bit slack I allowed myself liberties in various ways that would have been quite undreamt of in the earlier part of my spiritual journey. And then many people have been praying for me, all through my priestly life and my life in the Missionaries of Charity, many people have been praying for me and those prayers have been heard …

I can tell you, clearly as anything, my vocation and whatever integrity I've brought, survived and grew, not through my strength, but through the prayers of others and the grace that God gave to me. And as a result of that — I suppose it would have been in the '80s, 1980 — I had that conversion, that was rooted in a return to prayer, and that's sparked a whole new region and almost, a new stage in my life.

Because I can see at that stage in the early 80s my work with the Brothers was coming to its completion, beautifully fulfilled in many ways. The Society was established, and the young Brothers were taking over and reached a point they were going to take over and I would move out. That happened, but as a background to all that, was this wonderful grace that I received of a greater intimacy with God, a more gentle spirituality, and a great desire to journey with God and to find Him in greater simplicity and prayer and contemplation.[166]

Part – IV: From General to Troubadour (1976 – 1986)

THIRD GENERAL CHAPTER – 1986

Bringing together representatives of the whole society every six years is never an easy task. "Its purpose is to protect our heritage, to consider the state of the Congregation including its strengths and weaknesses, and its needs for renewal. It also elects the General Servant and his Council, deals with important matters and issues norms binding on all the Brothers."[167] It is announced by a letter sent by the General Servant to all communities one year before it is to begin and involves thorough preparation held during the preparation year.

Towards the end of 1985 the Third General Chapter was announced. This was definitely not going to be easy, especially with the General Servant not living in the generalate house and being unable freely to come and go to India due to visa problems. Some of the Indian regionals, therefore came up with the idea of having some of the preparatory meetings with Brother Andrew in Kathmandu, Nepal. Gathering there would be easier for all the parties concerned, given that Indian citizens did not need visas to enter the country. Around June and again in August, two meetings were held at a Jesuit retreat house in Kathmandu.

On another front things were not going as they should. Relations between Brother Andrew and some of the Brothers in the North American Region became more strained. In November 1985, Brother Andrew sent quite a strong, clear General Letter to everyone in the Congregation. Whether this letter had anything to do with the fact that some of the Brothers in North America were becoming involved in ministries to gay men and women is unknown. Brother Andrew was absolutely not in favour of evolving secular views that were at the opposite pole to Church teachings:

Dear Brothers,

Our vow of chastity has a very great significance in the permissive world of today. By your vow of poverty you present yourself as a strange sort of creature who wants no share in the mad race for wealth in a competitive society, nor the state handout of an equal piece of pie from a benevolent socialist state.

It's rapidly reaching a point in permissive liberal cultures where your vow of chastity makes you an even stranger contradiction.

Even among priests and Religious you can hear and observe ideas or ways of living that seem to be a negation of any kind of chastity.

A people that loses its sense of sexual morality is a people clearly in decline.

We are so much part of our culture that we can easily have become blinded to the extent of our own decline. This partly explains how priests and nuns can carry on as if the 6th commandment didn't exist — much less their own vow of chastity.

Everywhere today chastity is under attack. In smart sophisticated places it is merely a joke or a jibe.

The broken marriages, the single parents, the unwanted children, the young people burnt out under the pressures of unbridled sex, sex-caused diseases, can all be brought into our reflections on chastity and the witness we are called to give. But how few people anywhere make the connection.

We have to live our chastity in practice whether we are heterosexual or homosexual in our sexual orientation. One hears talk today which sounds as though Gay Liberation includes the licence to the free exercise of an active sex life.

Obscure and woolly thinking abounds. Gay rights legitimately asks for respect for any person with a homosexual orientation. And we must all agree to that

Part – IV: From General to Troubadour (1976 – 1986)

clearly. But the homosexual has no more right to exercise an active sex life outside marriage than does a heterosexual. This is also the position of Pope John Paul II … A reading of the chapter of our Constitutions on Chastity may be a worthwhile refresher. Let us pray for all the broken victims of our permissive society and world — and pray for each other for the joyful and free witness of our life of chastity.

God bless you all,
Br Andrew.[168]

Probably, this letter was intended more for the Brothers in North America (and to some extent in Europe) than for those in other parts of the world where such topics as gay rights were and still are taboo. Did Brother Andrew fear the outcome of only addressing it to the North American Brothers? Would those in the United States have taken it too personally and struck back? At the same time another, hotter issue was being raised in North America and this was even more worrisome for him. A significant rift was becoming apparent in the understanding of how Missionaries of Charity life should be led outside India. Some Brothers in the North American Region could not accept being "told" to live as Missionaries of Charity in North America with the same parameters as in Calcutta or elsewhere in India. The meeting in Nepal had already tried to tackle this issue. Andrew recognised that, "organization, techniques, structures, seminars, letters, etc., are not enough to preserve unity or to solve conflicts. Without love, none of these can succeed."[169]

A letter to Br Peter Murmu suggests that Andrew was aware that there was trouble afoot: "If they throw you out of the General Chapter, you can go to a quiet place. I may fly to some mountain — and sit beside my tomb. We shall suffer much at General Chapter but Holy Spirit will win."[170] A month later, on 14 October he wrote again to Peter. Having difficulty obtaining a visa to enter India, he was worried for the Brothers left like sheep without a shepherd. He was also aware of one influential but, in his opinion, confused

Brother attending the General Chapter who was susceptible to doing great harm both to himself and to the Society.

By mid-October he was reconciled with the idea that he would not get the visa, even though, as he personally confessed in a letter to Kathryn Spink, "The Visa was not the deepest issue. In fact, it finally came through — but very late, well after the start."[171] Mother Teresa and her Sisters in Delhi tried very hard to influence the authorities but to no avail. (What is puzzling is why Brother Andrew didn't try to enlist Mother's help earlier. Mother had used her influence with the Chief Minister Mr Jyoti Basu to obtain a permanent visa for Fr Rosario Stroscio, SDB, in 1979.)[172]

On 21 October 1986 Brother Andrew wrote a General Letter to the Congregation. In it he explained the difficulty of obtaining the required visa. He had also been wondering whether it was now time for a new General Servant. After all, he had been at the helm for twenty years. He was confident enough that the fifty elected Brothers were capable of finding a new General Servant and would not waste precious time discussing the possibility of re-electing him for another six years.

He exhorted the Chapter delegates:

1) Obviously most important in the Chapter is God's guidance. Therefore prayer on the part of the delegates is your most important part. I would hope that the daily Holy Hour is given prime place together with the Mass.

2) I have no heir or chosen successor. In fact, I am glad that being absent, I do not have to vote for anyone. I don't know whom I would vote for. It is for the Chapter, under the guidance of the Holy Spirit, to find the new General Servant.

3) I believe that our holiness is far more important than our organization or management. If Brothers grow in holiness, the Society will bear rich fruit. For myself I gladly move from a role of executive leadership to a more spiritual role.

Part – IV: From General to Troubadour (1976 – 1986)

4) All renewal and new life in God's plan begin with repentance and purification. John the Baptist begins: "Repent. The Kingdom of God is at hand." When Jesus begins His public life, one of His earliest acts is to purify the Temple of the money changers and those doing their own business. Purification doesn't mean seeing other Brothers' faults. It means seeing my own.

5) We MCs have never been a group that did good work through our own expertise. Yet there has been enormous fruit for many. There is a contradiction and secret here. We have a life-line. It comes to us from God and flows to us through the Church.

St Don Bosco said that wherever the Church flourishes three elements are always found. And the same three elements are always key points when the Church is under attack. They are: 1) The Tabernacle with Jesus present. 2) Mary, His Mother. 3) The Pope.

Mother Teresa has rooted MC firmly in all three. Her devotion to all three is clear to those who know her. Here is our life-line. It has always been under attack. It is under attack today from outside and inside the Church. I urge you to remember that.

6) From our own, human make-up at this moment I have two fears for the Chapter. Both come from the oldest and more developed regions of the Society. For that is where the power is. And where there is power there is the temptation to struggle for that power. The two regions are India and America. The other regions are young, weak and powerless at this moment in our history.[173]

Andrew was far from naïve. In India he feared, "the evils of casteism and groupism that could be used to manipulate for power. The whole country is torn apart by this disease. In past Chapters we have suffered great harm from the same thing."[174] In the American Church, Andrew was concerned about the powerful movement for an

American national church to develop independently of the Pope. He even sensed strong anti-John Paul II feelings amongst the Brothers.

In the absence of the General Servant, who under normal conditions presides at the General Chapter, the Vicar takes over as president. In the case of this Chapter it was Brother Jeremy, MC.

> This was the time leading up to the General Chapter in 1986. Visas were not the issue for Andrew's absence. I think that was a convenient excuse, but not completely true. While the visa regulations may have changed, had Andrew wanted to be there, it would have happened. I went to that Chapter in '86 expecting a painful experience. But after arriving in Calcutta, some days before the Chapter was to begin, I was stunned Andrew was not there. Two days before the chapter was to convene, he notified us he would not be coming and not to re-elect him. Another grenade thrown? That's how it felt.
>
> As Vicar General it fell on me to convey that information to the Brothers and then to deal with all their reactions to that. And to do all that without being able to share the background story. And that story was that Brothers in two different communities geographically far apart from each other, with no knowledge of each other's experience both wrote to me of Andrew's drinking and some unfortunate behavioural problems that resulted. As the constitution instructs I wrote to him gently and conveyed the concerns brought to my attention. Andrew's angry response (this is all occurring in the three months before the Chapter) and the way he was turning on me, was revealing and led me to assume the Chapter would be horrific.[175]

A thirty-two-year-old and only other Australian Brother, Geoff Brown, was elected as the General Servant, together with Br Jeremy Hollinger as Vicar or first councillor and Brothers Gary Richardson, Yesudas Mannooparampil and Prakash Lakra as general councillors.

Part – IV: From General to Troubadour (1976 – 1986)

AFTER THE GENERAL CHAPTER

When on 7 November the General Chapter concluded, Brother Andrew was still in Hong Kong. "And now what?" was perhaps the big question for the Brothers and for many who were close to him:

> Recently there has been a big change in my role. After 21 years as General Servant of our Congregation, I asked the Brothers at our recent Chapter to relieve me of this position …
>
> So now what about myself? What do I do now? Concrete images save pages of words; and I have two: — a smaller boat to ride in, and — a troubadour singing a new song. In fact, you can even put the troubadour in the small boat, and there you have it.
>
> I remain a member of the Missionaries of Charity — very much so, I hope. From being the 'General'— with all the burden of managing, disciplining, planning — I now become a troubadour in the small boat trying to sing the song of God's love and freedom, His joy and peace, His truth and beauty — for the Brothers in different places, for the poor, for Co-Workers, friends and other groups. I hope I shall be a support and encouragement to the Brothers.
>
> The idea of the smaller boat came to me a year or so ago when I was travelling to one of our remote communities on a small island off the Philippines. It involved transferring from a series of boats that got smaller and smaller as the waves of the Pacific Ocean got bigger and bigger. But I did notice that the fishermen often had even smaller boats; and with these they were able to go a long way; they could even get in under overhanging rocks of the sea cliffs where bigger boats could not go, to catch shell fish of many kinds.
>
> In one of these little boats I seemed to hear God suggesting that maybe I should be thinking of moving into a smaller boat.

The second idea of the troubadour came to me from a great friend who is a Trappist monk, and who for years has been helping my short-sighted vision with his broad perspective on the world as seen from the distance of his life of contemplation and closeness to God in the monastery, while I was spinning around the world making foundations in many countries.

He wrote after the change: "Well now you've changed from General to Troubadour!"

It's a tremendous help to get a name and an image on what is going on.

I don't know how far I shall get in this smaller boat.

But if it's God's will, that is more than enough.

So I'll write these letters and a few other things — if people want them. I'll be giving retreats and talks for the Brothers and other groups — again if people want them ...

In other words, I'll try to be a troubadour in a small boat singing a new song — if people want to listen ... a new song of truth and peace, of love and joy, of freedom and praise.

A new song of authentic love and freedom of life.

Love and prayers,
Brother Andrew, MC[176]

"Troubadour" is a generic term for poets and minstrels in southern France and northern Italy between the eleventh and thirteenth centuries. They were artists who elevated storytelling as an art. At that time, people had grown tired of the fact that the only works of art came from monks living in monasteries — hymns, sacred songs and the like. They needed something new, something they could understand in their own language and not in Medieval Latin. Troubadours sang their songs and played music on strange instruments. Originally, they were travelling musicians. No wonder then that, when Brother Andrew heard this allegorical

Part – IV: From General to Troubadour (1976 – 1986)

expression from Brother Nicholas, he liked it! Andrew was definitely a story teller, he was a traveller, he "sang" (even though he had no ear for music) a love song in a "language" that the small and simple people understood.

He did make it to Calcutta in December and even spent Christmas there:

> On Christmas morning it brought me to a gathering of well over a thousand children from the streets, slums and railway stations.
>
> Every year the Brothers have this party for the children they work with through the year. In fact there are a number of such gatherings.
>
> What the children get is simple: a bun and a banana for breakfast on arrival. There are a few songs and dances. Then they receive a packet to take home with a bun, a cake, an orange, a few candies, a balloon and a plastic cup. It is no big deal even for the poor of Calcutta.
>
> But very striking is the immense joy, peace and beauty that immediately becomes the atmosphere.
>
> As I walked around among those grimy, ragged children I realised there was something more than just those few gifts, more than the organization and music. There was an added respect, dignity and love.
>
> From there I went mid-morning to our Home for the Dying. Christmas Mass was just ending and the patients were already having their special Christmas lunch.
>
> The heavy cleaning work had already been done. Sisters and Brothers were helped by a large group of volunteers from India and abroad. Here too was a striking atmosphere of peace and calm, of quiet joy and contentment in a place with the startling name above its door: "Home for Dying Destitutes."

Again I was struck by that something more. Something more than the food, the clean bed clothes, the medicine, the decorations. There was life, dignity, love in the Home for Dying Destitutes.

I was standing quietly caught up in the wonder of it all, and I noticed that a thin, very emaciated man had just finished whatever he could manage of the special Christmas rice and curry.

I asked if he wanted water. He said "Yes," and I brought a glass. I poured it into his mouth Indian style. He drank eagerly.

As he finished I had this extraordinary experience myself. I felt myself filled with a deep joy and peace. It was Christmas — God's love and light came to me in that cup of water I had been privileged to give that utterly destitute man.

A cup of water. Nothing more. So common and ordinary. And yet it became the high point of a very beautiful Christmas for me.

It was only a cup of water. But here again was that something more added — which transformed the whole reality.

In a little third floor apartment opposite our house in Kidderpoor I have seen a high caste but poor Hindu family grow up over the past twenty years.

The father struggled with a meagrely paid government job to educate the four children. I was always struck by the goodness and peace of their family life.

The eldest girl married a couple of years ago. The two youngest, both boys, are still in school.

The second child, a girl of about twenty, always struck me for her joy, her beauty, her purity and her peace. If anybody ever shone with these it was she.

This New Year she went for a picnic with friends and was involved in a road accident. She was holding a small child in her arms. To save the child she continued to hold it; and not stretching out her arms to protect herself, her head struck the ground and she died of head injuries three days later. This pure child had given her own life in saving another.

I was deeply moved by her death. I felt myself touched in an extraordinary way by a saint. I still feel myself strengthened and enlivened by her living presence.

I was not the only one. Her grieving family bore the tragedy with an amazing strength and courage. They knew their daughter had not lived in vain. Neighbours stopped to reflect on the deeper beauty and values in life.

Again that something more was present. Here it was in that grim tragedy as it had been in the poorest children and the dying destitute.

It dawned on me that my Christmas pilgrimage around Calcutta had led me to that something more that lies hidden in the ordinary, common things and events — that lies hidden even in the most unlikely and even fearful things that happen.

And I realised that that something more is not just some thing.

It is Someone more. It is deeply personal — One who touches us, who speaks to us. It is One who transforms the whole reality and quality of my life.

It is not necessary to go to Calcutta at Christmas to find Him.

For He waits hidden now in the present circumstance of my life — wherever it be, whatever it be.

He waits for me to pause a little, to look, to welcome Him. And in that moment He transforms the whole reality of my life — and the world.

It's good to let myself be found by Him.

With love and prayers,
Brother Andrew, MC[177]

After that, he returned to Hong Kong, only to start travelling again to Europe (passing through the United States) around spring and then back to Hong Kong by the end of June. His European tour took him to Noto in Sicily, Finland, Sweden and England. By his own account, he was enjoying his "little boat":

> Sometimes people throw some stones at it, but so far it is still sailing. I appeared for 10 minutes one night on BBC TV in London.*** They said 10 million people watch at that time. Next day the man selling train tickets said, "I saw you last night." Kids in bus were pointing me to their mothers, etc. It was good to be able to say a few words to so many people. I hope they felt a little more that God loves them.[178]

The question arises as to why was he still travelling now that he was no longer General Servant? Most probably he took the liberty of still journeying and conducting retreats without any apparent consultation with the newly-elected General Servant because he had already organised them before the General Chapter. To his friend Kathryn Spink he confided his dilemma about what to do next:

> The retreats and performances have been going well — if judged by the invitation to return or appear at other places. So something seems to be stirring somewhere.
>
> At the moment I am wondering whether I should stay in the little boat and keep moving — or whether I should set up some sort of community — an ashram perhaps — or what in MC Language could be called a sort of spiritual soup kitchen for the spiritually hungry.
>
> You could then write some sort of comparison between Fr Bede and yours truly as Ashram-keepers!****

***   The Terry Wogan programme publicising *What I Met Along the Way*.
**** A reference to Fr Bede Griffiths (1906 -1993) who was a well-known British-born Benedictine monk who lived in ashrams in South India and who became a noted yogi.

Part – IV: From General to Troubadour (1976 – 1986)

> The Bishop of Helsinki came out with a bit of obvious wisdom this morning when he remarked, "Why can't you combine both?" This trip has had me in spring for nearly 3 months — and it is beautiful here.[179]

In another letter to her, he even mentioned a book he was already writing on the subject of "Peace". This book never found a publisher and the manuscript has not yet been discovered.

In June of 1987, Brother Andrew wrote to his good friend Leon, announcing his imminent arrival in Australia between July and August. He told Leon that retreats and talks were scheduled but that 4 August would definitely be free. What is very intriguing is the way in which he signed this letter — 'Ian' — his original, baptismal name. With Leon he could be his true self!

Thanks to Australian photographer John Casamento, we have some of the most beautiful black and white and a few coloured photographs of Andrew during this time. John was a photographer with *The Sun News-Pictorial* and on one of his trips he stopped in Hong Kong and made a photo-report of Brother Andrew's work. It was published as a double-page in The Sun of Thursday, 21 May 1987, and featured several photos of the Brothers and Andrew doing their rounds looking for poor people, an unusual scene on the streets of Hong Kong. Brother Andrew accompanied the Brothers that day just for the photo-report.[180]

Andrew's tensions at this point in his life were becoming evident. He saw himself as being steered in a small boat and yet he enjoyed the attention he was receiving as a result of books being written by and about him and the Congresgation, TV interviews and photo reports. He wanted to be unknown and small as much as he craved attention and affection. His sense of belonging to something bigger — the Congregation — started to dwindle. In India he was being set on a pedestal whereas in the West (especially in America) he was having problems with some of the Brothers. His sense of belonging was in a way reduced to the community in Hong Kong. It was as if his rise to "fame" isolated him more and more. He sought intimacy and needed friends but at the same time he was constantly on the move and so could not build long-lasting relationships. He might even have been running away from that same intimacy.

This moving from one place to another, opening many communities, consuming too much alcohol — were all definitely putting pressure on Andrew. As early as 1977, Geoffrey Solomon in *Brothers of Mother Teresa*, spoke of Andrew's depression and despondency (most probably due to the leaving of Vietnam). In a few letters Andrew had already mentioned loneliness. The one person in whom he could confide and speak freely was his friend Leon, and the last phrase of the following letter might shed light on the reason for his depression and loneliness:

Dear Leon,

Yours of 13/6 deserved a better reply than this. I understand a little your pain. I think I share it more & more. As this thing grows strangely I find myself more & more lonely — not belonging anywhere. Hundreds of people — and yet no one I can stay with — no special one. How long can it go on for[?] You are there alone. And I with so many am alone. It's like a trap — I go everywhere, and yet I know there is nowhere ever I can go. And you are about the only person in the world I can ever write this to.[181]

More than loneliness was on the horizon, however. On 24 September 1987, Andrew wrote to Peter Murmu:

Yesterday the mail brought an air ticket from Geoff for a summit meeting in Albuquerque with Jeremy. It was a great surprise. Also I think a great proof of the Spirit being with Geoff. (If you see Geoff, please tell him I am happy to come — and I feel peaceful about it.)[182]

Part – IV: From General to Troubadour (1976 – 1986)

*1. Calcutta 1980 – Elected Councillors
Isidore, Andrew, Christdas, Jeremy, Ferdinand.*

*2. Calcutta – Undated photo –
Andrew at the door of his office at Mansatala Row.*

3. Calcutta – Undated photo – Brother Andrew and Mother Teresa.

4. Los Angeles – 6 November 1976.

Part – IV: From General to Troubadour (1976 – 1986)

5. Los Angeles – 1984.

6. Los Angeles –1984 Br Anton (L of Br Andrew), Brs Gary, Jeremy and Sebastian in front.

7. Hong Kong 1987 – Mass with Brothers and Inmates (courtesy John Casamento).

8. Hong Kong 1987 – Br Andrew with Brothers Stephen and Robi (courtesy John Casamento).

Part – IV: From General to Troubadour (1976 – 1986)

9. Hong Kong 1987 – (courtesy John Casamento).

10. Hong Kong 1987 – (courtesy John Casamento).

11. South Korea – Br Andrew with members of Chain of Charity.

12. South Korea with Brothers and Inmates.

Part – IV: From General to Troubadour (1976 – 1986)

*13. South Koreas – 1985 Meeting of Regional Servants.
Br Peter Murmu (sitting on L).*

14. Dominican Republic c. 1984.

15. Guatemala c. 1984.

*16. Paris – One Troubadour serenading another –
Emile Msika—a clochard singing for Brother Andrew.*

Part – IV: From General to Troubadour (1976 – 1986)   345

17. Calcutta c. 1987 – Br Andrew with inmates and brothers.

18. Melbourne c. 1987 – Andrew, Aimée, Mary, Lucy.

19. Sydney c. 1986 - Andrew, his brother Leo and Peter Simons.

20. Sydney c. 1986 - Andrew and grandniece Kate Simons.

Part – IV: From General to Troubadour (1976 – 1986)

Endnotes

1. 19750522 LR to Mary Ennis.
2. 19770408 LF to Leon Allen.
3. 19770407 LF from Nguyen Minh Loan
4. 19990113 LF to Leon Allen.
5. 19801200 LF to Leon Allen.
6. Informal chats with Marcos Antonio Sutuj Boc, MC.
7. 20190123 IB James Besra, MC.
8. Ibid.
9. 19830103 LG.
10. 19820222 LB to Peter Murmu, MC.
11. The community in El Salvador opened on 14 June 1979 and Mons. Romero was assassinated on 24 March 1980. It would, therefore, be plausible to infer that the meeting was held on 23 September 1979 but around that time Andrew was in Korea and due to arrive in Los Angeles on 15 October (19791003 LB to Br Gary MC). In a letter dated October 1979, Andrew wrote, "I shall leave Los Angeles December 1. But today I am going to Guatemala & El Salvador for 2 weeks. Then I return here." (19791020 LB to Br Anima Prasad, MC) By 11 November he was back in Los Angeles. That dates the meeting as occurring on 23 October 1979 and not 23 September 1979.
12. 19871130 LF.
13. Kerr, Nicholas, *Through the Pain to Freedom — An Interview with Brother Andrew*, Sydney, Australia: The Catholic Weekly, 1990.
14. In April 1975, after the Brothers' evacuation from Saigon, they dispersed but later managed to go to Calcutta. There three of them made their first profession and were then sent to the U.S.A. with Br Jeremy as the first Local Servant. After making contacts on both East and West Coasts, they found themselves led to Los Angeles in California. In July two Brothers arrived there and stayed with Andrew's friends — Lloyd and Grace Tevis. Much help was given by the Co-Worker priest Fr Don Kribs especially in finding a very small wooden duplex house on Edgeware Road. This new MC community was born in the West out of the tragedy in Indo-China. The community slowly organized, with spiritual guidance given by Fr Kribs, and material help by Co-Workers. In November a first candidate came to live with the community and in December, after a visit to the Brothers, Timothy Cardinal Manning approved the little group. This was what Andrew found when he visited in November 1975.
15. 19760111 LB to L.A.
16. 19760126 LB to L.A. Brothers
17. 19790320 LB to Brother Jeremy, MC.

18. 19760218 LB to new Come-and-Sees.
19. 19760309 LB to L.A. Brothers.
20. 19760405 LB to L.A. Brothers.
21. 19760719 LB to Jeremy and Brothers.
22. 19760219 LF to Leon Allen.
23. 19790510 LB from Winston Street Brothers to Brother Andrew.
24. 19790804 LB to U.S. Communities.
25. 20120902 Email Jeremy Hollinger.
26. Ibid.
27. The Missionaries of Charity — Contemplative is a diocesan Religious Institute composed of Brothers and priests with equal rights and obligations, founded by Mother Teresa and Sebastian Vazhakala, MCC, on 19 March 1979.
28. 20120903 Email Jeremy Hollinger.
29. 19760209 LB to Brother Jeremy, MC, & Brothers.
30. 19760218 LB to L.A. Brothers.
31. 19760218 LB to L.A. Brothers.
32. 19760309 LB to L.A. Brothers.
33. 19760620 LG to Brothers.
34. 19760706 LB to L.A. Brothers.
35. Ibid.
36. 19760706 LR to Lucy Smith.
37. 19760710 LF to Leon Allen.
38. 19760730 LB to Brother Jeremy, MC, and Brothers.
39. Andrew confessed that at times he escaped from the difficulties that he faced living in Calcutta, among other things the heat, the monsoon, the limitations. 20171129 IJ Paul Chetcuti, SJ.
40. Years later, when Jim was transferred to Houston, Texas, Uncle Ian had the opportunity to visit the family there especially on his way coming from Central America (Honduras, El Salvador, Guatemala). 20180403 IR Jim, Gregory and Gabrielle Smith.
41. Ibid.
42. 20180102 IB Geoff Brown, MC.
43. Ibid.
44. Ibid.
45. 20181118 IB Peter Murmu, MC.
46. Ibid.
47. Lazaro Sung, MC, was one of the first Korean Brothers to join the Congregation in 1977. He professed his first vows in 1979. Even though as

a child he suffered from polio which left long-lasting effects, they were not considered as impediments by Brother Andrew. Unfortunately, he died of natural causes on 31 January 1989 in Seoul.

48 20180612 IF Liduvina-Hwang Kum Soo (When the author met Liduvina in her apartment in Seoul, South Korea, with Brother Lee Johan, MC, as translator, he asked what these young women perceived in Andrew that so attracted them, even though he spoke no Korean and they spoke no English. Liduvina and Lee Johan chatted in Korean between themselves. The author understood no Korean but one thing was evident: each time that the word, "Andrew" was mentioned Liduvina's eyes lit up.)

49 20180612 IF Park Mun Su, SJ; Born Francis Xavier Buchmayer in 1941 in the United States. He joined the Jesuits in 1960 and was sent to Korea in 1969. He was granted Korean citizenship in 1985 and adopted the name Park Mun Su.

50 Ibid.

51 Ibid.

52 Ibid.

53 Ibid.

54 Ibid.

55 Information recalled through the interview with Won Andrea, MC, and with Jeong John, MC, acting as translator — 20180608 IB Won Andrea, MC.

56 20180203 IB Prem Anand Naduvathette, MC.

57 20190508 IB Abraham Ellickal, MC.

58 20181118 IB Peter Murmu, MC.

59 19811120 LB to Peter Murmu, MC.

60 Titagarh a city about 20 kilometres north of Kolkata. In 1960 the Municipality of Titagarh leased a piece of land to Mother Teresa to establish a permanent centre for the mobile leprosy clinic she had started in 1958. Gandhiji Prem Nivas Leprosy Centre is run by the Missionaries of Charity Brothers and one of the main activities of the centre is the weaving on handlooms of the Sisters' blue bordered saris, bedsheets and other cloth.

61 20190807 IB Celestine Soreng, MC.

62 20180707 IB Michael Soreng, MC.

63 20180128 IB Lawrence Fernandez, MC.

64 Ibid.

65 Ibid.

66 19830412 LO to Shri Yadav.

67 Ibid.

68 Ibid.

69 20180708 IB Marcel Surin, MC.

70. 20181006 IB George Lugun, MC.
71. 20191209 IB Bob Theis, MC.
72. 20171202 IB Ben Harrison, MC.
73. 20190517 IB Robi Gut, MC.
74. 19840412 LJ to Patrick O'Sullivan, SJ.
75. 19840531 LG.
76. 19850308 LG.
77. 19730213 LG.
78. Spink, Kathryn and González-Balado, José Luis, *Spirit of Bethlehem*, London, UK: SPCK, 1987.
79. Ibid.
80. 19751027 LG.
81. 19731115 LG.
82. Duca, Carmel, "God's Troubadour, Brother Andrew 1928 - 2000" Los Angeles: Unpublished source 2013.
83. From a talk given by Brother Andrew circa 1994 or 1995 at Gracewood - God's Farm.
84. 19820529 LG.
85. Duca, Carmel, "God's Troubadour, Brother Andrew 1928 - 2000" Los Angeles: Unpublished source 2013.
86. 19730218 LG.
87. 19780529 LG
88. 19731115 LG.
89. 19720000 LG.
90. 19820531 LB General.
91. 19910528 LF Anonymous.
92. 20190201 IS Sister Joelle, MC; 20190209 IS Sister Camillus, MC; 20190218 IS Sister Joanne, MC.
93. 19690413 Interview with Malcolm Muggeridge.
94. Egan, Eileen, *Such a Vision of the Street: Mother Teresa — The Spirit and the Work,* New York, USA: Image Doubleday, 1985.
95. 19910421 LF Kathryn Spink.
96. Egan, Eileen, *Such a Vision of the Street, Mother Teresa — The Spirit and the Work,* New York, USA: Image Doubleday, 1985.
97. 19770930 LB to Brother Gordon, MC.
98. 19811101 LG.
99. 19811110 LS Mother Teresa to Brother Andrew.
100. Ibid.

Part – IV: From General to Troubadour (1976 – 1986)

[101] Solomon, Geoffrey D., *Brothers of Mother Teresa*, Homebush NSW: St Paul Publications, 1987.
[102] Ibid.
[103] 19770526 LS from Mother Teresa, MC
[104] 19770808 LS from Mother Teresa, MC.
[105] 19771209 LB to Brother Gordon, MC.
[106] https://www.nightingale.com/authors/angelo-scolozzi-lou-tartaglia.html. Web 16 October 2021. (Author: Consulting the official website for the Missionaries of Charity, the Spiritual Family founded by Mother Teresa of Calcutta is listed as follows: Active Sisters, Contemplative Sisters, Active Brothers, Contemplative Brothers, and Fathers. Associated with these are Co-Workers of Mother Teresa, Sick and Suffering Co-Workers, Lay Missionaries of Charity, Corpus Christi movement for priests. https://missionariesofcharity.org/ Web 16 October 2021).
[107] Solomon, Geoffrey D., *Brothers of Mother Teresa*, Homebush NSW: St Paul Publications, 1987.
[108] 19780926 LS from Mother Teresa, MC.
[109] 19850603 LG
[110] 19920126 LF to Kathryn Spink.
[111] 19771209 LB to Brother Gordon, MC.
[112] 19760819 LB to Brother Jeremy, MC, and Brothers.
[113] "Larrikin" is an Australian English term meaning mischievous young person, an uncultivated but good-hearted person. Some say it might have originated in the time when the convicts lived their lives, challenging taboos, breaking rules and being different.
[114] 19770518 LB to L.A. Brothers
[115] Michael Leunig is an Australian cartoonist whose human characters are drawn with exaggerated noses. Some of his works were political in nature but the majority dealt with the spiritual, religious, and moral themes.
[116] 19830516 LJ to Patrick O'Sullivan, SJ.
[117] 20180107 IB DT Xavier, MC.
[118] Egan, Eileen, *Such a Vision of the Street, Mother Teresa — The Spirit and the Work,* New York, USA: Image Doubleday, 1985.
[119] From a talk given by Br Andrew in 1993 at Gracewood - God's Farm, Australia. "Miracles just don't happen."
[120] 19760129 LB to Brother Jeremy, MC.
[121] 19710204 LG.
[122] 19711029 LG.
[123] 19790910 LG.

[124] 19829811 LG.
[125] 19840531 LG.
[126] 20190114 Email Val Noone.
[127] 19760405 LB to L.A. Brothers
[128] 19760427 LB to Brother Jeremy, MC, and Brothers.
[129] 20180319 IR Leone, Kate and Jane Simons.
[130] 19860121 LF to Kathryn Spink.
[131] 19870923 LG.
[132] 20180319 IR Leone, Kate and Jane Simons.
[133] 20180305 IR Anne and Julian Millership, Jim Smith.
[134] Brother Andrew MC, *What I Met Along the Way*, London, UK: Darton, Longman and Todd Ltd., 1987.
[135] The girl who came with a flower to the community in Seoul, was, at the time of research Sister Oliva, MC, Superior of the community of the Missionaries of Charity Sisters in Perth, Western Australia.
[136] Brother Andrew MC, *What I Met Along the Way*, London, UK: Darton, Longman and Todd Ltd 1987.
[137] Ibid.
[138] Ibid.
[139] From a talk given by Brother Andrew in 1991 at Gracewood - God's Farm – "Being Aware of Our Own Value".
[140] From a talk given by Brother Andrew in 1990 at Gracewood - God's Farm – "Jesus Healing the Lame Man".
[141] Egan, Harvey D., SJ, *Christian Mysticism: The Future of a Tradition*, Eugene, Oregon: Wipf & Stock Publishers, 1998.
[142] https://ldysinger.com Web. Jun. 26, 2020.
[143] Inaugurated in 1854, one hundred years before Brother Andrew set foot in India, Howrah Station is the oldest and largest railway complex in India and one of the busiest stations in the world.
[144] 19711200 LP Christmas 1971.
[145] https://www.goodreads.com/ Web. Jul. 30, 2020.
[146] Matthews, Iain, *The Impact of God: Soundings from St John of the Cross*, UK: Hodder & Stoughton 1995.
[147] 19770502 to Brother Gary, MC.
[148] 19860000 LG.
[149] Ibid.

Part – IV: From General to Troubadour (1976 – 1986)

[150] 19701200 LF Christmas.

[151] Brother Andrew, MC, *What I Met Along the Way*, London, UK: Darton, Longman and Todd Ltd 1987.

[152] From a talk given by Brother Andrew in 1995 at Gracewood - God's Farm – "Being Aware of Our Own Value".

[153] 19740400 LP.

[154] 20180116 IB George Dev, MC.

[155] 19850830 LG.

[156] Ibid.

[157] 19790804 LB to U.S. communities.

[158] Brother Gordon, MC, "Missionaries of Charity — Journal," Los Angeles: Unpublished Source, 1978.

[159] 19801200 LF.

[160] 19811200 LP.

[161] Brother Gordon, MC, "Missionaries of Charity — Journal," Los Angeles: Unpublished Source, 1978.

[162] 19850806 LG.

[163] Ben MC, Brother, "Mary Mother of the Poor," Calcutta: Unpublished Source 2014.

[164] 19711200 LF.

[165] Brother Andrew, MC, *What I Met Along the Way*, London, UK: Darton, Longman and Todd Ltd., 1987.

[166] From a talk given by Brother Andrew circa 1994 or 1995 at Gracewood - God's Farm, Australia.

[167] Missionaries of Charity Brothers Constitutions, 17.1, Calcutta: Unpublished Source 1999.

[168] 19851120 LG.

[169] 19860508 LG.

[170] 19860908 LB to Peter Murmu, MC.

[171] 19861105 LF to Kathryn Spink.

[172] Rosario Stroscio, SDB, (1922 – 2019). Salesian priest, born in Italy, arrived in India in 1939. A former history professor at the Salesian Institute of Sonada, he was accused of the crime of "conversion" during his missionary service in Maliapota in the diocese of Krishnanagar and risked being deported. Mother Teresa intervened with the Marxist government, asking to have him as chaplain to the Missionaries of Charity at their "Prem Dan" centre. The authorities withdrew the expulsion order, and, from 1979 on Fr Stroscio continued to reside in Calcutta. http://www. Infoans.org Web. 2 July 2020.

[173] 19861021 LG.

Part – IV: From General to Troubadour (1976 – 1986)

[174] Ibid.
[175] 20120902 Email Jeremy Hollinger.
[176] 19861100 LP.
[177] 19870211 LP.
[178] 19870518 LB to Peter Murmu, MC.
[179] 19870521 LF to Kathryn Spink.
[180] John Casamento was a photojournalist for The Sun News-Pictorial, Melbourne's daily morning paper with the highest circulation of any daily paper in the country. "In 1986 I had a phone call from a priest friend who the Australian bishops had asked to head a team organising Pope John Paul's visit to Australia in 1986. He asked if I could be a photographer covering the visit so I asked my editor if I could have a week off to do that, to which, he agreed. Before I left Melbourne to board the papal flight, I told my editor about Brother Andrew. Because Andrew was a Melbournian, he would be a suitable person for a story in our paper, well known for its pictorial content. Brother obliged and I arranged a flight to Hong Kong where he met me at the airport. I stayed with him for two or three days and the feature article appeared some weeks later." (20200827 Email John Casamento).
[181] 19771200 LF to Leon Allen.
[182] 19870925 LB to Peter Murmu, MC. Another letter with the same information was sent to Abraham Ellickal, MC, "Yesterday I received by mail an air ticket from Geoff in U.S. for a 5 day visit for a meeting with Jeremy as there has been some confusion over the new house in Oakland. It was completely unexpected. But it seems to me to be a wonderful step—and a sign that the Spirit is alive in Geoff." (19870826 LB to Abraham Ellickal, MC).

INTERLUDE – II

THE MEETING AND SEPARATION
(1987 – 1988)

We don't have to be afraid of our own history.
What has happened, I think
is one of the great things about MC.
For one thing we're not able to hide the things that go wrong.
I think we're able to handle the things that go wrong
without being hopelessly discouraged.

– **BROTHER ANDREW**

THE MEETING

When Brother Andrew arrived in Albuquerque on 20 October 1987, he found two Missionaries of Charity Brothers: Geoff and Gary. A diocesan priest was also present — a recovering alcoholic — from the archdiocese of Los Angeles, as was the former general superior of a Congregation whose main apostolate was helping priests and Religious in difficulty with, for instance, alcoholism. The latter had very generously offered arrangements for Brother Andrew to receive treatment at the centre run by his Congregation. It is worth noting that Brother Jeremy, the then Vicar General who was not on good terms with Brother Andrew, did not attend the meeting, feeling that his presence would lessen the likelihood of a positive outcome. Brother Yesudas, who was a councillor, stayed in India. Moreover, according to him, Brother Prakash who was the fourth councillor, was not even told about the gathering.

The specifics of the meeting have been subject to much conjecture since all those involved agreed that it would not be of benefit to share details. However, in a general letter to the Brothers written by Brother Geoff on the following day, the first information emerged. In it he assured the Brothers that neither he nor the general councillors had wanted in any way to attack or criticise the person of Brother Andrew, but that action had had to be taken "out of brotherly love and deep concern for the health of Brother Andrew, an action which was felt to be the best thing to do for him."[1] Brother Geoff explained:

> In this meeting I told Brother Andrew the facts of why I believe he is alcoholic. I told him that I was therefore assigning [him] to a place where he could receive the needed treatment. I also told him that, for the present, I would not be giving him the permission to continue with the apostolate he has been doing this year, i.e., giving retreats to various groups, even though I know much good has come from this work.
>
> The meeting was calm and peaceful. There were no angry or heated words. Though Br Andrew did not accept our action, he was understanding of our concern and our desire to help him. He was calm and outwardly at peace but I do not doubt the deep pain which he must have felt and continues to feel. I am very sad for the result of what happened but I did what I, with the advice available, believe I had to do and I accept responsibility for it.
>
> This event will bring sadness and shock to all of us and to the many people whose lives have been touched by him.[2]

Brother Andrew attached to the above letter, a brief note to the entire Congregation:

> The Society asked me on 20th October to go for treatment as an alcoholic. I did not consider this necessary. And this has led to my request for dispensation from vows in the Society. I do, however, confess to getting drunk a number of times over the past 12 years, and I regret the damage I have caused in this matter. I thank each and every one of you for all your kindness and acceptance over the years. I pray that the Society always remain close to Jesus and the poor in great simplicity.
>
> Br Andrew.[3]

Interlude – II: The Meeting and Separation (1987 – 1988)

Why didn't Andrew mention "over the past twenty-one years," namely, since the day he joined the Brothers? Why did he only mention the past twelve years, which could mean the time after leaving Saigon? Andrew was drinking more than he should. He admitted it. But was he an alcoholic? Without going into details of what makes an alcoholic, there exists the possibility that Andrew might have been experiencing Post-Traumatic Stress Disorder (PTSD). This is not a way of sugar-coating the fact that he was drinking or to justify his behaviour as a result of his drinking, simply a recognition of the role that trauma can play over an extended period of time.

Andrew never believed in all the pop or pseudo psychology in vogue in the 1970s and 1980s, so we are treading here on very delicate and dangerous ground. (If Andrew knew we were talking about a possible case of PTSD he would certainly ask God to send us fire and brimstone!) PTSD is a mental health condition triggered by a terrifying event, either directly experienced or witnessed. Symptoms may include flashbacks, nightmares and severe anxiety. At times alcohol, drugs or other destructive behaviours are used to mitigate the pain. Brothers who lived with Andrew after Saigon recall him shouting and screaming in his sleep. Various psychologists and psychiatrists were consulted, not to obtain a posthumous diagnosis of PTSD, but to gain some insights into the condition and some understanding of whether Andrew could have had such a disorder, given that he had lived through such tense times in Saigon.[4] Dr Joseph Saliba wrote: "The likely stress he encountered [in Saigon] probably would have been of a sufficient level to cause PTSD in a susceptible person. But then, having elected to stay behind when all the rest left, suggests that he was quite robust in that respect and faced the stresses rather than collapsed under them."[5] Whereas Dr Claudia Degrati wrote: "I think the best way to understand and explain your Order's founder is to do what you are doing, tell the story of his life and let it unfold in a way that will give context to his behaviours, adaptive and otherwise."[6]

During the meeting, Brother Andrew was presented with a series of situations in which he had drunk more than normal. It was an intervention of the kind where a supposedly alcoholic person is given an ultimatum after his drinking has created havoc in his family and/or surroundings. Usually such interventions take place only after all other attempts at breaking the denial fail. It is then that an intervention team is set up with family members, friends and professionals. It seems that Andrew had never previously been confronted about his drinking but had instead been enabled by some Brothers.[7] He was just set up directly for an intervention. Maybe this was the mistake — the way this help was offered by the superiors of the Congregation.

When the meeting was over Andrew had to make a decision. Thirty minutes of prayer were sufficient for him to come to a definite resolution — to ask for a dispensation from the vows that united him to the Congregation. Usually when a Brother starts showing the desire to sever his ties with the Congregation, he is advised against rash decisions. He might take a few weeks for discernment before asking for exclaustration. Even then this might entail a first year out of the "cloister" which may then be renewed for another year and then for a third and final year. After that a Brother is encouraged and even impelled to make a definite decision: either to reintegrate into the Congregation or to ask for a dispensation of vows and sever any legal ties with the Society.

Brother Andrew did not follow protocol. He asked for a dispensation there and then. It could be that he felt he was in an untenable position. He was being glorified by some Brothers in India and expected him to be another Mother Teresa. This he did not like. He knew himself well enough not to want to be compared with and morphed into another "living saint." He did not feel himself to be a saint. He alternately shunned and enjoyed the limelight and he knew his failures and shortcomings. Visas for India were hard to come by and Hong Kong had presented itself as a "safe haven" against this myth-making. He could no longer live the daily life as it had been formalized and established in India. Nor could he be a "normal brother", with no special rights and responsibilities. Brother Ben, who at this time was living in Noto, a small city in Sicily, recalled that, after Andrew had resigned as a General Servant but before this meeting, Andrew had visited the community: "We had a long walk one day and he was talking about his plans for the future, and I said something about I thought it is a good thing for a Brother who had been in a position, a senior position to live the normal life to show that it's possible for a Brother who had been in responsibility to return to the simple life of a normal Brother. And he looked at me with surprise and only later sort of realised that he was like probably shocked that I expected such a thing of him that probably he already knew that that was not within either his desire or the potential to live as a normal MC Brother because he was used to living on his own. He was used to being his own boss."[8]

Wasn't he impulsive in all the major decisions he took in his life? Perhaps not. When as a young man he was already thinking about becoming a priest and then lost everything on a horse, the occasion became his moment of destiny leading to the Jesuits. His almost immediate request to join the Indian mission after seeing a film about missionaries in the Philippines, was the moment that his teenage desire "to do something for the poor" finally took concrete form. Some five or six years later he wanted to live with the poor in a slum area in Delhi, and then he met Mother Teresa and the Brothers and in a matter of a week decided to join them. He knew what was happening in Indochina way before he read an article in a newspaper and decided to go to Saigon.

The decision to leave the Brothers may have been another case of his remotely preparing himself and discerning this very important step in his life. It is as if he had been waiting for a last sign from God and the process which made him take such a quick decision had already been in the making for a long time. For years Brother Andrew had felt it was time to move on. He believed his task was finished when in 1972 he left for Australia and on his return to India saw that the Brothers were thriving and had survived without his direct presence. He already wanted to leave the Brothers and the intervention meeting was his last "moment of destiny". What seem like his "rash decisions" were actually the outcome of an unseen discernment process which had previously taken place. When a colleague once asked Ignatius of Loyola how long he would need to recover if the Pope were ever to disband the Jesuits, his response was, "If I recollected myself in prayer for a quarter of an hour, I would be happy, and even happier than before."[9] A little more than a quarter of an hour was enough for Brother Andrew.

His decision was partly based on the fact that, by his own account, going to a rehabilitation centre meant two things: one, that he was an alcoholic in need of help, and two, that he accepted that therapies and centres were a solution — something he disbelieved to the end of his life. What he actually did not believe in was therapy *without God*. In a letter from the late nineties, written after a woman had talked to him about her schizophrenia, he was "struck by something that went beyond this woman to many other people today. I was struck by the futility of psychiatry without God."[10] In his case, however, was being offered a rehabilitation centre run by a religious Congregation and not by purely secular psychologists or psychiatrists.

In no time he was gone, leaving a confused Congregation. Back in India, Brother Geoff wrote another general letter. In it he explained to the Brothers that Andrew's seemingly quick decision to leave might not have been so impulsively taken:

> He [Andrew] said to me that many will not understand that his decision was a step in a process that, he felt, had been moving in this direction for some time. It has to do with his view of his vocation and, though I personally do not fully agree with it, I can understand it. Though Br Andrew is certainly sad to leave, he is not worried about his future, confident that God will show him the way. He will continue to be a priest, probably in Australia. When I spoke with Br Andrew by telephone on 31st October, he said he is continuing with his decision.[11]

Interlude – II: The Meeting and Separation (1987 – 1988)

On 1 November 1987 Brother Andrew sent his usual "Dear Friends" letter to Brothers, family, friends and Co-Workers explaining the reasons for his decision to leave:

> Suddenly and unexpectedly something caught up with me these days. It is one of those incredible stories that come out of the deep conflict between good and evil, light and darkness, life and death — which is in fact the deepest drama and reality of all our lives. I only wish I didn't have to inflict it on you. But because I have been sending these letters and sharing my story for a long time I don't have any choice.[12]

He then described in a nutshell what had occurred during the meeting. Totally conscious that a comparison with what Jesus went through was rash and absurd, he wrote nevertheless:

> In a poor way I understand how Christ was crucified for the truth of His being. He only had to deny that He was the Son of God.[13]

But above all there was the identification with the little ones:

> Perhaps this humiliating story of Brother Andrew who was admired, praised and loved by many wonderful people, may in a strange way offer a little comfort to other humiliated, hard-pressed, embarrassed people, struggling with a disgrace, a failure, a fall in their own lives or in their dear ones — a painful break-up of a relationship, abandonment, a lonely pregnancy, a police case, being written off.[14]

He ended the letter with a note which he had written to himself years before:

> My Radical Message: It's better to be small, weak, poor, foolish, out of control, because then I need the grace that Christ comes to give. If I am strong, clever, a success, master of it all, everything under control, then I have no need or place for Him. This is the radical Gospel or Good News.[15]

In Calcutta, as soon as Br Prem Anand Naduvathette received the news of Andrew's leaving, he went to convey it to Mother Teresa. Mother knew nothing about the events leading up to Brother Andrew's decision. She was not consulted and by the time she heard of it, it had all happened.[16] She was on retreat and one of the Sisters in the Mother House told Brother Prem Anand that Mother would not come to him. He insisted and Mother did finally come out. According to Prem Anand, she was very upset by the news,

> Mother cried in front of me, one hand on her forehead, and cried. I saw the tears coming down. Then after five minutes, she told me, "Come Brother" and we went to the chapel, we knelt, we prayed, I felt the pain there. Then we came to the bench outside the chapel again and Mother said, "Is Mother not your mother? Why Brothers don't talk to Mother? Why Brothers won't tell Mother?" The pain. I said nothing. I just listened to Mother, I asked her, can you write a letter for Brother Andrew to reconsider his situation? She immediately asked for a letterhead and wrote a letter and asked me to post.[17]

According to the Mansatala House Journal, 7 November 1987 was the date of Mother Teresa's visit to the Brothers in Mansatala. They remember her sitting in the refectory, elbows resting on the table with her chin cupped in her hands, looking downcast and saying, "I am very sad." She accompanied the novices and the Brothers in prayer and that day she also stayed for lunch.[18]

A few weeks later, Brother Geoff left for Paris to have a meeting with all the Regional Superiors. In a letter dated 20 November 1987, they expressed their feelings of sadness at Brother Andrew's decision to ask for a dispensation from his vows. At the same time they conveyed their "support and loyalty to our general superior and his council for what they did, and it should be clear that Brother Andrew was never pushed or pressured to leave MC. We were also informed that Brother Andrew thinks and feels that his vocation has changed over the years and that now he needs the freedom to put it into practice. This does not mean that he is completely happy about his leaving as you can read in the letter he has written to the Co-Workers, where he shows how he sees at the moment his life and departure."[19]

Anger and sadness would be normal reactions in such a situation but Andrew initially opted for silence. He felt that the more he talked about what happened the greater the damage he would be doing to the Brothers' trust. It seems, however, that he could not hold to this silence for too long. On 30 November 1987 he wrote a long letter, in which he finally acknowledged his anger. He had intended to making it public but the Congregation's authorities tried to stop the further propagation of the letter. In fact, even Andrew himself soon realised that it would be a mistake, since it was written out of anger, opting instead to send it only to a few close friends. According to him there were all kinds of responses:

One was from a Mercy nun who wrote something that steadied me greatly, even though it laid a heavy burden on me. She wrote:

> "The story is so bizarre, one has to conclude that it is very directly of God in some special sort of way — in the category of being asked to tie up small sons and burn them or being knocked off your horse and blinded. We have to ask why is God doing all this to his friend?
>
> The story of what may or may not have happened in the past is a non-issue.
>
> However, what will have enormous impact on our lives is the way you handle this crisis of authority, obedience, commitment, etc., and what it all means — not in some theological abstraction but in the reality of day-to-day living. What does one do when mutual trust and respect is irreparably damaged in a relationship? And what does one do when authority confronts in such a manner? We all know just how much lunacy and savagery exists in marriages and religious houses at times (as in the world at large). And whether it's marriage or religious vows, how

does one know when a commitment is no longer one's way of walking true to God?

It's as though the crisis has been created. Andrew has been plunged into the Western world's thorniest issue — and it's not for no reason. He has chosen someone who may be weak and unfaithful but is marvellously attuned to Him and marvellously gifted in communicating with his fellow men and women.[20]

Whilst the Brothers who arranged the meeting felt that Andrew had a problem with alcohol, Andrew seemed to think that the alcohol issue was a retaliation for his complaining to and about the American region. Through a letter sent to Jeremy from Hong Kong in June 1987, a few months before the Albuquerque meeting, we catch a glimpse of what was going on between them:

Dear Jeremy,

With this letter I want to make another attempt at reconciliation between us. And I begin this effort with a prayer for God's help.

I believe the situation regarding communication between us is that I have written three letters to you since the Chapter but have not received any reply.

We have a disagreement on your community: Firstly, on the approval it appears to be giving to active homosexual life-styles (as distinct from compassion and understanding of people with homosexual orientation and attraction for which they are not responsible); Secondly, in the practice of poverty in your community; Thirdly, in your community's acceptance of the Catholic Church with the Pope as its head and authoritative teacher as established by Christ.

These are big points indeed. They even raise the point of whether we share the same faith in the same Church and whether we share the same commitment to MC as founded by Mother Teresa — for these are vital points for her and therefore for MC.

Interlude – II: The Meeting and Separation (1987 – 1988)

They are very big points, vital points, in fact.

But still, Jeremy, I ask you whether differences over them should lead you and me to a total cutting off of a relationship such as ours for twelve years.

You and I, I believe, had a very close, trusting, loving relationship — to a point where I was even criticised for being too much under your influence.

We differ on these points now — big points as they may be — but what does this cutting of all communication say?

There must be something devilishly wrong there. There is the harm done to you and to me — harm that must be more destructive in the one of us in whom the rejection more originates. It can only poison us.

And there is the harm that is done to others — Brothers, Co-Workers, friends who can be and are scandalized as they see this awful break.

In the whole sad story, it is here that I find it most unreal. I still can scarcely believe what has happened.

That we have differences — even big differences — is one thing. That we cut a lengthy relationship such as you and I had and out of which so much good issued, that is a totally different thing.

Mature people, and Christians, should be able to have different views and even strive for them without cutting all relationship. We've spoken in the past of Liberation activists, for whom those who hold a different view instantly become the enemy.

An awful spirit has taken and is taking its grip. Love, unity, and brotherhood are its first victims. And one doesn't need to be too near to recognize the disastrous effects in the Nth [North American] Region. These will bring death, not life and growth. Already good friends of MCB in the U.S. are concerned.

> There is a life-line in the Church. It comes through the set-up of our MCB. Consts [Constitutions] with the key place of obedience. It comes through M.T. [Mother Teresa] and her vision and founding charism. Which in turn comes through the Catholic Church and its teaching and discipline which for M.T. are so very vital.
>
> Cut off from this life-line we shall die. For out of step with M.T. and the Pope who is the Rock of the Church, what are we? All that is left is our own initiative, or merely human initiative. The mystery is gone, the magic is gone, the life-line is gone. Our own MC history and make-up show that it is not just our thing or fancy.
>
> I just hope that the loving and life-giving relationship that you and I had for so long is not the first victim of a cutting of this life-line.
>
> The issue is a very serious one, with consequences beyond our knowing.
>
> That is why I express it in terms of what I honestly believe it all to be — even if it is very painful to do so.
>
> As it all concerns more than just you and me, I send a copy of this to Brs Geoff, Prakash, Yesudas, Gary and Anthony. (I don't want to put any burden of responding on any of these Brothers).
>
> May the Trinity's gift of Truth and Love in the Spirit be with us. For in that Spirit there is always hope.
>
> Andrew MC[21]

Andrew had thought (and hoped) that this Albuquerque meeting was an attempt at reconciliation. He and Jeremy had been very good friends to the extent that Andrew had been criticised by Brothers for doing what Jeremy dictated. Whilst still Vicar General of the Congregation, Jeremy wrote to Brother Yesudas on 30 December 1987 stating that "Brother Andrew has been attacking me for 1 year and 4 months. And he has been attacking the North American

Interlude – II: The Meeting and Separation (1987 – 1988)

region for that same amount of time."[22] It is telling that Brother Jeremy did not state a rough date of say, "a year and a half" but was specific with years and months. Such was the hurt he felt. He was clear when the attack on him and on the North American Region started — August 1986 — a couple of months before the General Chapter and after he had told Andrew that he thought he had "a problem with alcohol".[23] At the same time, it was quite certain that Jeremy was going to be elected as the next General Superior and Brother Andrew was starting to have doubts and fears about such a result. Brother Jeremy believed that Andrew was exaggerating the issues arising in the North American Region.

But then again, this was the '80s in California! In 1977 Harvey Milk had been elected city-county supervisor in San Francisco, becoming the first openly gay American elected to public office in California. He was assassinated the year after by the former Supervisor, Dan White. The controversy over the acquittal of White resulted in the 1979 San Francisco riots. In 1983 the Oakland City Council passed a Gay Rights Ordinance prohibiting discrimination, while in 1984, Berkeley became the first U.S. city to adopt a programme of domestic partnership health benefits for city employees. That same year West Hollywood became the first city to elect a city council, of which the majority of members were openly gay or lesbian. The list of "firsts" in California could go on. These were the situations that the Brothers in California faced. As early as 1979 Brother Gary had already mentioned to Andrew: "There is such a profusion of ideas, the church's encyclicals say one thing, and the moralists and theologians another, popular psychology another and gay lib another. But I need to look basically at the simple and beautiful evidence of spirit-filled people in front of me every day."[24]

On the issue of Church teaching, there were the tensions between the Vatican and the Church in the United States. Archbishop Hunthausen of Seattle who had participated in the Second Vatican Council was working closely with *Call to Action* — a group that advocated a variety of changes in the Roman Catholic Church with regard to mandatory celibacy for priests, the male-only priesthood, the selection process for bishops and popes, and artificial contraception. The Church thought that these tensions would be placated with the Pope's visit to the United States in 1987. At the same time the U.S. bishops were discovering their role and importance as moral leaders in public policy and debates on peace and the economy. Pope John Paul II started putting things in order after the turbulent post-conciliar era and was a leading voice for peace and a great influencer in the transformation of Eastern Europe and the Soviet Union. But to the other side of the globe, he did not appear to be so attentive. John Paul II did not approve of any political engagement by Latin American priests but did not censure Polish priests for the same activity. In the 1980s when the Brothers had already opened communities in Peru, Colombia, Guatemala, Honduras, Brazil, Dominican Republic, Haiti and El Salvador, civil wars in some of these countries were at their height. The civil war in El Salvador, for instance, left about 30,000 people dead in the course of the decade, including Archbishop Oscar Romero, four U.S. women missionaries and six prominent Jesuits.

For sure all these were conditions that made the young Brothers question their identity even within the same Congregation vis-à-vis the issue of enculturation. The existing communities in Los Angeles and surroundings were divided. Jeremy and his followers were advocating enculturation to the more or less middle-working class American/Western way of life since that was the kind of environment in which they were living; another group thought that enculturation should be at the level of the poorest in society (Skid Row and the immigrant neighbourhoods in which those Brothers were living and working). It was not necessary to live poverty at the level experienced in India, say, but at that experienced in other third world countries in the South and Central American regions. After all, these communities emerged from the North American region and still had strong ties to it. A case in point was the House of Prayer in Albuquerque: "Gary was just opening the house in Albuquerque, which also was causing concern for some Brothers, because the house was a nice house on a beautiful farmland, and was dedicated to prayer and service to the Brothers. Instead of serving the poor as [the Brothers] were accustomed, they lived a more contemplative life and viewed the Brothers who needed spiritual healing as the poor that they served."[25]

Going back to Andrew's letter to Jeremy, it started with an "attempt at reconciliation" between the two but soon turned out to be another lecture on the very issues causing the rift. Yes, the issues were serious and important, especially to consecrated Religious who had vowed obedience to the authority of the Roman Catholic Church. Of that, there are no doubts. But whether it was out of hurt at being rejected and maybe betrayed by his great friend in the Congregation or out of anger, Andrew did use harsh, strong and hurtful words when he said that there was something devilishly wrong on the side of the one from whom the rejection originated. He even implied Jeremy was immature and non-Christian for not being able to have different views without cutting off the relationship.

There are a few undeniable facts: Brother Andrew had been drinking and the Brothers in the North American Region were being led astray by the different philosophies, values, attitudes and practices of that particular period in history. According to former Brother Anthony Ceja, who was the MC Regional Servant of North America at the time: "Jeremy had already established his new community in Oakland and some Brothers seemed suspicious about him doing this. He really wanted to serve people that were challenged by AIDS. Everything that I could see when I went to visit him was that he was doing amazing service where it was so needed, but I got the sense that he was less and less tied to the MC traditions of austerity and traditional prayer in the chapel, along with daily Mass and Holy Hours. His expression of his spirituality was new, different and caused a lot of concern among the MC communities."[26]

But there is another even greater undeniable fact — Andrew and Jeremy respected each other and were possibly more like-minded than they thought. Anthony Ceja shared:

> I think that Andrew received complaints from Brothers in America about the conflicting dynamics among the Brothers. I am sure that some complained about Jeremy and Gary, and how things seemed to be changing so much. I would think that Andrew confronted Jeremy on these things. Andrew was very close to Jeremy and I felt they really loved and respected each other. One of the greatest character traits that I admired in Andrew was his acceptance of himself as an imperfect Christian man who was fully loved by God. Jeremy was different from Andrew, but similar in that they always made me feel valued and honoured as a human being. They both exuded a sense of peace and love when I was with them. They were both highly intelligent men, and I valued their logic and guidance. They both had an ability to carry a ton of stress from MC and dealing with all the craziness that comes from hundreds of different personalities and needs.[27]

Was the outcome of the letter successful? No. Jeremy and Andrew were not reconciled. Was the intervention meeting arranged by Jeremy — as Vicar General — on 20 October 1987 in retribution for this letter or were the two things independent of each other?

> Former Brother Gary who was at the meeting confided:
>
> I sometimes wonder what would have happened if Andrew would have taken our advice at the intervention in Albuquerque. Then, he would have been seen as a "broken person" in a way that he could not have controlled, in a way that he could not have manicured or designed, or manipulated in any way. It may have released him in such a way that he could have truly been re-made by a Force greater than himself. We (the Western Brothers) would not have been vilified; his whole history would have been an open book, and his stature would have been that of Mother Teresa. I sometimes play a soliloquy in my mind of a retort to Andrew after his answer to us at the intervention. It would have been to implore him to entrust Himself to Love,

to a Higher Power, to Truth, to God, and rest in that, and let that lead to his next step. To those that have been given much (poverty, brokenness) much is asked (to surrender, let go of ego, let go of one's own plan, let go of one's own image of oneself). But he held on to himself, his ego, his way, there was rancour, division, confusion, drunkenness, broken relationships with no hope of healing as a result. At the end of his life and vocation, Love called him (that intervention was a fraternity, a summit of Love). Our leader was asked to show us the way to even more heights of Love, and maybe to an even more sublime corridor of our calling as an MC. Maybe his failure is teaching us even now.[28]

SEPARATION AND DISPENSATION FROM VOWS

The day after the meeting, Brother Andrew presented his request for dispensation:

To General Servant,

Dear Brother Geoff,

With this letter I am asking you to arrange the dispensation of my vows in the Missionary Brothers of Charity — as we have discussed in these days. I shall write to the Archbishop of Calcutta concerning issues rising from my priesthood. I thank you and the Society for so much love and kindness all these years. And I pray that you may all remain close to Jesus and the poor in great simplicity.

With my love and prayers.
Brother Andrew[29]

Instead of "as we have discussed in these days," it would have been more correct to write, "as we have discussed in the last 24 hours!" A short, terse, to the point letter. He was decided. There was no going back on his decision — as with a lot of his other decisions in life.

After the meeting he returned to Hong Kong to finish some practical concerns. One of them was money. He wrote to his sister Mary (who was in charge of donations coming in his name from benefactors in Australia), instructing her to take all the money in the bank, close the account and deposit it in the bank account of the Missionaries of Charity in Calcutta. From Hong Kong he was expected to be in the United States until the end of January, maybe, February. He then returned to Hong Kong (where according to some Brothers he stayed in a hotel) and afterwards went on to the Philippines. He was expected to land in Australia around March/April:

> Don't worry about my health. I am in good form. There were a couple of rough weeks after the bomb burst, and I had to work through quite a bit. Now I am feeling very relaxed and positive about things. There is no bitterness between the Brothers and myself. On the contrary there is much love and concern. And they keep on doing all the beautiful work with the poor as before. I believe that the Lord allowed this for a special purpose, and much good will come of it. It already is. I shall write to everyone later. It is still too early. And I think that as the time is passing the story becomes all the more wonderful. You can tell by the way I sound on the phone that I am OK and have my tail up. Love to all the family for Christmas. I'll contact you when I get the chance. But all is moving pretty nicely now.
>
> Love & prayers
> Ian.[30]

One of the last letters he wrote that year was to his friend Br Peter Murmu:

> What strange stories we human beings write with our lives.
>
> I can at times hardly believe what has happened. And then sometimes I laugh. I guess that proves I am mad!
>
> Now I feel more peace. The most difficult thing has been to avoid saying things in anger that would do more damage.

Interlude – II: The Meeting and Separation (1987 – 1988)

> For me it's a rich grace that has made me more free — And also the Gospel reads so differently for me now. I see it all in a different way and it is wonderful.
>
> I see there is pain for many Brothers. They want me to return, but I can't do that it seems.
>
> If I am so dangerous and destructive then it is not a loss for the Society that I am out.
>
> But truly, Peter, I don't feel any less part of MC. Yes, legally I am out, but in heart and spirit I feel the same or even more close to you all. And that is more important than the name in the Register.
>
> So we go on — tail up and head down.
>
> I'm going to America on 29th — some retreats there. Back through H.K. in Feb. Then maybe Australia.
>
> The small boat got smaller — And it's not easy to say where it will go. But the wind is the Spirit and that is enough.
>
> I know your love Peter and I rejoice in you as a wonderful man and Brother. And we don't need much more than that.
>
> Love & prayers
> Andrew.[31]

Written on Christmas Eve of 1987, the letter to Peter gives the impression that he was fairly at peace. The Brothers, who were absolutely shocked, however, needed a scapegoat and the authority figures and the American MCs were the "appropriate" ones. But then, the Brothers (especially those outside the North American region) could not be entirely blamed for an attitude based on lack of information. In an age of faulty, full-of-static land lines (or communities with no telephones at all) and slow snail mail, some did not get the news until more than a month after Andrew had left. Blame eventually gave way to shame and for years after the event, the Brothers were ashamed to mention that their co-founder had left them. A very few opted to leave the Congregation.

Questions lingered. What would have happened if Brother Andrew had not agreed to go to rehab but had not asked for a dispensation? Most probably, as a last resort the General Superior would have had to exercise his authority in the presence of two witnesses and order him to go to the rehab centre or else be dismissed and expulsed from the Congregation. Andrew knew of these procedures in Canon Law and probably did not want to create rifts in the community. He still loved the Congregation.

To lose Andrew was a terrible blow for the Brothers, but to lose him in such a way was humiliating. Heads hung low in shame. Maybe words like "shame" and "humiliation" have lost their emotional significance for the West, but in Eastern countries such as India "shame" still carries an immense weight. The meeting was all staged by Western Brothers with two American "professionals", without any representatives of other nationalities, not even from the General Council. It was organised with what seems like little consideration for the impact that such a meeting and ultimatum would have on the majority of the Brothers who were of Indian and Eastern origin.

In the Indian culture *izzat* — roughly translated as a sense of honour and reputation — is still very strong: a reminder to stay quiet in uncomfortable situations and maintain a "good" image. What will other congregations say of us now that our founder has left us? What will our own MC Sisters say?[32] Shame is also linked with the "fear of abandonment" and exclusion from social association that is a common practice especially in most Indian villages: will our Congregation be shunned as a result of such an event?

Another consideration is the emphasis that cultures place on individualism and independence versus the collective and interdependence. Maybe the Brothers who conducted the meeting were able to separate themselves from the problem that they presented to Brother Andrew because they came from a culture which is individualistic and independent. In the United States and Australia there is a clear distinction between "what belongs to self" and "what belongs to the other." Not in India. What happens to one, happens to the group.

Interlude – II: The Meeting and Separation (1987 – 1988)

Brother Geoff took a few months to write to the Archbishop of Calcutta requesting the dispensation, because he was still somewhat hopeful that Andrew would have a change of heart and mind. After meeting with his general council, he asked Andrew to reconsider his decision. If he remained he would be officially assigned to the Mansatala community. But many people knew that Andrew couldn't be "contained". Doing so would have destroyed his psyche, crushed his spirit. Andrew needed to leave. Andrew's reply to Geoff's invitation was a negative one.[33] Brother Geoff finally wrote to Archbishop Henry D'Souza on 15 January 1988.

Brother Andrew's formal dispensation letter arrived on 24 March 1988 — on the eve of the 25th anniversary of his priestly ordination and the foundation of the Brothers' Congregation.

> Dear Br Andrew,
>
> Having considered your petition of 11th March 1988 in which you have asked permission to leave permanently the Diocesan Congregation of the Missionaries of Charity (Brothers), and having consulted the Superior General of the Congregation, Br Geoff, I grant you dispensation from the vows taken in your religious profession. As you are an ordained priest I hereby incardinate you into the Archdiocese of Calcutta with immediate effect. You are also given the faculty for Mass and confessions until revoked. You are now to accept formally this indult so that its provision might take effect. Kindly sign two copies of this letter (one for me and the other for Br Geoff) to indicate your acceptance of the same. Assuring you of my prayers and with good wishes,
>
> Yours sincerely,
> H. D'Souza[34]

The indult was accepted of Brother Andrew's own free will and understanding and duly signed by "Br Andrew — Ian Travers-Ball" on 10 April 1988.

Thousands of miles away, in Melbourne Australia, on that same Tuesday, 20 October 1987, a group of ladies were together in prayer. Pat Rowland belonged to this little group, which since the '60s had met in a private home. That night one of the women, "a very prayerful lady said, 'Pat, Brother Andrew, there's something with Brother Andrew and he needs a lot of prayer, it's like as if he's covered around, he's trying to break his way out of something.' So we prayed for a long time, a couple of hours I think (I got back home at 1 o'clock that night). At one point one of these spiritual ladies said, 'It's OK, something has been broken, it's like a chain has been broken.' We didn't know why that was or whether or not it was anything bad."[35] Pat decided to write and tell Brother Andrew about the little prayer group in Templestowe and how on that specific day and at that time they had felt in prayer that he had big decisions to make and were deeply moved to intercede for him. Andrew wrote back:[36]

> 20-4-88
>
> Dear Pat & Thelma,
>
> It was lovely to get your letter & news. Your prayers for me have without doubt been part of a very wonderful story of Grace. I was amazed when you wrote that you were moved to pray for me especially on that Tuesday night. It was a Tuesday that it all happened — and would have been very likely the one you mentioned as "about 3 weeks before my letter".
>
> Only God knows what is effected through you all with Mary. I am very well. It has all been such a grace. The Brothers continue their MC life around the world beautifully. And I am set free to be some sort of pilgrim with Our Lord.
>
> In a few days I am returning to Australia. It is good to feel I can come gently & quietly and let God show what He wants. I feel at this point called to walk very simply and prayerfully — without any need to set things up. I do have a sprinkling of retreats through this year. And that will be good. Probably something again at Templestowe. What

Interlude – II: The Meeting and Separation (1987 – 1988)

wonders happen through prayer! Quite often it's not quite what we were expecting — but it's even better. Please give my love and great appreciation to all you Prayer Group and to the Co-Workers. We may well meet before too long.

Love & prayers
(Br) Andrew[37]

∂

The second Interlude of his life had come to an end: a loss distinct from the first Interlude, nevertheless not unrelated to it. In fact, Andrew, as ever intuitive and enlightened, managed a few years later to see the connection between the two:

There is a line in the book of Solzhenitsyn *The Twin Circle*, it is the story of those prisoners in Russia who they [the authorities] had a special prison for: scientists and people with great professional skills. They wanted to get out of them their work, so for that, the conditions in the prison where these scientists were held were very good: good food, and good meals, there was heating, and warmth, as distinct from the labour camps which were freezing, and of course it was a wonderful thing for them to get into this prison. Solzhenitsyn writes in the novel and much of it is his own experience surely, and there were three men towards the end of the book who were scientists and they were in this camp but they had done something and as punishment they were being sent back to the labour camps with all the harsh conditions. And Solzhenitsyn describes them going away and he makes this tremendous remark, he says, "But they went with the freedom of men who had already lost everything that was precious to them,"— their families, their homes... and I read that book. It was at an interesting time in my life, it was in Vietnam after the fall of Saigon, and I had stayed on to try to keep the works going there and it was clear that I was not going to be allowed to stay, and I was going to be expelled and the houses we had, there were women and children — racially mixed children of the American soldiers—and there was a tremendous sadness, you could see that the houses were going. These people, the women and the children who had found a home at last... and you could see it was all going. And there was a great sense of loss, and it was at that time that I was reading this book of Solzhenitsyn. And that line, made such a tremendous... [impact] ...the freedom.

For me, after that, having gone through that, that tremendous loss, then when I went through this, the next episode of a few years ago, which was sort of a painful loss, I could see very very clearly how I had been prepared. And in a way it was much worse, I realised how that previous loss in Vietnam and the separation and being sent out away from those people, that loss ...I noticed for myself at that time ...there is nothing now that I, if I ever had to lose, that I couldn't lose with freedom.

And when I went recently through the other one, a few years ago, I was very aware that I was strengthened to go through it, through the previous loss.

It is not a sort of fatalistic despairing hope. In a strange way it's a hopeful thing, it's sort of a liberation. The pain is there, the sadness, the grief, the hurt — all that is there — but one somehow knows that it's not the end.[38]

Interlude – II: The Meeting and Separation (1987 – 1988)

Endnotes

1. 19871021 LG from Geoff Brown, MC.
2. Ibid.
3. Ibid.
4. Dr Clelia de Stewart (Psychologist in Guatemala), Dr Francisco Bravo Alva (Psychiatrist in Peru), Dr Joseph R. Saliba (psychiatrist in Malta) and Dr Claudia Degrati (Clinical and Forensic Psychologist in the United States).
5. Joseph R. Saliba, MD FRCPsych — a psychiatrist from Malta (EU).
6. Claudia Degrati, Ph.D — Clinical and Forensic Psychologist in the United States.
7. Until 3 July 2020, only former Brother Jeremy Hollinger and Br Robi Gut, MC, confided to the author that they had confronted Andrew.
8. 20171202 IB Ben Harrison, MC.
9. Lowney, Chris, *Heroic Leadership: Best Practices from a 450-Year-Old Company That Changed the World*, Chicago, U.S.A.: Loyola Press 2003.
10. 00000026 LP.
11. 19871104 LG from Geoff Brown, MC.
12. 19871101 LP.
13. Ibid.
14. Ibid.
15. Ibid.
16. 19910528 LF Anonymous.
17. 20180203 IB Prem Anand Naduvathette, MC.
18. Informal chat with Thomas Pullickal, MC, (January 2017) in Tangra (Kolkata) and Prosanto Pereira, MC, (30 April 30 2019) in Nairobi (Kenya).
19. 19871120 LG from Regional Servants.
20. 19871130 LP.
21. 19870625 LB to Jeremy Hollinger, MC.
22. 19871230 LB Jeremy Hollinger, MC to Yesudas Mannooparampil, MC.
23. Ibid.
24. 19790512 LB from Gary Richardson, MC.
25. 20201118 Email Anthony Ceja.
26. 20201117 Email Anthony Ceja.
27. Ibid.
28. 20201130 Email Gary Richardson.
29. 19871021 LB

Interlude – II: The Meeting and Separation (1987 – 1988)

[30] 19871202 LR to Mary Ennis.
[31] 19871224 LB to Peter Murmu, MC.
[32] While the author was travelling (2018-2019) the world and meeting Religious, friends and others who knew Br Andrew, one MC Sister Regional expressed surprise that the Congregation was undertaking such a venture: "But Br Andrew was an alcoholic!"
[33] 19880115 LB from Br. Geoff to Archbishop Henry D'Souza
[34] 19880324 Letter of Archbishop Henry D'Souza.
[35] 20180303 IF Angela Bonnie and Pat Rowlands.
[36] When the author met Pat Rowland she mentioned having received a letter from Andrew confirming the date of the meeting, after she had informed him of what had happened. The author hesitated to ask for the letter, thinking she might feel he needed proof because he did not believe her. After confiding in Sister Shekinah, MC, (who helped the author find people who knew Brother Andrew) he plucked up the courage to ask Pat Rowland if she still had it. She had indeed preserved it.
[37] 19880420 LF Thelma and Pat Rowland.
[38] From a talk given by Brother Andrew in 1991 at Gracewood - God's Farm, Australia – "Fear of Our Anger."

PART – V

BROTHER ANDREW - SANNYASI
(1988 – 2000)

*So I walk along as a hermit in exile
carrying the burden
of myself in the world
among people
assaulted and exploited
by the powers and interest groups.
I am a hermit not in a solitary place, but on a solitary journey...
experiencing the awful poverty and emptiness
of my own poor heart.
A hermit living alone with Him,
walking alone with Him.
And so I am immensely rich in Him.
I am in solidarity with the powerless alkies, junkies,
punters, perverts and deviants.*

– BROTHER ANDREW

People who knew Andrew started asking, "What will become of Brother now?" In one of his earliest letters, after his dispensation from vows with the Missionaries of Charity Brothers, the idea of the Indian *sannyasi* came to Andrew's mind. This lifestyle is typified by asceticism and renunciation. The purpose is for a *sannyasi* to spend his last years in peace and spiritual practices trying to achieve *moksha* — a liberation of self.[1] A *sannyasi* does not cut himself off from society but abandons the ritualism and customs of the social world. He leads a simple lifestyle, detached, itinerant, going from place to place. In the Indian context, he may possess a walking stick, a container for food and drink, and a patched saffron-coloured robe for protection.

> That concept [Sanyas] speaks powerfully to me now. I have completed my work with the Brothers, and they have grown

to adulthood. The Lord seems to have gently but firmly moved me out on to the road. I am not exactly journeying with an empty bowl, but I do welcome the element of insecurity and uncertainty as discipleship of a poor Christ, whom I have long professed to follow in poverty. It is a rich grace indeed to be given for the years of the final chapter. And I have so long and so richly lived on God's Providence that I can have no doubt that this Providence will ever be shortened. Of course, I am not following Sanyas in pure or traditional Indian detail.[2]

Andrew's life project from now on was presented (maybe without Andrew being aware) in the posthumously published book, *Rebuild My Church*, edited by Frank Maher, SJ.

I never sat down to write a book. Suddenly one day — the Monday morning after Pentecost in Korea — I realised it was in fact written.

It was there in a book of notes, a sort of diary that I had put down as I travelled my life this last year and a half. In fact it started on New Year's Day in a new note book. The one before having been stolen along with a few other valuables in a pub in Dubbo.

I had spent a couple of weeks in Bourke in the home for Aboriginal men who had lost their place with family, mainly through drink. I was on my very hot way by bus to Melbourne with a ten-hour stopover in hot Dubbo. To pass the time I went to the church to pray a little. I had a sleep in the park under a tree, then I went to the TAB to pass a bit more time with a few bets on the horses. It was my day. I backed plenty of winners and emerged with over $100 in my little bag. All this was very hot work so I went for a drink. That was where the Aboriginal girl came asking me for two dollars for a pie. Then she was gone. A couple of minutes later I noticed that my bag was gone with my note book, my winnings on the horses, my bus ticket to Melbourne and my spectacles. For all this I deserved no sympathy. My stupidity in leaving the bag, my worldly distraction in the pub and TAB can take the blame.

This story of foolishness and thoughtlessness catches a thread that will run through these pages because it runs through my life and the lives of so many of us. The amazing thing is that we survive our own stupidity and worse, our sin. That is because of God's intervening love and protection. Even more, He uses it for our spiritual growth and that of others.

One Saturday in Melbourne I made a triple pilgrimage to places made holy by three Saints: the site where Blessed Mary MacKillop was born in Fitzroy, the tomb in Saint Patrick's Cathedral of Archbishop Daniel Mannix and Burnley Street Richmond where Eileen O'Connor was born.

I walked my pilgrim way hoping for a word from God — and I ended with a prayer in the words of the tax collector in the parable of Jesus: "Lord have mercy on me a sinner that I am."

This awareness of my poor self is heavy; but it is a gift. It is in truth a joyful freedom.

It leads me to trust in your mercy Lord, Your grace — not in myself. And I can trust You.

Saint Augustine prayed: "Give me self-knowledge; then I shall know You." The current focus on self needs to be not exaltation of self but emptying one's self.

Coming back from Bourke to several weeks of Christmas mail — after wondering, as I so often do, about my role, I saw from letters that I am playing a role of calling people into holiness and faith. I am not to organise anything. It is out of holiness that new life will come.[3]

There is the mention of Korea implying that Andrew was travelling abroad to conduct retreats. He "wandered" to Bourke, a place and people (the Aborigines) he loved and where he always hinted he wanted to spend his last days.[4] There is the vocation to writing, maybe not specifically a book.[5] There are the TAB and the drink; there is the mention of Andrew's three favourite Australian "saints", Mary MacKillop, Daniel Mannix and Eileen O'Connor, and the acknowledgement of his foolishness and thoughtlessness.[6] But above all there is the revelation of his deep desire for the emptying of self.

He would still go around as much or maybe more than during the previous ten to twelve years, but his comings and goings were now different. There was not the rushing and "craziness": no external expectations or pressures of either leading or forming any religious congregation or opening up new communities. It seems that this time the journey would take him more inside himself:

> Walking a lot on the Australian road these days is a great gift. It is good at this stage of life to be free from administration and organization. It is the opportunity to be more contemplative and prayerful, to make intercession for heavily burdened and oppressed people, to try to be a mediator between people and God. Engagements for retreats, etc., make a good balance, while leaving ample time and space to walk prayerfully with our Lord and to be part of the beauty and pain of fellow pilgrims' lives.[7]

As J. R. R. Tolkien would say in his book *The Lord of the Rings*, "Not all those who wander are lost."[8] Our sannyasi had no fixed residence but his wanderings had a purpose. He was not lost:

> On the road I meet others who walk with God, people of peace, love, truth. They have no power, they want no power. They are like salt that gives flavour. Other souls, other underground springs of the living waters, live in a room, a unit, a nursing home, a hovel, perhaps they still live in their home of former days. They too are powerless. But they are true, loving, praying. They hold the values. They too, in their powerlessness, radiate life in a poor world.[9]

His pilgrimage would take him to the Australian outback, to places like Adaminaby and Delegate; to "informal" retreat houses like Joseph's Place in the rainforest of Tallebudgera, and to Gracewood - God's Farm in the Western Australian bush. Outside his country, he would travel to Pakistan, South Africa and Europe, and end his itinerary with his last retreat in India — the place where he had started. The Philippines, particularly Munting Bukal, would be his Bethany, his place of rest amidst many journeys in and out of Australia.

He still maintained his contact with the Chain of Charity in Korea, while in his native Australia he tried to start new informal and loosely-organised groups: the Pilgrims of Mary and a House for Broken Priests. Spending time and sharing with his family members, whether around Melbourne or in Sydney, occasioned great joy for him (as much as for them). Being rather reserved, he cherished a few deep friendships. His love for MC was also still there; he would never sever his ties with the Congregation especially with the Sisters in Australia and the nearby Papua New Guinea, the Philippines and Cambodia.

In these last years of his life, Andrew discovered new insights and new understandings, particularly in the realm of his powerlessness, weakness and compulsions. Did he eventually attend any self-help groups? We don't know, even though he extensively quoted the literature from such programmes. But then, nobody, who knew Andrew at this stage of his life ever saw him abusing alcohol. One Brother strongly believes that Andrew underwent some kind of conversion around 1990, after his visit to the Marian shrine at Naju in South Korea.[10] Neither in Andrew's writings nor in testimonies of people who spent time with him, however, is there evidence of a specific "conversion".

But as Tolkien wrote, "The old that is strong does not wither, deep roots are not reached by the frost. From the ashes, a fire shall be woken, a light from the shadows shall spring."[11]

THE CHURCH IN AUSTRALIA and the "UNDERGROUND PEOPLE"

It was only after the Second World War that Roman Catholics in Australia saw a rapid increase in number. New parishes were established and the number of Religious, priests and nuns grew. This growth was linked to educational accomplishment and prosperity since quite a number of religious congregations were involved in education. The huge immigrant influx from non-English-speaking countries, especially from Italy, Malta, the Netherlands, Germany, Croatia and Hungary, had different needs and aspirations from the already-settled Irish Catholics. These changes also coincided with those happening after the Second Vatican Council which, according to some scholars, were slower to arrive in Australia than in the United States and Europe.

Three major issues were at stake both inside and outside the Australian Catholic Church: the nature of the Eucharist and doubts surrounding the Real Presence of Christ in the Blessed Sacrament; priestly ordination — specifically male ordination — as a necessity for the celebration of the Eucharist, (rather than the possibility of having ordained women); and the Church's teachings vis-à-vis sexual morality.[12] In 1986 Michael Gilchrist published *Rome or the Bush* which, according to Malcolm Muggeridge's introduction to the book, was "a powerful indictment of how the modernists are destroying the Catholic Church."[13] According to Gilchrist, the Roman Catholic Church in Australia, unlike other parts of the world, did not need drastic reformation, only fine-tuning. The book was written on the eve of John Paul II's first visit to Australia in 1986.[14] At the same time, new forms of ministry started emerging, especially in areas with large Aboriginal, refugee, asylum-seeker and immigrant populations. Other efforts targeted young people who were homeless, drug-dependent, and recovering from abuse. Beginning in the late 1980s, cases of abuse within the Catholic Church in Australia started to emerge, but it was only in 1996 that the Church issued a document called

Towards Healing, intended to create a compassionate and just environment for dealing with relating to abuse.

Many people in Australia who were interviewed for this book lived through the changes. Some were good; others were modifications that shook their faith and put them in powerless situations. Several of these people related many instances when they asked their parish priests to conduct a Holy Hour and expose the Blessed Sacrament. And these priests, who had started to doubt the True Presence of Jesus in the Eucharist, refused to oblige them. Others commented on the many times a group of women would go to the parish to pray the Rosary, only to have the priests chase them from the church. One MC nun even recalled a priest who would have two communion processions: one for adults to whom he would distribute the consecrated wafer and the other for children to whom he gave a lolly.[15] At this time many prayer groups met and flourished in private houses. Groups of mainly middle-aged persons (mostly women), not otherwise affiliated with any other group, would meet at someone's house and conduct a weekly prayer session and maybe pray the Rosary there. These were people who still believed in the teachings of the Catholic Church but who were not finding a space in the Church they loved. It was and to some extent still is, a sad situation.

Against this backdrop, Brother Andrew arrived in Australia in 1988. From now on, his ministry would be to these people, whom he started calling the "underground people", the small people, who could not find a place in the Church and yet who, with their prayers and devotion, would bring salvation to the whole Church. It was for these people that he started conducting retreats, days of prayer and missions. To some extent he also gave spiritual direction (although he could not commit himself to face-to-face spiritual direction because he was travelling most of the time). On occasions he would visit the prayer groups which were evolving in different family houses. It was through these contacts that the idea for the Pilgrims of Mary started forming in Andrew's mind.

In his view, at times even some bishops were directing their flock in wrong directions:

> A recent letter caught the grief and concern of many good people today. It was from a woman of faith who all her life has been a great worker for the needy. She lamented the loss of Christian belief in her children and grandchildren. She was pained over removal of the tabernacle in her parish church to an obscure corner.
>
> Several parishioners expressed their regret to their bishop, pointing to a link between loss of interest in the Church by the young with loss of reverence for the sacred in our churches.
>
> The bishop wrote a firm reply making the extraordinary point that too much attention to the tabernacle takes away people's concern for their neighbour. I wonder what he would say about Mother Teresa, Jean Vanier, Archbishop Oscar Romero, Charles de Foucauld,* Blessed Mary MacKillop and many more who had a remarkable devotion to the Blessed Sacrament—and who also spent their lives radically with the poorest of the poor.
>
> The woman who wrote to me — herself a compassionate carer — expressed sadness at the downgrading of Jesus in her church.[16]

In an undated letter (possibly composed towards the end of his life) he seemed to be echoing Gilchrist's criticisms even of Church art and music. After quoting from the Catechism of the Catholic Church, articles 2500, 2501 and 2502 about Sacred Art, Andrew wrote:

> Recalling all this, one may be struck by the question, "Where is this beauty and uplifting art, poetry and music today?" We have enormous quantity, produced and funded, but

---

* Charles de Foucauld (1858 – 1916) was a French cavalry officer in the French Army, an explorer and finally a Catholic priest hermit who lived among the Tuareg in the Sahara in Algeria. He was assassinated in Algeria in 1916. He was canonised as a saint in 2022.

> for the most part it does not inspire, it is not uplifting, it is not freeing. One would have to say even that it is often violent; degrading, ugly and depressing — despite all the sponsorships and technology behind it.
>
> This century seems to be particularly impoverished in this area. Who is the Shakespeare, the Rembrandt, the Beethoven who will be remembered? We have a succession of extravagances that are forgotten in months never to be thought of again. It is no coincidence that the impoverishment goes hand in hand with our massive loss of faith in the newness of Christ.
>
> So we await a new creativity, a new freedom, a new joy and burst of life.
>
> Church history — 2000 years of it now shows that a new spring does come ... In the darkness of our night, in the drug-ridden despair and nihilism of the young and not-so-young, we await this dawn, this new spring, this bursting forth of colour and joyful song to replace the black clothes and screeching music that is not even human ...
>
> All the darkness, the ugliness of our long night without Christian poetry, music, art is the dark night that amazingly becomes the preparation, the hopeful anticipation of the great dawn that the Incarnate Saviour always is.[17]

While he might have been right about all the above, he gave the impression that he was closed to those believers who were comfortable with the changes, feeling that he was right in what he was witnessing and prophesying and they were on the wrong side of the road. This tendency was something which was confirmed by some of his fellow Jesuits.

These and other world situations — not directly related to the Roman Catholic Church — would have a deep impact on Andrew, especially on his writings during these last twelve or so years of his life. Doom, despair, gloom would be common topics in his letters. One written in 1994 is a typical but not exclusive example:

It seems to me a Dark Age is upon us. People everywhere are shrouded in despair, death, violence, breakdown. Epidemics rage across the world: massacres, economic chaos, political absurdity from leaders, family breakdown, mental breakdown, suicides, drugs, AIDS, abortions, despoliation of lands, forests and seas. Monsters abound that devour the weak, the poor and defenceless, such as the ever-growing intrusion of TV systems, mind control, takeovers and centralisation ... The list is endless; and, political saviours, experts, financiers offer dim hope.[18]

Whereas such themes were rampant in his letters, interestingly they did not figure in his talks during retreats.

RETREATS AND MISSIONS IN AUSTRALIA

Run by the Passionists Fathers, the Holy Cross Retreat centre in the Melbourne suburb of Templestowe was the venue for Andrew's first retreat organised by Margaret Ryan, RSM, in 1988.[19] Margaret remembered Andrew as,

> a deeply disappointed if not entirely a broken man at that point. I didn't understand what had happened. When he came to Australia I saw him almost straight away and I thought, "He can do some retreats here till he decides what he's going to do." So in 1988, I organised a retreat very quickly at Templestowe. There were five priests on that retreat, this lovely Sister who had been my principal in College, and the Barnes — Jenny and John. It was a beautiful retreat. He used to give the most beautiful retreats, on the Gospel. He would walk through the different Gospels ... he was so alive in his way of explaining.[20]

Sometime afterwards, John and Jenny Barnes took over the organisation of his retreats in Australia, particularly those at Templestowe and, as we shall see, later on in Glowrey House. They always tried to keep the costs down as much as possible because most of the people who participated were not rich and sometimes could not afford to pay for a three- or seven-day stay in a retreat house. So Jenny Barnes, with the help of other volunteers, would cook some of the food ahead of the retreat, developing a communitarian spirit in the process.

About the cost of retreats, Andrew had something to say. In one of his retreat talks he described how,

> there was a four-day seminar on the Gospel a few weeks ago where you had to pay 560 dollars. You do not have to go to that because that excludes the poor. That's for the elite. The poor can't afford 560 dollars for a four/five day seminar. We have to be careful in the Church today that it does not become for the elite that excludes the poor. We talk a lot about the poor, about doing things for the poor. The poor are at the heart of the Gospel … And if you have to go and pay a lot of money, that's not the Gospel. Jesus came for the fishermen. We need to shock ourselves because we are doing violence to Jesus.[21]

After this first retreat at Templestowe, priests, nuns and lay people started to get to know Andrew and request his regular presence at retreats. The main venues were Glowrey House, Joseph's Place, Gracewood - God's Farm, and the Missionaries of Charity Sisters' houses. Others included Goulburn House of Prayer, Perpetual Adoration Sisters' convent at Fortitude Valley and Shalom House of Prayer in Carcoar.

Melbourne - Glowrey House

Mary Glowrey House on Nicholson Street in Melbourne still belongs to the Catholic Women's League (CWL). The house was named in honour of the first CWL's president, Dr Sr Mary Glowrey JMJ, and it provides a 17-bed, low cost, short-term accommodation often used by country people visiting relatives who require hospitalisation.[22] Within walking distance of Glowrey

House there are a number of other charitable organisations including the Missionaries of Charity Sisters on 101 Gore Street and 69 George Street — a shelter for women and soup kitchen respectively. Because of their involvement with the MC Sisters and Co-Workers, John and Jenny Barnes came to know Glowrey House, and eventually took up the job of caretakers.[23]

It was in the large hall on the ground floor of Glowrey House that Brother Andrew started conducting regular days of prayer. These usually consisted of a talk given by him, time for prayer in front of the exposed Blessed Sacrament, and a Mass. When the dates of Andrew's retreats were decided for a whole year, John and Jenny Barnes would contact persons and venues, and print and distribute the information to people they knew.

Tallebudgera - Joseph's Place

"I used to like reading his [Brother Andrew's] letter that he wrote to a magazine published in Melbourne called, *The Two Hearts*. So when I tried to discern what to do with this property, I was praying to God, 'Who shall I talk to,' to help me discern, and I wrote Brother Andrew a letter in 1989."[24] This started a spiritual friendship between Geraldine Ryan and Brother Andrew that lasted for more than ten years.

Born around 1945 in Brisbane, Geraldine Ryan moved to the Valley in Tallebudgera when she was thirty-two because of a marriage breakup. She dedicated her life to prayer and then one day, "I had this call, 'Go back to your land, there's nothing here, and wait. I have a work for you to do.' I didn't know what it was, so I sought out the Redemptorists. I used to come and go bush-walking, and then one day I felt I needed to act on this and I asked my son, would he build me a little cabin."[25] At that time Geraldine was quite sick and required nursing care. When after three months she came back, she was surprised to find that her son had built quite a bit of a cabin for her.

Part – V: Brother Andrew – Sannyasi (1988 – 2000)

One evening while sitting on the front porch amid lots of candles because she had no electricity, "Our Lord said, 'When are you going to build me that shrine you promised?' I remembered I had promised to build a shrine when I was married because my husband was a carpenter and I thought if he built the shrine in honour of St Joseph, St Joseph would bring him back to his conversion. (But he had refused to build the shrine. Our marriage broke up.) I simply said, 'I can't, I'm physically unable.' I had only a few dollars in the bank but knowing it was from God, I sought out a builder friend."[26] It cost Geraldine 500 dollars, the exact amount of money she had in her bank account. Some women helped bring the rocks from the creek and her friend put up the framework. "Brother Andrew hadn't started coming at this point, and we had an opening day to bless the shrine. I had no intention that this would go on to the monthly things and yearly retreats."

Tallebudgera Valley or just Tally Valley is an outer locality in the City of Gold Coast in Queensland, bordering with New South Wales. The Valley is a rainforest with lush green farmland and natural forest with a warm and temperate climate but a lot of rain even during the driest months. It is a most beautiful and serene place to spend time in prayer. On 17 September 1989 the land was blessed by Peter Ryan, CSsR, and on 21 March 1993 six priests and about 250 pilgrims attended the blessing of the wayside shrine of St Joseph, the statue of the saint having been donated by the parish priest, Fr Martin Doyle. (The chapel was built in 1994 as a gift of the Damon family and afterwards blessed by Brother Andrew on 1 September 1995).

Andrew's and Geraldine's relationship from 1989 until 1994 consisted of letters dealing with her discernment about the place. It was only in 1994 that Andrew wrote to tell her that he wanted to visit it. She strongly believed that Brother Andrew was sent to her by God — a specific act of God to help her "rise" from her broken state into the work God had entrusted to her. Geraldine recalled that during the first retreat it rained the whole weekend so everyone was huddled in together. Nevertheless, Andrew had insisted on trying to keep silence.

Andrew was one of the few who understood Geraldine's mission to propagate the devotion to St Joseph.[27] "He told me one day, 'Geraldine, you'll be so pleased your property is a private property. Because,' he said, 'if you came under the auspices of the official Church, you would have to fall into line.' 'And,' he said, 'if you give it to a religious order, they have their own charism, and they won't understand the mission you've been given. They might love St Joseph and everything,' he explained, 'but as soon as they take over, Joseph's Place will no longer be what God meant it to do.'"[28]

Why did Andrew opt for Joseph's Place and who were the people attending his retreats?

> Well, Brother Andrew revealed that to me over the years. When I asked him, "Why do you come here?" he said, "Our Lord always went to the fringe-dwellers, those who weren't part of the normal structure, those that weren't supported in the Church." Now, the people that came here came from all areas. Some would travel up from down in Kempsey, others from Brisbane, and once they heard Brother Andrew was here, they would travel. Some would come in caravans, while others … I would, as part of my job, find homes in the parish to accommodate them. They were mostly middle-aged, because the younger people didn't feel the crisis [in the Church] see … people like me, who were brought up in the Church of the 1950s and in the 1960s … suddenly all the new changes, the new liturgical reforms, and the new theologies were coming in and it confused people of my generation … He wasn't here to give a theological retreat. It was more the nurturing of brokenness.[29]

According to Geraldine, since her marriage breakup her son had resorted to substance abuse:

> You see, my son was a drug addict and an alcoholic. He came here with his mates who didn't have the faith; he was a troubled boy since our marriage breakup. Now the people who came here, most of them were practising Catholics.

And who does Andrew go to, to have a conversation with? He goes straight to these boys. He just goes to the most broken. He had the intuition of, you go to the ones who are not fitting in, the one that's on the periphery. See that's a sign of holiness because it's like what Jesus would do. It's a dismantling of the norm, the structure that happens in retreats. I think when people fit into structures, they miss those opportunities, like Jesus going to Matthew the tax collector. That was Andrew. He was just drawn to the most broken — a characteristic he definitely shared with Mother Teresa![30]

Gracewood - God's Farm

It must have been in the late 1980s when Betty Peaker — a renowned organist at a Congregational Church in Busselton — was received into the Roman Catholic Church. Betty was married and had already given birth to twin sons before she converted. (She later adopted three Aboriginal baby girls.) But her call was deeper. She felt that God was calling her to bring people of faith closer to Him. After much searching, she found 200 acres of land approximately halfway between Dunsborough and Margaret River in the wine-producing country of the south-west of Western Australia. And that's how Gracewood - God's Farm was born. The retreat house, along with caravans and cabins, is a place of silence, solitude and stillness. Kangaroos abound in the nearby bush. It was in this setting that Andrew gave retreats in the last twelve years of his life. The first time Betty met him was around 1987 when she flew to Melbourne to attend one of his retreats. From then on, he would go to God's Farm at least once or twice a year. Out of all the memories Betty has of Brother, she recalled in October 1993 taking him to speak in Perth: "Right before one of the talks, a couple came over to me and said, 'Would you ask him what the answer is to committing suicide?' and I said, 'I wouldn't dare, he's about to start talking.' But after taking a cup of tea, I told him and he gave an impromptu talk about suicide prevention."[31] (This ability spontaneously to adapt also impressed several Brothers who used to see Andrew going around the block in Mansatala just before Mass. He would then come back with a beautiful reflection on what he had just seen on the streets around Kidderpoor and tie it in with the Gospel reading of the day).

In one of his last talks given at God's Farm, he touched on this topic of spontaneity which he described as being empty for God to work through him rather than just improvisation.

> I've been doing a lot of preaching like this in the last ten or twelve years, and Betty records them, and I tell you, the experience I have is the experience of having nothing to say. And that is frightening. You are so empty and you've got to come in and talk for forty minutes. You have a subject, but you don't know how it's going. That experience of being totally empty. And you wonder, what on earth is going to come out?[32]

Thanks to Betty we have over ninety recorded talks which Andrew gave during the retreats at God's Farm. Two persons, who attended all his retreats there and who provided many insights, were Peter and Maria Kiely, a married couple from Coogee, Western Australia. "It was in 1988 and we used to get the Catholic newspaper, a weekly publication called *The Record*, when we saw Betty's advertisement ... One thing led to another and I rang Betty and that was the first year that we attended the retreat. We had no idea who Brother Andrew was. We found it one of the greatest experiences. I can think Brother Andrew was the ongoing formation of my faith."[33]

At God's Farm, Andrew would give a weekend retreat, a mid-week retreat and another weekend retreat. Usually he was there for two weeks. He would give about six retreats in all.

> Brother's talk was never less than thirty minutes ... but you never felt you'd had enough. The tapes of Betty were forty-five-minute tapes and more often they clicked off and had to be turned over. But I never felt bored. What I liked was the fact that he came for more than one retreat and he divided

them in small groups of people — twenty or twenty-five — and so we all fitted in that meeting room of God's Farm. He'd sit on a chair, with his legs crossed, resting his elbows sometimes on his knees. Normally there was a talk after breakfast in the meeting room, then we'd go off for a bit of reflection and then Mass mid-morning; after the Gospel, he would give a talk on the Gospel. In the evenings there were a couple of talks. I recall one evening, it was, I can't remember what the talk was about, and I said, "Good talk." "It's the Holy Spirit not me," he said. He never took any credit.[34]

At God's Farm (as at Joseph's Place) a substantial number of the people who came to the retreat were single or divorced women with problems. Brother Andrew appealed to them. Peter tended to think that these women were looking for reassurance that they still had value to God and Jesus, and that was Andrew's message for them. Peter asserted, "Married couples were an exception; we would have been the only married ones on many occasions."[35]

Out of all the retreats Peter and Maria attended, only on one occasion did they hear someone complain about Andrew's talks; she was expecting someone with great gifts of oratory, someone who would raise his voice while preaching. For Peter, Andrew's greatness was that he wasn't a preacher, he was a talker. It is true. Andrew was not a preacher in the conventional sense. Even though his retreats were not very long, he tried to build a relationship with the people who attended them.

After Brother Andrew died, "We bought some of his recordings that Betty had made on tape, I thought it would be good to get them from Betty and get them all [into a] more modern, accessible medium [CDs]. And listening to his talks as I was recording, there is certainly repetition of what he'd said, but it never felt like that. Each time you'd go back, it's like reading the Scripture, we read in the Scriptures the same message but we always get something different."[36]

Missionaries of Charity Sisters

Whenever a Religious leaves a congregation there is always an initial time of transition, during which the former Religious is advised by the authorities of the Congregation not to visit the community. This applied to Andrew too.[37]

But was Andrew ever banned from visiting the MC Sisters? Did Mother Teresa ever instruct the Sisters not to accept Andrew in their communities, or forbid them to attend or ask him to give retreats and seminars? The answer is no. In fact, in 1992 Mother Teresa asked Andrew in a letter, "to help our Sisters in Australia & Papua N.G. [New Guinea] to deepen their personal love for Jesus through prayer and fidelity to the spirit of our society."[38] This is not the only missive from Mother to Andrew after he left the Society. What is most poignant about these letters is the fact that she wrote all of them and their envelopes (in long hand) herself, without going through the Sister acting as her secretary.

Thus, the MC Sisters continued to ask him for retreats, seminars and days of prayer whenever he was in the vicinity of any of the communities.

Sister Shekinah, MC, recalled a retreat with him in Queanbeyan. "It was my job to sweep the front part of the house. He was staying in the presbytery close by. It was winter, and he'd come every morning to our convent with a bag. His jacket was shorter than his jumper. He was really a poor man. It was just lovely to see him coming in every morning like that. He was beautiful, same as always. That same thing, it's ok to be poor. Lots of stories and reflections [during the retreat]. Because he was such a reflective man, he'd see something or deliberately go, like when he sat on the station all night. Just go to observe and see and think about it."[39]

Here are Sister Eliezer's memories of Andrew: "When I was in Queanbeyan and heard there was a retreat going on somewhere like in Goulburn, we would go for that, not the whole retreat but maybe the afternoon. When I was superior, I would invite him for Mass. I remember another time giving a retreat in Darwin. He was funny even during the retreats. Once he was telling us how some communities are big butcher shops! Yes, he was really understanding."[40]

Sr Milada, MC, recalled the first time she met Brother Andrew when she was still in her initial formation around 1989 in Melbourne. The Sisters attended a retreat he was giving for the Co-Workers. Intuitively she felt he was not yet fully peaceful about the whole situation of leaving: "I felt that he was still struggling, but at the same time he was always very charitable. I did not hear him say back any negative things. Then in 1994 when I was a junior, we had a retreat with him and I remember that was very beautiful. I remember it helped me a lot in my own spiritual journey and the main thing was Brother's great simplicity and his great insights into life. The last time I met him was in Darwin in 1998."[41]

"He came to Tenant Creek in July 2000 to give a retreat to our Co-Workers, and he stayed with us. When in his presence, I felt it was similar to Mother's presence: totally accepted and at home with him, never judged. I had a retreat with him in 1998 and a seminar for the superiors in Sydney. I had just become a new superior for the first time. Sister Dorothy was the regional and she loved Brother Andrew, so she really invited him a lot. In the year 2000 I was going through my own struggle, and I didn't have many spiritual helps."[42] It was at the suggestion of Sister Dorothy, MC, that this MC Sister started corresponding with Andrew because he was never in one place for long enough to maintain a constant and continuous relationship with anyone seeking formal spiritual direction or accompaniment. She sought his advice through letters. "He was very faithful. I always got an answer. So, then I met him in person. He came in 2000, before he died, so I was very blessed."[43]

Catholic Parochial Missions

Parochial missions are not intended to make converts to the Roman Catholic Church but are instruction extended over a number of days by authorized missionaries to existing Catholics in their parishes. As early as the birth of the Church, we find such saints as Gregory Nazianzus and Gregory of Nyssa, Basil, Chrysostom, Ambrose, Leo, Augustine, and Gregory the Great instructing and exhorting. In Australia missions were recommended by The Plenary Council of Australia held in Sydney in 1885, and were mostly conducted by Redemptorist Priests. If the mission only lasted two weeks, the first week was usually exclusively for women and the second for men. The sermons usually dealt with salvation, sin, repentance, hell, death, judgement and heaven — with special instructions on matrimony, temperance and Christian education.

Brother Andrew was invited for the first time in 1992 to the Holy Spirit Church in Manifold Heights, a residential suburb of Geelong, Victoria to conduct a five-day mission. At the time Fr Frank E. Burns was the parish priest and Philippa McDonald, RSM, was the parish assistant.[44] Before that, Father Burns had been a curate at Norrington where Brendan (Andrew's brother) and his wife Marie were living. It was Father Burns who invited Andrew to give that first parochial mission after Andrew had admitted to being at a bit of a loose end on his return to Australia.

According to Father Burns, Andrew's preaching and teaching were: "Very simple, straightforward, very organised and he had wonderful crowds. The place was full that first mission when he came. The year was 1992, I think, and in the church there were a lot of Protestants that came too, and you could hear them saying, 'Alleluia, Praise the Lord.' He was always the same Andrew, he was excellent and very patient, very beautiful preaching, very simple and down to earth business and he'd sit in the confessional for hours."[45] From then on, other parishes started to come to know of Andrew and the word spread.

GRAZIERS IN DELEGATE

I've got another week in Delegate. It's a real luxury — all alone except for Mass in the Church. It's a lovely place and the people are friendly. The ones that are still coming to Church are the sort that nothing could really shake them and they are the solid people who keep on going and who — if the truth be known — keep the whole world going.⁴⁶

The fact that very few Australians know where Delegate is comes as no surprise. Located some 239 kilometres south of Australia's capital — Canberra — in the Snowy Monaro Regional Council, it is a small town in New South Wales, but lying just a few kilometres from the state border with Victoria. In 2016 Delegate had a population of 351 people and fewer than ten of them were Catholics. There is still a church dedicated to St Joseph but unfortunately no priest resides in the rectory. The one who was instrumental in bringing Andrew to Delegate was Jean Manning, after she had been to some of his retreats and talks. He accepted the offer and from then on would go both to spend time on his own and to give talks to the people in the area. At that time Jean already had an ecumenical prayer group meeting. In fact, the people who came for Andrew's retreats and talks were not necessarily all Catholics. What is interesting is that Andrew would go to Delegate even if it was just for a few people in the middle of nowhere. Even a small group was important to him and worth visiting and spending time with.⁴⁷ Delegate for Andrew was another Bethany. "I think he also wanted to come here for a quiet time, and we were fortunate enough to benefit from that … like Jesus when he stopped at Martha and Mary."⁴⁸

Some 176 kilometres to the north of Delegate lies Adaminaby, which is one of the highest towns in Australia with regular snowfalls. Small like Delegate, Adaminaby has a population of 301 people. Whenever Andrew was not abroad during Holy Week, he used to spend the whole week with the few parishioners in Adaminaby because it had no resident priest. Celebrations with Andrew were simple. When one of the parishioners in charge of preparing the fire for the Easter vigil celebration asked Andrew what she had to do because she had never done it before and was concerned she would make a mess, he just encouraged her with, "Don't worry, I don't know what I'm doing myself but we'll get through." Parishioners all found him very approachable. Nothing was a problem for him.

The people around this area are graziers, owners of large properties on which livestock graze in preparation for market. Because they are tough men who work alone and hard in difficult situations and weather conditions, conventional wisdom has it that they only show their feelings to their faithful working dogs. My experience with one of them proved to be different. Seventy years old, weather-beaten, bolt upright in his chair, he remarked with eyes moist with tears, "He understood me. He was easy to listen to. Something always struck you, maybe something you didn't understand, or the way he used to tell it. He was down to earth."[49]

Between Delegate and Adaminaby lies Cooma from where a dirt road takes to you Kybeyan. There Gordon Southern had a 100-acre property called *Pinewood* where Andrew would occasionally spend some time in prayer.[50] Gordon had met Andrew through a mutual friend, Peter Taylor. Both Peter and Gordon were involved with *Faith and Light* and *L'Arche*. In November 1988, Gordon attended a retreat given by Andrew in St Joseph's House of Prayer in Goulburn where they struck up a friendship.

By the end of 1989, Gordon had left his career and bought *Pinewood*. Along with his wife, he intended providing hospitality for people with special needs, people "on the journey", and refugees from Bosnia — an idea which Andrew always supported. Gordon still remembers the first time Andrew arrived in Nimmitabel, some twenty kilometres from *Pinewood*, and phoned Gordon to let him know that he was on his way: "He thought he could just get on the road and walk. But that was typical of him, that simplicity. Everything was simple for him. Once he gave a retreat for locals in our shearing shed (which was converted into accommodation for refugees), and another time he gave one in the Town Hall in Kybeyan Valley, which was in disuse and had seen better days and gave a bit of retreat there for people in the neighbouring areas. But most of the time he was with us in Pinewood, in our property."[51]

Being realistic was one characteristic of Andrew that Gordon remembered: "During a retreat at Marlo [the retreat house was also an ostrich farm], near the southeast coast of Victoria, around '98 or '99, I remember him saying to me one afternoon, 'I wouldn't bother coming to this afternoon's talk, Gordon, you've heard it.' At the same retreat, we had a lot of pious ladies who were so busy meeting their schedules for devotions, clutching lots of booklets and flushed and breathless as they rushed from one place to another, that Andrew said to them one afternoon in his gentle way, 'Sometimes, one *good* Hail Mary is enough.'"[52]

According to Gordon, Andrew was also gifted with great insights into current affairs. "But mostly he had a very great deep, empathy with people who struggled emotionally. It was very significant. Emotional struggles. He would talk about the hole in the soul, and meeting Christ at our deepest point of pain. That theme was so deep, such an important one. Such an essential point in the human condition."[53]

For Gordon, Andrew was very similar to St Francis in his practice of poverty and simplicity, but

> he wasn't simple the other way. He could talk about, for example, Dostoevsky, and his classic novels *The Brothers Karamazov* and *Crime and Punishment* and in context always, not just to talk about. And to me that is wonderful. At Pinewood, he would sit down in the lounge with the Bible and sit for hours. Hours just reading. And then he'd get up and go for a walk. And before dinner every evening, praying his Rosary; he would stroll around our large garden but also sometimes he walked to the letter box which was about a kilometre away, still on the dirt road. And back. On his first visit to Pinewood I said to him, Brother Andrew, would you like a lamp by the bedside in your room in case you want to read? And he just said, when I go to bed, I go to sleep. It's a little detail. So wise.[54]

In *Pinewood's* Guest Book Andrew left the following entry, dated 10 November 1997:

> Truly an oasis of peace, grace, natural beauty, warm hospitality — and much more. It is God's farm — and I have been touched here by Him. With my love & prayers, Brother Andrew.

HOME FOR BROKEN PRIESTS

It was in the late 1960s that Father Gerard (Gerry) Monaghan started corresponding with Brother Andrew, after reading an article Andrew had written in *Madonna* magazine. In the introduction to the letters that Gerry sent to the Missionaries of Charity some years after Andrew died, he wrote: "Brother Andrew wrote to me over many years but I only have the file of those I collected in the last six. While they are particularly personal to me in my particular situation and written as it were man to man, I believe they would benefit others — especially men in similar predicaments."[55] A trove of over fifty letters has been recovered thanks to Gerry. They are beautiful letters between two priests, two men, and two persons who share things in common. They are serious letters, letters with deep insights, encouragement and at the same time, letters full of humour.

Even as both shared their experiences, difficulties, strengths and hopes, one theme started to emerge — the possibility of opening a home for priests coming out of prison:

> I've been thinking of the possibility of some opening for priests in difficulties. The enclosed eventuated as some kind of opener for a start, for comment or for the trash basket. So I send it off to you — for yourself or perhaps to be passed on to some of the guys in prison or to the bishop or anyone. It's a sort of flag raised to see if there's any Indians in the bushes.[56]

At the beginning of 1995, Andrew issued a letter to priests about this idea. The thinking behind this home is not very clear because there are two suggestions in the letter. One was the problem in the Church in Australia faced by young men considered too pious or orthodox in their religious practices who were not therefore being accepted into seminaries. At the same time, there is mention of the situation of priests released from prison and wanting to continue in their ministry but unable to do so.

A few ideas have come to me, which I simply put out here as points for thought:

- A more or less loose bonding of priests available for priestly ministry or supply. A sort of Priests Anonymous or Mission Band of priests.
- They could live privately or there could be a simple rented house with some community prayers, the Blessed Sacrament.
- If something more formal was wanted there could be a mission society of priests in Australia (cfr. Columbans, Maryknolls).
- Perhaps an evangelizing dimension.
- For young men with a vocation a house near to a suitable seminary where they could attend lectures.
- To provide a base for priests after prison terms who want to continue as priests — available for supply. To avoid liability on the part of dioceses, there would be no need for official diocesan approbation.

Much of this may sound like wild proposals — and it may be. Yet the situation in the Church — and in Australia too — is dire and desperate enough to call for one of those interventions of the Spirit that have marked Church history through the ages. The more administrative and official side of the Church clearly cannot undertake such initiatives. The question that I don't really want to hear is whether the Spirit may be calling some of us to look into this. That catch slogan of a prominent brand of shoes says, "Just do it." What does the Spirit say — today — amid the pain and urgency of souls?

Let's pray it
Brother Andrew[57]

To Gerry Monaghan he explained a bit more. While Andrew was in Finland, he spoke to an American Trappist priest living as a hermit in the mountains of Norway and an elderly French priest who had been in prison during the war. They discussed the idea of such a grouping, a support, a house for priests, and both immediately understood and approved the move. Andrew told Monaghan that he, Andrew, was ready to go ahead because he was not incardinated in Australia and had nothing to lose. But wasn't he being a little naïve considering that the house would welcome priests coming out of prison after serving time for sex crimes? Was he aware of the laws and regulations by which these men would have to abide? The end of the letter had a certain urgency of tone, "The beauty is that we could find a place now and start. Allowing the Spirit to show us the way as we proceed and listen further." — Here again was the Exodus formation idea of developing something while living it, without any formal organisation or preparation beforehand!

Andrew was at his best, wanting to start something new, knowing well that he would not be able to take charge of it or lead it. It's as if he were only a catalyst for reactions. He did receive some responses to the letter:

> A number of priests wrote to thank me for my letter and my solidarity with the community of the publicans, tax collectors, and sinners. This is a belated reply. I have been travelling and as I am, in fact, a one-man band without office, secretary and the like, letters can be late. The response I received was low-key but good. I believe I saw a quality in the way a number of priests simply expressed thanks for someone taking the trouble to share.[58]

One priest who happened to live in the Philippines even,

> painfully bared his struggle amidst his tears, I could identify with him in my particular brand of unfreedom; I could

Part – V: Brother Andrew – Sannyasi (1988 – 2000)

> express my personal solidarity in that communion, not of iron supermen, but of the poor, the wounded, the broken battlers — which is where Jesus seemed to spend much of his time ... "Two men went up to the synagogue to pray. One was a Pharisee, the other a tax collector".[59]

Another person to whom he sent the letters concerning the possible house was Geraldine Ryan. Geraldine as mentioned earlier, had already opened Joseph's Place for retreats. It seems, however, that for a time there were no retreatants and so Andrew raised the possibility of starting the home for these broken priests at Joseph's Place. He did not spell it out in his letter but Geraldine confirmed that he did hint at the idea a few times.

> Thanks for calling me forth further the priests. You are playing a role here. For I cannot see the details how to proceed. I am getting enough response to go on with — including two bishops — more priests in prison — others — as well as some lay people. It's enough to keep me at it. I'll try to let God write a letter to send out.
>
> In fact, today I am spending on this with Him — trying to listen. And I'm writing this to you — with Him in the middle of us.
>
> There are the priests in prison — others who are fearful or discouraged over their past mistakes — there are priests trying to preach the truth who are being pushed out — silenced. Young men who want to be priests but who don't find a genuine seminary. And there are plenty of lay people wanting & supportive of genuine priests.
>
> Most leadership in the Church — including many bishops in Australia — are too confused, timid or afraid to take a genuine stand.
>
> The poorest & weakest are priests now in prison who have been so humiliated publicly — who don't know where they'll go or who will want them when they come out.

> It won't be difficult to have a place or places for them to stay and live — where they can pray and have Mass privately. I guess it will be a matter of taking one at a time and letting it fall into shape. Some bishops will be very helpful. Maybe this is where it will all start — with the poorest and the weakest. That's where Mother Teresa and Jesus would start. Jesus in the poorest showing us the way. I'll keep tossing out letters. We'll wait and listen. St Joseph is a key person here.[60]

It is rather sad that he gave the impression of being inclined to side more with the brokenness of the victimizer. Andrew saw the Church as being formed of two elements — the Divine element comprising the Trinity: the Father, the Son and the Holy Spirit, but also of the human element which comes through the Divine element and dwells most powerfully in people who are the family of God through baptism. Being a human Church only means that there are weaknesses, presumptuousness, limitations and jealousies.

> We are very much aware of the failures of the Church, there are moral failures of the Church, brought up with great relish by the media and the people who are hostile to the Church …
>
> There have always been scandals in the Church in the realms of morality. In our day we hear about them because as I said, the media and those who are hostile to the Church make tremendous capital out of it and want to destroy the Church and so publicise those things. It's all a very sad story but we will be wrong if we think that it's only in our times that these things have popped up.
>
> Today with the media they make more damage and it's more destructive because in the past we knew how to deal with things — not putting out all the dirty linen out in the front garden for everybody to see — that's not just hypocrisy, that's common sense. We don't need to destroy ourselves unnecessarily but these things are not new. That's why Our Lord instituted the sacrament of confession. He gave it to

> us because He knew we would sin. He gave it to us out of His great love and mercy ...
>
> In the parable of the publican and the sinner, Jesus is teaching us to say, "Lord, have mercy, I am a sinner." If I say that I go home justified and pleasing in the sight of God ... this recognition of the human element is very, very important and of course today the enemies of the Church, the hypocrites of the media ... they may be quite correct, but what about themselves? The media cannot stand up as paragons of chastity or purity or innocence and modesty. It's a lot of hypocrisy.[61]

While he might have been right in that the media is no model of chastity or purity, he could not water down and downplay the damage such abuse had done to innocent victims. A simple "Lord, have mercy on me, I am a sinner," will never heal the psychological damage inflicted on victims of abuse.

For over a year and a half there was no mention of the home for priests in any of the letters to either Gerry or Geraldine. But then in March 1997, after mentioning to Gerry that he had succumbed again to stupidity and misery, the idea came back. This time the desire was also triggered after he had heard

> of two women on the dole who get their fortnightly payment and go off at once and it's all gone in one session. It's a grace to feel one with them in Christ. Such beauty, grace and love comes out of one's poverty.[62]

He called the idea "some grouping of wounded, tabled priests — compulsives included." Andrew ended the letter to his fellow pilgrim Gerry after realising how failure could shed light:

> Funny ... a failure can be so illuminating. I guess it reduces one to the very simple uncomplicated core — which is Jesus. And in His light no bullshit stands. It is a wondrous liberation that comes to us where and as what we in fact are — poor compulsive, screwed-up — whose only hope is Christ the Saviour — for us and for all. But it is a precious

revelation we've been given. And we really can't sit on it. You know all this so much better. It is a grace to be able to share it together.[63]

This would be the last time that he mentioned the possibility of starting the home.[64] In his compulsive behaviour — whatever it was — Andrew was one with them. In fact, to this last letter Andrew attached a photocopy of one of Leunig's cartoons — a man in bed with some kind of virus starts mentioning all the others who have the virus: aunts, uncles, people at work, at garages, in stores. The list of those who have it goes on *ad infinitum* and eventually the man dozes off to sleep with a smile on his face, while saying, "We've all got the virus. We're a community. I belong to a community."

PILGRIMS OF MARY

By the end of 1990, Andrew was fairly "settled" in his new life of going around giving talks and retreats, and had embraced this new lifestyle with trust and gratitude. He considered it a gift from God, especially the fact that he was able to journey with minimal possessions which afforded him a highly valued liberty:

> a freedom that can allow much space and time for God my God and for my brother and sister. There is really nothing — or even no one — apart from Him. I have nothing to live for, nothing to possess me, except Him. And that is a great wealth that gives back everything.[65]

He had, for years, travelled extensively within Australia (and as a Brother in most parts of the world), and was able to understand the longing of the people he met — the small ones, the ones without a voice even in the Church, but who had a spiritual life, who prayed and loved the poor. And for the first time there is the mention of the "Pilgrims of Mary":

> There is the Church of Jesus, mother of saints and the little ones.
>
> There is the beauty of nature and one's own life journey that mirrors the beauty of the Creator.

Some of us are trying to walk in this simplicity, love and light.

We have found our life in the Church, which like a loving Mother, gives us precious treasures that cannot be bought — three in particular: the Blessed Sacrament, Mary the Mother of Jesus and the Pope who is the promised guarantee of Jesus amid many confusing voices.

We may call ourselves Pilgrims of Mary — if she wants it.

One or two of us are pilgrims on the road who in fact have no house or place where we can say we live. I go from place to place preaching retreats, etc., where I am invited, staying in communities of welcome, prayer, hospitality, in parishes.

Some live in their home, or room, or with family. They are living and/or seeking a life of deeper prayer and the freedom of a greater simplicity or poverty. They love the poor, the broken, and the scattered — in their own ways.[66]

Prayer of the Rosary was seen as essential for the Pilgrims of Mary — for those who walked the roads and market-places and for those who stayed at home. The Blessed Sacrament, Mass and an hour before the exposed Blessed Sacrament where possible, were Andrew's other recommendations. He never thought that people would start writing to ask him more about this "new movement". Around Easter of 1991, he wrote a letter elaborating a little more about the idea of the Pilgrims of Mary and making it clear that it was not a new organisation or a new structured movement but: "a loose bonding in prayer and the desire to do little things in love for God and others: a smile, a kind word, a visit, a phone call, a few moments of prayer."[67]

He himself was surprised by the reaction received from people touched by the term "Pilgrims of Mary," admitting that he was not sure what had prompted him to use it. Among the people who responded to his new idea was a widow who had become deaf and was living a hidden life of prayer and intercession. There was the layman striving to live a spiritual life, and a woman from a country town who felt she fitted nowhere and who was drawing strength from the "unseen spiritual community of the unfit and misfits". Another lay woman considered herself one of Andrew's "little people, the voiceless, powerless, and suffering little people." She felt at peace, as if somebody were speaking directly to her. She even urged Andrew "not to stop talking," and when the underground was formed, wanted to belong to it. A nun wrote of her yearning to lead a simpler life amidst all the materialism with which she found herself surrounded. A woman in America, a Quaker man serving others in Africa, and an Indian man involved in relief work in his native place — all responded to Andrew.

For Andrew, the pilgrims who started writing to him at this time had a few common characteristics. They experienced a deep hunger and desire for God, for prayer. They were concerned and pained at the poverty, misery, and brokenness. They were ordinary folk, not public figures — not noticed, much less listened to, by political or church leaders. There was not much in terms of Christian formation for them. They were ridiculed or brushed aside if they even dared to question aspects of religious education, parish life or Church priorities. Yet they had always been the cradle of vocations, a source of Church support and vitality through their fidelity and commitment to the Church they loved. Without his planning, Andrew found himself among a community of voiceless people. Yet, he wrote, "It is a delight, a grace and an experience of hope in a land and a Church that are in decline in a number of ways. It is a story of hope rising from below."[68]

Soon an undated, anonymous booklet *Pilgrims of Mary* started circulating. Written by "a deacon, to fulfil the promise to serve," it contained one person's meditations on what it meant to be a Pilgrim of Mary. His words echoed Andrew's ideas of walking hand in hand with Mary in their day-to-day journey of life.

RETREATS OUTSIDE AUSTRALIA

Over the years, Brother Andrew was even asked to give retreats outside Australia. He kept up his annual retreat for the Chain of Charity in Korea. Other places he visited were South Africa in 1989; Vancouver, Canada in 1990; Papua New Guinea in 1994; Scandinavia in 1990 and 1995; Japan in 1998. It is worth mentioning in some detail four retreat locations in particular: the Philippines, Pakistan, Cambodia and India.

Munting Bukal – Philippines

For Lily Manalo, better known as Ate Lily (Aunt Lily), 1980 would be a year of coincidences or possibly providential meetings. That was the year when she was in Calcutta and met Brother Andrew. She chatted with him and he invited her to stay for Mass. One of the questions Ate Lily asked him was why the Brothers had not yet founded a community in the Philippines, considering that Jaime Cardinal Lachica Sin was open to the possibility. That same year she went to America and while she was visiting one of the communities in Los Angeles, Brother Andrew happened to arrive from Guatemala. Soon afterwards, in December of that same year, Ate Lily met Andrew and two Indian Brothers at the airport for the foundation of the first community in the Philippines.[69]

Later, in 1985, again influenced by Brother Andrew, Ate Lily started Munting Bukal (lit: little spring). Munting Bukal is a place where anybody can spend time in strict silence. The original idea was for it to serve as a refuge for priests and Religious, especially those undergoing crises or needing a time for solitude. Tagaytay, the town south of Manila where Munting Bukal is situated, is known for its mild climate since it sits on a ridge above Tall Volcano Island with elevations of about 650 metres above sea level. Little wooden houses built in typical old Filipino style are dispersed about the property, and in a small, remote corner stands a statue of Our Lady of the Broom.

Brother Andrew used to come for personal prayer time, usually "for silence" in between trips to other countries, even after 1988 when he had left the MC Congregation. He would stop by for a few days and though he might meet other people and talk to them, he went there strictly for himself.

Lily recalled how one day she asked Andrew why she was always low and never high. He told her to stay low as being high would be dangerous for her. According to her, Andrew was direct and understood her concerns right away without explanation. Later she asked him if he would like to be her spiritual director. He replied, "No, we don't like that word, the only director is the Holy Spirit."[70]

One day, Brother Andrew told her, "When you talk about me please talk about what's wrong with me and what's right with God."[71] He called himself "Brother misery" and her "Sister Misery". It was Ate Lily who gave him a little monstrance that he used to carry round with him — a monstrance made from wood found on the Munting Bukal property. Interestingly, Ate Lily, Geraldine Ryan, and Betty Peaker were in contact thanks to the intervention of Brother Andrew. They visited each other over the years and helped each other start or maintain their houses of prayer.

During Sr Nirmala Ghosh's time as General Superior of the Missionaries of Charity Sisters, acting on Andrew's suggestion, Lily decided to donate half (or more) of her property to the Sisters for their retreats. Nowadays a statue of the Good Shepherd stands at the entrance to the main chapel of the MC Sisters' section, underneath which is a plaque dedicated to Brother Andrew, "Friend of the Poor and Wounded".

India, 1991

Three years had passed since his departure and maybe wounds and hurt had started to heal. In 1991 Brother Andrew was asked to give retreats around Calcutta to the MC Brothers and to the priests of the diocese. In Dhyan Ashram, Andrew directed another retreat for

Part – V: Brother Andrew – Sannyasi (1988 – 2000)

the members of Asha Niketan (*L'Arche* in Calcutta) and Antara. He gave another to the Franciscan Clarist Sisters in Kodarma, where he also met his old Jesuit friends. He felt wanted and loved by the Brothers, Sisters and Mother Teresa herself.

> Dear Peter,
>
> I was in India for 2 months. It was so good — much love from Mother Teresa, from Brothers & Sisters — And the poor. Many kept saying, "Come back to us." And I said, "Don't you see I am here?" I feel very much an MC — without any fences or boundary walls now.
>
> It was good to see so many "old" Brothers: Varghese, Martin, Motha [fat] Thomas, Jayaprakash, Bernard, etc. . . they are still committed, Peter and MCB still stands. Many good juniors too.
>
> Yes, the day of seminars & courses is here. But the "Truck" will come around the corner again. I see many communities still have the poorest & most helpless and they have Jesus in the Holy Hour. So it's alive.
>
> I didn't really leave, Peter. We all just got our feathers shaken like some old murghas [hens].
>
> You are so much needed with your joy and your smile — and your perseverance. Life is like this and MCB is in the middle of life.
>
> I was in Korea for Chain of Charity retreat. They too have grumbling & mumblings. They are changed — and yet it's still the same.
>
> No plan or news from Peru for retreat. I'm getting old & slow. No worry we'll be with the angels soon — flying.
>
> Love & prayers.
> Andrew.[72]

A most valuable outcome of his visit to India was a letter he wrote to Mother Teresa, her Sisters and the Brothers, on the primacy of the poorest of the poor in the formation and spirituality of the MC family. By this time the Brothers and the Sisters were already opting for outside specialized courses which could help them in the work for the poor.

Dear Mother, Sisters and Brothers,

[…]I would like to speak here rather of a third great grace that I received among you. It was the opportunity to be touched and enriched by the poorest of the poor—by Jesus present in the poor.

Thomas Merton once wrote that there are two people not so easy to find: one is God, the other are the poor. And MC offers the chance to meet both.

The meeting with the poorest is very humbling. It revealed to me my own great poverty. It is always painful. And yet it makes one free. It is liberating. It is the Good News which is Jesus Himself.

I observed one new development in both Sisters and Brothers MC, this time, which is a greater attention to training and formation. This is important and is appreciated by Sisters and Brothers. It offers the chance to have more confidence and ability in serving the people. In the Brothers' development it corrects a weakness in my vision and priority for many years in the past.

It is surely progress to have more scope for training in the society.

The point I wish to make here does not oppose this development. Rather it wishes to focus light on a very vital part of this training. It is the place of the poorest of the poor in MC formation and spirituality.

I would even speak of the primacy of the poor in this formation — after God, of course. But since we speak of Christ present in the poor, to speak of primacy is not robbing God of His place.

MCs do not discover the heart of their vocation in courses or studies. It is the destitute dying person in Kalighat, the leper, the starving child, the broken, the rejected, the handicapped in their own dirt — it is these who are the first and necessary teachers of the MC vocation. They call to the newest candidate to meet the most urgent and pressing need they have: bathe me, feed me, cover my nakedness, spend your time with me now.

In addition these are simple things that the newest candidate can immediately do. They are simple things that are still valid and necessary for us older ones if we are to be faithful to the special MC call.

There is a miracle in MC. It has carried MC across the whole world in less than a life time. It is very different from the Jesuit way, or the Salesian or any other religious family. It cannot be explained by the professional skill, equipment, efficiency of the members — not even of Mother, as she always says herself. There is a miracle. It is important that MCs recognise it themselves ...

MCs, however, should know it, and make the connection with the source of their power ... May Jesus in the Eucharist and in the poor and Mary His Mother continue to be the heart and soul of MC.

Your brother in Christ,
Brother Andrew.[73]

This would be Brother Andrew's legacy on formation and spirituality to the MC Family. The letter seems to be derived from the following meditation written sometime after a bus trip from Hazaribagh to Gaya:

On a visit to India at the end of last year, I was travelling on a Sunday morning from Hazaribagh to Gaya, not much more than 100 km, but it would take a good three hours. The mini-bus was crowded and I got the last seat.

At a stop along the way three young tribal couples, each with two or three small children including a nursing baby, caught the bus.

They were poor, really poor — dressed literally in rags, the children had sores, running noses; they were dirty. One woman's threadbare blouse was miraculously held together at the shoulder by an old safety pin. They were going or coming back from contract work digging and moving earth manually as a team. The husband digs the earth; the wife carries it in a basket on her head. The pair of them, for a day's work would not get anything like five dollars.

They were illiterate, voiceless and defenceless. They paid their fares, but the smarter conductor extracted more still from their meagre cash.

They were packed into the already crowded bus. The men were put to sit on the roof. The women and children crowded inside.

Passengers didn't want these grubby people touching them and so the women tried to occupy as little space as possible. They realised that I didn't mind if the children clutched my trousers when the bus lurched. They stood holding their babies, and the small ones who could stand clutched their saris and legs — or mine.

The mothers were silent; the children too. I wondered, was it the silence of fear or timidity — or was it the silence of dignity? I watched the face of one mother who managed to sit on the floor feeding her baby. I saw Mary the Mother of Jesus.

As the bus raced, and lurched on, I was graced with the awareness of being close to the sacred, to the Holy One, to God.

It was all wordless. There was a wordless understanding among us. They realised that I didn't mind them catching hold of me. For me, they were Jesus. I was overwhelmed by His touch and His grace on me in them.

I was thinking to give them some money as they got off. I didn't. I was meant to remain powerless myself, not to be any benefactor with cheap money.

I was to recognise that I was poor — so poor, so graced — humbled and graced — graced and made rich by their poverty.[74]

Sheer beauty — Andrew at his best!

Pakistan, 1993

Around the beginning of 1989, Abbé François Vandekerkove, a Belgian missionary priest and spiritual director of Christ the King Seminary in Karachi, Pakistan, was invited for a meeting in Tagaytay, at Lily Manalo's Munting Bukal. While he was there, Lily gave him one of Andrew's general letters to friends, and he immediately wrote to Brother Andrew asking him about the possibility of directing a retreat for the seminarians.

In answer to that first letter, Andrew promptly wrote agreeing, and in a subsequent letter of 10 June 1989, it was decided that the retreat would take place around March 1991. Unfortunately, the Gulf War (started in August 1990) was at its peak around January and February 1991, so Andrew was advised to cancel his visit. He and Abbé François considered other possible dates. Amazingly the first open slot was in 1993.

The visit to Karachi finally happened between 22 March 1993 and 6 April 1993. Apart from giving the retreat for seminarians, Andrew was invited to speak at St Patrick's Cathedral and at St Lawrence's Church in Karachi.[75] He also met with a group of alcoholics, drug addicts and their families.[76]

The relationship between Andrew and Abbé François continued via letters. They had Munting Bukal in common and the fact is that they both worked "on their own". Andrew always encouraged

François (he had already dropped the title "Abbé" or "Father" in his letters):

> It is good that you go to Europe for your spiritual vitality. You work alone in Karachi— and you need to meet people of faith at times. Also take 2 or 3 days in solitude even in Pakistan. You need this... Here in Australia I find myself isolated from priests, Jesuits, etc. But received by the humble souls. God is alive. We can trust Him — And let Him use us.[77]

Cambodia, 1997

It might have been around the time of Mother Teresa's death in 1997, that Andrew gave a retreat for the MC Sisters in Phnom Penh in the house in Cham Chao. According to Sister Elenita, MC, after the retreat Brother Andrew visited the Chroy Changya Bridge (also known as the Cambodia - Japan Friendship Bridge) in Phnom Penh where according to a journalist, the postulant Brian Walch was seen for the last time. There Andrew prayed. Two other visits were to Tuol Sleng Detention Centre and Choeung Ek Genocidal Centre (one of the Killing Fields).

> On the last day of a recent visit to Cambodia for a retreat preached to Mother Teresa's nuns working there, I was moved to visit one of the notorious Killing Fields and the Detention Centre that has become a sort of museum to Pol Pot's atrocities.
>
> My intention was not curiosity or sight-seeing. I knew it was a pilgrimage to a holy place and that I would be greatly — if painfully — graced by it.
>
> I have seen a lot of raw misery in my time, but this was totally different. Much of what I saw cannot be described because it would be too distressing for the reader and also because I cannot find the words.
>
> On the day of my visit I had read St Thérèse of Lisieux:

"There are scents that you can't expose to the air without losing their fragrance, and there are experiences of the soul which you can't express in human language without losing their inner meaning, their heavenly meaning."

I was overwhelmed by the enormity of the human suffering and the human evil. I was also gripped in an amazing way by the spiritual power, grace and even beauty of these countless suffering souls. I experienced Christ Crucified and Christ Risen. Together there was the hopelessness and the hope. I was humbled, chastened and deeply grateful to God and to my suffering nameless brothers and sisters.

This one of the many Killing Fields in the country, on the outskirts of Phnom Penh, now has a Buddhist stupa, a tower-like structure about two stories high with shelf upon shelf of skulls taken from the mass graves ten metres away which now lie open and empty with lush monsoon grass mercifully covering them.

A notice in poor English says that just short of 9,000 bodies were taken from them — men, women and children. Reports of the number of victims in Cambodia vary from one to three million. It's not so long ago (1976-1981). I saw still in the earth at the side of the graves items of clothing that still had not rotted.

I cannot bring myself to write here or speak of the methods of execution of the adults and children. It seems to make the gas chambers of Hitler look almost humane.

To stand on that ground and try to think of the suffering and death of those people was to be gripped and graced by the passion of Jesus. And how much I needed to remember His Resurrection on the third day. Without that only despair or anger or hatred would remain.

From here I went to the Detention Centre in the heart of Phnom Penh. It was once a large primary school with three stories of classrooms. Here too the lush green grass mercifully carpets the ground and a few portulaca flowers here and there gently bring their colour.

Here men, women and children were interrogated and tortured. Crude instruments of it all are kept in their actual place. Again it is totally impossible for me to attempt any description.

But one may ask, Why were the women, children and babies brought here? ...

We are led to believe that today our social awareness is enlightened and that we have moved into a higher level of humanity. It is salutary to remember that mass graves and Killing Fields are as contemporary as Bosnia, Rwanda, terrorism, Stalin, Hitler's Holocaust. They run through human history. But we forget — understandably. Pol Pot is possibly still alive ...

As I walked that bloodied and sacred ground of the Killing Field and thought both of the victims and of the perpetrators, I realised that this is the human race of which I am a member. The perpetrators of these atrocities are my brothers. This is humanity. It always has been, is now, and probably always will be — despite Cultural Revolution that would reshape in utopian mode the whole of humanity. Solzhenitsyn has pointed out the murderous fruits of utopianism that won't look at the grim realities of human experience from the first Fall.

As I stood on that hallowed but bloody ground, and still now, I am powerfully gripped by humanity's need of a Redeemer who doesn't merely talk and organise, but who transforms the reality of our/my heart. And that is Christ, God-man, who came to do for us what we cannot do for ourselves. Politics, reformed economics, technologies, brilliant universities — nothing merely human can change the flawed and lethal possibilities of human hearts in pursuit of wealth, power and pride.

Those countless Khmer victims in their frightful suffering and death, have been Christ to me in a powerful way. They shine an enormous freeing light on my poor, shallow, self-occupied existence ...

Out of all this wondrously shine forth signs of hope. At the nun's place in Cambodia I heard shrieks of joyful laughter from the young woman recovering from T.B. I saw the grass and the flowers on bloodied ground. I saw rice fields cultivated again in Cambodia after years of war. I saw vital life and rebuilding in Phnom Penh even in the midst of the current crazy fragile political scene ...

In that awful pilgrimage I have been deeply graced and touched by Christ in those many victims whose bones and death cells and torture rooms I visited.[78]

Last Visit to India, 1999

The Fifth General Chapter of the MC Brothers between 4 and 23 November 1998, elected Brother Yesudas as General Servant. One of the first things the newly elected General and the Chapter decided was to invite Andrew to come to India and give retreats, days of prayer and talks. During the meetings of the General Chapter, the possibility of asking Andrew to re-join the Congregation was discussed. (General Chapter discussions are kept confidential, so it is not known why Brother Andrew was invited to come back to the Congregation of the Missionaries of Charity Brothers. Obviously questions arise: Did the Brothers realise that they had made a mistake when Andrew was asked to go to a rehabilitation centre for alcoholics? Did the Brothers see Brother Andrew as a recovered alcoholic?) Over the years individual brothers had asked him to come back, and he had always answered that he never felt that he had left. In fact, even during his retreat talks, he often spoke about his time in the Congregation and would do so as if he was still a member.

He promptly agreed to give retreats but gently declined the second invitation.

> We can wait to see if God wants anything to follow this visit. It will be good for a start.
>
> I can see that living with the Brothers would have many benefits — Not the least for me, as it would mean a security in my declining years — which I do not have in Australia. It would not, of course, be a role of any administration, but a spiritual life lived and shared.
>
> But I have a conflict, because I am ministering to people in Australia who are suffering and who receive very little spiritual help. In a way, they are poorer than MCs. For, although you have the weakness and spiritual poverty in the Society, you do have great riches in the spirit of Mother Teresa, in the prayer life & sacraments you have in the way that the Gospel is alive and lived among you, in your nearness to Jesus in the poor. Many hungry souls here live without this and are rejected by theologians, Church activities, etc...
>
> The people I am working with are the spiritually poor and lowly who have much pain and are left alone. So there is need of guidance and light from the Holy Spirit.[79]

By June 1999, the retreat dates were confirmed but Andrew confessed to feeling more frail:

> I am not as strong physically as I was, but with God's grace and the kindness of the Brothers I should be able to travel around India. I am looking forward to be with you all. It will be a great spiritual grace for me.[80]

His trip to India was indeed exhausting and during his travels he was occasionally sick, which he blamed on the change of food, the weather, and the effusive love and attention he received from the Brothers, Sisters and all the people he was re-encountering after eight years. He did not know at that time that he already had stomach cancer.

Part – V: Brother Andrew – Sannyasi (1988 – 2000)

There were two main retreats for the senior Brothers — one in Madras and the other one in Kalyani (some sixty kilometres north of Calcutta). He also visited different communities in all the four regions in India. During the retreat in Madras, a Brother recorded and filmed Andrew's talks only to have them stolen on the train on his way back to Cochin.[81] Luckily, some of Andrew's talks during the retreat in Kalyani were also recorded and transcribed.

Most of the Brothers, who either attended one of his retreats or met him otherwise, spoke of two things: asking him to come back to the Congregation, to which he jokingly answered that if he came back he would come back as a grandfather and not a father; and Andrew's assertion that he would bring back the "Truck". Some Brothers also shared that when he saw the big building in Borivali (Bombay), he said that if he were still in the Congregation, such a building would not have been erected!

Of interest is Andrew's last talk to the Brothers in Kalyani. Appreciation and gratitude runs through it. He narrated the beginnings of his vocation as a MC and how Mother Teresa had asked him to take charge of the Brothers and went on to speak of the development and growth of the Congregation. He also perceived the maturity in how the Brothers dealt with his leaving the Society.

> And so that 1986 Chapter. I didn't come. There was a visa problem but I think I can honestly say I don't think that was the deepest reason. The deepest reason was, for right or wrong, that I felt that it was time to move on. I've never regretted that decision. I've never, I have no reason now, the way the Society has grown and developed since then, I have no reason whatsoever to regret having made that decision.
>
> What happened after that ... there was a confusion which led to my moving out. That too was painful for everyone concerned, for the Brothers, for the Society, for myself at the time. I can honestly say now, and I'd like to say this, if it were possible to go back and re-play the whole thing like a cassette tape and act it all out again and have it all,

> would I want that part to be left out? I could honestly say, no. Yes, there was pain, there was hurt, there was loss of vocations which is the most regrettable part of it all but I believe God's there in that.
>
> If we see what has happened, the Society made a total transition from the founding General Superior. And it survived that and a leadership took over the Society ... Some were saying, I think that there were priests in Calcutta saying, "Well, this will be the end of the whole thing, this will be the end of the Brothers." It wasn't. On the contrary it's been a deepening.[82]

He ended by reassuring the Brothers that he was in the place which God had "destined" for him and that, even though physically he was far away from the Society, he still felt that deep bond which had always existed.

> What about the future? What happens next with Brother Andrew? I must say, the way it seems to me is that the present status, the present situation doesn't need to be changed. It's a bit like bishops in Australia, you know. My status, canonically, I'm a diocesan priest of the Archdiocese of Calcutta. My archbishop is Archbishop Henry D'Souza. I don't belong to a diocese in Australia.
>
> According to Canon Law, because I have faculties to celebrate the Sacraments from Calcutta — any priest who has faculties from one diocese has faculties to exercise in any diocese — unless the bishop in that place issued an order to the contrary. So in Australia no Bishop has done that and they know that I have faculties in Calcutta so that allows me to hear Confession, celebrate Mass, minister there ... that's the relationship with bishops but more importantly the relationship with the Brothers and the Society. I hope these few words — they've been jumping all over the place — but I hope that they would, if they could reassure you, if there's any reassuring needed, of that bond, that very deep,

strong bond that exists between us and to me that is a very, very precious thing.[83]

THE SPIRITUAL JOURNEY CONTINUES

Was Andrew becoming increasingly orthodox in his spirituality? Was he more conservative in his teachings? Some people think that he was. Andrew talked very little about the problems he was facing with being labelled and attacked by some liberal and hostile nuns as ultra-conservative. However, in a public letter dated 15 August 1993, he did mention that the Adelaide Diocesan Retreat Executive had expressed regrets at finding it necessary — because of his views — to cancel a retreat that he was to give under their auspices. Some people disagreed nicely; others angrily. According to Andrew these were mostly nuns.

Fr Greg Beath thought that towards the end of his life Andrew was depressed about the state of the world and its suffering. He was also becoming very upset with the hierarchy, ordinary priests included: "I think this distressed him to see what was happening to the official Church especially by priests, and as a result of that when he wrote his letters, he was expressing that sort of depression that went with the reality of what was happening, for example, about basic principles and basic theology that we believe in. At that stage we had a number of priests around Australia [who] were doubting the Real Presence. That upset him — really broke his heart to see what was happening as he moved around Australia and sort of experienced seeing what was happening to the priesthood — official priesthood — at that stage."[84]

Patrick O'Sullivan, SJ, seemed to agree with Father Beath. He and Andrew were very close but eventually drifted apart when Patrick sensed Andrew's conservatism. Father Patrick believed that Andrew stopped updating himself on theological issues and topics, Andrew himself believed that people were still "following" because: "It has been given to me to proclaim and introduce a living personal

God in Christ rather than a theory, a theology, a technique, a course or a plan."[85] On the other hand Gordon Southern pointed out that Brother Andrew's conservatism was not in any way near to that of SSPX — the Society of Saint Pius X founded by French Archbishop Marcel Lefebvre. When Andrew used to visit Gordon at Pinewood, they would pray the Office together at 5:30 am and then the two of them would have Mass in a converted shearing shed. There is no way that an ultra-conservative with all the associated scruples would say Mass in such a setting.

The Pope, Mary, the Mass

In these later years of his life, his spiritual focus continued to revolve around three essentials — the Pope, Mary and the Mass.

> I love the Church, I love the Church more and more as I grow old. The Mass, the Blessed Mother, the Pope, the Saints, the devotions in the Church, I find even as I get older, a growing appreciation of the richness we have got in there. And it's all so personal.
>
> I suppose I'm a fool to be saying this, I think in a way theology is the trap.
>
> Theology is abstract. It's debate, discussion, opinions, arguments, and scholarship … there that we get into trouble with the Church.
>
> What I love now are the stories of saints, the saints are the great people of history. They are the great people in God's story and dealings with us, and saints are always meeting the front problems of the times. I guess that's where the Holy Spirit has it. So I've got so much to thank God for.[86]

If Andrew's emphasis on these elements in Roman Catholicism meant becoming more orthodox, then he was. We could also consider it a return to the centre, to the basics of what it means to be a Catholic. His premise came from his reflection on Christianity:

1) The Oriental Orthodox split 1000 years ago keeping the Mass and Mary ... but rejecting the Pope. 2) The Protestant Reformation 500 years ago which got rid of the Mass and Mary, but kept Christ. 3) Now the split in the Catholic Church jettisons Christ ... denying His Resurrection, miracles, Real Presence, if not His Divinity ... while Buddhism, New Age, Relativism are embraced.[87]

Saint Joseph

Saint Joseph always had a special place in Andrew's heart. He continued to carry with him the small statue of St Joseph given to him by his friend Patrick O'Sullivan, SJ. But this was not the only indication of Andrew's deep devotion to the saint. St Joseph featured frequently in Andrew's retreat talks, and it was in Geraldine Ryan, another devotee of Saint Joseph, that Andrew found a soulmate. He even dedicated a whole Christmas Letter (1994) to Geraldine and Saint Joseph. For Andrew, Saint Joseph's life, as shown in the Scriptures, clearly revealed one who knew the drama of life:

> ... This is not the story of some unreal flowery figure. It is the human drama lived in its fullness, struggle and beauty.
>
> St Joseph is indeed a role model for men ... Joseph offers the model of a man who devotedly and lovingly parented a child that was not his own. In these times of struggling single mothers, many would understand the worth of Joseph.
>
> The Bible and the Catholic Faith have a timelessness that shallow moderns write off to their own great loss.
>
> Joseph is one who shows a way different from the popular voice of our troubled times. The permissive laissez-faire economics of unbridled Capitalism with its greed in pursuit of wealth has long been hailed as the way to prosperity. The inequalities, misery and oppression stretching across the world give the lie to that.

St Joseph, the working carpenter in Nazareth with a lifestyle of simplicity and moderation, points to another way.[88]

The letter draws attention to an example related to St Joseph that Andrew frequently cited. It is the story of a young man in Australia who was going to marry, when his fiancée unfortunately became pregnant by another. The young man decided to go ahead with the marriage but he eventually lost his job as a teacher in a Catholic School because he was marrying a pregnant girl with another man's child. Listening to Andrew recounting the story, one cannot miss the delight in his voice, when he concludes with what the young man told the priest at the Catholic School, "Isn't that what St Joseph did?"

God amongst Us — A Spirituality Based on the Incarnation

> An awful sight I've seen in India a number of times. You know in India they don't have the things we [Australians] have and when it is a question of a prisoner being taken from one place to another, to a court or transferred to another prison, they don't have the police vans, so at times they would take a prisoner by public transport — train or bus — and you see sometimes on the railway stations, because railway stations in India are always very crowded, lots of people travelling up and down.
>
> And you will see this sight of two policemen taking a prisoner and they have him tied, he's tied with a rope, sort of a rope around his waist and hands and one policeman will be holding and he'll be taken through the crowd to get on the train.
>
> I've never, I think, felt the loneliness of somebody so intensely. That prisoner is so alone. Everybody else is going about their business, quite free, going up and down, people may look. That man is there in public, in that humiliating way bound and tied, and taken along, absolutely alone

... And I thought about that lonely prisoner in Calcutta in the railway station, so alone and yet Jesus knows that experience.

Our God has come and endured that — so that whatever we really suffer, disappointment, sadness, misunderstandings, rejection, loss of a loved one, physical pain, humiliation, whatever we suffer we really cannot ever say we are alone because Jesus has been through it. And Mary his Mother who was always there, the compassionate, she was always there with him.[89]

For Andrew this is where Christ the Lord comes to us, the extraordinary story of God who comes among us. He leads us from suffering to transformation and He does this, not while sitting on His throne of glory, but by becoming one of us and entering into the great ordinariness of our lives. The greatness of the story of the Incarnation is the fact that God enters into our human experience, particularly into three areas familiar to us all: family life, work and labour, and suffering.

Twelve-Step Spirituality

Twelve-Step meetings are anonymous in nature and it is a tribute to that anonymity that it is not known whether Andrew attended meetings on a regular basis. However, there is an increase in Twelve-Step language in his letters and writings and especially in his retreat talks.[90] As early as 1990 he started mentioning the wisdom of Alcoholics Anonymous. In an undated article (but possibly from *The Herald* of September 1990) called "Pain", he wrote of the priceless key which the AA wisdom offered for all. "But alcohol is only one of countless unmanageable areas that afflict us all one way or another." (In 1999 Brother Andrew was even invited to give a talk on the Twelve Steps at Morwell — a town in Victoria).[91]

Whereas earlier in his life he spoke a lot of woundedness and fragility, now he spoke more of powerlessness, helplessness, foolishness and compulsions. The first three steps in the recovery programme of Alcoholics Anonymous assume an admission of powerlessness in the face of the compulsion and unmanageability of life, the realisation that only God can restore the person to sanity, and the decision to give one's life and will to the care of God.[92] In his short article, "Pain" he outlined these first three steps.

Whether he regularly attended Twelve-Step meetings is irrelevant. What is important at this point is that he actually applied the Twelve-Step spirituality and philosophy to his life, and that he offered his experience as an appeal to people undergoing the same struggles and trying to make sense of their lives. In so many retreat talks he mentioned the Twelve-Step approach and other programmes that adopted the same AA philosophy and tradition. "I believe that AA is one of the greatest movements of our day — a spirit-inspired God-given movement,"[93] he said in a talk at Gracewood – God's Farm. In another retreat talk he not only mentioned AA material and gave an explanation of the Serenity Prayer — a prayer often recited at AA meetings — but he also quoted from and read two meditations published by Hazelden Publishing, a leader in addiction recovery and self-help resources.[94] He must have had the meditation books.

> I believe, he confessed, we all have some unmanageable area where we can't manage. And all we have to do is just change that word alcohol to whatever it is. Change alcohol to whatever, drugs, gambling. That's one of mine, I'm a compulsive gambler, can't handle it. I just don't have a few bets. I can't go into a TAB. I can't even read the racing page in a paper, because if I do, I'm off, and it's not one or two bets, and it may be more than one [compulsion], I mentioned gambling, there are a few more, but I won't mention them.

> They cluster, and there are different areas but they all come from the same source — whatever it might be — and it is deep between my wounded self.

Part – V: Brother Andrew – Sannyasi (1988 – 2000)

> Will power does not work. And I know myself with that gambling, will power does not work. I've got to keep away, and I have to keep asking God to help and I can't do it myself ...
>
> In AA they speak the same language, they understand, they have great compassion yet they call a spade a spade. If there's one place where you cannot pull wool over anybody's eyes, it's an AA meeting. If an alky goes and he tries to pitch a yarn, they are on him like that! They know all the excuses, all the gags, the tricks, everything and they'll tell him, don't try that here, we've been there, we've done all those things ... so that tremendous honesty. And that's in a way their strength.[95]

A striking parallel exists between the process of how Andrew worked through his addictions and those of Venerable Matt Talbot. Whether or not Andrew had a devotion to Matt is not clear, since he only mentioned him once in a letter to the general public dated January 1994. Matt Talbot, who was born into extreme poverty in Dublin in 1856, was one of twelve children. His father was a heavy drinker who could not sustain his family. They had consequently to move quite frequently from place to place with the result that Matt only attended school for one year. At twelve he got his first job in a beer bottling company and by sixteen he was a fully-fledged alcoholic. Twelve years of hard drinking followed until one Saturday afternoon while walking home and finding himself with no job, no friends and without a drink, he had a moment of intense clarity and grace. He was twenty-eight years old. That same day he walked to a church and made his confession to a priest, who helped him "take the pledge" to renounce alcohol for three months (which he then renewed for life after six months). At the time there were no Twelve-Step programmes, or rehabs or support groups, and it is here that the strongest identification between Andrew and Matt lies: they both adhered steadfastly to daily Mass, devotion to the Eucharist, a love for Mary, and spiritual reading. The term "urban ascetic" is often used in relation to Matt because he lived a quiet life of devotion, holiness and generosity with all those around him, whilst exercising austerity — characteristics also applicable to Andrew.

Andrew's life was a sacred journey. It was a journey about change, growth, discovery, movement, and a continuously expanding vision. He stretched his soul, listened to his intuition and made courageous, and at times crazy, decisions at every step along the way. Andrew's "pilgrimage shrine" was not the Jesuits; Andrew's "holy place" was not the Missionaries of Charity Brothers. Andrew's pilgrimage was into the labyrinth — a journey to the centre of his deepest self and back into the world with a broadened understanding of who he was.

Something must have happened in Andrew between the time of leaving the Brothers and the first few years in Australia. It could be that "the meeting" in Albuquerque was a wakeup call which made him realise that he needed help in another area or other areas of his life, not necessarily alcohol, to which he could apply the AA spirituality and philosophy.

Maybe this realisation was also one of the reasons why Andrew wanted to be small, unnoticed and unimportant. It gave him the freedom he always yearned for to be one with those he sang of — the poorest of the poor, because like them he needed God's love and mercy.

> Perhaps this humiliating story of Brother Andrew
> who was admired, praised and loved
> by many wonderful people,
> may in a strange way offer a little comfort
> to other humiliated,
> hard-pressed, embarrassing people,
> struggling with a disgrace, a failure,
> a fall in their own lives or in their dear ones—
> a painful break-up of a relationship, abandonment,
> a lonely pregnancy, a police case, being written off.[96]

FRIENDS

People who knew Andrew described him as a private sort of person but who at the same time enjoyed the company of others. He knew his boundaries and he respected others' boundaries. People felt at ease with him, looked up to him. They sought him for direction and for retreat preaching. But there seems to be a small group of people with whom he felt very comfortable and whom he most probably considered friends.

There was Margaret Ryan, RSM, who met him on his first visit home to Australia in 1972, and kept in touch with him through letters even while he was in Saigon and Cambodia, and for the remainder of his life. Margaret had come to know Andrew through a mutual friend, Fr Patrick O'Sullivan. Andrew and Patrick's relationship became strained over time. In fact, there are no letters between them from 1993 until Andrew's last letter to Patrick in 1999, in which he confessed, that they "used to cross half the world to meet — Now we don't even make it 200 yards up or down Power St. We've moved along I guess — Not back. I hope."[97]

Andrew experienced some estrangement with Val Noone. This time it was over the political issues concerning Vietnam, but Andrew could not live with this discordance and he eventually wrote:

> For a few months now I've been thinking of writing. We seem to have broken relations some years ago. Not so violently, but still in a way that was effective enough. And I think Our Lord tells us we shouldn't do that. So I guess this is a clumsy sort of effort to make a bridge. Which doesn't mean I have any expectation for you to come rushing across. We seem to have gone separate ways on account of differing ideas on how to love our neighbour. Which really strikes me as being a bit silly of us.[98]

It seems they did make up. Val and his wife invited Andrew to their home in Gore Street, Fitzroy, and in 1986 Andrew and they enjoyed several visits together.

Would Fr Daven Day be considered a friend? Probably not. Such was the relationship between the two that had started as early as 1952 in Watsonia that he was more like family. Even Andrew's nephews and nieces call Daven, "Uncle Daven".

Gerry, John and Leon

There is ample evidence to suggest that those closest to Andrew (each for different reasons, especially during the last twelve years or so of his life) were Gerry Monaghan, Leon Allen and John Barnes.

With Gerry there was definitely a sense of the fraternity of the wounded and compulsive, the ones who had been through hard times because of their "foolishness".

> I'm sorry you caught me out of sorts when you rang at lunchtime. Actually you were lucky you didn't get me or you might have been bitten by "the black dog" that had hold of me. We'd spoken about how we, when we're sick are pretty awful company — so pathetic in our self-preoccupation.[99]

Letters to Gerry were, according to him, very personal in his particular situation. They understood each other: "I write to share with you an experience of my own stupidity and misery. No need for details. You know it all."[100] What brought Gerry and Andrew together was their addictions, but what bound them together was not their addictions but their solutions: a trust in God and at the same time a service to the ones who still suffered — addicts or not. Again, Andrew wrote to Gerry:

> That 'stinking thinking' will always be with us. It's our wound. It's the reality we cannot change. But through comes all that grace you write of. And that's even more wonderful reality.[101]

Reminiscing about Andrew, the day Gerry received the news that he had died, he recalled, "At our last meal August 15 in a Greek cafe in Surry Hills [Sydney], we were on our old topic of addiction and compulsions. He claimed he still struggled to walk past a TAB without entering and gambling. It was this tremendous sense of

Part – V: Brother Andrew – Sannyasi (1988 – 2000)

his own weakness and unworthiness that made him so dear to the thousands who wrote to him from around the world ... Just before we parted after our meal on that Assumption Day, Andrew uncharacteristically mentioned that he was feeling weak and felt there was something wrong in his stomach."[102]

Andrew's relationship with John Barnes was different. John was the closest to him geographically. Andrew loved to pop into Glowrey House occasionally for a cuppa and a relaxed chat without having to be "Brother Andrew" or "Father Andrew", even though the Barnes persisted in calling him "Brother". There still exists a nice photo of John and Andrew doing some manual work on the outside railings of Glowrey House. John's presence and valuable assistance was of utmost importance during Andrew's last days at the MC Sisters in Gore Street.

The other deep relationship was with Leon Allen. Leon had lived with Andrew during the most difficult and most beautiful times in Vietnam. They understood each other at that level of pain and beauty. In the last Night Points that Andrew gave to the Brothers during his final retreat for them in Kalyani in October 1999, he talked extensively and passionately about Leon:

> There's another Australian who I think would feel exactly the same. Some of you remember Brother Leon who spent a few years with the Brothers. Very special sort of a man. Very sensitive person. Something of a poet. A very delicate make up. Physically, life was very difficult for him in Calcutta and then in Vietnam. Health-wise, food he couldn't take and the air. He had asthma and all sorts of things affected him. And also he was a very sensitive man in that he had great difficulty in sort of revealing himself. He kept a certain distance and suffered greatly.
>
> Finally he left. He left India and he went back to Australia. Then he came back to Vietnam thinking it might be a bit easier to manage there but eventually it was all too much and he had to leave.

I don't think I've ever known a Brother who has a greater appreciation of the Society and of the Brothers than Leon had and he conveyed that to me. He had a great appreciation particularly of the simple Brothers, perhaps because he was a wounded man himself and often felt threatened by strong people. He had a great appreciation for the simple Brothers and he would go with them for work and he could see them operating. He could see them working with the children at Babughat and places like that and the leprosy work. He could appreciate the way in which the simple Brothers related to the people and worked with them.

When he left he got a job. He was a nurse. He got a job in a government mental institution and a very good job and well paid and he did well financially. He never married. For a long time when he went back he wouldn't write. He didn't want to. He said it's too painful for him to be reminded of the beauty of that life with the Brothers. And he told me later, "I've got all that I need here materially" but he said "there's only one place in the world that I want to be and my body won't allow me to be there."

So that tremendous appreciation of the Brothers and that love. As I say, I think I loved the Brothers from the beginning but he certainly helped me to love them and to appreciate them and he was one, as I say, a bit of a poet and poets are people who see into the depths of things. They don't just see a tree there or a flower. They somehow see a depth of beauty within whatever it is and Leon, the poet in him, was able to see the beauty of MC and he still writes to a few Brothers here and there that he knew from long ago and he treasures those contacts.[103]

Andrew respected Leon but above all he loved Leon. He made it a point of meeting him whenever he was in Sydney and he looked forward to such encounters. For Andrew it was a delight to be with Leon, a delight that he confessed to in various letters written to him, "You can't imagine how much it meant to me to meet you again in

Part – V: Brother Andrew – Sannyasi (1988 – 2000)

Sydney. So you'll have to take that on faith."[104] Andrew could be himself with no frills and titles attached. He enjoyed being with people who treated him as another man, another human being — and Leon seems to have been one of them: "I'm going to OZ on 30th. I have enough public appearances, but a meeting like we had last year was so pleasant and relaxing that I would enjoy a repeat. It's nice, I guess, to be able to be myself with someone, without any expectations."[105]

When for some reason such meetings were not possible Andrew would despair:

> I got here yesterday. Your note was here to the Simons. And the latter are away for school holidays. Normal family confusion has led to your note not being dealt with. I phoned last night to your good mother. And she said you are on night duty this week — at which point I went into despair. I'm just here till 26th. At any rate I send this off this morning — still believing in miracles. The weekend even Sunday morning would be possibilities — a Friday. In a bit of haste to get this off.
>
> Love & prayers Andrew.[106]

At the same time there was no chance of misinterpreting this despair because they both knew each other and the respect they had for one another:

> My thanks for your words. It was a delight to meet in Sydney. We really do know each other well enough not to have to be too concerned about how we clod-hopper around. It's nice when it's like that. No need of expectations. I was delighted with your being there at the Retreat — and happy to see that you are still Leon.[107]

BEATIFICATION OF MOTHER TERESA

When Mother Teresa died on 5 September 1997, Brother Andrew was in Munting Bukal (Philippines) for some days of prayer. Brother Geoff — who was the General Superior at that time — tried to contact him via the Brothers in Manila to inform him and ask him whether he wished to go to her funeral. Brother George, MC, and Brother Benedict, MC, tried to talk to him and encourage him to attend. But Andrew preferred not to go. (After Mother's death, Sister Gertrude, one of the first group who had joined Mother Teresa, gave Sister Joseph Maria a relic of Mother's blood to give to Brother Andrew. Andrew would not take it. He travelled so much that he felt unable to take care of it properly. He also told Sister Joseph Maria that after Mother's death he felt her so close to him that he did not need her relic.)

In time, Gillian Pacheco and Brother Andrew were nominated in Australia to be witnesses for Mother's beatification.[108] They had both at one point in their lives formed part of the MC family. For this occasion, Brother Andrew prepared the following document:

> I had a close and privileged contact with Mother Teresa from December 1965 when she invited me as a Jesuit priest ordained in 1963, to be the superior and formator of the congregation of the Missionary Brothers of Charity that she was establishing. I filled that role until 1986, when the leadership passed on to the next generation of Brothers. These years and that role naturally involved close personal association with Mother Teresa.
>
> The birth and growth and apostolic fruitfulness of the Congregation of Brothers came from Mother Teresa's inspiration, charism, missionary purpose and spirituality, as well as from the detailed practicality of her approach in the work with the poorest of the poor, in the daily life of prayer, community living and simplicity. Evidence of all this and the fruitful reality can be readily observed in the history of the Brothers and in the current daily reality of their apostolate in many places. For the purpose of my submission here, I will try to outline something of her impact on me personally and spiritually. For this clearly comes from her holiness, from Christ alive in her. It is the

Part – V: Brother Andrew – Sannyasi (1988 – 2000)

fulfilment of the prayer of Cardinal Newman, 'Radiating Jesus' that she said every day.

As I began to formulate this submission, I came to realise more clearly the impact of Mother Teresa on me. Awareness of this grows stronger with the passage of time. It has become a grateful rich awareness of having been graced by her life and her life-giving in so many ways and in such depths that it is impossible to describe with due adequacy. Mother Teresa introduced me to Christ in the poorest of the poor in a new and thrilling way. She did this with a simplicity and personal directness that I can see now as a wonderful touch of God upon me. She led me — not by lecturing or theoretical teaching — to a closeness and friendship and intimacy with Jesus that is a priceless gift. She led to a simplicity and poverty of lifestyle in practical details that is a great freedom. I would describe it as part of the evangelical freedom of the poor in spirit that Jesus offered to His disciples. It is not that I received these and many more graces from Mother Teresa, and then lived and practised them fully or even adequately. Quite the opposite. And it humbles me now, at 70 years of age, to realise that having been so specially blessed by God in this association with Mother Teresa, in spite of such grace, I responded so poorly and inadequately.

This leads to a special consideration on Mother T*eresa's magnanimity and generosity of heart. For she trusted me greatly, she gave of her time and love abundantly to me. And I was so poor and ungenerous in my response. "To whom more is given, more will be expected."

So often I was petty, disagreeable and presumptuous in decisions and positions that I took. Part of this was my pride as a man in his 40s who wanted to assert himself in independence and individuality. I know that I disappointed Mother Teresa in many such ways. And yet I saw and experienced in her the extraordinary humility of a great spiritual and effectively caring person who allowed me the space to disappoint her and even frustrate her intentions and initiatives.

Her meekness, her tolerance of poor human nature, her trust that God would bring good even out of frustrating human behaviour from others — even from those who were her collaborators. On-going grace from all this is the call I am being given now as I write these two years after her death. Like so much else it is the on-going influence of Mother Teresa's life and life-giving holiness. I am aware that this grace flows on and through me — poor as I am — in my ministry of Word and Sacrament and in shepherding souls. All this clearly seems to me to be the fruit of a soul so filled with Christ and so surrendered to Him that he radiated through her on to those graced to be close to her.[109]

Andrew's oral testimony was submitted in Melbourne and Gillian's in Sydney. When afterwards they met, they both agreed that if Mother were canonised, the MCs would owe them big time!

Part – V: Brother Andrew – Sannyasi (1988 – 2000)

1. Br Andrew with Cardinal Kim Sou Hwan in South Korea.

2. Melbourne 1988 - First retreat at Templestowe.

3. Andrew at his best.

4. (Undated) Retreat at God's Farm.

Part – V: Brother Andrew – Sannyasi (1988 – 2000)

5. *(Undated) With Betty Peaker at God's Farm.*

6. *Sydney 1992 Br Andrew with Timothy Hughes.*

7. Calcutta 1991.

8. Pakistan 1993 Abbe Francois Vandekerkove.

Part – V: Brother Andrew – Sannyasi (1988 – 2000)

9. Melbourne c. 1999 Br Andrew and John Barnes.

10. Melbourne c. 1996 – At work at Glowrey House with John Barnes.

11. Kalyani (India) 1999 - Bros Geoff and Yesudas.

Endnotes

[1] Sannyasa is the fourth state in the Hindu system of life stages or ashramas, the first three being brahmacharya (celibate student), grihastha (householder) and vanaprastha (retired person).

[2] 19880312 LP.

[3] Maher, Frank, SJ, (ed.) *Rebuild My Church,* Victoria, Australia: Hampton Marian Centre, 2002.

[4] 19950100 LP. "What did I do for Christmas? I went to Bourke which is the end of outback Australia. A hot, harsh, dusty town. Of the ten days I was there only one was below 40 degrees. I stayed in 'Bethlehem' which is the home for homeless men, mostly Aboriginal, run by Mother Teresa's sisters. It is built of iron sheets, has a ceiling and a simple cooling system. Considering all of which it is surprisingly liveable. Because it was too hot to go outside, I had plenty of time for prayer and reflection. It was dormitory living, and I was there with the men who would be on their beds or just sitting without much talk. I was struck by their peace and serenity. Their capacity to be silent."

[5] 19911113 LF to Kathryn Spink. "Enclosed is a recent booklet. I think I've moved across that edge too — or fallen over it. No more publishers & booksellers. It's little booklets and free distribution. Divine Providence is, of course, helped by aging bachelorhood, celibacy or whatever it may be."

[6] Eileen O'Connor. (1892 - 1921). Born in Melbourne, at the age of three she fell injuring her spine, and was largely paralysed. With limited education and no formal theological formation, Eileen embodied a distinctive spirituality marked by an unwavering devotion to Our Lady and her own willingness to endure a lifetime of suffering. Father Edward McGrath met Eileen through his duties as priest-in-charge of St Brigid's Church, Coogee, NSW. He became convinced of her saintliness during his frequent visits to the family home. The plight of the sick poor was especially close to Eileen, whose family had been plunged into precarious financial circumstances following the death of her father in 1911. Father McGrath too came from a disadvantaged background and had a deep empathy for those experiencing similar difficulties. Our Lady's Nurses of the Poor began its ministry from Our Lady's Home at Coogee in April 1913. Despite her growing disabilities, Eileen continued to guide the work of the fledgling society from her bed until her death aged just 28. Father McGrath finally returned to Australia in 1941 and continued his fruitful vocation as a MSC priest in Melbourne, where he died on 17 May 1977, aged 96 years. (https://www.ourladysnurses.org.au/founders Web. 29 July 2020.); Mary MacKillop's life will be quoted later on in the book.

[7] 19880815 LP.

[8] Tolkien, J. R. R., *The Lord of the Rings,* London, U.K.: Harper Collins Publishers, 2005.

[9] 19890125 LP.

10. 20190517 IB Robi Gut, MC.
11. Tolkien, J. R. R., *The Lord of the Rings,* London, U.K.: Harper Collins Publishers, 2005.
12. "The Real Presence of Christ in the Eucharist" is a term used in Christian Theology to express the doctrine that in the Eucharist the whole Christ is present, not merely symbolically or metaphorically — but truly present, body, blood, soul and divinity under the appearance of bread and wine.
13. Gilchrist, Michael, *Rome or the Bush,* Ormond, Melbourne: John XXIII Fellowship Co-op. Ltd., 1986.
14. Michael Gilchrist is editor of the Australian monthly *AD 2000* published by The Thomas More Centre begun by B. A. Santamaria. The reasons for starting the magazine are described in Santamaria's first editorial, "An Act of Folly or an Act of Faith?" In Andrew's Christmas Letter of 1990, after admitting that he was sorry publication of The Advocate had stopped, he recommended *AD 2000* to the people as a good magazine giving a Christian perspective on life in contemporary Australia.
15. 20180227 IS Sister M. Shekinah, MC.
16. 19950700 LP.
17. 00000003 LP.
18. 19941100 LP.
19. 20180308 IF Margaret Ryan, RSM.
20. Ibid.
21. From a talk given by Brother Andrew in 1990 at Gracewood - God's Farm, Australia – "Jesus Meeting People"
22. Mary Glowrey, (1887 – 1957). Born in Australia. She graduated with a Bachelor of Medicine and Bachelor of Surgery in 1910, specializing in obstetrics, gynaecology and ophthalmology. In 1916, the Catholic Women's League was formed at a meeting in Brunswick Street, Fitzroy (Melbourne). Glowrey became the inaugural president, giving lectures and writing articles about economic and social problems faced by women. In 1920, after reading a pamphlet about the life of Agnes McLaren, a Scottish missionary doctor in India, Mary gave up her career as a doctor in Australia to go to India to care for the poorest women and children. She became a Sister with the Society of Jesus Mary Joseph in Guntur (India) and for many years ministered to thousands of patients who would not otherwise have received care. She even trained local women to be compounders, midwives and nurses. In 1942 she founded the Catholic Health Association of India. She never returned to her native Australia and died at the age of 69 in Bangalore, India. She was declared a Servant of God in 2013. http://maryglowreymuseum.info/Who-was-Mary-Glowrey Web. 21 July 2020
23. John Barnes, (1935 – 2012). Married to Jenny Barnes who at the time of writing still lives in Mill Park, Victoria. He died of mesothelioma due to

Part – V: Brother Andrew – Sannyasi (1988 – 2000)

exposure to asbestos while working as a carpenter.

24 20180324 IF Geraldine Ryan.
25 Ibid.
26 Ibid.
27 20180326 Email of Geraldine Ryan to author. "The main theme of my writings is that through St Joseph, who is the vicar for the Eternal Father, God wants to restore a holy manhood on earth ... both for fathers of families and the priests of the Church, who embody his virgin fatherhood over the Incarnation Mystery. What has happened since that time, which is decades ago, it's more pertinent than ever to invoke Saint Joseph for this to occur as the fathers of politics, science, medicine, religion, communities and government organizations have essentially abandoned people and children in particular, pursuing worldly and evil goals and even legalizing abortion, euthanasia, etc. In Queensland, our state, the government recently brought in a law making abortion legal up to full term. The fatherhood of our societies has been corrupted by deceptive ideologies which have been propagated in our schools and universities. I didn't realize years ago how bad it would become; but I'm aware now that it is critical to invoke the father of Jesus to imbue all men with his holy paternity for the sake of women and children; because this virgin fatherhood like God the Father was first deposited in him through his espousal to The Immaculate Conception, his wife."
28 20180324 IF Geraldine Ryan.
29 Ibid.
30 Ibid.
31 20180328 IF Betty Peaker.
32 From a talk given by Brother Andrew in 1999 at Gracewood God's Farm, Australia – "The Dryness of Prayer."
33 20180420 IF Peter and Maria Kiely.
34 Ibid.
35 Ibid.
36 Ibid.
37 19881012 LB to Peter Murmu, MC. "I had a lovely time in Korea with C. of C. [Chain of Charity] and an open retreat for some nuns. MC Brothers are confused and embarrassed to meet me — And so it is kindness to keep away from MC houses as Geoff has asked me to do."
38 19920719 LS Mother Teresa to Brother Andrew.
39 20180227 IS Sister M. Shekinah, MC.
40 20180321 IS Sister M. Eliezer, MC.
41 20180325 IS Sister M. Milada, MC.
42 20180317 IS MC Sister (Anonymous).

43 Ibid.
44 20180312 IF Fr Frank E. Burns. Fr Frank Eduard Burns was born in 1938 in Shepparton in Northern Victoria and ordained in 1967. His mother, who lived in Mt. Martha, was good friends with Marie Travers-Ball — Brendan's wife.
45 20180312 IF Fr Frank E. Burns.
46 19950115 LF to Fr Gerard Monaghan.
47 The small group the author met consisted of Peter and Joyce Reed, Clive and Lorraine Cottrell, Jenny Wright and Sandra Walker.
48 20180316 IP Peter Reed.
49 Ibid.
50 Gordon Southern, 73 at the time of interview, was born in the United Kingdom, but immigrated to Australia in his early twenties and was working in the insurance business. Upon the author's arrival in Australia, Gordon insisted that he should visit his place. The author was initially reluctant to do so because of pressure of time but in the course of a number of long phone calls, the name Delegate came up. Gordon was asked to elaborate because Delegate was on the author's list of priorities to visit. It turned out that Gordon was actually living in Delegate and would provide a wealth of insights about Andrew. Such was Divine Providence!
51 20180302 IF Gordon Southern.
52 Ibid.
53 Ibid.
54 Ibid.
55 Fr Gerard Monaghan was ordained priest in 1961 (aged 26) for the Canberra-Goulburn diocese. He worked in parishes, conducted marriage encounter groups and had an official responsibility in family planning. According to the website http//: www.brokenrites.org.au as visited on 7 July 2020, "these roles enabled him to glean intimate details about the lives of women parishioners. He also visited hospitals where he became acquainted with women patients." Broken rites stated that Monaghan had sexually abused one of these women. In an interview with the author Father Greg Beath shared: "Gerry reached out to a lot of priests who sort of went through crises and a lot of priests were around. Gerry was a very faithful visitor to priests in jails — particularly the Junee jail. At one stage they had something like four or five priests and Gerry made an apostolate to go and visit them to sit with them and talk and correspond with them and he even established a whole prayer card for prisoners as part of his whole desire to intercede on behalf of the priests especially priests in jail." 20180315 IF Fr Greg Beath.
56 19950407 LF to Fr Gerard Monaghan.
57 Undated letter but possibly early 1995.

58. 19950815 LP to Priests.
59. Ibid.
60. 19951110 LF to Geraldine Ryan.
61. From a talk given by Brother Andrew in 1995 at Gracewood - God's Farm, Australia – "God Planned for the Church to be Human."
62. 19970316 LF to Fr Gerard Monaghan.
63. Ibid.
64. Posthumously a small booklet was privately published by Betty Peaker under the title of The Song of the Wounded Healer. In it there is a short mention of A House for "Named Priests", in which Andrew wrote: "A special harshness for offending priests, even when they have served sentences, cries out for Christian compassion. Bishops find it difficult to place them in any Church establishment for fear of further litigation. Someone crazy enough and with nothing to lose might have a simple House of Prayer and hospitality . . . not under the authority or title of the Church but in the name of private citizens. There is no law against people praying in a house, having the Celebration of the Eucharist, Divine Office. It just could be a citizen's House of Prayer. It would be a house open to the Spirit. I believe such a house would be a spring of much grace and spiritual life. The crucifixion of these men, their humiliation, and their endurance in faith may be the formation of a great renewal in the country. The Gospel finds its native soil on such ground."
65. 19900908 LP.
66. Ibid.
67. 19910400 LP.
68. Ibid.
69. The official foundation date of the Lorraine community in the Philippines is actually 27 April 1981.
70. 20180522 IF Lily Manalo.
71. Ibid.
72. 19911110 LB to Peter Murmu, MC.
73. 19911105 LS/B.
74. 19920400 LP.
75. Christian Voice, Karachi, 7 March 1993.
76. From a talk given by Brother Andrew in 1996 at Gracewood - God's Farm, Australia – "A New Creation."
77. 19940913 LF Abbé François Vandekerkove.
78. 00000011 LP.
79. 19990203 LB to Yesudas Mannooparampil, MC.
80. 19990622 LB to Yesudas Mannooparampil, MC.

81. 20180126 IB Devasia Baby.
82. 19991024 Brother Andrew "Night Points," Kalyani (Calcutta): Unpublished Source, 1999.
83. Ibid.
84. 20180315 IF Fr Greg Beath.
85. 19920815 LP.
86. From a talk given by Brother Andrew circa 1994 or 1995 at Gracewood - God's Farm, Australia.
87. Ibid.
88. 19941200 LP
89. From a talk given by Brother Andrew in 1993 at Gracewood - God's Farm, Australia – "Upside Down Kingdom."
90. Twelve-Step meetings are those which apply the philosophy and the Twelve Steps of Recovery of Alcoholics Anonymous to any compulsion or addiction.
91. From a letter 20010107 from Sister Joseph Maria, MC, to Br Yesudas Mannooparampil, MC.
92. 1. We admitted that we are powerless over alcohol — that our lives had become unmanageable. 2. Came to believe that a Power greater than ourselves could restore us to sanity. 3. Made a decision to turn our will and lives over to the care of God *as we understood Him*. (*Alcoholics Anonymous*, Alcoholics Anonymous New York City: World Services Inc., 1976).
93. From a talk given by Brother Andrew in 1990 at Gracewood - God's Farm, Australia – "Jesus Healing the Lame Man."
94. The Hazelden Betty Ford Foundation provides a holistic and forward-thinking approach to the disease of alcoholism. Part of the foundation is the publishing house that produces material on different types of addictions and self-help resources.
95. From a talk given by Brother Andrew in 1990 at Gracewood - God's Farm, Australia – "Jesus Healing the Lame Man."
96. 19871101 LF.
97. 19990112 LJ to Patrick O'Sullivan, SJ.
98. 19830622 LF to Val Noone.
99. 19979827 LF to Fr Gerard Monaghan.
100. 19970316 LF to Fr Gerard Monaghan.
101. 19980522 LF to Fr Gerard Monaghan.
102. 20001004 OF Remembering Brother Andrew – Fr Gerard Monaghan.
103. 19991024 Brother Andrew "Night Points," Kalyani (Calcutta): Unpublished Source, 1999.
104. 19850903 LF to Leon Allen.

Part – V: Brother Andrew – Sannyasi (1988 – 2000)

[105] 19870623 LF to Leon Allen.
[106] 19860121 LF to Leon Allen.
[107] 19810824 LF to Leon Allen.
[108] Gillian Pacheco, an Indian living in Australia, aged 72 at the time of the interview, was formerly known as Sister Cabrini, MC. She joined the Missionaries of Charity in Calcutta in 1962 and for many years was a novice mistress in Mother House. She knew the Brothers when they were still in Shishu Bhavan. She used to meet Brother Andrew whenever he was in Sydney. The last time was in August 1999 when he was giving a retreat. Usually they would go out for a meal, but that particular time, he asked her to bring him a homemade Indian meal which her mother prepared. (20180322 IS Gillian Pacheco)
[109] Andrew, Brother, "Submission of Brother Andrew on Mother Teresa," Melbourne: Unpublished Source, c. 1999.

PART – VI

THE JOURNEY COMES TO AN END

I have always preached the importance of suffering:
Its redemptive value.
But I have always been somehow outside of it.
I have always been in control.
When I was superior and in these years,
I could contact anyone, make a phone call, go anywhere —
now I can't even walk up a few stairs.
It's so peaceful here.
I have the Lord with me, the birds singing,
the jasmine outside the window.
You wouldn't believe it's in the middle of the city.
And yet still the devil comes in sometimes to confuse me.
To make me think bad thoughts about others and what not.
He is really a spirit of confusion. I just have to throw him out
(with a hand gesture). Then there is peace.
– BROTHER ANDREW

24 September 2000

It must have been the end of September when Brother Yesudas, MC, received a letter from Andrew:

21/9/2000

Dear Yesudas,

This may only catch you after some time on your travels. And there is some uncertainty about me.

I have cancer and it has developed very quickly and continues that way. Nothing can be done medically. I have tried to clear up all my papers and things — And now there is nothing left.

God is so good and I feel great peace. It is a humbling experience to see one's own pettiness, self-concern at this moment. And how I fail to be able to concentrate on God. Faith goes deeper.

I really have nowhere to be now that I am becoming helpless. So I go to the MC Sisters for a bed. They are wonderful — And such a welcome.

After all my wandering and pride in going away I now come back as a poor man who needs help. It is very beautiful. God is so good.

I don't know how much time there will be. At this point, I feel it will not be long.

So now I thank you and all MC. I cannot imagine the grace MC has been for me. I am sorry that I have responded so poorly all these years. But God will make up for all my lack of love.

We are still brothers. We shall meet again for all eternity.

Love and prayers.
Brother Andrew[1]

A few weeks before, Andrew had been conducting a retreat in Sydney but unable to finish it. His trip to the Philippines for the end of September was cancelled. He had given his last day of prayer at Glowrey House on 29 July.

His nephew Julian had by now sensed that something was not right:

He was pretty crook. He only announced literally weeks earlier that he was dying. He knew there was something wrong twelve months before in August 1999 when he was going back to India. He even rang me before he went on that last trip to India and he said, "Just in case I don't come back, under the bed at Lucy's there is that and the other thing, in a box." But he didn't get himself diagnosed or tested until literally the September before the October he died. And I remember sitting watching football with Mum in the middle of September, after he told us, and it was a

Part – VI: The Journey Comes to an End

heck of a shock, and I remember saying, "Oh, he can be fixed, we'll get him to ... " No one realised how far down ... but it was God's will.[2]

When his niece, Leone was given the news that Uncle Ian's health was deteriorating rapidly, was in very bad shape and not expected to last long, she immediately rang, "'I'll come down to you, Ian.' And he said, 'No dear, don't. We know how we feel.' And it was just so beautiful. He just realised he didn't have the strength probably and he would not have wanted me to put myself out because of my family — quite unselfish and I felt that was very nice, the way he just said, 'We both know how we feel.'"[3]

On 20 September Andrew approached the MC Sisters in Fitzroy to let them know that he had "cancer of the stomach and it's racing." Death was imminent and his wish was to spend his last days with them. His family members thought it was the right decision because his "other family" would give him the best care he could have. The Sisters had just a few days to prepare what they would later call "the upper room," — an allusion to the place where Jesus celebrated His Last Supper with His apostles. They were overwhelmed and started to prepare a room in the refuge next door to their convent at 101 Gore Street. A section of the house had previously been occupied by the aspirants, until May when they went to Sydney, but was now vacant.

It is thanks to the MC Sisters' love and devotion to him, and their intuition, that today we have a day-to-day journal of Andrew's final journey. For this we are indebted to the community in Fitzroy at the time of his death: Sister Dorothy (Regional Superior), Sister M. Eliezer (Local Superior), Sister M. Sybil, Sister M. Maximilian, Sister M. Josie, Sister M. Agnes Joseph, Sister M. Jeramile, Sister M. Archana, Sister M. Lymark and Sister Joseph Maria. We owe the same appreciation to John and Jenny Barnes, who were with Andrew during those days. John also kept a personal journal. What follows is an almost verbatim combined account of these last days. It is to be noted that both the Sisters and John Barnes refer to Brother

Andrew as just "Brother". This might be due to the Missionaries of Charity Sisters' tradition of referring to any authority figure within the Congregation, regardless of level, as "Sister". This tradition does not exist within the Missionaries of Charity Brothers.

THE LAST DAYS
Saturday, 23 September 2000

Our Co-Workers have an annual [day of recollection] "Day with Mary," with exposition of the Blessed Sacrament all day and this year it happened to be on 23rd September. It was on this day that Brother arrived, in the late afternoon. He came to the convent, not wanting to meet all the Co-Workers who were gathered for prayer in the refuge next door. As Sister was reposing the Blessed Sacrament, another Sister led Brother up to his room, as he felt he needed to lie down. He said, "It's a day of grace." Later on, "I'm overwhelmed by all the preparations made for me. I feel like a king. I feel a great peace here." He said he was glad to have been able to come, having settled all his affairs. Asked if he were having pain, "Not really pain. Just a feeling of being uncomfortable." He said he didn't have any medicine, but that Sister had suggested paracetamol. "One will be enough, when you're not used to taking medicine." There was a noise outside. We hoped it would not be noisy. He said, "Oh, I don't hear the noise. Anyway, I don't sleep much. I'll sit up here sometimes," (in the armchair near the window.) I showed him the little heater and how to turn it on. He felt he wouldn't need it. Every word is spoken with such a deep gentleness and peace. Brother has always been gentle, but it seems to have taken a new depth.

Sunday, 24 September 2000

Brother said Mass in our chapel [the convent] this morning, at his request. He had to sit for the Gloria and almost all the rest of the Mass. But in everything there is a complete acceptance and peace. No irritation or regret at his state. One Sister's tears were falling to

Part – VI: The Journey Comes to an End

see Brother so weak. He said, "We'll all have a good cry now, and everything will be alright." He is always kind and gracious with a beautiful smile. After Mass we took the Blessed Sacrament over to his room. Jesus was in Brother's small monstrance [given to him by Ate Lily] and He was placed in the tabernacle lent to us from the Cathedral the night before for Brother's use. As Sr Eliezer entered the room with the monstrance, Brother's eyes were only on Jesus. His whole body relaxed and he walked over and sat on the bed, near the tabernacle, just gazing at Jesus. His face was joyful, grateful and he gently nodded to each of us as we left and he sat looking lovingly at Jesus. Later, he said, "I'm so grateful to be here. This place is so perfect. If I went all around Australia, I couldn't find a more perfect place. I love space, and there's space in this room to move about, to walk a bit. All the things you have prepared are lovely. I feel that I'm in heaven. I don't know when purgatory will come. I suppose it must. But for now, I'm in heaven." Brother spoke of a Sister in India involved in the foundation of a congregation like ours which spread rapidly, working for the poor. She had cancer. Just when he got the news of his own cancer, he received her obituary. Her superior had offered that she could have any treatment, but she had not wanted it. Brother said, "It was like a light for me. It confirmed what I was thinking at that time and for many years now — that when the time came I would not go around seeking this and that treatment, but just accept it." I recalled a talk on the Cross he had given once. "I have always preached the importance of suffering. Its redemptive value. But I have always been somehow outside of it. I have always been in control. When I was superior and in these years, I could contact anyone, make a phone call, go anywhere — now I can't even walk up a few stairs." "It's so peaceful here. I have the Lord with me, the birds singing, the jasmine outside the window. You wouldn't believe it's in the middle of the city. And yet still the devil comes in sometimes to confuse me. To make me think bad thoughts about others and what not. He is really a spirit of confusion. I just have to throw him out (with a hand gesture). Then there is peace." I told him about my own problem of negative thoughts. "St Michael is the best helper for that." We talked about the Chain of Charity, a small community for disabled [women] Brother started in [South] Korea. "Ah, Chain of Charity, yes. Their numbers are very small at the moment. But at the time they started there was nothing for the handicapped at all. Now there are quite a few groups for the handicapped. So they have become small. But that's OK. Like John the Baptist." Asked if he felt Mother near, he nodded, "Not fully present here, but as a quiet presence in the background. Like the other saints I have told people about over the years — Little Flower [St Thérèse of Lisieux], whose picture you've got here so beautifully, Edith Stein, Eileen O'Connor. They're all here with me now."* John Barnes came to meet Brother Andrew and they were talking about the retreats that would not take place and commitments that had to be cancelled. "All part of God's plan," he said. He spoke about [John] Negri, MD, and how understanding he was of his situation — that he didn't want any hospital treatment, especially chemo. The doctor had said it would be useless anyway. During this chat John received the greatest compliment he could be given by Brother Andrew, "We don't need any words, you and I, we understand each other."

Monday, 25 September 2000

Brother felt too weak to go down the flight of stairs which led to the back door of our convent, so we went up to his room for Mass. Brother was seated on a chair throughout the Mass, but was pausing, labouring through the Eucharistic prayer. After communion, he was silent for a long time. He was gazing up about our heads, his eyes almost unmoving, except that sometimes he would glance down at us and then up again. Sometimes his head would move from side to side, as if listening. After the last blessing he said, "There's

---

* Edith Stein (1891 – 1942) was a German Jewish philosopher and atheist who converted to Catholicism and became a discalced Carmelite, changing her name to Teresa Benedicta of the Cross. She died as a martyr in Auschwitz and was canonised by the Catholic Church. Br Andrew seems to have had a devotion to and admiration for Edith Stein. In 1999 he even dedicated a whole retreat talk to her.

Part – VI: The Journey Comes to an End

a picture of Mother Teresa on the wall here, but she's not smiling. I've been trying to get her to smile for a few days, but she hasn't smiled. But now, with all the Sisters here, she's smiling." That was Brother's last Mass, as the next day he felt too weak to be able to say Mass. The Co-Workers [John and Jenny] wanted to bring a reclining chair, but Brother preferred not to have it. He said, "The world is full of 'stuff'. There was a cartoonist [probably Leunig] who said that the world today is cluttered up with 'stuff'. But we don't need it. That's the beauty of MC and the Gospel. The witness of simplicity, of needing nothing but (pointing to the tabernacle, into the air) . . . the spiritual. That's the way of Jesus. That's why so many people don't like Him." Later on he said, "God has given me the gift of a deep trust. Trust in His Divine Mercy. A faith, hope and love that go beyond feelings." Brother then said, "Trust Him, whatever may be. He loves you so much." We said we were going to write "Welcome Home!" on the blackboard, but in the end, we wrote "Welcome." He said, "I feel that I've come home. And I've come with nothing. Empty-handed." We offered a small table, set up for Mass. "No need any extra table or extra anything. This table (in the room) is enough." All is said with the sweetest and most gentle smile. That day, Brother had requested John to come and help him with his shower.

Tuesday, 26 September 2000

The decline is so quick. It's a great grace that he's here, with the MCs. Brother spoke of the chaos the devil causes even after we have given everything away and have nothing to worry about. He brings to mind irritations from the past and even from the present. All has to be laid at Jesus' Cross. He brings good from it all. Then Brother advised me that all mistakes, failures, etc., must be placed at the foot of the Cross. The devil tries to create chaos but we must quickly bring these things to Jesus. "Here (in this house) I can share some things with the Sisters, but the people outside wouldn't know what I was talking about." Regarding feelings, he said that feelings are nothing. "We can feel anything — lust, anger, etc. — but we must go much deeper. Feelings are nothing. It's deeper in our heart, it's our relationship with God that matters." After a very fervent Holy Communion, Brother said, "Do you think I have lovely thoughts? No. I feel nothing. But it's deeper than that. Look at Little Flower."** Regarding keeping notes, "They are no use to us. I don't use notes for retreats. What is in your heart comes out as life. What is not in your heart comes out dead." He has an old prayer book in large print and commented that some things are good to keep. John Barnes started coming daily to help Brother take a shower or sponge bath. When John was getting the soap and water ready, Brother suddenly went into a spasm or fit. His head went back, his eyes were fixed wide open in a stare. I thought he was dying and I held him and called the Sisters. It lasted for about one minute or less and was over when Sr Eliezer arrived. John proceeded with the shower. Brother was able to help with his washing and drying, so John helped him back to the bed and he said, "You don't know how good that feels." Today we began our twenty-four-hour watch with Brother, taking it in turns to be with him. John and Jenny helped us with this, too.

Wednesday, 27 September 2000

Early in the morning, "Jesus is here. He's going to take me. Perhaps today or tomorrow or next week. All is well. Jesus is everything. There is peace." He asked for water. "I understand 'I Thirst' now." He continued, "Now for the practical things. I don't want any medical things. No drips or anything. Jesus is taking me. Let Him do it peacefully, without struggle." (Concerning this matter, Brother wrote a letter to his doctor and handed it to him on one of his visits.) "I just want Jesus to take me soon. But not my will, but His be done. I don't want healing. They must all be praying for me in Calcutta for healing (smiling). But that's alright. God will use all those prayers

---

** It is a known fact that St Thérèse of Lisieux (Little Flower) at her death bed had thoughts of suicide.

Part – VI: The Journey Comes to an End

for good. Surrender is more important." "I always thought with cancer, there would be a lot of pain — sharp pain. But there isn't, it's a dull pain. It's very hard to get a comfortable position to lie in. But that's alright. Whatever he wants. I feel like I have no body from here (indicating chest) down. No stomach, no legs. It's very funny. Like I'm in pieces. (Smiles and laughs) But that's alright." Brother is still able to walk over to the armchair near the window, sit or talk for a while, then walk back to bed. But he is very feeble. He said that a Sister had written to him saying strongly to come "back to MC" — he smiles. I said that he must have missed MC all those years. "I never really felt that I was away from MC. The love was there and the relationship. That's the important thing." How did you feel at that time you left? "Not so bad. That's all gone now." When John came this morning, Brother didn't want to go into the shower, so we decided to wash him on the chair. He was still very much in control. We moved him from the bed to the chair and he had another short spasm. He was still able to lift himself and help with washing. During the afternoon, Brother was visited by the retired Archbishop of Melbourne, Archbishop [Frank] Little. Later in the evening, he was visited by the present Archbishop, Archbishop George Pell. Brother was happy to see them. The Sisters were looking in on Brother every hour, but during a time when he was alone Brother had a fall. It was decided that he had to have someone in attendance at all times.

Thursday, 28 September 2000

Brother has been very peaceful throughout the day. He said, "Have a little rest." The atmosphere in the room is very peaceful. The night before, a sister on duty had sat just outside Brother's open door, so as not to disturb him, ready for any need. Today he said that the Sister doing the night duty could stay inside the room with the chair near the Blessed Sacrament. Brother said he is, "experiencing 'I thirst' in a beautiful way." He would often drink water from the jug beside his bed or ask for juice or glucose drink. Although there were short periods of intense pain it was mostly discomfort, and it meant he had to move his arms and legs constantly. While John was sitting with Brother during the afternoon he heard him whispering the prayer of Jesus on the cross, "I Thirst — I Thirst — I Thirst!" Jenny and John stayed till 9:30 pm. On the night of 28/29 September, Brother started to have more severe pain in his chest and body.

Friday, 29 September 2000

In the morning, "How are you, Brother?" (Slowly) "Waiting … waiting … waiting for Jesus, Mary and Joseph." "Jesus is here." He was having pain, but had taken one pain killer tablet at 9:40 am. Around midday, he still had pain, but didn't want to take anything for it. Said that he didn't think that he would be able to suffer, but he could. He offered all for the greater glory of God and for the good of souls. He said three times, "Sacred Heart of Jesus, I place my trust in you." Today, John washed Brother on the chair. He was in and out of bed and onto the chair. His breathing was much louder and his rest was constantly disrupted. He had family visitors and Fr Daven Day, and Fr Tom Lees, and local Fitzroy parish priest, Fr Pat Harvey. Brother suggested to John that they together listen to the 5:00 pm. news on his little radio. Brother still in control.

Saturday, 30 September 2000

Brother was experiencing more and more pain. During the day. I was in the room with Brother, and offered to say a short Rosary. I would say the prayers — he could just lead the decades. He led only the Agony in the Garden and the Crucifixion. At night, 30 September – 1 October, 3:00 am. In great pain, with each breath, "O Lord … Lord … Lord … " "O Yes … O Yes … O Yes." Still in a lot of pain, he got up and sat in the armchair. He asked for a cold orange juice. As he drank it, he said, "That's good! Beauty!" John and Jenny stayed all afternoon. Brother dictated to them details he wanted for after his death.

Part – VI: The Journey Comes to an End

Sunday, 1 October 2000

The first rose in our garden bloomed, and we put it near Brother's tabernacle. He said, "It's a gift of Little Flower." His breathing was very difficult and painful. We began to give him water by a sponge on his lips. Jenny and John were at 101 at 9:00 am. Brother knew who they were and acknowledged their presence. Most of this time Brother's eyes were partly closed and there was no conversation. John washed Brother in bed after quite a wait, and then sat with Brother all afternoon. A doctor-friend of Brother's came to visit him in the afternoon and said she felt he had about 24 hours to live. His own doctor was to come to see him in the evening. The doctor was travelling down from the country and was to call in on Brother on his way home. About 7:00 pm Brother made a phone call to Julian (his nephew) and told him to ring Tobin Bros [undertakers] and start getting things ready. This was his last phone call. At 7:40 pm, we were all, eight sisters and John and Jenny, gathered in Brother's room, feeling the end may be near. Brother said in a loud voice, "I think when doctor comes, he'll just want to see me and go quickly because he's had a long day. If he could just do his work and go it'll be nice." Later, "Sister, you will need a towel and some soap ready for the doctor at the end of his visit." At about 9:00 pm, Doctor Negri arrived and discussed with Brother about whether he wanted to start injections for pain. Brother said he did want to start. Doctor said that it may cause chest congestion. Brother said, "Doctor, there's one big question — euthanasia." Doctor assured him that this was not an issue, as the injections would be administered solely for pain relief. Brother asked John's opinion, "Are you happy with that John?" John said it was only for controlling pain and that would make him more comfortable. He then agreed to have the injections. The doctor gave the first injection and included something to ease Brother's hiccups. Sr Maximilian (who had previous experience) was to administer the injections every four hours if necessary. Before leaving the doctor was obviously moved by Brother's peaceful acceptance of everything. He said to Brother that it seemed that Brother's many and varied life experiences had prepared him for this moment. He felt Brother had a tremendous amount of "courage and faith — especially faith." Brother was now much more comfortable, moving around less and able to rest. John and Jenny stayed with him. After the Sisters had left for the convent (next door) Brother suggested that they open the little tabernacle door and have some special time—just the three of them and Jesus. John and Jenny stayed with Brother until about 10:00 pm and then went to rest next door. They got up at 12:45 am to sit with Brother until 5:00 am. John and Jenny had arranged with the sisters to stay at 101 Gore Street and to share the time with Brother. That night, Brother slept peacefully.

Monday, 2 October 2000

John and Jenny were up at 8:00 am. Brother's breathing was much more difficult and his eyes were mostly closed and there was no conversation. He still knew who was in the room at this stage. The injections were allowing him to rest. His throat had become very raw due to all his breathing through his mouth. Jenny obtained a spray from the local chemist which eased the situation, "I know your love. I just want to say thank you ... I just want to thank God for everything. Everything is alright." "I just need to let everything work out." Brother was visited by Fr Daven Day, Jesuit Provincial and Fr Tom Lees. After they left, "I wanted to ask Fr Tom Lees to say Mass for me, and he came." After Holy Communion, "Jesus, my love. Want to thank you for that. Thank you for everything. Amen. Thank you, Jesus." During a time of prayer with the tabernacle open, "Jesus, I thirst for you. Father, I surrender myself to you. Into your hands, O Lord, I commend my spirit. You will be with me in paradise. Take, O Lord, and receive, all my liberty, my memory, my understanding and my whole will. Jesus I love you. Jesus, I thirst for you. Mary, Queen and Mother, pray for me." During the afternoon, we realized that Brother could no longer see. He had been sitting for a short time on the armchair. He had one of those moments when his body would become rigid and his eyes fixed.

Part – VI: The Journey Comes to an End 475

This had been happening about once or twice a day for six days. When he was relaxed, three of us were helping him back to bed. He said, "I've got just one problem in God's world — where are the Sisters? All the Sisters?" We said, "Here we are, Brother!" "Where? How many are you?" We put our hands on his and counted, "1 … 2 … 3 … Alright?" "Alright. Remain." 10:00 pm. Sr Dorothy and Sisters arrived from Sydney. Brother greeted them warmly. They asked, "Any message for us, Brother?" "God loves you all. Thank you all. God bless you. I just ask God to bless you. Thank you now. I can see you all now. I understand you now. Ok, I'll think of you all now. I love you. Sister, I just love you. Sister, everything is good." That day, John went home. There were fourteen messages on the family's answering machine. The news of Brother's illness was getting out quickly!

Tuesday, 3 October 2000

Brother was becoming weaker. His breathing was difficult. His eyes were turned upwards, half opened. They remained so until just before his death. His face looked strikingly similar to the old picture of the Sacred Heart on the wall beside his bed, above the tabernacle.

DEATH AND FUNERAL

Wednesday, 4 October 2000

John and Jenny Barnes were with Brother from 1:00 am to 5:00 am. About 1:30 am Brother was quite restless so John and Jenny called Sr Maximillian to give Brother an injection (this was to be the last). Brother settled down and he slept, breathing evenly, not painfully as before. When John and Jenny left, Sr Joseph Maria, Sr Archana and Sr Maximilian took over. Around 5.30 am Brother jerked suddenly and became restless. He began to gasp at intervals instead of breathing evenly. He suddenly turned round in one movement like drawn by a magnet, he was too sick to be able to do it by himself. His back was up from the pillow, sitting in that position not supported by anything, his eyes opened so much that you could see the white all the way around, like amazement. One Sister was saying, "Thank you, thank you for everything," again and again. Sister Joseph Maria was gently repeating. "Jesus, Mary and Joseph, assist me in my last agony. Jesus, Mary and Joseph, may I breathe forth my last sigh in peace with you. Amen." During this time Brother was in an ecstasy. Sr Maximilian had gone to call John and Jenny and when they arrived, he was still like that. John had tears in his eyes and was repeating ejaculations to the Sacred Heart and Immaculate Heart that Brother used to say at the end of his talks. He then fell back onto the pillow and he gasped three times and it was over. It was 5.45 am. There was a great peace and calm. The other Sisters arrived and said that two Sisters had already left to go to the airport to pick up Brother Geoff. We all knelt around Brother's bed and prayed the Rosary. Then we prepared Brother's body and just as we finished, Brother Geoff arrived. Jenny supplied a camera with which Brother Geoff took photos, as he was very concerned to share these moments with the brothers. Archbishop Pell arrived about 7:00 am. He had not been told, he just called in on his way to the airport. About midday, Brother's body was taken to the funeral parlour. Sometime later, they returned with the body in a coffin. We had prepared a place for Brother in the large dining room downstairs. Many people came to pray with us that day and the next. (Here ends the daily account of the MC Sisters).

Andrew died seven hundred metres away, on the same Gore Street in Fitzroy as his paternal grandfather Henry Ball almost one hundred years previously.

Rumours started spreading in Melbourne, even amongst the Jesuits, about Brother Andrew not wanting to follow medical treatment and that he would not go to a doctor. Fr Daven Day still feels strongly about the issue to this day,

Part – VI: The Journey Comes to an End

That Ian did not go to the doctor, so he allowed the cancer to go and to offer it up and had a death wish, he wanted to die — all that is nonsense. I can speak strongly in all this because I said to him, "Why didn't you go to a doctor?" … When he was going around in India and he was desperately ill, vomiting, diarrhoeas, and he said, "I didn't. I did realise that I couldn't go back to the Brothers anyway because I couldn't. I was so weak." And he said, "I think it's because I have been away so long from them. My health just seemed to collapse on me." And I said, "Did you know you had cancer?" and he said, "No, I didn't. I wouldn't have kept going." He said quite clearly to me. "No, I didn't, I didn't realise." And the doctor to whom he spoke didn't tell him that. He thought that it was an emotional thing because the Brothers were so highly emotional with him, and he couldn't cope with it. That's exactly what he said. I think that is a very important thing to write in the book because as the Jesuits were saying, "He gave in and he wouldn't look after himself, and he had a death wish, and so he wouldn't take medicine." The last couple of days, he didn't want to take the morphine because he was offering it up, but then he also did give instructions to the doctor that if he thought he should have it, he should do it.[4]

6 October 2000, was the day of the funeral. At 1:00 pm the undertakers came and sealed the coffin. The crucifix on the lid of the coffin was removed before the burial and given to his family, who in turn gave it to Brother Geoff to take back to Mansatala.[5] The Requiem Mass was held at the Sacred Heart Church in Kew. Although Brother Andrew had not wanted a fuss and tried to keep his illness quiet, news of his death had spread by word of mouth so the church was full. About thirty priests concelebrated, many of them Jesuits. The Archbishop had also planned to be there but was held up in Sydney for a meeting. Daven Day, who was the main celebrant gave the introduction and the homily:

This is not a eulogy, rather a short reflection on how Ian Travers-Ball, Br Andrew, has touched the lives of each of us in a special way, and how that, on this day that he leaves us, it is important that the witness of his whole life speak to each of us. I, too, have been largely moulded by Ian — by his humour, common sense, and idealism in our novitiate and by the advice given in brief meetings over many years as our paths crossed in India, Hong Kong, and the Philippines. More recently it has been the comfort of sometimes spotting Ian from a Melbourne tram as he went for his walk round Hawthorn, easily recognisable in his old pullover and hat — and feeling a security — ah Ian's home for a while!

In a kernel, Ian showed us all how to live simply and how to be truly simple. This was not something pious. He rejected all forms of showiness and with vehemence never allowed the mantle of guru to be placed on his shoulders. He was a sophisticated man, well versed in the ways of the world with his mother's charm and compassion and his father's eye for the fine things of life. His simplicity was his transparency — he simply made God the main priority of his life. At twenty-three he fell in love with God and through bad days and good he never took his eyes off God. Ian did this so effortlessly that he has been able to cajole all of us to have a shot at doing the same, but always in our own way.

There are many hurdles to jump before one can become free enough, not to worry about oneself, what one will wear, how one will survive, how one can be completely free and available to God, and Ian didn't conceal his own hurdles from us, and how on the really big ones he had to take several run ups before he could get over them — He shared his vulnerability with appealing candour and great Australian humour.

This is not to praise Ian, it is rather to encourage you and also myself. Ian shows us that we really can follow the Lord very closely, that it doesn't matter what career we follow in life we can be transparent in our priorities, simple in our lifestyle — we can be free to love God. Above all, in some way we all carry Ian's mantle — there is a real possibility that we can bring some of the Travers-Ball charm, humour and laid-back style in our life stories. I suspect it's already there. Ian's magnetism has always been contagious. Ian would laugh, but for better or worse — it depends on what we do with it — some of his holiness has surely rubbed off on all of us. Avanti, Brother Andrew, into God's future but please keep us all within your horizon.

Brother Andrew was laid to rest in the Boroondara General Cemetery in Kew in the Roman Catholic Compartment A No. 1730, above his grandparents and beside his parents and his sister Mary.

TRIBUTES

In keeping with Andrew's desire not to have a grand funeral, tributes and funeral notices were published either on the funeral day or some days afterwards. Obituaries were posted separately by his family members in *The Age* and *Herald Sun*.

A few interesting obituaries include ones in the *L'Osservatore Romano* (18 October 2000), the Vatican's official newspaper; in the weekly Perth Catholic newspaper *The Record* written by Peter Rosengren; and in *The Times* in England on 17 October 2000 — "BROTHER ANDREW, Gambler turned priest who set up a charity with Mother Teresa." Although not exact in some of the details, but still engaging is one written by a certain Tom Carey, in a newspaper most possibly published in the Shepparton district of northern Victoria. The article was entitled "Arcadia's Saint of Calcutta" on the first page and "Arcadian Selector's Grandson Dies" on the next. Carey praised Andrew as the grandson of James Miller and Mary Ann Daly, farmers in the district at a place called Arcadia. He describes Andrew as "a remarkable Arcadian [who] achieved the pinnacle of his life's desire with his death a fortnight ago," as the male counterpart of Mother Teresa.[6] An obituary that gave quite a detailed and accurate résumé of Andrew's life was published on the day after his death in *The Hindustan Times of Ranchi*: "World has lost a brother, and his caring touch."

People who had been close to Brother Andrew started writing and distributing memoirs of their time with him, among them Betty Peaker, Lily Manalo and Gerry Monaghan. This is what Gerry wrote:

> Andrew lived a spirit of poverty. Most people know how light he travelled. All he owned was in a small cloth carry-bag that you could take on planes or buses. What was in it? Our Lord in the Blessed Sacrament in a tiny wooden monstrance about five inches high. He spent time in prayer before the Lord at least twice a day and in the last years he confided to me that when he woke in the night he would spend time in prayer before getting back into bed.
>
> He carried a tiny Mass kit — chalice, Missal, bread and wine — a Bible, a home-brand small writing pad, the current wad of letters held by an elastic band that he was answering; then he'd have the current book or articles that he was reading, some changes of underwear and a couple of shirts and some pyjamas.
>
> When he came to stay, all he wanted was a plastic bucket to wash out a few articles of clothing every couple of days. He hung on to nothing. Because he travelled so much on buses and planes and waited at airports and terminals, he wrote notes to people on scraps of paper and backs of envelopes. It was amazing the comfort or encouragement he could give in one line.
>
> Another example: One day I was preparing a meal for us. The cheese had gone hard and a bit green at the edges, so I cut the pieces off to get at the good part. Andrew started

Part – VI: The Journey Comes to an End

eating the bad bits, gave a sheepish grin and said, "Can't help it — too bloody long living in Calcutta."

I won't dwell on the painful way the Lord helped him to relinquish the leadership of the Missionary of Charity Brothers that he co-founded with Mother Teresa. He was accused of being an alcoholic and was told he should get treatment. Andrew asked for a half-hour to shower and to pray. He knew he was not an alcoholic and asked to step aside from the leadership. The Archbishop of Calcutta gave him a place in his diocese and permission to go where the Spirit led him. So for the last ten years or so he has simply accepted invitations to go and supply in a parish, give a mission or retreat to a group or a parish.

On his second or third visit to Bega [for a retreat], there was not much of a turn-up and a friend of mine was quite hurt on his behalf and said so. Andrew's profound and simple response was "Numbers don't matter — only God matters."

Andrew's way of self-effacement was disarming. People seemed to be immediately comfortable with him. He gave you his full attention and you felt you were of worth and what you had to say was important. A cousin of mine with a large family phoned. I told her Andrew had died and she said, "When I listened to him I felt he saw right through me — but kindly." A nun who phoned said that he was the most Christ-like person she had ever met in her lifetime. The lovely thing was that he was flawed and could so share his brokenness that we felt free to unburden ourselves. I think of the good he did listening and being confessor to the people that came to him.[7]

A few months after Andrew's death, John and Jenny Barnes decided to travel round parts of Australia where Andrew used to give retreats, with the intention of meeting people and sharing with them his last days before his death.

"When spirits are low, pain appears to rule and even the incarnated deity seems inattentive and distant, it is you, my friend, who are the tangible sign of God,"[8] wrote his friend Kathryn Spink almost nineteen years after his death:

> He was a gambler who, in his youth, lost everything he had on racehorses, a gentle, prayer-filled man whom Mother Teresa described as "very, very holy". As a priest he was later instrumental in founding a community of Brothers devoted to the service of the poorest of the poor. He shared their lives in Saigon, Cambodia and many other places of violence and suffering, and wrote sublimely of the "beautiful" unsung people he met along the way, whom he believed to be the hope of the world. With fear and trepidation he appeared on prime time television. The interviewer and the audience were manifestly touched. A public platform beckoned from which he could have spoken powerfully on behalf of the voiceless of the world, until some of those close to him called him to account. There had been times when he had drunk too much and set a bad example. They wanted him to go into a clinic. Acknowledging with characteristic humility his frailty, he nonetheless declined. For him to do so would, he said, be a denial of the truth of his being. I have never met anyone whose being was so truthful. He opted to relinquish the leadership of his Brothers to become instead a "troubadour in a small boat". Possessing nothing, leaving God alone to arrange his life, he journeyed with the wind and tide, took retreats and wrote small booklets and letters. We met only a handful of times; we corresponded for some twenty years. His words increased in beauty, wisdom and light in a way that surprised him most: it could only, he was sure, be the Spirit at work through his weakening humanity. He died of stomach cancer, opting not to have expensive treatment but to end his life as he had lived it: in communion with the poorest of the poor. His voice still

sings to me with richness, love and compassion from the pages of his letters.⁹

POSTHUMOUS WRITINGS and POSSESSIONS

According to Betty Peaker, around 1998 Brother Andrew had given a rough manuscript of some of his writings to a friend of hers in Western Australia to put on her computer in preparation for printing. Months later he enquired whether it was ready, but health issues had prevented her from even starting the project, to which according to Betty he replied, "Don't worry at all. Forget it. I don't really need the hassle of publishing again. Your health is more important." The manuscript never resurfaced until after his death when the typist was clearing her desk and the manuscript jumped out of the beyond. It was then that it was published by Betty Peaker as *Song of the Wounded Healer — A Tribute of Highest Esteem and Honour for Brother Andrew*.

Then, in September 2002, the small book *Rebuild My Church* was published by Frank Maher, SJ, through Hampton Marian Centre. In his foreword Father Maher wrote that a year or so before Andrew's death he had told Maher that he [Andrew] was working on a small book that he hoped to publish. Some months later he decided against it. In Father Maher's understanding, this might have been because of ill health. In the beginning of 2002, however, Father Maher was approached by a lady named Paula from Western Australia who told him that she had a manuscript that she had typed for Brother Andrew which she thought that Father Maher might be interested in publishing. Later, Father Maher found out that both Betty Peaker and John and Jenny Barnes had similar incomplete copies. Jean Manning of Delegate confirmed the fact, adding that according to Brother Andrew the manuscript was very dear to his heart.

For more than eighteen years the MC Sisters in Melbourne (same as the Melbourne Jesuits who archived Andrew's letters) preserved Andrew's possessions at the time of his death. In 2018 they were handed over to the MC Brothers in India after the author's visit to Australia. Among some clothes and other personal items, there was a whole package of holy pictures. Quite a number of these cards were of known Carmelite saints like St Thérèse of Lisieux, St John of the Cross and St Teresa of Avila. Andrew seems to have had a special devotion to St Teresa of Jesus of the Andes.[10] The following is a prayer written by her and hand-copied by Andrew:

> "Boldly cast your faults and sins into the abyss, into the ocean of divine mercy.
> "Jesus will take compassion on your miseries. He knows your poor heart thoroughly.
> "So don't be afraid; for fear dries up love"
> — St Teresa of the Andes

Part – VI: The Journey Comes to an End

1. 101 Gore Street, Fitzroy where Andrew spent his last days and died.

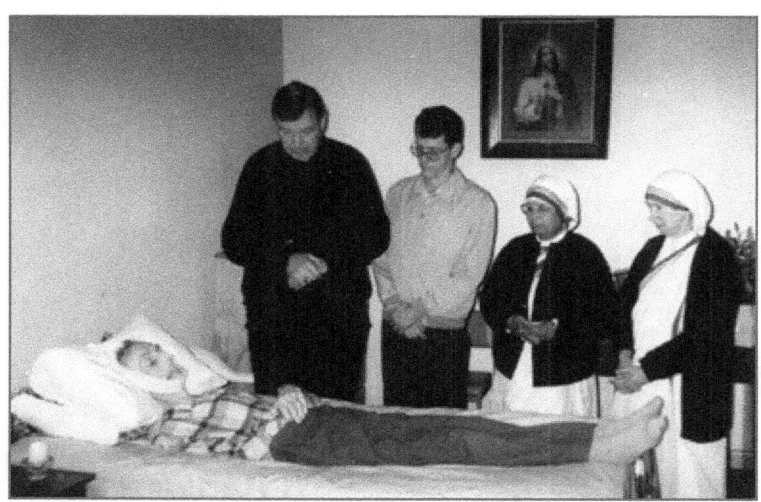

2. Melbourne 4 October 2000 –
Archbishop Pell, Br Geoff MC, Sr Dorothy and Sr Eliezer MC.

*3. Melbourne 6 October 2000 –
The body of Br Andrew coming out of 101, Gore Street.*

4. Sacred Heart Church - Funeral Mass.

Part – VI: The Journey Comes to an End

5. Arriving at Boroondara Cemetery.

6. Family Tomb.

7. *Family Plaque on Tomb.*

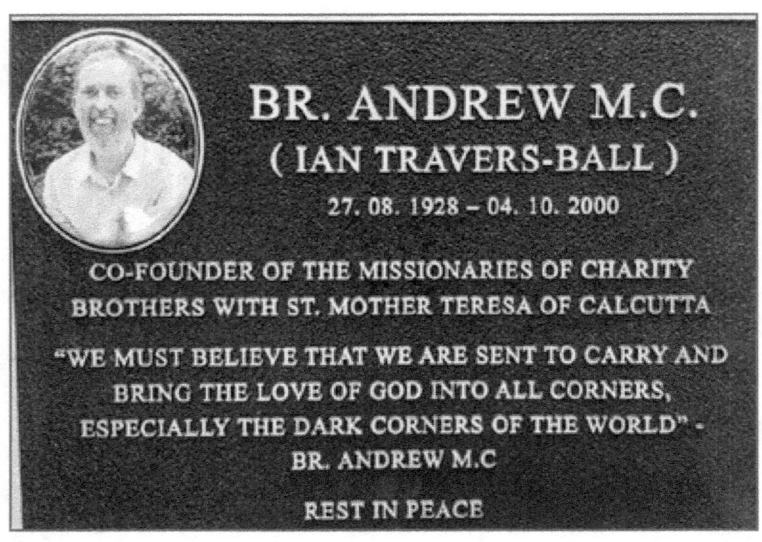

8. *New Plaque prepared by the Co-workers in Melbourne and was intended to be blessed on October 2020. (Postponed due to COVID-19).*

Part – VI: The Journey Comes to an End

Endnotes

1. 20000921 LB to Yesudas Mannooparampil, MC.
2. 20180305 IR Anne and Julian Millership, Jim Smith.
3. 20180319 IR Leone, Kate and Jane Simons.
4. 20180320 IJ Daven Day, SJ.
5. When the Brothers in Mansatala received the news from the Sisters in Shishu Bhavan, they immediately contacted Brother Yesudas who was on one of his official visits in Madagascar (Africa). Various Sisters who were around Andrew or had come to visit him from nearby communities said that he longed to meet Brother Yesudas. Unfortunately, his wish was not granted because Brother Yesudas could not get a visa at such short notice. So, he asked Brother Geoff to go to Australia and represent the Congregation.
6. The photocopied cutting of the obituary does not bear the name of the newspaper.
7. 2001004 OF Remembering Brother Andrew - Fr Gerald Monaghan.
8. Kathrynspink.com/com/notebook Web: 7 September 2021.
9. Ibid.
10. Juana Fernández Solar, (1900 – 1920). Born in Santiago de Chile. At 14 she was inspired by God to consecrate herself to him as a Religious with the Discalced Carmelite nuns, taking the name of Teresa of Jesus (later on known as Teresa of Jesus of Los Andes). Her desire was realised on 7 May 1919, when she entered the tiny monastery of the Holy Spirit in the township of Los Andes, some 90 kilometres from Santiago. She was clothed with the Carmelite habit on 14 October the same year and began her novitiate as Teresa of Jesus. She had known for a long time before that she would die young. The Lord had revealed this to her. A month before she was to depart this life, she related this to her confessor. She died aged 19 on the evening of 12 April 1920. Why Andrew had a devotion to her is not known but most probably because "not much was accomplished" by her. Her holiness shone out in everyday occurrences, wherever she found herself: at home, in college, with friends, among the people she stayed with.

PART – VII

THE FIORETTI AND EPILOGUE

THE FIORETTI OF BROTHER ANDREW

I remember the letter he wrote about Johnny Walker, one of our mentally-challenged boys. Andrew comes out with such an enriching and beautiful reflection. We were seeing the boy every day and we did not see any of this beauty in him. Once I asked him about it and he told me, "You have to meet people at a deeper level, some may talk, some may not talk, but if you observe them, watch them if you are really present, then you will get these insights and you will be able to love them more and you will know how God sees us."

– **MC Brother**[1]

∂

Cambodia. We were a few Brothers travelling past Pochentong Airport, headed over a dangerous road to a refugee camp some thirty-five kilometres from Phnom Penh. We saw a taxi on the road with Andrew in it headed towards the capital. He hadn't announced his arrival, and we had locked up the school room that we had been living in at École Miche. In the early evening when we arrived back to our school room, there was Andrew, lying sound asleep on the bare tile gallery floor by the door to our living quarters. It struck me as so tender, and he was so vulnerable, and when we woke him he was joyful at seeing us and would not listen to our apologies. We loved having him with us, and he communicated the news from the other community. The homilies he gave during Masses when he was with us were very potent. They were truly our food.

– **Former MC Brother**[2]

∂

There was one Brother who during his tertianship was postponed to take final vows, but Father Andrew then put him as a superior in one of the communities. I could not understand the logic, so I asked him, why he was putting him as a superior if he was postponed from taking vows? And he told me, "Postponing him from vows does not mean that I lost my love and respect for him. It only means that there are certain things he needs to work on. Putting him as a superior might help him become a better Brother. I talked to him, I sat with him and explained."

– MC Brother[3]

∂

On Fridays we used to have public confessions, Andrew was the first one to kneel down and kiss the ground and say publicly his faults, for example, whatever electricity or water he had wasted.

– MC Brother[4]

∂

Brother Andrew didn't like to be in the limelight and was quite critical of more established religious orders. He used anger a lot to correct us but always ended up with a smile. He would take a quiet walk to balance his tasks but normally didn't join in our apostolate. He would however take a broom, move the rubbish (*lap sap*, he knew that in Cantonese) and also wash dishes. He liked a cup of tea very much and would share about little joys with little people. I think he treasured a lot of good stuff we experienced together. He never joined us in recreation-games but preferred to sit with a book on the floor. He loved good books and passed them on to me for reading. I remember Andrew couldn't sing well but he managed to sing, "Soul of my Saviour" that was the only one he managed. He never cooked, he was satisfied with bread and tea, if nobody was cooking. But when we first came to Hong Kong, we settled in the flat and he showed us how to make instant noodles.

– MC Brother[5]

∂

His tendency; his opinions that he had held strongly for instance about Brothers not getting further education, about his suspicion of training courses, the thing about littleness and accepting people as

Part – VII: The Fioretti and Epilogue

candidates without any vetting or without knowing about them — a very laidback attitude — or on those points that he spoke strongly about, he really was overbearing, and even used his homilies to bat his own points. The biggest incident that I remember was when we had an All Formators Meeting in Korea in winter of 1985. I forgot what the issue was, he was doing that a lot. One afternoon we had Mass and he used his homily to harp on some of those things that he was hot on. It made me so angry that I walked out of Mass, probably otherwise, I don't know what I would have done. Afterwards we were all right, he understood why I left and teased me about it. He said he saw me getting whiter and whiter. So it wasn't a barrier to the friendship and trust that there was between us but it was very irritating.

– MC Brother[6]

∂

We were in the refectory once when one Brother was criticizing my lack of English. I was a bit upset and I said that in the Gospel there is nothing written that you have to know English before you came to follow Jesus. From the other end of the table I noticed that Brother Andrew had a smile of understanding on his face. Another day when we got a good catch of fish from our pond in Noorpur, Brother Andrew saw that we were eating the fish, but had not given to the residents in our home. He was upset with us and he told us, "Share. You eat and you also give to the patients."

– MC Brother[7]

∂

Brother Petrus, MC, (RIP) told us this story, that in the beginning the Brothers' house in Bokaro was very small. They did not even have a toilet and were all going outside in the fields like all the natives. The first morning when Andrew went to visit the Brothers, Brother Petrus got up as usual and went with his *lotha* [a small tin container for water] to the fields, where he met Brother Andrew coming back from his morning ritual, trying to hide the *lotha*.

The only problem was that the people did not dare to go for their morning rituals as usual because they were scared of Andrew, thinking he was one of the sahibs from the company who owned the land, and who came from the city to inspect the area.
– **MC Brother**[8]

∂

We were sent, two Indian Brothers and two European Brothers to start a community in Europe. It was a struggle to live together, blending two different cultures. In those days, the European Brothers were exaggerating on poverty and some of them would go around and collect all the rotten fruit from the market and come and provide it for lunch. Also they never put the heater on in the room because according to their understanding, it went against the practice of simplicity. We Brothers from India struggled. We were only allowed to have hot water, for a proper bath, once a week.

So when Andrew heard of our struggles, he phoned from Hong Kong and told the Local Servant to allow us Indian Brothers to have rice at least once a week. He was concerned about us. The day he was supposed to arrive, we were all excited. He brought a suitcase, put in on the table in the refectory and then before opening, he asked, "Can you imagine what is in my box?" We said, maybe some chocolate, but when he opened, out came a big fried chicken. He was carrying a fried chicken all the way from Hong Kong to Paris. He said he was lucky that nobody had opened and inspected his bag at customs in the airport. The superior then went and brought some beer which we shared. And we laughed and laughed. Andrew had a great love for the Brothers whether Indian or European.
– **MC Brother**[9]

∂

Andrew loved our house for the alcoholic aboriginal men in Bourke. Once he came to visit and we were not there, so he had just lain down in a field around and had a nap — the alcoholic men in our

Part – VII: The Fioretti and Epilogue

house thought he was a "long grass."* They even encouraged him to stay with them and assured him that, "We'll fix you up."
– MC Sister[10]

∂

When I arrived in Hong Kong, we crossed over to Macau. That evening Brother Andrew took us for a walk after supper. In Macau there were many casinos. One was a floating casino near our community. We were interested to see. So we went in together with him. He allowed us to play with a few small coins; soon we lost all the coins. But we enjoyed ourselves. And you know what Brother Andrew said, "Gambling is like this, so do not be tempted, do not come here anymore." That was a very interesting experience for me.
– MC Brother[11]

∂

Whenever Brother Andrew used to visit the community, he would first go to the ward, say hello to the patients and greet them. Then he would go to the chapel and lastly to the refectory.
– MC Brother[12]

∂

When I was in Taiwan he brought a girl to our community, whom he probably had met in a bar. We had a small house, a small flat. Four rooms, one chapel, one kitchen. Brother Andrew wanted to take her in, in our community. And he told us to keep her with us for one month in the house. He wanted to save her from the bar. Did he realise we were young Brothers? Well, she stayed for one month and she did not go back to the bar again!
– MC Brother[13]

∂

---

* "Long grass" is a British idiom originally used in politics meaning "to put aside, defer." In this sense it is used for people who are living on the streets, the down-and-outs.

One day there was a day of prayer for the Co-Workers in Sydney. He did not know that we [MC Sisters] were going to attend. As soon as he came in and saw us in the chapel he turned around and he said, "A sight for sore eyes." He was so happy to see the MC Sisters. He was really happy. You felt he never left us, that he was still part of the family. He was still an MC, although he wasn't. We never had this feeling that he wasn't one of us, because of the way he lived.
– **MC Sister**[14]

∂

You know, he used to smoke, so sometimes he used to ask me to get him one particular brand of cigarettes — Wills Flake — the cheapest brand.
– **MC Brother**[15]

∂

Brother Andrew shared that one day Mother and he went to the bishop's house, Archbishop D'Souza, and they had a disagreement about something in front of the bishop and the next day when he went to Mother House for something, he was in the car, and Mother came out to the car and then she said to him, "Wasn't that a wonderful chance Jesus gave us yesterday?" Mother felt that they had humiliated themselves by arguing in front of the bishop and what a beautiful chance it was to be humble.
– **MC Sister**[16]

∂

It must have been around 1988, and one Sister and I went to the bus station in Melbourne to receive our Regional Superior. She was arriving around three or four in the morning. A bus arrived and Brother Andrew jumped down. We were so surprised and happy to see him. He thought we had come to pick him up and when we said that we were waiting for our Regional Superior he just said, "That's good for my pride." He always travelled carrying the Blessed Sacrament in the bus, in the train, anywhere, walking. He said, my

Part – VII: The Fioretti and Epilogue

Adoration is that. Our Regional Superior once wrote a letter to us about the time she was travelling with Brother Andrew in the bus and she said it was a privilege to be able to have Adoration in the bus.
– **MC Sister**[17]

∂

How many times did I tell him to get himself a new cardigan because the one he always wore, the grey coloured one, was worn out? We were insisting to get him one, but he said, "No, this cardigan is still warm for me."
– **MC Sister**[18]

∂

It must have been around 1981. I remember the day we were having class in Titagarh. He was not happy with how Titagarh was running. We heard him. He was upset with Brother Christdas who was managing Titagarh at that time. He was saying that in the future the Brothers will not be able to handle it because how it was developing it seemed to Brother Andrew too big. He was in favour of something simpler and smaller.
– **MC Sister**[19]

∂

We [MC Sisters in Australia] had two homes — one was for women in crisis and the other was called "The Home of Mercy" and Brother Andrew used to help in the soup kitchen and night shelter for men — drug addicts and alcoholics. Brother Andrew occasionally used to celebrate the Mass for them. He would talk to the men and eat with them. Whenever I saw Brother Andrew lining up for food, I was so touched — he was one of them. And I used to chide him, "Brother don't line up there, we'll prepare another place for you." And he would say, "No, I would like to be with them." This was my agony, Brother Andrew was not accepting our offer. So we would let him be there. He would insist to eat with the poor.
– **MC Sister**[20]

I was superior of the house when one of our junior Sisters was renewing her vows. Brother Andrew was invited to celebrate the Mass for us. So before the Mass, I went over and I said, "Brother, you know, after the homily we'll kneel down." "Ah yes, Sister, give me riding instructions," he joked. That was Brother, Brother had a good sense of humour; that's why if you offloaded a problem on to Brother he would tell a funny story. One time I told him that I was annoyed with someone. He told me that this Jesuit would come into the city every week, from a remote village in India with the excuse of sending a letter. Each time he turned up in the Cathedral presbytery he said, "I've just come in to post a letter," and one day they told him, "You know this is not a post office." He told me stories like that just to get me laughing. Brother was funny, he had that sense of humour. When the Co-Workers would have their days of retreat with Brother, afterwards he'd come around for the afternoon tea. He knew that we can't eat, we were very strict in those days, so he came around with the plate in front of us! One time all the juniors were out on retreat and he came to visit us in Orange and we were only two Australian Sisters, and when we went to meet him at the bus stop and he saw the two of us, he said, "Not you two!" That was Brother. He had that lovely sense of humour.

– **MC Sister**[21]

∂

Terrific memory he had for names. He always remembered you. I would be walking to the kitchen [during a retreat] and he'd say, "Hi, Pat." That was a great gift!

– **Retreatant**[22]

∂

In those days of late '80s we were a lot of juniors. One day, he arrived while we juniors were having a retreat. It was very cold that day, and when he arrived in the evening we had the heater on in the chapel. That, together with the presence of about twenty-five of us, meant that it was very warm inside the small chapel. Brother was in

Part – VII: The Fioretti and Epilogue

the middle of us Sisters kneeling, no chair or anything. There were Sisters on both sides. We were praying the rosary and little by little we could see Brother nodding off and falling, falling.... And there was one Sister who was quite big, and she was kneeling on the side, and she would be pulling him back in place, until he would restart again! I was at the back and I couldn't stop laughing. He could have asked for a chair but no, he knelt down like us. After the Adoration we had a good laugh with him.

– MC Sister[23]

∂

I remember once I had some questions about my faith and so I got in touch with Brother Andrew. We decided to meet at a McDonald's but unfortunately we were at different McDonald's. When I realised and ran to the one on Flinders Street [Melbourne], there he was waiting in front of the door, and he said, "Oh good, I have been praying to St Joseph." We went to the first floor of McDonald's and we just forgot the people around us. I took a coffee and a pastry, but he declined the pastry. He only took coffee because he was fasting, he said. After our long chat, he said, "Today we have sanctified McDonald's."

– Retreatant[24]

∂

I found Brother Andrew to be the most lovely man, full of compassion and understanding. But my most outstanding memory was of his humility, in a world where humility was and is sadly lacking. Funnily my enduring memory of Brother is the state of his shoes. They were the most threadbare pair of runners I have ever seen but he seemed so blissfully unaware of this fact. He was more concerned with souls than soles! I think that we had a morning tea or something with Brother and he said he didn't want any fancy food just tea, coffee, and plain Marie biscuits, nothing else. Just my kind of bloke.

– Retreatant[25]

My husband Ed and I arranged visits, and travelled with him, by bus and plane, to Co-Worker groups in Rhode Island, Kentucky and Tacoma, Washington [in the United States]. As we entered each city during our travels, Andrew used to ask Ed to buy him a copy of the local newspaper, so that he could read about the key issues in whatever city or town he was speaking. He wove those issues into his homilies/talks, which then made his audience feel noticed. At the last stop of our tour with him, he asked Ed to write a cheque for a rather large sum. Ed did so, trusting Andrew enough to not even question what he was going to do with the cheque. In true Andrew-fashion, he then explained to Ed that he was uncomfortable carrying the large sum of money he had received in currency and coins as donations — and handed Ed an envelope which contained the exact sum of the cheque. His honesty with money and his attentiveness to the happenings in each city endeared him to us.

– Co-Workers of Mother Teresa[26]

∂

Once when I went to Melbourne with a friend of mine to participate in one of Brother Andrew's prayer days at Glowrey House in Fitzroy, we decided to visit Melbourne's St Patrick's Cathedral before the day of prayer. After showing my friend around the Cathedral we arrived at the place where Archbishop Mannix was buried, and just happened to find Brother Andrew praying there. Brother Andrew had great devotion to Mannix. We acknowledged each other, but as he was praying we did not bother him. As he got up to leave I couldn't help but notice the simplicity of his dress. He had a usual simple pair of sneakers on, a jumper which had one of the elbow patches hanging off, a scarf around his neck as it was winter, and small bag in which I'm sure he was carrying his small booklets to hand out to the participants at the prayer day.

– A fellow-priest and retreatant[27]

∂

Part – VII: The Fioretti and Epilogue

He was a strong character. I don't know. He wasn't a man who displayed any temper in front of me. But I can tell, he certainly wasn't a cream puff. He was a human being of course. When he was over at my parish, there were a few blokes there and they would be talking in the sacristy about all types of psychological tests, which I thought was a load of crap, rubbish.... Andrew would just leave. Andrew did not subscribe to such things.

– A fellow-priest [28]

∂

I can still remember asking him, "How can you put up with all this — the heat, the hopelessness, the situation, the limitations, all the chaos?" For me Kidderpoor was very chaotic, and also the work, and Calcutta itself for me.... It was very painful to be there, the monsoon, the heat, the scabies, and I thought, "How can you put up with it as a life journey?" And he told me, "You know, I don't put up with it, because I often go away. So it's not hard because I escape." And I think I found that much more profound and authentic kind of spirituality than bearing with it all in a heroic way. He didn't have any ideals or any aspirations to become a hero, but he just lived what he had to live. And when he can't take it anymore, thank God that he had to go abroad and find a better climate. So he could joke about it — even if it doesn't seem to be such a lofty idea but it's a human technique or mechanism of survival. He was surviving like all the others and that is a much deeper sense of poverty than building up an aura of "look-how-self-sacrificed-I-can-be."

– A fellow-Jesuit [29]

∂

I was a parish priest in a place called Mohodan — a very remote place, and Ian who was already an MC Brother at that stage, was visiting me. We were being welcomed into the village, drumming and dancing girls, and all this sort of thing. So, as they were dancing, the two of us were going, "Yeah, what are we doing here?..." Ian leant over to me, and he said, "If only they knew what bastards we are."

And I said, "They actually do."

– A fellow-Jesuit[30]

∂

I used to visit him in Calcutta, at Mansatala Row. Once I was there for a month and went on to help with the visiting to Howrah Station and leper spots and all that sort of thing. And we used to go and have a beer together, and it was like, here he is running the novitiate, and the whole show on Mansatala Row, and he would be, "Let's go for a beer." It was fun. He hadn't lost it — that human funny touch. So we would go down to one of those places near the docks and we would have a couple of beers together. And then I visited him in Saigon and there was Ian and me one day.... He was facing the inevitable downfall of Saigon, and he took me out and he took me to the bars where he used to go, he said, "You have to buy a drink for the girls." We sat down at a table and two girls came and joined us, then I bought them something, probably Coca Cola at an incredible price. We chatted with these bar girls. They were both Catholics. Ian chatted with them, talked to them about their children, they said, "Well, we can only afford to put them in a Catholic school if we work in a bar like this."

– A fellow-Jesuit[31]

∂

I knew Andrew mostly in Macau. Knowing that I was an ardent reader he normally brought over books he had read, not necessarily spiritual. He brought Bombay mix all the way from India for the community but mostly for the Indian Brother in our community. He loved keeping the morale high even with simple gifts like snacks. He showed appreciation for everything, be it as little as it could be. He would appreciate all meals and tell us. Once after a beautiful day out with the community on a feast day, he asked the treasurer to give each Brother a small amount of money so we could gamble in a dog track down the street. He thought that it was good clean fun and at the end of the day [we would] see which Brother would win the most. I thought that this was not appropriate and told him so and that I would not go. He was angry and told me that I had ruined the day. Another day when I criticised the way that money was being spent on the community's rare simple celebrations he told me, "You want to be poor with the poor. You have never seen the poor celebrating with the little they have." I once spent a whole day meticulously putting the few spiritual and other books in order according to subjects. Another brother who was more inclined towards what he thought looked good than according to subject decided in anger to put the books in a more symmetrical mode. Andrew was amused about the whole thing.

– Former MC novice[32]

∂

I attended a couple of his retreats. He was a very quiet man. The first time I saw him I was down at God's Farm. I was walking down towards the chapel and I saw this man raking the leaves from the path. I thought he was the gardener and I said to him, "Hello." And then I saw Betty and I said, "I met a chap down the road, I think he is the gardener," and she said, "No, no, no. That's Brother Andrew." He did all those sort of things.

– Retreatant[33]

∂

I was the director of a theological library in Melbourne — The Caroline Chisholm Library — from 1993 - 2006. In the early days we were very short of money and wondered whether we would survive. We held lunchtime talks there and Brother Andrew was among the speakers. One day — I think it was around 1995 — I was assessing the finances and saw we were really in dire straits without rent for the next three months and no sign of any donations. I decided to ring the landlord and let him know the situation with a view to closing down. Because I did not want to worry the other people working in the library at the time I decided to make the call from home. When I got home, I found a letter in my mailbox with a cheque for the exact amount for the next three months' rent! It was from Brother Andrew with a short note explaining that someone had left it to him in their will "to be given to a good cause." What's more, I then went to my local church (St Joseph's West Brunswick) to give thanks for God's provision and saw that the Sacrament of Reconciliation was on. I thought I would take the opportunity to go. Who was in the confessional (in a church that was not his parish) but Brother Andrew so I had the chance to thank him personally on the same day!

– **Director of a Theology Library**[34]

∂

I remember Brother Andrew's visit to the Catholic Worker [in New York] in November 1973. My husband Patrick and I were both at St Joseph House at the time of Brother Andrew's visit. We lived directly across the street from the Worker, and he came over to our apartment for a visit. We both recall a sense of deep peace and attentiveness in him, a warm and personal manner, a recognition and appreciation of a profound bond between his vocation and that of the Catholic Workers.

– **Catholic Worker member**[35]

∂

When Andrew stayed in our home, he told us that we were for him like a five-star hotel, because we had a bucket. He, like St Mother Teresa, had only two sets of clothes. He would wear one set one day and wash them the next day in the bucket. He had a shirt and trousers and wore a simple crucifix on his pocket. We asked him what happened if he was invited to a function where there were "dignitaries"? He replied that if that were a problem to them, they would not invite him back. That would not worry him. However any discerning person could see that simplicity in an affluent society made a big statement as to the fact that "the kingdom of heaven belongs to the poor in spirit." Andrew was a man who suffered much, but deep down there was a quiet joy that radiated from his humble smile.

– **Retreatant**[36]

Part – VII: The Fioretti and Epilogue

The first time I met Father/Brother Andrew, I had never been to God's Farm and I was sort of not sure where to go and Brother Andrew came out with a torch to guide me in and walk me in and then he rushed to get my suitcase and carry that in, and I was very impressed and I thought, "Wow, this is not what normally happens," and he was busy putting out rubbish bins and sort of doing all these small jobs which normally don't get done by someone like Brother Andrew and of course we had his talks, which were useful with lots of insights, but the big impression which left on me was the fact that he welcomed me in the most humble way.
– **Retreatant**[37]

∂

Uncle Ian was stubborn, and he knew that he was stubborn. I think a lot of the Travers-Balls were stubborn. Lucy was stubborn, I remember my mother [Aimée] was also. You know sometimes you have to do things that you don't want to do. The Travers-Ball family didn't do what they didn't want to do! And they all got it from Pop (Ian's father) … But then even Mother Teresa was stubborn. Ian used to say, "You don't want to cross Mother." If Mother wants something to be done Mother will get it done. But all said in an affectionate way. They were very similar.
– **Family member**[38]

∂

I tell the people in our parish who come to me with their troubles, about Andrew. The day of his funeral … a married couple came to see me at twelve noon, very distressed because their teenage daughter was self-mutilating with a knife and they were afraid she would kill herself. I told them that I would need to leave soon to go to the requiem but that we would ask Andrew to care for Z., and I would see them again on Monday. When we met on Monday, they had experienced a dreadful weekend. When I said that I was sorry and that I had hoped Andrew would care for her, her father replied, "We asked Andrew to keep her alive and he has done that for us." — And she is still alive today.

– Mercy Sister[39]

∂

Andrew was very different from anyone else I had met at that time in my life [1972]. He seemed to live fully in the present moment, with a great stillness of soul about him. In India, such a quality might go unnoticed, maybe in fact, it was principally India's gift to him. But from my perspective at the time, the first meeting with him was unforgettable for the leadership he offered. He tendered a different set of values to that post-Vatican II Western living that I struggled with as a young, idealistic, and newly professed sister.

– Mercy Sister[40]

∂

Cambodia. Myself, another Brother and Andrew were driven by a Catholic Relief Services employee to a distant refugee camp, again, over a dangerous road with military activity all around us and even overhead. We had a Cambodian interpreter with us. I could see Andrew was quite nervous and, was coping by smoking cigarettes. We had food in the trunk of the car and selected some people who looked particularly wanting that were living in a refugee camp. We handed them the food and they were surprised and overjoyed. My first small act on behalf of the Brothers in the midst of an immense tragedy that was unfolding around us. I was so privileged to witness, to be able to participate in some small act to bring comfort in some small way. And so it was with the Brothers in Cambodia. It was a contemplative participation … being in such a place at such a time … being amidst the suffering and the horror. Andrew helped to tend my soul, my mind, which allowed me to remain vital and alive in such an ambient. That tending has left an imprint which has remained with me all these many years later.

– Former MC Brother[41]

∂

EPILOGUE

My journey with Brother Andrew comes to an end. It took me to many countries: from Peru to the United States and England, from South Korea to the Philippines and from Cambodia to Madagascar and Kenya, and to Andrew's native Australia — from big cities such as Melbourne, Sydney, Canberra, Brisbane and Perth to the outback town of Delegate. I crossed India from Mumbai and Delhi in the West to the northern-most Raj Bari city of Cooch Behar and to the southern-most tip of India — Kanyakumari. I met and interviewed over 300 people — family, friends, Religious, acquaintances, fellow students, volunteers and Co-Workers. It has been a most instructive, interesting, and enriching journey — an emotionally laden pilgrimage with Brother Andrew.

When I started travelling around India, my first stop was Vijayawada in Andhra Pradesh. One Missionaries of Charity Sister asked me, "Any miracles?" meaning "Any miracles thanks to the intercession of Brother Andrew?" I was taken aback and I promptly answered, "I hope not." Now, *she* was shocked. I went on to explain that if there were to be a miracle, that would further complicate things. Others thought I was the postulator for Andrew's cause. I had to explain, to their disappointment, that I wasn't.

Around ten years ago, Richard Lucas — a middle-aged teacher from Australia and at the time the Canberra Branch Chairman of the Knights of the Southern Cross, wrote to Br David Roberts, MC, the then General Servant of the Missionaries of Charity Brothers, to Daven Day, SJ, who was the Provincial of the Jesuits in Sydney, and to the Archbishop of Canberra and Goulburn, Mark Coleridge.[42] He was asking their help in initiating the cause for Andrew's canonisation process. He had first met Brother Andrew at a retreat at Nudgee Junior Christian Brothers College, Indooroopilly, in Brisbane, in January 1991. Richard says that he was impressed by Andrew's humility and gentleness. "He was a bloke without pretentions. His simple but such appropriately warm loving language made me feel that I was the only one at that wonderful retreat."[43] After that first retreat Richard attended many. He is a simple man with no knowledge of the canonisation process. He did not even have a computer to type the letters. Archbishop Mark Coleridge directed him to the Missionaries of Charity Brothers and to the Jesuits; Brother David expressed his concern that the Brothers did not have people competent to undertake the task. He also felt that Andrew himself would not have agreed to the venture.[44]

Daven Day was willing to be interviewed and strongly supported the idea of a professional and competent study of Brother Andrew's life, including theological and spiritual competence. Daven was the same person who told me in an interview, "Let me say from the beginning, I'm not only a great admirer of him [Brother Andrew] also a great friend of his. But he's the only person in my long life, I'm eighty-four, that I really think was a saint."[45]

In desiring to see Andrew canonised, Richard Lucas made a pertinent and poignant point: Australian women already have a female saint as a role model in Mary MacKillop, whereas for Australian men one still needs to be found. According to Richard Lucas, Andrew is the one. When I met Richard, I remember telling him that there was no way that Rome — meaning the Church's hierarchy at the Vatican — would ever consider a man who had had issues with alcohol and gambling and who was sort of "forced out" of the same Congregation he had helped to build. It was then that Richard suggested that I read the life story of Mary MacKillop.

Was it sheer coincidence that Mary MacKillop was born in the same Fitzroy, Melbourne, where Andrew's grandfather lived and died and where Andrew himself died? She was born on 15 January 1842, and died in Sydney on 8 August 1909. She was the eldest of eight children born to Scottish immigrants. During her teens she worked as a governess, a shop assistant and a schoolteacher. It was while she was teaching in Portland, Victoria, that she met Fr Julian Woods who invited her to teach in a new school in a small

Part – VII: The Fioretti and Epilogue 511

town called Penola — an innovative setting in which the Church provided free education for all children. The success was immediate. Mary was soon joined by other young women and together they founded the first Australian Order — the Sisters of St Joseph. They soon spread all over Australia providing free schooling for children. Unfortunately, not all Church officials were happy with the new venture, especially the more conservative Catholics, to the extent that Bishop Laurence Sheil, OFM, of Adelaide declared that Mary was to be excommunicated and that the Order was to be disbanded. Among the allegations he provided were financial incompetence and rumours of a drinking problem. In fact, it was widely known that she drank alcohol on doctor's orders to relieve the symptoms of dysmenorrhea, which often confined her to bed for days.

Mary and her sisters were to find support from different people ranging from Emanuel Solomon — a Jew — who gave them a place to stay, Joanna Barr Smith — a prominent Prebyterian, and even the Jesuit Fathers, who in defiance continued to offer spiritual help and direction to the group. After two years, Bishop Sheil on his deathbed asked the Church authorities to lift the excommunication of MacKillop, and completely exonerated her. After this experience in 1873 Mary sought official approval of the Catholic Church from Pope Pius IX who provisionally blessed the constitution of the order. Only in 1888 did Pope Leo XIII give final approval. In 1909 Mary suffered a stroke and died in the convent in North Sydney. She was canonised by Pope Benedict XVI in Rome on 17 October 2010, becoming the first Australian saint.

Yes, Andrew could well be the male counterpart of Mary MacKillop.

The majority of Missionaries of Charity Brothers would be in favour of promoting Andrew's cause for sainthood for a few reasons: they would take pride in the fact that their co-founder (together with Saint Teresa of Calcutta) was a saint. It might also lessen or eradicate the stigma and shame they have felt for more than thirty years. At the same time, it would make a nice success story!

I do not believe it is for me to offer an opinion as to whether or not Andrew could be considered a saint. Still without drawing any conclusions, it may be worth pondering certain points. In Andrew's own words saints are, "people who lived very close to God, people whose will, there is a harmony between their will and the will of God … Each saint expresses some special light on holiness."[46] According to the Oxford dictionary, a saint is a person acknowledged as holy or virtuous and regarded in Christian faith as being in heaven after death. But then, anyone who is in heaven including our loved ones may not have lived a perfect life but amid their failures and faults, they kept on striving to move forward towards God.

In fact, not only the Christian faith has the notion of sainthood. Religions across the world attribute a state of holiness to certain people. The Jews speak of *tzadik* the "just or righteous one". Moslems speak of *wali*, the "friend of God". For the Hindus and Sikhs there are the *rishi* and *guru* respectively, the "seer," or "sage". People are strongly and powerfully attracted to these persons who in turn touch their inner lives simply by being who they are, and who they were meant to be.

John A. Coleman, SJ, states that saints usually have a few common characteristics: from being exemplary models to extraordinary teachers.[47] They are a source of benevolent power, intercession, and an example of detachment. They also have a special relationship to the holy. The Catholic Church goes a step further and confers the title "Saint" on a person who has been formally canonised and included in the official list (the Canon) of recognised people to be venerated. This is where it all becomes complicated. Whereas Andrew can easily and definitely be considered a saint or *tzadik*, *wali*, *guru*, *rishi* or *bodhisattva*, to be included in the "Canon of Saints" in the Roman Catholic Church is another matter. The Catholic Church states that she does not "make" or "create" saints, but rather recognises their heroic virtues by first considering them Servant of God, Venerable, and then, Blessed. Things get more complex: there are financial needs to support the research and study, and the further proof of two

Part – VII: The Fioretti and Epilogue

posthumous miracles obtained from God through the intercession of the candidate for sainthood.

Whether Andrew becomes a declared saint in the Catholic Church is not fundamental. The relevance of Andrew's life — with all its complexities and flaws — lies in the fact that the weak, the lonely, the unloved, the dejected, the rejected, the alcoholic, the gambler, the addict and others would find solace in an ordinary man who was also weak, felt lonely, rejected by his own, and who struggled with alcohol, gambling and with his own character imperfections, while at the same time maintaining a deep trust in God.

I truly believe that such experiences deeply changed and shaped Andrew's relationships with people and with God: the fact that his birth was soon followed by the death of his sister and his daily facing "death" in India, Vietnam and Cambodia; his unexpressed pain at leaving for India less than two months after the death of his mother and the parting from Ba Kim in such tragic circumstances in Vietnam; his loneliness and sadness; his compulsion to gambling; his stubbornness and his occasional bouts of anger towards Brothers; his ego and pride when taking particular decisions; his not being able to settle down in one place and the need constantly to be on the move; his not accepting the help offered by his Brothers when his alcohol consumption increased; his not being able to mend broken relationships with specific friends; his internal struggles with political ideologies and his becoming more conservative in his theology. These situations would eventually be reflected in his writings and his talks: morality, darkness in the world and in the Church, compulsions, death, suffering, misery and redemption.

As with Dostoevsky, his hope came from a source that was intangible and transcendental: beauty. It was a beauty wrought from pain. He maintained that if the two were to be separated there would be something missing:

> In a paradoxical way, it is the secrets of beauty, richness, love and grace that are more difficult to deal with. These are treasures that I long to share with others, but communication is difficult ... So I live with my secret — not sharing it in any depth even with family and friends — not even with myself perhaps. This causes pain, because love and beauty want to share themselves.[48]

It was ultimately the voice of Beauty that summoned him. He even confessed to Gerry Monaghan that he couldn't grasp such Beauty for more than three seconds before he wandered off again. But Beauty stayed. Beauty revealed herself in the charm of Nana Ball and the love of his family and friends, and the fun he had as a young Jesuit with Crotty; through the effusive love and admiration of the MC Brothers and Sisters. Beauty appeared in "the mountains, the green of the trees, the rich blue of the sky, the silence with no traffic, the quiet clear nights with no electricity — and above all the gentle Kaqchikel Indians" in Guatemala.[49] Beauty instructed him in the teachings of the Church, the Sacraments, and the Eucharist and in the Holy Family of Nazareth. He discovered Beauty in the richness and depth of the Twelve Step Spirituality.

But above all he perceived and touched Beauty in the misery of the poor, the wounded and the broken because there lay the Presence of the Divine. It was this gradual discovery of Beauty in the suffering person including himself that would lead Andrew to redemption. It was because of his woundedness — and not despite it — that he could claim a total trust in and surrender to a loving God. Through his darkness — and not despite it — lay his hope of light.

> For it is a strange thing that I can be more open to the beauty and grace of Christ when I am a loser and wounded than when I am winning with my own strength. In the end it is in the misery that He reveals Himself to us — in our need, our total need of His grace.[50]

Part – VII: The Fioretti and Epilogue

[1] 20180203 IB Prem Anand Naduvathette, MC.
[2] 20201130 Email Gary Richardson.
[3] 20180203 IB Prem Anand Naduvathette, MC.
[4] 20181118 IB Peter Murmu, MC.
[5] 20190520 IB Robi Gut, MC.
[6] 20171202 IB Ben Harrison, MC.
[7] 20180201 IB Benjamin Indwar, MC.
[8] 20190506 IB Charles Dung Dung, MC.
[9] 20180116 IB George Dev, MC.
[10] 20180328 IS Sister Shekinah, MC.
[11] 20190510 IB Oh John, MC.
[12] 20190213 IB PT Varghese, MC.
[13] 20180506 IB Mariadas, MC.
[14] 20180321 IS Sister Antonine, MC.
[15] 20190108 IB Simon Hembron, MC.
[16] 20180515 IS Sister Joseph Maria, MC.
[17] 20180328 IS Sister Oliva, MC.
[18] 20180328 IS Sister Oliva, MC.
[19] 20180521 IS Sister Ruth, MC.
[20] 20171120 IS Sister Soledad, MC.
[21] 20180321 IS Sister Eliezer, MC.
[22] 20180303 IF Angela Bonnie and Pat Rowland.
[23] 20180325 IS Sister Milada, MC.
[24] 20180303 IF Angela Bonnie and Pat Rowland.
[25] 20190831 Email Emanuel Howard.
[26] 20190526 Email Ed and Dorothy Baroch.
[27] 20171212 IF Adam Carroll, MCF.
[28] 20180312 IF Fr Frank Burns.
[29] 20171129 IJ Paul Chetcuti, SJ.
[30] 20180320 IJ Phil Crotty, SJ.
[31] 20180320 IJ Phil Crotty, SJ.
[32] 20180427 IF Eugene Galea.
[33] 20180330 Email Jan Cole.
[34] 20180628 Email Kate Cleary.
[35] 20190221 Email Kathleen and Patrick Jordan.
[36] 20181103 Email Paul and Christine Hodgkinson.

Part – VII: The Fioretti and Epilogue

37 20180330 Email Pauline Caldwell.
38 20180305 IR Anne and Julian Millership, Jim Smith.
39 20001105 LF Sr Margaret Ryan, RSM to Br Geoff Brown, MC.
40 20001105 LF Sr Margaret Ryan, RSM to Br Geoff Brown, MC.
41 20201103 Email Gary Richardson.
42 The Order of the Knights of the Southern Cross is a national organisation of Catholic laymen who operate with the support of the Australian bishops. Its members strive to serve the wider community and support those in need, promote the advancement of Australia, foster the Christian way of life throughout the nation; promote the welfare of members of the Order and their families; encourage spiritual, social and intellectual activities amongst its members; and conduct and support educational, charitable, religious and social welfare work.
43 20180320 IF Richard Lucas.
44 Part of the letter written on 20 September 2013, by Marc Daniel Delapeyre, MC, the General Secretary to Richard Lucas: "We discussed the matter at our recent General Council meeting. At present, it is the view of Br David Roberts, our General Servant, and also of his council, that we do not wish to begin a cause for canonization. The reason would seem to be the following: a) It is a very complicated process and we struggle to maintain our current apostolates without adding any further work! b) We do not think Br Andrew would want us to try to canonize him. c) It is not long since Br Andrew died and of course many of our Brothers have known and lived with him. We hold him in great esteem, for his leadership, vision, writings and care of the Brothers. At the same time, naturally, quite a few Brothers have memories of times when he was not so saintly and so it is, in a way, too early to attempt canonization."
45 20180320 IJ Daven Day, SJ.
46 From a talk given by Brother Andrew in 1999 at Gracewood - God's Farm, Australia – "Edith Stein".
47 Coleman, John A. "Conclusion: After sainthood", in Hawley, John Stratton, ed. *Saints and Virtues* Berkeley: University of California Press, 1987.
48 00000019 LP.
49 00000106 LP.
50 19960100 LP.

APPENDIX – I: MILLER AND TRAVERS-BALL FAMILY TREES

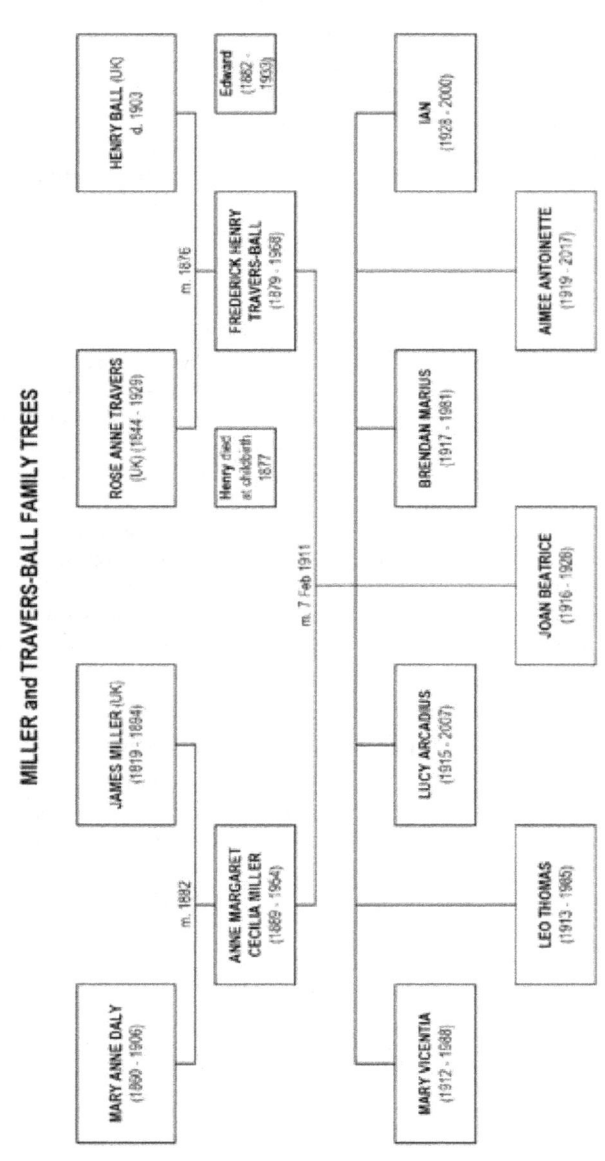

APPENDIX – II: INTERVIEW WITH BROTHER ANDREW

Extracts from an interview conducted on 29 January 1969 by Fr Val Noone co-editor of *Priest Forum*.

LOOKING FOR SOMETHING

Fr Noone : Brother Andrew, how did you come to do this work?

Br Andrew : Mother Teresa wanted a priest to come and take over the training. She was buttonholing pretty well every priest she got hold of and then finally I came on the scene and I was looking for something, some sort of work with the poor. It wasn't exactly what I was thinking of, not by any means, but it all worked out.

FVN : What was it that you were thinking of at the time?

BA : Even before theology I had a desire to work for the poor without knowing where. Ordination came and I still didn't see where or how. I was thinking of living in a slum, taking work and sort of starting from there. I really wanted to try that but then this came along and somehow everything fell into shape.

PEOPLE WHO ARE REALLY DESPERATE

FVN : What is the work that the Brothers do?

BA : One of the biggest is the mobile leprosy clinic which treats about 2,000 people in different centres in and around Calcutta. Then we do fairly simple medical work in the slums for people who don't get any medical attention. Also primary schools for some of the children who don't go to school at all, and the group with the biggest percentage of dropouts is class one and two. Then there's work on the streets and stations for abandoned boys who live by begging, stealing, scavenging in trains and things like that. Then there's a relief programme providing a cooked meal each day for families and for people who are really desperate. We've got a home where there are a number of handicapped or disabled destitute men. About thirty or forty of those boys live in one of the Brothers' houses — also a youth club. We've got the beginnings of adult education work with workers in the docks. On a voluntary basis a retired Hindu doctor who was thirty-five years professor in leprosy at the medical college supervises our mobile leprosy clinic, but he has trained the Brothers so that they can pretty well run the clinic on their own.

FVN : One of the brothers referred to a 'mini' school. What is that?

BA : A school which starts in a slum, for the children who don't go to school at all or who can't come regularly, for example, they may have to go out to work, they may have to mind the babies at home while the parents go for work, they may have to cook the meal and they haven't got the clothes to wear to go to a school even though most of the schools are free. So we start these schools wherever we can, even under a tree or on a bit of a veranda, perhaps afterwards we get a chance to rent a little hut in the slums. Our aim is to get the children into other regular schools. But there are still plenty that can't fit in, so we try to give them in two or three years, something whenever they can come. Brother Benedict has a house near here. He uses the downstairs rooms as classrooms by day — and in the winter takes in families off the street to stay the night.

FVN : (While we talked we were interrupted several times by people who came to see Andrew). Could you tell us about that boy who was here?

BA : That boy is Sri Khanto. He came for money to buy a geometry set. Two years ago we met him on the station begging and in pretty terrible health. His father had died. Mother married again, the stepfather gave him a terrible time and he ran away. His mother finally committed suicide. The Brothers brought him home. He settled down very well. He's studied just one or two years in school so we've sent him to a local school but here's a boy of 16 with the little kids in third class. Then we got a chance to put him in a technical school that takes boys without too much background. He is doing a course in turning and fitting now, and says it's coming along nicely.

WASHING BITS OF COAL

FVN : Could you tell us more about the people of Kidderpoor?

BA : This is the dock area of Calcutta so all the dock workers live around here. There are a number of factories too. In parts of Kidderpoor the ratio of men to women is 80 to 20, because the men from the villages inland leave their families there and come to the city for work. This creates all sorts of problems, prostitution and all the rest, with some businessmen making a tremendous thing out of that. There are very bad slums where people live in shocking, unbelievable conditions, some have got absolutely nothing. I can never work out how some of them can live. You may get a man who is sick, out of work, with a number of kids, the wife perhaps earns something, washing dishes in a house or ragpicking, picking up coals from the ashes that are thrown out and then washing the bits of coal that are left and selling that. They get practically nothing and yet the whole family lives on that.

FVN : About how much would they get?

BA : You get families living on less than thirty rupees a month. How they do it I don't know. Thirty rupees that's about four dollars a month and there may be four or five children there. How they live I don't know? You go into a house or a hut and you'll find not a grain of anything, not a skerrick of food anywhere in the whole house and people just sitting there. The cooking vessels there just empty. That cooked meal we provide for many people that is all they get, and even that is not a full meal. Often more people come along than we have food for. You spin it out which means everybody gets a bit less. Still people will keep some of that for the next morning.

Recently one of the Brothers was telling me about a very poor family he used to visit. He'd help a bit with medicine and whatever he could. One day he found there was another young couple there with two or three children so he asked the wife of the house who they were. It was winter, and she said, "Oh, last night I saw them sleeping under a tree just close by, I knew how cold it was, so I brought them in."

It was in the evening that that Brother met them, just sitting there. They had had a bit of black tea and a bit of bread in the morning for breakfast. Nothing else all day. Even that bit of breakfast they had shared with that other family. Things like that really make you feel extremely small. We know many lepers, some living by begging. Naturally a man who lives by begging has always got to try and get a bit more, reasonably enough. But you have to build up a bit of a defence, which they know we've got and that doesn't spoil the relationship at all, but sometimes someone will come and ask for something, help with the house rent or for some food supplies. Then the others will chime in and say, oh you help this one, she is in a very bad way. They forget themselves, and push the other person's case.

DON'T YOU GET DISCOURAGED?

FVN : Yesterday, we started to talk about the symbolic value of what you are doing. Could you explain that?

BA : Well, that's an idea that came to me clearly at least only recently. We had a bit of a session with that ecumenical institute from Chicago when they were in Calcutta. They were saying how they understand their work in the ghetto with the Negroes of Chicago as having a value that goes beyond the immediate work that they are doing for the people. It struck them that our work is the same that it has a value for society at large and the Church at large. People such as this group have often asked, "Don't you get discouraged with the overwhelming enormity of the problem of poverty in Calcutta?" One thing that perhaps helps us to avoid falling into despair is the number of people both in the Church and non-Christians, who have been tremendously inspired by the work they've seen the Brothers do. Many of them are not highly qualified, yet the way in which they work, and the way they go to the really poorest has an impact on people who see it. For instance, people in India, Christians and non-Christians, and visitors from overseas are tremendously struck with anything done with lepers.

START AT THE BOTTOM

FVN : That the effect of your work goes beyond the actual work done is borne out by the goodwill both the Brothers and the Sisters have built up with the government. And also now you have been elected one of the West Bengal delegates to this all India seminar on renewal of the Church. Our readers would be interested to know about the latter.

BA : The Conference of Bishops is planning a sort of Vatican Council of our own for May 1969. Our preparations in West Bengal were in two phases, one a general theological reflection on renewal, the other on concrete spheres of life, for example, works of mercy, liturgy, youth, labour, etc. It was open to anybody. Extremely hard work. It was a real experience of the Church. Really wonderful. Openness. Something I haven't had before. Nothing spectacular. It took us all where we are — the Church with differences of opinions. But a real effort to look at the problems ahead of us. Even living in Calcutta with poverty at your doorstep it is possible to become used to it. You don't realise that there is a call coming to you in the misery of

Appendix: II – Interview with Brother Andrew

people. But when anything like that was suggested, many people would immediately say there are existing societies for this, St Vincent de Paul's, Legion, YCW [Youth Catholic Worker]. A number of us began to feel there is not much chance to renew working through existing organizations. I was very struck by the Gospel one morning during the seminar — Our Lord saying that you can't put new wine in old skins. That came a bit of a light. We need new groups forming to meet and tackle the new problems of today. There is a danger that people are saying, well not. The Bishops should tell us what to do, or somebody should do such and such. But I wonder to what extent renewal comes from the top. We have got to start at the bottom. For instance, in the labour workshop I met three or four others interested in labour problems in Calcutta. The only hope is to start with them. There is no chance of it coming from the top.

TALKING ABOUT THE ENCYCLICAL

FVN : What do you mean by the renewal of the Church?

BA : The first word that comes to my mind is simplification. A lot of things that have come in have complicated the Gospel and we need to get back to the simplicity of the Gospel.

FVN : One of the things we said in our first editorial was that we thought the question of being progressive or conservative was not the really important one, that this was often a matter of temperament and education but the important issue was that we be faithful to the Gospel and faithful to Christ. Now this....

BA : You've met Fr Van? Now he is running Boys Town and doing a wonderful job. The other day we were talking about part of the encyclical Humanae Vitae and a lot of theologians. He said, "If I were the Pope, I would just say, what do you hold? If you didn't toe the line, then clear out. I wouldn't care if there was only ten per cent left in the Church." And I said, "Well I do hope you don't become Archbishop because if you do, it will become the end of us." There is a man working completely for the poorest but tremendously conservative. We are able to laugh over it. "I had the training in Rome," he said, "That was the line we had there, I suppose you got a different line." It is good to be able to laugh over these things and remain friends.

WHAT DIFFERENCE DOES CHRIST MAKE?

FVN : Following on about the renewal of the Church, what is it that strikes you about Christ?

BA : Since I have got into this work the miracles of Christ have taken on a tremendous meaning. I always tell the Brothers, these are miracles, the work for the lepers, the curing of the sick, the feeding of the hungry, the giving shelter to the poor. What are we Brothers? We are a group of people without anything, without any position. People are always asking us where you get the finances. That's the least problem. Somebody gave us an ambulance for the mobile leprosy clinic. Medicine comes. These are miracles. All sorts of little Catholic papers run articles and as a result donations come. It's all one work — the work of the spirit in the Church. Christ is the one who brings love. He brings that victory over our own selfishness. Christ asks of each one in a different way and added together that is the Church.

FVN : The question is a pretty tough one. To come at it in another way, what difference do you find it makes that you believe in Christ?

BA : If I can turn the question a bit to, what difference does Christ make to these people around here? 99% are not Christians. We've got in our rules, and it is a big point in our spirituality to realise that when we do the works of mercy, when you give a meal to the hungry or an injection to the poor man with T.B. or whatever it is, giving shelter, if you're united with Christ you are giving more than bread, you are giving more than an injection; you are also giving the charity of Christ which is redemptive. Just as in the Gospel Christ's touch transformed a man. The charity of Christ touches the heart of the man, the poor man, the suffering man. You do see a difference in the dying, in the lepers. They realise that there is a meaning behind it all and they can recognize the charity of Christ.

STOPGAP APPROACH?

FVN : Some communists would say that feeding the hungry and caring for people the way you do is only a stopgap measure instead of working for the radical and revolutionary change in the structures of the society which produce this poverty.

BA : That underestimated the work of the Brothers and their effect on the attitudes of the people. The works of mercy go beyond the immediate effect on the man in need. They bring hope to the man who is helped if done in the right way; they change the man who does the work, so that he then begins to realise the need to go to the roots of the problem. Then, too, it is easy to become pragmatic. A Hindu said to me recently, "I'm ready to help you but don't ask me to help in hopeless cases of cripples and defectives ready to die – better to let them die." Our work for the hopeless cases is a testimony to the value of each human life.

FVN : Do you meet many of the local communists?

BA : There are all different types. One, a local doctor helps us a lot. He is ready to give medical care to people of any caste or group. He is genuinely concerned with people and is on the city council. He has asked us to help him in providing shelter for prostitutes who want to get out of that game. But there is another communist councillor in the next ward who seems ready to try anything for his political purposes. He works on the narrow communal interest of Hindu and Moslem and plays the one group against the other.

OUR OWN DARKNESS

FVN : You haven't finished that train of thought on Christ.

BA : In the slums, as everywhere else, again and again you come up against real darkness, ignorance, prejudice, superstition. Basically good people are held back. That applies to ourselves doing this work. Christ really is the light of the world. He brings tremendous light into the darkness of our own lives. The life is a bit hard, yet there's tremendous joy and happiness for ourselves.

For more information on the Missionaries of Charity Brothers
https://mcbrothers.org

For more information on the Missionaries of Charity Sisters
https://missionariesofcharity.org/
https://www.motherteresa.org/

NAME INDEX

A

Agnes Joseph, MC, Sister 465
Agnes, MC, Sister 132
Allen, Leon 178, 179, 180, 187, 197, 202, 208, 231, 232, 248, 249, 252, 259, 335, 336, 348, 440, 441, 442, 443
Aloysius, MC, Brother 121, 141
Amrit, MC, Brother 190, 194, 203, 205, 206, 212
Anima Prasad, MC, Brother 137
Antoine, SJ, Father Robert 101, 149
Archana, MC, Sister 465, 475
Arrupe, SJ, Father Pedro 103, 136

B

Ball, Henry 26, 35, 476
Bara, Father Thomas 87
Barber, SJ, Msgr. Eric 132
Barnabas, MC, Brother 249
Barnes, Jenny 394, 395, 396, 465, 474, 475, 481, 483
Barnes, John 21, 394, 396, 440, 441, 465, 468, 470, 473, 474, 475, 476, 481, 483
Baroch, Ed 502
Barone, Frank 190, 194
Basu, Jyoti 326
Ba Thi 316, 318, 319
Batley, Michael 179, 187, 197
Beath, Father Greg 431
Beattie, Max 142
Benedict, MC, Brother 141
Benedict XVI, Pope 511
Bernard, MC, Brother 121, 179, 419
Besra, MC, Brother James 249
Bianchi, Bishop Lorenzo 136
Blondiaux, Joel 192
Bowling, SJ, Father Theodore 84
Boyd-Turner, Father John 229
Boylan, SJ, Father John Rolland 115, 133
Brady, SJ, Father Michael 88
Brown, MC, Brother Geoff 260, 261, 262, 328, 336, 357, 358, 362, 364, 373, 377, 443, 476, 477
Burns, Father Frank E. 404

C

Caldwell Moore, Edward 97
Carey, Tom 479
Casamento, John 335
Casey, Bishop Eamon 299

Ceja, Anthony 371
Charlebois, Father Robert 188
Cheshire, Leonard 70
Christanand 85
Christdas, MC, Brother 268, 499
Clement, MC, Brother 190,
    194, 203, 205, 206, 212
Coleridge, Archbishop Mark 509
Collins, Don 85
Collins, SJ, Father Jim 64
Costigan, Margaret 134
Cowan, Father Don 179, 188
Crotty, SJ, Father Phil 65, 70,
    73, 76, 84, 101, 103, 514
Cuni, Filomena 152
Cuni, Luca 152

D

Daly, Mary Anne 36, 479
Daly, SJ, Father Michael 64
Daly, SJ, Father Stephen 64
Damien, MC, Brother 121, 141
Dasgupta, Dr. Satrujit 148
David, MC, Brother 121
Davis, Dr. R. B. 148
Day, Dorothy 70, 133
Day, SJ, Father Daven 24, 47,
    440, 472, 474, 476, 477,
    509, 510
Deakin, Archbishop Hilton 170
De Bertodano, Teresa 304

De Coster, Mother Odille 88
De Fonseca, Angelo 91
De Foucauld, Saint Charles 392
Degrati, Dr. Claudia 359
De Hueck Doherty, Catherine 70
De Keyser, SJ, Father 90
De la Bédoyère, Michael 85
DeMartini, Paul 188
De Mello, SJ, Father Tony 82
De Pypere, SJ, Father Joseph
    76, 78
De Smet, SJ, Father Richard 73
Dev, MC, Brother George 314
Dey, Gobinda Chandra 142
Dezza, Father Paolo 115
Dilip, MC, Brother 249
Dincher, SJ, Father Carl 101
Dipchandra, MC, Brother 146
Doherty, SJ, Father Peter 65
Dominic, MC, Brother 121
Dorothy, MC, Sister 403, 465
Dostoevsky, Fyodor
    313, 407, 513
Doyle, Father Martin 397
Doyle, Mary 177
Doyle, SJ, Father Michael 64, 86
D'Souza, Archbishop Albert V.
    92, 125, 132, 498
D'Souza, Archbishop Henry
    377, 430
Dullard, SJ, Father Maurice
    87, 89

Name Index

Dwyer, SJ, Father Bill 65, 69, 87, 89
Dynon, Moira 152

E

Eather, Michael 78
Egan, Eileen 21, 37, 184, 187, 282, 283, 295
Elenita, MC, Sister 424
Eliezer, MC, Sister 402, 465, 467
Ellickal, MC, Brother Abraham 267
Ennis (née Travers-Ball), Mary Vincentia 22, 36, 37, 178, 182, 198, 207, 220, 229, 230, 374

F

Fallaci, Oriana 18
Felicia, MC, Brother Benedict 444
Felix, MC, Brother 135
Fellini, Federico 97
Frame, Neil 227
Frederick, MC, Sister 255

G

Gabric, SJ, Father Michael 101
Galea, Eugene 18
Gandhi, Indira 146
Garrick, Gordon 19
Geilenfeld, Mike 192, 203, 206, 212, 213
George, MC, Brother 141, 190, 194, 203, 206, 212, 232
Gertrude, MC, Sister 444
Ghosh, MC, Sister Nirmala 418
Gilchrist, Michael 390, 392
González-Balado, José Luis 301, 302
Gracias, Cardinal Valerian 96
Grogan, SJ, Father Kevin 64
Groués, Henri Marie (Abbé Pierre) 70
Gut, MC, Brother Robi 272, 273

H

Hamilton Smith, SJ, Father John 66
Hammarskjöld, Dag 316
Harrison, MC, Brother Ben 23, 320, 361
Harte, SJ, Father John 47, 194
Harvey, Father Pat 472
Hawkins, SJ, Father James 41, 319
Hendriks, SJ, Father Hans 20, 22, 65
Henry, SJ, Father Julien 121, 132
Ho Chi Minh 171
Hollinger, Jeremy 167, 187, 188, 191, 197, 206, 213, 215, 223, 227, 254, 255, 268, 292, 328, 336, 357,

366, 367, 368, 369, 370, 371, 372, 381
Hsu, Bishop Francis 136
Hughes, Dick 227
Hurney, SJ, Brother John 64, 76, 79
Hwang Kum Soo (Liduvina) 263

I

Ignatius, MC, Brother 121
Ignatius of Loyola 307

J

James, MC, Brother 121
Janssens, SJ, Father Jean Baptiste 65
Jayaprakash, MC, Brother 419
Jeramile, MC, Sister 465
John, MC, Brother 121
John of the Cross, Saint 310, 484
John Paul II, Pope 325, 328, 370, 390
John, P. M. 148
Jordan, Patrick 506
Joseph, Annie 150
Joseph Maria, MC, Sister 444, 465, 475
Joseph, SJ, Father Thomas 21
Josie, MC, Sister 465
Jo Young Sim (Alexia) 266

K

K.A. SJ, Father Sebastian 82
Kelly, SJ, Father Austin 63, 65, 66, 76, 81, 87, 88, 119, 134, 141
Kennedy, John F. 97
Keogh, SJ, Father Tom 40
Kerketta, Archbishop Pius 88, 89
Kerketta, SJ, Brother Stanislaus 76
Kiely, Maria 400
Kiely, Peter 400, 401
King, SJ, Father Harold 66, 67, 70, 71, 73, 81, 82
King, SJ, Father Kevin 152
Knox, Cardinal James R. 92, 142, 144
Korinek, Jindriska 315
Korinek, Karel 315
Kotria, Iva 315
Kotria, Zdenik 315
Kozanek Palackeho, Petr 315
Kraemer, Hendrik 97
Kribs, Father Don 184, 185, 187, 213
Kullu, Father Patrick 87
Kump, Patty 187

L

Lachal, SJ, Father Lou 88
Lachica Sin, Cardinal Jaime 174, 417
Lakra, Father Placidus 87

Name Index

Lakra, MC Brother Prakash 328, 357
Lalor, SJ, Father Harold 45, 46, 102, 116, 172, 173
Lees, SJ, Father Tom 472, 474
Lefebvre, Archbishop Marcel 432
Leo XIII, Pope 69
Leunig, Michael 292, 414
Lievens, SJ, Father Constant 65, 74
Little, Archbishop Frank 471
Lon Nol 192, 211
Lopez, SJ, Father Francis 82
Lucas, Richard 509
Lugun, Father Marcus 87
Lugun, MC, Brother George 444
Lymark, MC, Sister 465

M

MacKillop, Saint Mary 387, 388, 392, 510, 511
Maher, SJ, Father Frank 483
Manalo, Lily (Ate Lily) 417, 418, 423, 467, 480
Manning, Jean 405, 483
Mannix, Archbishop Daniel 38, 41, 387, 388, 502
Mannooparampil, MC Brother Yesudas 328, 357, 368, 427
Marcel, MC Brother 136
Marko, Drana 152
Martin, MC, Brother 419
Marti, SJ, Father John 70
Maximilian, MC, Sister 465, 473, 475
McDonald, RSM, Sister Philippa 404
McLoughlin, Garry 148, 149, 177
Menzies, Robert Gordon 42, 172
Merton, OCSO, Father Thomas 44, 45, 420
Michael, MC, Brother 121
Milada, MC, Sister 403
Miller, Anne Margaret Cecilia 35, 36, 39, 514
Miller, James 35, 36, 479
Millership, Anne 152, 301
Millership, Julian 40, 152, 301, 464, 473
Millership, Keith 43
Millership (née Travers-Ball), Aimée Antoinette 36, 37, 40, 43, 63, 117, 152, 507
Mobbs, Dr. Frank 64
Monaghan, Gerard 292, 408, 410, 413, 440, 480, 514
Morales, DC, Sister Estela 184
Morgan, Patrick 96, 232
Moyersoen, SJ, Father Iannes B. 101, 134
Muggeridge, Malcolm 44, 143, 281, 302, 390
Mulhearn, SJ, Father Michael 64, 86

Murmu, MC, Brother Peter 250, 261, 263, 267, 268, 325, 336, 374, 419
My Le 184, 185, 217

N

Naduvathette, MC, Brother Prem Anand 266, 364
Negri, Dr. John 468, 473
Ngo Dinh, Diem 171, 172
Ngo Dinh Thuc, Archbishop Pierre Martin 172
Nguyen Minh Loan 248
Nguyen Thi Kim, (Ba Kim) 176, 199, 202, 217, 229, 231, 248, 316, 513
Nguyen Van Binh, Archbishop Paul 167, 232
Nguyen Van Thuan, Cardinal Francis Xavier 172, 232
Nimmo, Derek 305
Nixon, Richard 192
Niyogi, M. Bhawani Shankar 74
Noone, Val 11, 176, 179, 298, 299, 439, 519

O

O'Connor, Eileen 387, 388, 468
O'Connor, SJ, Father Edmund 86, 88, 103, 139
O'Mara, SJ, Father Thomas J. 37
O'Sullivan, SJ, Father Patrick 207, 211, 273, 431, 439

P

Pacheco, Gillian 444
Park, SJ, Father Mun Su 263, 264, 265
Paul, MC, Brother 121
Paul VI, Pope 103
Peaker, Betty 399, 400, 401, 418, 480, 483
Pell, Cardinal George 471
Pescais, Father Edward 141
Peter, MC, Brother 121
Petrus, MC, Brother 495
Philip, MC, Brother 146
Picachy, Cardinal Lawrence 290
Pran, Dith 192
Prinster, OCSO, Brother Nicholas 21, 142, 153, 175, 182, 184, 187, 197, 203, 204, 212, 213, 223, 224, 229, 230, 256, 287, 290, 318, 331
Priscilla, MC, Sister 255
P.T., MC, Brother Thomas 190

R

Ramousse, Archbishop George 200
Rayan, SJ, Father Samuel 149
Reed, Peter 25
Reilly, SJ, Father John 87, 89
Richardson, Gary 187, 188,

Name Index

192, 328, 357, 370, 372
Riddick, Ray 188
Riordan, SJ, Father Edward 47
Roberts, MC, Brother David 509
Roger of Taizé 133
Romero, Archbishop Oscar
    250, 370, 392
Roncalli, Angelo Giuseppe
    (Pope John XXIII) 80, 97
Rosengren, Peter 479
Rowland, Pat 378, 500
Rumi 310
Ryan, CSsR, Father Peter 397
Ryan, Geraldine 396, 397, 398,
    411, 413, 418, 433
Ryan, RSM, Sister Margaret
    24, 181, 188, 394, 439
Ryan, SJ, Father Michael 78

S

Saliba, Dr. Joseph 359
Santamaria, Bartholomew A.
    95, 96, 172, 232
Scolizzi, Father Angelo 290
Sevrin, SJ, Bishop Oscar 65
Shanti, SJ, Father Peter 68
Sheil, OFM, Bishop Laurence 511
Shekinah, MC, Sister 402
Sihanouk, Norodom 192
Simon, Boris 70
Simons, Jane 22, 300
Simons, Kate 22

Simons (née Travers-Ball), Leone
    39, 299, 300, 465
Singh, Sundar 150
Smith, Gabrielle 260
Smith, Gregory 152
Smith, Jim 22, 152, 260, 352
Smith (née Travers-Ball),
    Lucy Arcadius 22, 36, 40, 63,
    120, 152, 259, 464, 507
Sölle, Dorothee 310
Solomon, Geoffrey 41, 79, 101,
    176, 191, 197, 287, 290,
    302, 336
Solzhenitsyn, Alexandr
    233, 379, 380, 426
Sontag, SJ, Father Peter 70, 84
Soreng, MC, Brother Michael 269
Southern, Gordon 406, 407, 432
Spink, Kathryn 11, 23, 92,
    276, 283, 291, 299, 302,
    326, 334, 482
Sri Khanto 521
Stanislaus, MC, Brother 121
Stein, Edith 468
Stern, Karl 97
Stroscio, SDB, Father Rosario 326
Sung, MC, Brother Lazaro
    263, 266
Sutuj Boc, MC, Brother Marcos
    Antonio 249
Sybil, MC, Sister 465

T

Talbot, Venerable Matt 437
Teresa, MC, Mother 13, 19, 21, 26, 37, 44, 91, 92, 101, 102, 116, 118, 119, 121, 124, 125, 126, 127, 128, 129, 130, 132, 134, 143, 146, 148, 152, 169, 184, 185, 187, 189, 205, 253, 256, 263, 275, 277, 278, 280, 281, 282, 283, 284, 286, 287, 288, 290, 291, 292, 294, 297, 301, 305, 315, 316, 319, 320, 326, 327, 360, 361, 364, 366, 368, 372, 392, 399, 402, 412, 419, 424, 428, 429, 443, 444, 445, 446, 469, 480, 481, 482, 506, 507, 519
Teresa of Avila, Saint 484
Teresa of Jesus of the Andes, Saint 484
Terziani, Tiziano 218
Tevis, Lloyd 184, 213
Thérèse of Lisieux, Saint 468, 484
Thich Tri Quang 232
Thomas, MC, Brother 419
Tigga, Ferdinand 150, 189, 215, 230, 232, 258
Tirkey, Father Deonis 87
Tolkien, J. R. R. 388

Travers-Ball, Brendan Marius 36, 40, 87, 88, 89, 299, 404
Travers-Ball, Frederick Henry 35, 36, 38, 39, 40, 43, 63, 64, 66, 67, 71, 115, 116, 119, 142
Travers-Ball, Joan Beatrice 36, 37
Travers-Ball, Leo Thomas 36, 37, 39, 40, 299
Travers, Rose Anne 35
Trojan, OFM, Father Ladislav 315

V

Vandekerkove, Abbé François 423
Van Don, MC, Brother Anton 195, 202, 206, 207, 211, 212
Van Exem, SJ, Father Celeste 122
Vanier, Jean 133, 392
Vanigasooriyar, Father Aloysius Hari 123, 129, 526
Van Nghi, Father Huynh 167, 180, 182, 206
Varghese, MC, Brother 419
Vazhakala, MCC, Father Sebastian 141, 149, 254, 255, 288, 289
Venet, Père Robert 212
Voillaume, Father René 133

W

Walch, Brian 187, 195, 196, 205, 207, 209, 424

Name Index

Walker, Johnny 493
Walker, SJ, Father Des 47
Walsh, Bernie 197
Watson, Dr. Roy 37
Watson, Matron E. M. 37
Wenisch, SJ, Father Paul 70
Wineman, Gordon 19, 167, 173, 194, 197, 206, 213, 215, 223, 290, 292
Wogan, Terry 305
Woods, Father Julian 510

Z

Zorza, Victor 173

OUR DISTRIBUTION CENTRES

ANDHRA PRADESH

Subodha Nilayam Communications
Eluru
Tel: (08812) 232261; Mob: 8465963301
subodhanilayam@stpauls.in

Jeevandhara Book Centre
Vijayawada
Tel: (0866) 2477805; Mob: 7382208802
jeevandhara@stpauls.in

ASSAM

Pohar Prakashan
Jorhat
Mob: 9435051054; 9435051056
poharprakashan@stpauls.in

Subha Sandesh Prasarani
Guwahati
Tel: (0361) 2895029; Mob: 9706447972
sspcentreguwahati@stpauls.in

Pauline book & Media Centre
Guwahati
Tel: (0361) 2739878; Mob: 6913324994
paulineguwahatibc@gmail.com

DELHI

St Paul Int. Book Centre
New Delhi
Tel: (011) 23320381 & 41513127
spbcnewdelhi@stpauls.in

Pauline book & Media Stall
New Delhi
Tel: (011) 25851260; Mob: 9868301987
paulinesdel@gmail.com

GOA

Pauline book & Media centre
Panjim
Tel: (0832) 2231158; Mob: 7507548572
pauline18junegoa@gmail.com

Pauline book & Media centre
Panjim
Tel: (0832) 2432608
paulinesgoa@gmail.com

Pauline book & Media centre
Mapusa – Bardez
Tel: (0832) 2253329; Mob: 8806775642
mapusabc@gmail.com

GUJARAT

Pauline book & Media centre
Ahmedabad
Tel: (079) 26563701
ahmedabadbc@gmail.com

JHARKHAND

Divyodaya
Ranchi
Mob: 7759819601
spbcranchi@stpauls.in

KARNATAKA

Better Yourself Books
Bengaluru
Tel: (080) 28392175; Mob: 9538302195
sales@betteryourselfbooks.com

Pauline book & Media Centre
Bengaluru
Tel: (080) 25587106; Mob: 7026682915
paulinebangalore@gmail.com

Pauline book & Media Centre
Bengaluru
Mob: 8861859264
paulines.stjohnbgl@gmail.com

Pauline book & Media Centre
Mangalore
Tel: (0824) 2440517; Mob: 8296608349
paulines.mangalore@gmail.com

KERALA

St Paul Book & Art Centre
Kochi
Tel: (0484) 2366589 & 2362549
spbckochi@stpauls.in

St Paul Book & Art Centre
Kozhikode
Tel: (0495) 2720941
spbccalicut@stpauls.in

Pauline book & Media Centre
Thiruvananthapuram
Tel: (0471) 6451315; Mob: 9072897510
dsptrivandrum@gmail.com

MAHARASHTRA

St Paul Book & Art Centre
Mumbai
Tel: (022) 26407127; Mob: 9619463430
spbcbandra@stpauls.in

Title Waves
Mumbai
Tel: (022) 26510841
info@titlewaves.in

St Paul Book Centre
Pune
Tel: (020) 26343146; Mob: 8408889837
spbcpune@stpauls.in

Pauline book & Media centre
Mumbai
(022) 26404049, 8433537946
paulinebcbandra@gmail.com

Pauline book & Media centre
Mumbai
(022) 28980744, 8657824706
borivlibc@gmail.com

Pauline book & Media centre
Vasai Road
(0250) 2380011, 8149793217
paulinesvasai@gmail.com

Pauline book & Media centre
Nagpur
(0712) 2555047; Mob. 9545540726
nagpurbc@gmail.com

MEGHALAYA

Pauline book & Media centre
Shillong
(0364) 2223637; Mob. 9378185450
pauline.shillong@gmail.com

PUNJAB

Jyothi Books & Media Centre
Jalandhar
Tel: 8951679184 / 9872996865
spbcjalandhar@stpauls.in

TAMIL NADU

Good Pastor Int. Book Centre
Chennai
Tel: (044) 25388547; Mob: 9840351482
goodpastor@stpauls.in

Pauline book & Media centre
Trichy
(0431) 2410017; Mob. 9750278943
paulinebctrichy@gmail.com

Telangana

Pauline book & Media Centre
Secunderabad
Tel: (040) 27804057; Mob: 8297168363
secunderabadbc@gmail.com

UTTAR PRADESH

St Paul Book Centre
Allahabad
Mob: 7292881493
spbcallahabad@stpauls.in

West Bengal

Pauline book & Media centre
Kolkata
(033) 22265471; Mob. 9062760361
kolkatapaulinebc@gmail.com

SALES OFFICES

MUMBAI
ST PAULS
BETTER YOURSELF BOOKS
58/23rd Road, TPS III
Bandra (W)
Mumbai – 400 050
Tel: (022) 26407127
Mob: 99694 03426
sales@betteryourselfbooks.com

BENGALURU
BETTER YOURSELF BOOKS
St Pauls Campus, 8th Mile,
Tumkur Road, Nagasandra P.O.,
Bengaluru – 560 073
Tel: (080) 28392175
Mob: 95383 02195
sales@stpaulsbyb.com

GUWAHATI
ST PAULS
BETTER YOURSELF BOOKS
Subha Sandesh Prasarini,
9th Mile, G.S. Road, Hastinapur
Guwahati 781 023
Tel: (0361) 2895029
Mob: 97064 47972
sspcentreguwahati@stpauls.in

ST PAULS/BETTER YOURSELF BOOKS
Marketing Division, 58/23rd Road, TPS III
Bandra (W), Mumbai - 400 050
Phone: (022) 2651 0023, 2640 3312, 2643 6106
Mob: 99694 03426
E-mail: marketing@stpauls.in | marketing@betteryourselfbooks.com
www.stpaulsbyb.com | www.betteryourselfbooks.com

Scan the QR Code to browse our website

www.stpaulsbyb.com
www.betteryourselfbooks.com

www.ingramcontent.com/pod-product-compliance
Lightning Source LLC
Chambersburg PA
CBHW060827190426
43197CB00039B/2528